UPROOTED

The Shipment of Poor Children to Canada, 1867-1917

Roy Parker

This edition first published in Great Britain in 2010 by

The Policy Press
University of Bristol
Fourth Floor
Beacon House
Queen's Road
Bristol BS8 1QU
UK

Tel +44 (0)117 331 4054
Fax +44 (0)117 331 4093
e-mail tpp-info@bristol.ac.uk
www.policypress.org.uk

North American office:
The Policy Press
c/o International Specialized Books Services
920 NE 58th Avenue, Suite 300
Portland, OR 97213-3786, USA
Tel +1 503 287 3093
Fax +1 503 280 8832
e-mail info@isbs.com

British Library Cataloguing in Publication Data
A catalogue record for this book is available from the British Library.

Library of Congress Cataloging-in-Publication Data
A catalog record for this book has been requested.

ISBN 978 1 84742 668 0 paperback
Previously published in 2008 (hardcover) by The Policy Press

Cover design by Robin Hawes
Front cover: image courtesy of City of London, London Metropolitan Archives
Printed and bound in Great Britain by Hobb the Printers, Southampton

The front cover photograph shows boys parading before departure to Canada from the St Nicholas (Catholic) industrial school at Manor Park in London in 1908. This party was organised by the Catholic Emigration Association.

The International Council for Canadian Studies (ICCS) has contributed financially to the publication of this paperback edition.

Contents

Part VIII: A Review

Acknowledgements

First and foremost I must thank my wife, Jo, who has borne with patience and unflagging interest the slow progress of this work. Furthermore, she has been a perceptive and constructive critic as well as assisting with many archival searches. I owe her a great deal. I am also most grateful to Patricia Lees who has unfailingly brought her meticulous expertise to bear on the often untidy manuscripts that I have sent to her. I have valued her continued support and friendship.

My interest in child migration was first captured many years ago while I was at Carleton University in Ottawa, supported by a Government of Canada scheme for visiting professors. It was also there that I first learned about various aspects of Canadian social policy and its history, encouraged by many of its staff but in particular by Professor Jim Albert.

The study would not have been possible without the financial help of the Economic and Social Research Council (ESRC). The British Association for Canadian Studies also assisted with certain travel expenses. I am grateful to both. I have relied heavily on a variety of archives, both private and public. The Public Record Office in London was invaluable and its staff always helpful. Similarly, the Scottish Record Office in Edinburgh and the London Metropolitan Archives were most accommodating. A particular mention must be made of the Special Collections and Archives Department of the University of Liverpool where the records of several of the voluntary children's organisations are now deposited and where Adrian Allan has been particularly helpful. I have been accorded generous access to the archives of Barnardos, the Catholic Children's Society, The Children's Society, Fegans Child and Family Care, the National Children's Homes, Middlemores, Nugent Care, Quarriers and the Together Trust; I am grateful to them all.

In Canada I have received equally ready help from the staff of various archives: from those at the National Archives in Ottawa and from the record offices of Ontario, Nova Scotia, New Brunswick, Québec and Manitoba.

Over the years, and at different times, many colleagues have given me their advice and encouragement. In particular, I would like to thank Professors Noel Whiteside, Hilary Land and Roger Bullock. Drs Jean Harris-Hendriks and Alan Rushton gave me wise advice about the history of child psychiatry. My membership of the Centre for Social Policy at Dartington has provided me with invaluable facilities for the completion of the book, an assistance not always so readily available once one has retired.

Permission to reproduce the photographs that have been included was given by Barnardos, the City of London, London Metropolitan Archives, National Archives of Canada, the National Children's Homes, Quarriers, and the Together Trust.

Of course, I alone am responsible for what is written and therefore for any errors or omissions that the reader may detect.

List of Abbreviations

ANB	Archives of New Brunswick
ANQ	Archives Nationales de Québec
AO	Archives of Ontario
BES	Bristol Emigration Society
BPP	British Parliamentary Papers
CAS	The Children's Aid Society
CCRS	Catholic Children's Rescue Society (Salford)
CCSW(A)	Catholic Children's Society Westminster (Archives)
CEA	Catholic Emigration Association
CLEC	Colonial Land and Emigration Commission
CO	Colonial Office
COS	Charity Organisation Society
CPR	Canadian Pacific Railway
CSA	The Children's Society Archives
CSSL(A)	Catholic Social Services Liverpool (Archives)
ESRC	Economic and Social Research Council
FA	Fegans Archives
HC	House of Commons
JHANB	Journals of the House of Assembly of the Province of New Brunswick
JHCC	Journals of the House of Commons of Canada
JPHANS	Journals and Proceedings of the House of Assembly of the Province of Nova Scotia
LCCPS	Liverpool Catholic Children's Protection Society
LGB	Local Government Board
LMA	London Metropolitan Archives
LUA	Liverpool University Archives
MCL	Manchester Central Library
MSBG(A)	Manchester and Salford Boys' and Girls' Refuges and Homes (Archives)
NAC	National Archives of Canada
NAS	National Archives of Scotland
NB	New Brunswick
NCH	National Children's Homes
NCSA	Nugent Care Society Archives
nd	No date
nm	No month
nnb	No number
np	No page number
npb	No publisher
NS	Nova Scotia

NWMP	North West Mounted Police
NWT	North West Territories
OLA	Ontario Legislative Assembly
OR	Official Record
PANS	Public Archives of Nova Scotia
PLB	Poor Law Board
PLC	Poor Law Commission
PRO	Public Record Office
QA	Quarriers Archives
RC	Royal Commission
SCES	Southwark Catholic Emigration Society
SP	Sessional Papers
SPCK	Society for Promoting Christian Knowledge
SSCC	Social Services Council of Canada
TTA	Together Trust Archives

Preface

Thousands of children are being uprooted as I write. Some accompany parents who are starting new jobs; some go with their parents as optimistic migrants; while others flee as refugees, sometimes with their parents, sometimes not. Whatever the reason many children feel distressed at having to move. They have to leave behind the familiar, with the unknown ahead. Even when they reach a new location, there can often be a different language to be learned, and a perplexing culture to be understood, as well as the challenge of making new friends and being accepted by them. However, the children for whom such moves are likely to be the most harrowing are those who have to go away unaccompanied by parents, relatives or friends; but if the settings are not too unfamiliar and essentially benevolent, and if the children do not feel abandoned, some may be able to settle.

War has been, and remains, a major cause of disruptions like these. Its effects may range from evacuation out of a danger zone to ethnic cleansing or forced enlistment as child soldiers. Apart from the upheavals created by armed conflict some children are sold into virtual slavery or prostitution, while girls may be obliged to leave home as child brides. Many get caught up in a downward spiral of constant movement, despair, fear and deprivation, not least those who run away from intolerable situations.

It goes without saying, of course, that the consequences of such uprooting affect children differently. Nevertheless, certain themes recur. There is uncertainty, even when mixed with excitement and hopefulness. For others there is a sense of being cast adrift, of being unprotected and therefore profoundly vulnerable. Yet one of the beliefs that adults have held, and which some still do, is that children, especially young children, are essentially pliable and adaptable. They are assumed to settle easily into new situations because they are at a stage of rapid development and because they have little past to put behind them. Of course this ignores the fact that, just as much as adults, they have their own unique histories, however brief and fragmentary, that remain a crucial part of their sense of identity. Their knowledge and understanding of their past may be incomplete because they have 'not been told', or have been given confusing, false or contradictory accounts of what happened to them. Nonetheless, what they do know or believe is not easily forgotten, be it people, places, experiences or possessions. Although movement – especially from one culture to another – ruptures a past, it does not extinguish it; indeed, it is likely to intensify the desire to know and to remember the details of that past.

How children react to the trauma of uprooting will, of course, depend on many things: for example, their age, their personality, the completeness of the severance from their past and, not least, on the kinds of misfortunes that have already befallen them. Much remains to be understood about the influence of such factors, about their interactions, and about their short- and long-term psychological and physical consequences. There are certainly many risks associated with moving children from the familiar to the unfamiliar, especially when that movement is tantamount to severance. Nevertheless, it has to be recognised that some situations may be so bad and so dangerous that it becomes necessary that this be done; but that still leaves open the question of where and to whom they should be moved and what kind of restorative care they require. Sadly, these matters have often not been uppermost in the minds of those who have made the arrangements, particularly in times of grave danger or when the motives in play derive from unchallenged convictions or blatant exploitation.

Although the circumstances surrounding the uprooting of a particular child demand to be understood, the wider picture is equally important. In sociological, political and economic terms there is a need to appreciate the variety of reasons why children are moved from one place to another. Furthermore, it is necessary to understand the contexts in which these upheavals occur. The organised emigration of children from Britain to different parts of the Empire, separated from their parents, is an example of one remarkable episode in the history of 'child saving'. It was at its peak during the second half of the nineteenth century and the early years of the twentieth, and continued on a reduced scale up to the 1960s. The destinations included Australia, New Zealand and Natal, but Canada in particular.

This book is concerned with the organised emigration of British children to Canada during the 50 years from Canadian confederation in 1867 to 1917 when the wartime dangers of crossing the Atlantic eventually caused a halt to be called. Although by now there will be very few, if any, survivors of this trans-shipment of 80,000 children a small number of their letters still exist. Examples of these are interspersed in the chapters that follow, particularly where they illustrate themes or issues. However, it should be made clear at the outset that this is essentially a study that seeks to explain the complex forces and competing interests that gave rise to the expatriation of so many children, typically between the ages of 10 and 14.

In order to explore the various aspects of the inception and evolution of the child emigration movement considerable use has been made of public and private archives in both Britain and Canada. These obviously reflect the perceptions and the preoccupations of those who compiled them, and this has to be borne in mind throughout. Nevertheless, they do provide a rich source of information about the way in which their authors (often key figures in the shaping of child welfare history) regarded their responsibilities; how they approached and conceptualised the issue of 'child saving'; and how they thought about the nature of childhood itself. Not least, however, these archives offer evidence of the manner in which different organisations interpreted the problems of the day and endeavoured to pursue their favoured solutions. They also offer an insight into the conflicts of interest, the unfolding decisions and the status of the contemporary law affecting children and families more generally. Thus, in succeeding chapters the reader will be introduced not only to what might be regarded as the 'story' of child emigration to Canada but also to the forces that lay behind it and influenced its development, including those that impeded it as well as those that sustained it.

In a real sense, therefore, what follows is a study of the politics surrounding this remarkable chapter in the treatment of children that casts light on far more than is suggested at first glance and that still has a resonance today. Indeed, an important purpose of this book is to show how the interests of children – and thereby their well-being – can fall victim to prevailing expediencies, fashion or exploitation.

I spent a good deal of time searching for an accurate and appropriate title for this book. Eventually, *Uprooted* seemed to capture best what many children felt about their experience. The use of the words 'shipment' and 'poor' in the sub-title were chosen because the former was the term that was often used at the time and the latter was certainly a true reflection of the circumstances from which the children came. I also thought long and hard about including the real names of some of the children and a few parents. While I have observed the injunction not to give names when this was a condition of having access to private archives, when names appeared in the public domain, for example in newspapers or open public archives, I decided to include them unless it was likely to cause unnecessary distress to descendants. The reason for doing this was my conviction that it would be a small gesture towards the preservation in the public memory of at least a few of the children caught up in this upheaval. Furthermore, I thought that it might enable just a few of their present-day families to obtain a glimpse of what their forebears had experienced. I hope that it will be felt that I have made a wise judgement.

Part I
Setting the Scene

ONE

The Background

I Prelude

While the late 1860s might be taken to mark the start of the child emigration movement, that would be misleading, for there were many earlier examples. The trans-shipment of unwanted pauper children to the plantations of Virginia is reported from the beginning of the seventeenth century and, somewhat later, children were also taken to the West Indies.[1] There is, however, little evidence that these practices continued much into the eighteenth century. This was partly because, by then, the demand for servant and plantation labour was increasingly being met by the spread of black slavery. Even so, prisoners continued to be transported to the colonial plantations, and children were included along with adults. But after the American War of Independence Britain's convicts were no longer welcome and alternatives had to be found. Banishment to West Africa was tried but rejected as impractical. Australia, on the other hand, offered not only the prospect of a fresh colonial settlement but also a destination for the burgeoning population in prison at home. By 1787 the transportation of felons to New South Wales had begun. Thereafter, children arrived in the new colonies together with the adults. For example, 1,500 boy convicts were sent to New South Wales, Western Australia and Van Diemen's Land (now Tasmania) between 1842 and 1853, when the transportation of children was effectively abolished.[2]

During the first half of the nineteenth century charitable organisations were also arranging the transfer of children to various parts of the Empire. Foremost among them was the Children's Friend Society that was established in 1830 under the name of 'The Society for the Suppression of Juvenile Vagrancy'.[3] Until its demise in 1841 it sent 70 destitute children to Australia, 440 to the Cape of Good Hope and about 150 to Canada. Later, in 1849, a government grant was made to the Ragged School Union to enable it to send 150 boys and girls to Australia; but it was not renewed, largely because of fears that it would set a precedent that would encourage further calls on public expenditure.[4] Thereafter the Union could send only small parties of children abroad. Nevertheless, another organisation, the Royal Philanthropic School, did manage to emigrate a steady stream of older reformatory boys throughout most of the 1850s and 1860s with the help of profits from its farm and charitable donations.[5] Schemes such as these were, however, generally short-lived, defeated by the lack of financial support and by fears or charges that the children's subsequent well-being would suffer from the want of adequate protection from exploitation.

One might have expected Poor Law guardians to try to reduce their costs by emigrating children from their workhouses and schools, but there were considerable obstacles. Before 1834 parochial funds could not be spent in aid of any emigration. Afterwards, the new legislation permitted Poor Law unions to obtain loans in order to meet the cost of emigrating poor people.[6] At first there was a flurry of interest, but the number of people assisted in this way was never great and declined rapidly. There were two major disincentives. First, the decision to raise a loan for emigration purposes had to be approved by a meeting of rate-payers and, second, the new legislation encouraged the construction of workhouses that competed for capital funds. Furthermore, pauper emigration in general, and child emigration in particular, received no special encouragement from the Poor Law Commission. Nevertheless, from 1842 the Australian colonies had been pressing the recently formed Colonial Land and Emigration Commission (CLEC) in London to find ways of increasing immigration;[7] but as a result of the Imperial government's decision to raise the price of colonial land after 1840 sales plummeted, severely limiting the principal source of the Commission's income.[8] Its ability to promote and assist emigration was, therefore, severely curtailed. Whereas by 1841 emigration from Great Britain and Ireland to Australia had reached 32,500, by 1845 it had fallen to 800,[9] leading to an acute shortage of labour. Yet one longer-term need was clear: for young single women and girls to become servants and wives. Not only would they increase the reproductive capacity of the colonies and offset the preponderance of men but, it was argued, more women would help to combat immorality as well as many other social ills.[10]

In 1848 Colonial Land and Emigration Commissioners were instructed to see how far an emigration of girls from Irish workhouses could be organised.[11] Masters of workhouses were asked to compile lists of those between the ages of 14 and 18 who wished to go to Australia. Over 4,000 Irish girls were sent to New South Wales and South Australia between 1848 and 1850. It was no coincidence, of course, that the British authorities should look to the Irish Poor Law for the supply of some of the female labour that the Australian colonies sought, or that they should have chosen girls in particular. The famine had left the workhouses in Ireland full to overflowing, especially with orphaned and deserted youngsters.[12] Without charitable or official help they were unlikely to join the exodus of people from Ireland that occurred during these years. Furthermore, in the absence of a significant middle class the demand for girls for domestic service was significantly lower in Ireland than it was in England. It would therefore have been hard to shift girls and young women out of the workhouses. However, the use of emigration as a means of relieving the Irish workhouses of their abundance of young female inmates did not last. It was halted partly as a result of Protestant opposition in Australia, partly because of revelations about the depredations that the girls had suffered on the voyage and partly in consequence of allegations of their immorality and waywardness when they arrived.[13] The scheme was brought to an abrupt end in 1850 and no more contingents of pauper girls sailed from Ireland to Australia although, as we shall see, smaller groups were dispatched to Canada from time to time.

Hard on the heels of the Irish initiative, changes were introduced in England at the behest of a number of enthusiastic boards of guardians that gave them and other boards new powers to assist emigration from their rate funds without raising loans and without having to call a meeting of their rate-payers.[14] In 1852 alone over 3,000 paupers were helped to emigrate. However, in 1854 the Poor Law Board (PLB) had a change of heart and no longer sanctioned local expenditure on emigration. Both pauper children and adults were affected by this prohibition that continued until the mid-1860s. There are several explanations for the government's withdrawal of support for pauper emigration.[15] First, there was the growing objection of the colonies to receiving such people and, second, there was the political conviction, expressed by successive presidents of the PLB, that it was no longer wise to encourage the export of labour when there would later be a need for more workers at home. Furthermore, in any case there was a considerable volume of spontaneous emigration, particularly to Australia. This accelerated after gold was discovered in 1851. By 1850 emigration from Britain and Ireland to Australia had risen slowly to 16,000; two years later it had climbed to almost 88,000.[16] The government was also concerned about levels of public expenditure, particularly with the onset of the Crimean War in 1853; and spending on colonial activities already accounted for a substantial part of the annual budget.

Despite the government having set its face against pauper emigration, proposals continued to be put forward for sending children in the care of the guardians to the colonies. For example, in 1849 the Kensington board of guardians in London proposed a scheme for pauper children to be sent to industrial schools in New Zealand, or, indeed, to any other colony with 'properly conducted' industrial schools.[17] Although its draft Bill was never adopted its more general aims were reflected in a clause that was included in the Poor Law Amendment Act later that year. This made the conditions under which guardians could emigrate abandoned and orphaned children quite explicit, but also added the requirement that before approval would be given children had to appear before at least two justices to give their consent. Up to a point, therefore, the way now seemed to be more open for the development of child emigration by Poor Law unions; but there remained a disinclination, both on the part of the central authority and most local guardians, to move ahead with any such schemes.

Three years later, in 1852, the PLB received another proposal, this time from the CLEC for the trans-shipment of pauper youths to New Brunswick (NB), Canada.[18] It was explained that several hundred children between the ages of 14 and 18 could be placed with the families of 'respectable farmers'. The inspector of the metropolitan Poor Law schools promptly drew up a long list of children who, in his opinion, would be eligible candidates. This was sent to the immigration agent at St John, NB, as an example of the scale of what might be done.[19] However, the President of the PLB, Viscount Courtney, did not consider it to be desirable[20] – arrangements for the children's supervision were felt to be 'unsatisfactory'. In 1856, however, the CLEC returned to the question of sending young people from Poor Law schools to the colonies, but this time just girls. They asked the central PLB how many girls would be available and what the home demand was. The gist of the reply was that it was doubtful whether girls of an appropriate age would still be in the schools, and if they were, this was because they were likely to be seen as 'defective' or had 'intractable tempers'. It was felt that it might be possible to send some girls aged 14 if they could be maintained in colonial schools until they were ready for service, but since the home demand began to operate at about 14 or 15, very few girls would actually be available.[21]

The reluctance of the PLB to lend its support to schemes of pauper emigration throughout the 1850s and the early 1860s affected the emigration of unaccompanied children as well as that of adults and families and may be explained in several ways. First, there was the conviction that the home labour market should not be denied this potential source of recruits. This was especially so in the case of the girls. Second, emigration (particularly to Australia) was still expensive. Guardians were neither encouraged nor usually inclined to incur the extra expenditure, even though it might be offset by longer-term savings; the Treasury was certainly unwilling to shoulder any additional 'colonial' expenditure. Third, the difficulties of ensuring reliable supervision of the children once they had reached the colonies gave the central authority ample grounds for rejecting the few proposals that were presented for its approval. However, by the mid-1860s the worsening economic situation led to a widespread resurgence of interest in emigration that created a much more favourable climate in which schemes for child emigration could flourish.

II The Pressure for Emigration Grows

The commercial crisis of 1866, which lasted at least until 1871, created widespread unemployment and a fear that social upheaval would follow. Many came to see emigration as an attractive and rapid solution, especially in London. Indeed, the east end of the city was regarded as the heartland of this distress and discontent. Its shipyards and docks had suffered badly, as had many of the associated trades. Several initiatives were taken in order to encourage the emigration of those who were thrown out of work. For example, an East End Emigration Fund was established in 1867 in order to help the 'deserving' unemployed to emigrate (especially to Canada) or to move elsewhere in Britain. The East London Family Fund was established a year later. However, it was the East End Emigration Fund that went from strength to strength. Its activities were extended to any distressed district and its title changed accordingly to the British and Colonial Emigration Fund. Between April and August 1870 it assisted over 5,000 people to emigrate to Canada.[22]

The activities of both these organisations illustrate the growing interest that was shown in emigration as a solution to the problem of unemployment. It was widely advocated and many other schemes and local clubs sprang up for its promotion and facilitation. There was also an active lobby aimed at establishing state-aided emigration that was consolidated in the formation of the National Emigration

League at the end of 1869.[23] Further evidence of the considerable attention that emigration attracted during this period is provided by two parliamentary debates – one in the Lords in 1869[24] and another in the Commons the year after.[25] In introducing the debate in the upper chamber Lord Houghton (a socialite with an interest in issues such as reformatories, mechanics' institutes and penny banks) drew attention to the advantages of emigration as a means of relieving the growing number of paupers. In Canada or Australia they would become 'producers and consumers – consumers of our manufactures – instead of being a burden'.[26] Furthermore, since the colonies 'felt very strongly the want of labour' they could be told, Houghton contended, that 'they must take an inferior article, whether they like it or not'.[27] Earl Granville, the leader in the House of Lords and Secretary of State for the Colonies, replied for Gladstone's government. He was unenthusiastic about Houghton's proposals. Once trade had improved, he explained, the most readily re-employable workers were also those who were most likely to have been regarded as desirable colonists. The more casual labour that was taken on only when trade was thriving was the first to be thrown out of work and the most likely to become – and remain – pauperised. They could be spared for emigration. Yet these were just the people whom the colonies were least willing to accept.[28]

It was plain that there were strong business interests that regarded emigration as an over-reaction to a time of economic recession that would pass and that would be succeeded by a period of economic growth when there would be a need for extra labour. Emigration was opposed because it led to a permanent reduction in the size of the labour force and, sooner or later therefore, to a scarcity of labour and consequently higher wages. Yet emigration did offer a solution to the cost of poor relief. The problem was that it could not be organised so that it included only those regarded as the long-term unemployable without offending colonial sensibilities.

In the following year the Commons also debated a proposal seeking state support for emigration. The discussion followed much the same pattern as it had in the Lords, but the motion was defeated by a large majority. Among other things this reflected the fact that there were now signs of economic recovery and that, in any case, Gladstone's government was preoccupied with an extensive legislative programme. Over and above such factors the government was convinced that a state scheme for emigration would jeopardise colonial relations. This view was based on the discouraging responses that had been received to a circular on the subject that the Colonial Secretary had sent to colonial governments earlier in 1870.[29]

How then did the resurgence of interest in child emigration in the late 1860s fit into this picture? There was the more favourable light, of course, in which emigration was being regarded in many quarters, but several other influences were also at work. First, much of the growth in pauperism was actually among children. For example, the number of children accommodated in workhouses or workhouse schools in England and Wales had risen from 40,000 to 60,000 in the 10 years of the 1860s. Indeed, overall, by 1871 poor relief was being paid in respect of 400,000 children.[30] Second, many destitute young people who had not been swept up (or retained) in the Poor Law system resorted to semi-vagrant lives, sleeping rough, begging and engaging in minor delinquencies. The discipline of the school had yet to be imposed and parents lacked the means or the inclination to provide the care or to exercise the control that might have forestalled their children falling into such desperate situations. Surely, it was contended, these sources of child suffering could be relieved by emigration? Furthermore, sending the children overseas to start new lives would prevent them becoming criminals, paupers or the harbingers of social disorder as adults. The added attraction was that it appeared easier to overcome some of the difficulties confronting the emigration of the adult poor, not least Canadian fears that the arrival of people from the pauperised or criminal classes would become a public burden rather than an economic asset. In contrast to such unwelcome adult immigrants, children, albeit from similar backgrounds, might be regarded (or described) as innocent victims who were not yet indelibly scarred by the poverty, destitution or criminal associations into which they had fallen.

However, there was one other important development that helped to advance the cause of child emigration. This was the evangelical revival that occurred from about 1859 onwards. For those who chose to devote themselves to child saving in general and child emigration in particular, religious commitment provided both a reason for doing so and a powerful public justification. Within the kaleidoscope of all these interests and opportunities it is hardly surprising that several individuals and societies turned their attention to organising the emigration of boys and girls. Foremost among them were Maria Rye, Annie Macpherson and Father Nugent. However, before these developments are explored in the next chapter it is necessary to look briefly at Canadian immigration policy at the time and then to consider official reactions at the PLB to various pressures on them to sanction and then to encourage the emigration of so-called pauper children.

III The Ups and Downs of Official Policies

One incident serves to underline how easily overseas attitudes towards certain types of immigration could be soured, even when labour was in short supply. In 1865 the clerk of the Limerick Poor Law Union in Ireland wrote to Buchanan, the chief emigrant agent at Québec, to inform him that 70 workhouse girls would be embarked for Canada in the near future.[31] He replied that the arrangement was 'most unsatisfactory and unbusinesslike', and considered it necessary to bring the matter to the attention of the PLB in London. This he duly did, as well as writing to the Poor Law inspector for the Limerick district complaining about the off-hand way in which the girls had been sent, and telling him that

> ... the conduct of a great many of them was most disgraceful
> – they sold their Boxes, Bonnets, Combs and any article of clothing

they could dispense with to procure drink and not only became shamefully intoxicated but were guilty of the most depraved acts of immorality.[32]

Canada, Buchanan informed the inspector, was willing to receive 'any number of well conducted young women, however poor ... but a continuance of the present system of sending us none but the worst characters will ... render it incumbent upon the department [of agriculture – and responsible for immigration] to adopt measures to keep the evil in check'. However, this was not the end of the matter. Some of the Limerick girls had been sent on to Ottawa from where the local agent made another adverse report to his department. On arrival several of the girls were intoxicated and 'their appearance was anything but respectable'.[33] A similarly outraged report was submitted by the agent at Kingston, where a section of the party had also arrived. Some, for whom placements had been found, returned the next day, refusing to work. 'Is it not', the agent asked, 'very much to be regretted that the Poor Law Commissioners still persist in sending out such poor helpless inexperienced girls to Canada, who have never been accustomed to any kind of household work?'[34] If further confirmation of the girls' behaviour were needed, he added, he had seen a number of them on the steamer to Toronto 'lying on the deck dead drunk and several sitting on the laps and in the arms of some artillery soldiers ... and this too in broad daylight'. In due course the Limerick guardians replied to this catalogue of complaints, but confessed themselves mystified by the sudden outbreak of depravity. Most of the girls, they protested, had been in the workhouse since infancy.[35]

This particular episode is important because it brought to a head a simmering discontent about pauper immigration. As a *cause célèbre* it served as a reference point for official Canadian attitudes for some time. Indeed, the tone of the government's opposition to such immigration continued to be expressed in no uncertain terms. In 1868 Taché, the Deputy Minister in the Department of Agriculture, wrote to William Dixon, the Canadian immigration agent in Britain, telling him that he should oppose to his 'utmost capacity the sending to our shores of a pauper ... immigration'.[36] This injunction was reflected in the Immigration Act of 1869. Among other things it debarred from entering Canada those who had been convicted of a crime, had been paupers or who were without the prospect of earning a livelihood; this certainly included children from the Poor Law system or from reformatories, although not necessarily other children as long as they could be put to work. Yet, all this notwithstanding, most areas continued to face shortages of labour, especially with respect to men to work on the land and women to labour as domestic and farm servants. As we shall see, in the case of immigrant children this gradually led to the legislation being circumvented.

IV Maria Rye's Appearance on the Scene

We must now introduce Maria Rye (1829-1903). She was the first dedicated emigrationist or, as some would refer to her, child emigration agent. However, her early activities arose from a concern to improve the employment opportunities for middle-class women, including her own. In 1859 she had been a founder member of the Society for Promoting the Employment of Women. As Hammerton explains, the Society's initial aims were to 'endow more suspect occupations with a new air of respectability and thereby open them to women of a higher social class'.[37] As part of that endeavour Rye established a law-stationer's business in 1859. There followed a veritable flood of applications for the jobs it provided and, in 1861, she began to assist some of those who were turned away to emigrate. Later in the same year she described what she had done in a paper entitled 'Emigration for Educated Women', which she delivered at the annual conference of the National Society for the Promotion of Social Science. It was subsequently reissued as a tract and also appeared in the newly established feminist publication *The English Woman's Journal*.[38]

By 1862 Rye had obtained sufficient support to form the Female Middle-class Emigration Society and, until 1868, she devoted much of her time to organising parties of women for emigration, chiefly to Australia and New Zealand. At first she concentrated on middle-class women seeking work as governesses or teachers. However, it soon became clear that there was little colonial demand for such occupations; the first and foremost requirement was for domestic servants. This led Rye to turn her attention instead to the emigration of working-class women and older girls. As a result of these activities she was widely travelled, able to run a venture on business lines, was familiar with the nature of the demand for female labour in the colonies and confident in her dealings with the men who occupied the key official positions at home and abroad as well as within the shipping companies. For a middle-class woman of 40 her experience by 1869 was, in these respects, probably unique.

Marion Diamond's biography of Rye (*Emigration and Empire*) explores her personality but also describes the dilemmas that confronted middle-class Victorian women who were determined to break free from the many social and economic constraints that surrounded them. In Rye's case this represented a particular challenge. Not only was she a spinster but she also lacked financial security. She was, however, energetic and strong-minded, much influenced by 'her intense Evangelical faith' and by the conviction that she was an 'instrument of God's will', a will, as Diamond suggests, which 'seemed to parallel quite closely her own half-acknowledged ambitions'.[39] Another of Diamond's observations is particularly relevant to understanding how Rye went about her activities:

> ... officials – all, of course, men – found [her] difficult to work with because she stood outside the usual bureaucratic hierarchies. Instead, she operated through networks of friends and patrons.... She was

impervious to rules and regulations, and she had no idea of the normal working of bureaucracies – how could she, after all, when women were excluded from such knowledge?[40]

Let us now turn to Maria Rye's involvement in certain events in Wolverhampton. In April 1868 the clerk to the Poor Law guardians wrote to the PLB seeking approval for eight young women from its workhouse to be sent to New Zealand with Rye.[41] In reply the Board wished to know how the emigration was to be arranged and whether the shipping company would sign the contract that was required to guarantee the proper conduct of the voyage.[42] All this was relayed to the next meeting of the guardians. The discussion that followed, as reported in the local press, captures the many cross-currents of members' opinions.

On the one hand, there were those among them who supported the plan because it would be 'a good riddance' to a class of young woman 'with whom the house was over-crowded'. However, it was argued that those who were honest, industrious and well trained should not be emigrated since they could easily be found domestic employment locally. Others welcomed the proposal as a means of reducing expenditure while at the same time offering some girls the chance of bettering themselves. Furthermore, some felt that were young women to remain in the workhouse they were likely to stay or, if discharged, to return with babies or infants in train. Nevertheless, there were some guardians who opposed the scheme on the grounds that the expenditure was not warranted, partly because the young women would soon make their way back (the intention by now being that they should go to Canada). There was also the fear that once it became known that it was possible to be funded to emigrate if one were a pauper in Wolverhampton, those wishing to go abroad would flock to the area. Rye endeavoured to dispel some of these misgivings, in particular writing that the girls would be going so far away from Québec (the port of disembarkation) that there would be no chance that they could find their way back to Britain. In any case she would not assist them to do so. After several more meetings of the Board Rye's offer was accepted, 14 being in favour and three against. In the meantime the clerk, probably aware that this would be the outcome, had continued his correspondence with the PLB and with Rye, sending her the necessary contract papers for the shipping company so that she could get them completed.[43]

The local press coverage of the issue had been considerable and it inevitably came to the notice of William Dixon,[44] the chief Canadian immigration agent in Britain who, at that time, had his offices in Wolverhampton. Given the past history of pauper emigration to Canada and the insistent instructions that he had received from Ottawa to oppose the immigration of undesirables at all costs, the tone of the Wolverhampton guardians' discussions was more than enough to spur him into action. It was not only that the young women who had been selected seemed to be those of whom the guardians wished to be rid that concerned him, but also that the agent involved was Rye, a woman with whom he had already had hostile communications and whose motives he did not trust.

Earlier in 1868 he had called on her in connection with her advertised plan to take a hundred young women to Canada. He had told her that since the demand for domestic servants was so great, Canada would take a few workhouse girls, but that because of the Limerick incident they would have to be chosen with considerable care. However, from what Rye had told him Dixon understood that she did not intend to have anything to do with girls from workhouses. So, when he read of her activities under his very nose in Wolverhampton he exploded in an outraged letter to the secretary of the PLB. She had, he complained, not advised him of her intentions, 'although the workhouse is within twenty minutes walk of my residence'. He had asked her for an explanation, whereupon she replied that she had selected the girls herself, thereby ensuring their worthiness. Having been made aware that Rye had applied to other boards of guardians for girls Dixon wrote to her asking for the names of the unions in question. She declined to provide them. In the light of this he pressed the central Board to investigate the matter and to provide him with assurances that any pauper girls emigrated by Rye would be 'of good character and not such as are likely to prove a burden or an annoyance'.[45]

The PLB asked the Wolverhampton guardians for their observations. They, in turn, claimed that the girls were not of the class to which Dixon objected and that, in any case, the ship-owners had refused to sign the contract required by the PLB.[46] As a result, it was explained, nothing further could be done and that appeared to be the end of the matter. Nevertheless, Rye did take a party of over a 100 girls and young women to Canada at the end of May 1868, although it was not supposed that she included any from Wolverhampton. While in Canada she set about mobilising political and financial support for further ventures. She arrived armed with a letter from Lord Shaftesbury introducing her to John Macdonald, the Canadian Prime Minister. She forwarded this to him together with a covering letter in which she explained that in order to bring out another group she needed £600, which she hoped the government of Canada would provide.[47] In the event she was granted $500.[48] However, Rye wrote that she did not feel able to accept it since she had expected more. Were more not to be made available she would be obliged, she said, to bring her work in Canada to an end;[49] but no increase was forthcoming. Nevertheless, later that year she asked for the $500 to be paid into her Montreal bank,[50] but was told that payment would be made only when she arrived with her next party.

Back in Britain Rye set about assembling her second party of 100 girls and young women. She advertised her plans through the correspondence columns of *The Times* and the *Standard* but was 'taken up' by Dixon. Recounting to Stafford, the chief immigration agent at Québec, the exchanges that he had had with her in letters to these papers, he explained that he had written under pseudonyms as he considered it better to avoid squabbles in his own name. He was sure, however, that she would have known who was 'exposing her doings'. 'I am not', he told Stafford, 'aware that she has been taken up in this way before and will trust that it may do her good and cause her to be more particular in the future'.[51]

In gathering together her second party, however, Rye had not abandoned the plan of recruiting Poor Law girls. She had now succeeded in getting the Allan steamship company to agree to sign the undertaking that the PLB required. She informed the Wolverhampton guardians of the fact and they, in turn, instructed their clerk to get matters moving again. He duly wrote to the PLB asking whether they would give the necessary approval.[52] The reinstatement of the Wolverhampton scheme came to Dixon's notice and he promptly wrote to the Board in London asking them to withhold their permission.[53]

The matter was referred to the President of the Board, George Goschen (in office from 1868 to 1871) who, although sympathetic to the cause of emigration, referred the issue to the Colonial Secretary. He, however, was not prepared to give advice without first consulting the Governor of Canada,[54] although he did suggest that a circular be sent to all boards of guardians exhorting them to be especially careful in their selection of children for emigration. The PLB did not believe that such a circular was necessary since there were too few cases. While these exchanges were taking place Dixon had also written to the Department of Agriculture in Ottawa protesting that since 'Miss Rye thinks fit to act in this reprehensible manner and is making Canada a receptacle for refractory paupers I would ask you to refuse free inland passages for the party which is to sail on ... the 22nd'.[55] However, Rye had already laid plans for its distribution, as had some of the immigration agents in Canada. Nevertheless, Dixon continued to fight his rearguard action. He visited the PLB in London to protest against Rye's activities and was promised that he would be told the outcome of the consideration being given to the matter by the Colonial Office. However, as he wrote in exasperation to Stafford at Québec, 'If I report it [the outcome] to you and you report it to the Dept it will make a very pretty round & all to prevent Miss Rye shipping refractory paupers'. In the same letter he told Stafford what he thought about Rye and her operations, asking him to pass on the substance of his misgivings to Taché, the Deputy Minister, for he felt certain that she would 'bring pressure to bear on the Department for funds to assist her ...'. Of Rye he wrote that she was not a philanthropist but 'a passenger agent of the sharpest description'.[56] Dixon ended his letter, rather despairingly, to the effect that he had done all in his power to work with 'this woman', all to no avail.

While the matter was being referred back and forth between the authorities, towards the end of October 1868 Rye had arrived in Canada with her second party of 90 young servants, although it was not clear how many workhouse girls or women were included. In order to facilitate the work she had again appealed for funds in the columns of *The Times*, where she reported that she had only been able to obtain $500 from the Canadian government and was therefore obliged to call on people's benevolence at home.[57]

During these events the Canadian government took no firm decision about the immigration of pauper children or young women. Perhaps the demand for labour was so great that paupers – as long as they were not outrageous in their behaviour – were welcome alongside other immigrants. Yet because of the suspicion and popular hostility that they attracted, there could be no official encouragement, hence the lack of guidance. The activities of people like Rye allowed the Canadian authorities to avoid any accusation that pauper immigration was being promoted under their auspices. Even so, Dixon still felt that he had instructions that required him to exercise the greatest caution in facilitating any such immigration. Furthermore, he was now locked in a personal battle with Rye. As the emigration season of 1869 approached therefore, and as information began to filter through of further proposals to emigrate workhouse girls, he returned to the fray. His local guardians at Wolverhampton provided his best target, but the Liverpool guardians were also active in the matter. Fearing that the appeal of child emigration from the Poor Law system would spread, Dixon again conveyed his disquiet to the PLB where the justice of his complaints seems to have been recognised.[58] Even so, the Board was not inclined to curtail pauper emigration. Indeed, the general lack of enthusiasm in the matter that it had exhibited throughout most of the 1850s and 1860s had begun to change from about 1868.

There were several reasons for this. One was that George Goschen, an avowed emigrationist, had become President of the Board in the new Gladstone government that was formed in December 1868. He was succeeded two years later (in January 1871) by James Stansfeld, yet another convinced supporter of the emigration remedy and a member of the National Emigration League. Second, the Board became the target of lobbyists from various emigration interests, especially in connection with the regulations that required shipping companies conveying Poor Law-supported emigrants to sign contracts that provided for the retention of half the passage money until safe landing. Indeed, it was proving difficult to find ship-owners who would agree to these terms given the general growth in their emigration business during these years. The outcome was that a relaxation of these regulations was implemented in a circular in 1870, together with specific instructions about what guardians had to do when they proposed people for emigration, not least that the approval of the British-based agent of the colony or dominion in question had to be obtained in respect of each prospective emigrant. In addition, a medical certificate had to be supplied vouchsafing the emigrant's fitness.[59] Clearly, there was considerable concern that colonial sensitivities should not be offended, but also a desire not to obstruct Poor Law emigration.

The 1870 circular cleared away the difficulty of finding shipping companies willing to convey paupers and emphasised that care was to be taken over their selection. It also signalled to boards of guardians that emigration had been given the hallmark of approval. Nonetheless, that approval was somewhat unexpected. On the face of it there were good reasons for the PLB to suppose that any sign of official British encouragement of pauper emigration would be met by a hostile Canadian reaction, especially in the light of the Limerick episode. But the events surrounding the 'Wolverhampton case' give an insight into the complexity of the issues as well as illustrating the contradictions in the Canadian position and the important role of a freelance entrepreneur in exploiting official indecision and vacillation.

Several conclusions may be drawn from this account of the events that sprang from the decision of the Wolverhampton guardians to send some of their workhouse girls to Canada with Maria Rye. First and foremost, it had become clear that given certain rather weak reassurances about their moral and physical fitness, pauper children would not be debarred from entry into Canada. Neither the British nor the Canadian government was going to stand in the way despite the prohibitions codified in the Dominion's immigration legislation. Second, there was no unanimity among the local guardians, although the dominant view in Wolverhampton was that emigration was an excellent solution to the problem of what to do with 'young women' admitted to the workhouse for comparatively short periods but who were liable to return. However, the narrative shifts between references to young women and to 'girls', illustrating the confused terminology around the age of 16.

It is also noteworthy that in 1868 the prevailing mood in official Canadian circles was opposed to any pauper immigration. Dixon, the chief emigration agent in Britain, was given instructions reflecting these sentiments. He saw himself as his government's watchdog and so came into conflict with Rye. Yet he received no support from Ottawa. Several of his requests for guidance were ignored and his channels of official communication were unclear. Within the Canadian administration his immediate superior appears to have been Stafford, the chief immigration agent at Québec; but he also communicated directly with Taché, the Deputy Minister of Agriculture. Such difficulties and uncertainties were exacerbated by the newness of the Canadian state after Confederation in 1867.

Thus, given such a complicated yet vague system, agents like Rye could play off one interest against another, could ignore the Canadian 'representative' in Britain with impunity and, in travelling back and forth across the Atlantic, work with the kind of personal contacts that were less readily available to the officials of either Canada or Britain. Indeed, the apparently confused state of affairs owed a good deal to the ambiguities of communication between the two countries until 1880, when the first Canadian High Commissioner, Sir Alexander Galt, was appointed. Before that Canada's interests in Britain were represented by various 'agents' (like Dixon) without diplomatic status.[60] The most important of these was Sir John Rose.[61] He had been Minister of Finance in Macdonald's government until his resignation in order to join a London bank. Two of his particular responsibilities in London were to oversee the purchase of Rupert's Land from the Hudson's Bay Company and to encourage British emigration. However, first and foremost, his activities appear to have been concerned with securing capital for Canadian development, especially in the north west. Yet his precise dealings with the British government and the extent of the communications that he sustained with Ottawa remain somewhat obscure. His informal status, together with his close ties with the upper echelons of the British financial and political world, made him quite a different figure to William Dixon in his small office helped by a mere handful of staff. One suspects that messages about the major issues of British – Canadian relationships in these years travelled along an informal route via Rose and that Dixon and his successors were frequently by-passed.

The difficulties that this *ad hoc* system of representation created were considerable. The principal formal channel of communication was that between the Colonial Secretary and the Governor-General. That meant, for example, that if the Local Government Board (LGB) (which succeeded the PLB in 1871) or the Home Office wished to exchange views with, say, the Canadian Department of Agriculture, they were obliged to do so via the Colonial Office. When the Governor-General received a dispatch it was either referred to the appropriate minister or, if more important, taken to the Privy Council for decision. This was a time-consuming process.

Up to 1880 therefore, and, to a lesser extent thereafter, the complex system of trans-Atlantic communications, superimposed as it was on the inherent tension between the provincial governments and the federal government in Canada, offered excellent opportunities for enterprising emigrationists. The innumerable divisions, misunderstandings, delays and uncertainties that arose could be readily exploited by those who were shrewd enough to perceive them and determined enough in their objectives.

V The Scene is Set

Various circumstances thus conspired to create the opportunity for a reconsideration of emigration as a solution to the intensified social and economic problems of Britain in the late 1860s. Children came to be regarded as an especially appropriate group of candidates. Child-saving motives could be blended with the wish to see the poor rates relieved and society protected from the dangers of unbridled street-children. Compulsory education was still in the future, while in both the industrial towns and in the countryside new technologies reduced the call for child labour. Perhaps more than any earlier decade the 1860s in Britain witnessed a crisis in the social control of children of the under-classes. It was no accident that the movements for the inauguration of compulsory education, reformatories, industrial schools and emigration reached their most active phases during this period, albeit often given added impetus by the evangelical zeal of their proponents.

Abroad there were countries of the Empire whose economies had not yet reached the stage where there was sufficient capital or labour to introduce and establish the technology that in Britain was changing the economic position of the child and the family. A time lag existed between the economic development of countries like Canada and Britain. This created the practical possibility that the social problems surrounding poor and destitute children in Britain could be transformed into economic solutions in Canada. In many ways the passage across the Atlantic not only transported children to another country but also to an earlier period in their own country where their toil represented an important element in the agricultural labour force. Yet that analogy is somewhat misleading because, as we shall see, the farming and domestic work that the children found themselves doing in Canada was based essentially on the family unit and on relatively modest holdings of land; not at all like the large farms of East Anglia, for example, which had traditionally employed gangs of female and child workers. Even so, it remains important to stress that it was the differences in the economic and political development of Britain and Canada that created an emigration gradient down which an increasing number of children were to be sent until the First World War.

TWO

Early Initiatives

I London: Rye, Macpherson and Stephenson

It was Maria Rye and Annie Macpherson (1824-1904) whose names have been most often associated with the inauguration of child emigration to Canada, although they did not collaborate and were never closely acquainted. Their styles of operation were markedly different. Rye, although subscribing to evangelical sentiments, was a tough-minded entrepreneur with a sharp eye for political opportunities. Macpherson, as Wagner describes her, was a 'twice-born Christian, a committed evangelical who shunned the secular world'.[1] The depth and pervasiveness of this evangelism is compellingly illustrated in her letters that appear in the 'record' of her work written by her helper Clara Lowe.[2] In contrast, Rye's letters are robust and businesslike with only an occasional reference to evangelical sentiments.

After training as a Froebel teacher Macpherson was introduced to social work in the East End of London through the revival movement, and from 1865 she was involved in various schemes to assist destitute families, and children in particular. There was visiting, feeding, classes and bible instruction. She publicised the plight of the small children whose poverty-stricken parents were obliged to set them to work making matchboxes.[3] In 1868 she opened a small Home for boys, then a second for girls, followed by a third for older boys. Donations came mostly from the readers of the evangelical paper, *The Revival*; indeed, the Homes were called 'Revival Homes'. Funds from similar sources were collected in 1868 in order to rent a warehouse that was to become the 'Home of Industry'. The aim was to combine work for young people and their mothers with elementary education and the propagation of the Gospel. However, by 1869 Macpherson, like many others, had come to the conclusion that emigration was an important remedy for the distress in east London and a fund was established to send selected families to Canada.[4]

Thus, although they had arrived at the idea of child emigration by different routes both Rye and Macpherson were, by 1869, in a position to appreciate the opportunities that child emigration seemed to offer. Rye had more practical experience of organising emigration parties and a better understanding of the nature and scale of the demand for child labour in countries like Canada. Macpherson had much more direct experience of the suffering of the poor, was now running three children's Homes as well as the Home of Industry and was acutely aware that these provisions could be filled many times over. In order to continue and expand the work acceptable destinations had to be found for the children who were already being accommodated in the Homes. Rye did not have to take this into consideration because at the start of her endeavours she had no Home to run in Britain. There were other factors that led her to her involvement in child emigration. Nonetheless, one experience from their separate visits to the US helped to convince both women that the emigration of poor children was not only desirable but also practical.

While in the US Rye and Macpherson were introduced to schemes for the relocation of destitute city children (particularly from New York) in the developing areas of the west. These undertakings, instigated by people like Charles Loring Brace of the Children's Aid Society and van Meter of the Howard League for Children, had been operating since the end of the Civil War. Both women had met van Meter and heard from him about the success that he had had in placing children with farm families. Not only were such schemes possible (the existence of a growing railway system being especially important) but they also appealed to romantic notions of a return to a golden age – to a time of simplicity, strong moral values, firm religion and family unity, all unthreatened by the apparent sinfulness and disorder of the great cities. If children were to be rescued from the unhealthiness and moral corruption of urban life, where better to send them than to the farms and homesteads that clamoured to receive them? As Loring Brace wrote in 1872, 'the best of all Asylums for the outcast child is the *farmer's home*' (original emphasis).[5] Such claims, together with the examples of what could be done, left a deep impression on both Rye and Macpherson and on others like Father Nugent whose contribution is described later. The appeal of the American example lay in the fact that the rescue of deprived and endangered children, although couched in terms of religious objectives, could be manifested in tangible acts of geographical relocation. Rescue could be *seen* to have been accomplished, and that was important in attracting donations, sustaining enthusiasm and deflecting criticism.

Nonetheless, this shared experience from the US and a common evangelical commitment were about the only similarities between Rye and Macpherson. Rye usually took girls, Macpherson boys. More importantly they approached the task of winning support and overcoming opposition in quite different ways. Chapter 1 provided a taste of Rye's approach. Here this is illustrated more fully and then compared with how Macpherson went about matters.

We have seen how, after bringing her last party of women to Canada in 1868, Rye set about lobbying Prime Minister Macdonald in order to prepare the ground for bringing girls rather than women, and to obtain financial support from his government. Although she was awarded a grant of $500 it remained unclear whether this was to help her to provide women or girls, again reflecting the uneasy definition of which was which at around the ages of 14, 15 or 16. In any case birth certificates were sometimes missing and girls unsure or mistaken about how old they were.

Nevertheless, with her plans laid for landing with a party of girls in 1869 Rye had to neutralise any official opposition. First, she wrote to the Principal Secretary of the government of Ontario asking whether there would be any objection to her bringing children into the province; there was none.[6] Then she wrote to the Secretary of State in Ottawa describing her scheme, enclosing a copy of the reply that she had received from Ontario and seeking permission to land the children.[7] At much the same time she also communicated with Sir John Rose, the Minister of Finance (later to be the High Commissioner in London), who had already helped her to defray the cost of conveying the women whom she had brought to Canada from Québec to Toronto as well as having sanctioned the $500 grant. She hoped, she wrote, that he would continue to lend her his support with respect to her new venture in child immigration.[8]

So, Rye had now alerted the Secretary of State and the Minister of Finance to her scheme, already having been granted financial assistance in connection with her work in the emigration of women. Now the matter was referred to the Minister of Agriculture, J.-C. Chapais, who was doubtless considering William Dixon's request from London for more precise instructions as well as Dixon's evident distrust of Rye's motives. Perhaps because of this Taché, the Deputy Minister in the Department of Agriculture (that is, the senior civil servant in the department), wrote back to Rye to say that the children could *not* be landed since, because they were helpless and dependent, it would be in violation of the immigration legislation.[9] However, despite this rebuff she went ahead with her arrangements for taking her first party of girls to Canada in the autumn of 1869, her position having been strengthened because the government of Ontario had sold her the old prison at Niagara cheaply for a reception Home. Despite all this Dixon still endeavoured to thwart Rye, entreating Taché 'to compel the return of the children to England'.[10] He also wrote to Stafford, the chief immigration agent at Québec, suggesting that he ask for instructions about what to do when Rye's party of children arrived.[11] At the same time Stafford received a note from Rye informing him of her expected arrival and telling him that she would be seeking his help. Could he, she asked, confirm that her party would be passed on free to Toronto?[12] Contrary to the letter that Taché had written to Rye, Stafford was now instructed to allow her party of children to land and also to accord them free transport.

Thus, by a combination of political lobbying and bravado Rye had cleared the ground in Canada for the inauguration of her child emigration enterprise and for others to follow. She had circumvented the 1869 Immigration Act, won the support of the government of Ontario and (eventually) the federal government in Ottawa, established a precedent for the free travel of her parties from Québec and had obtained a reception Home. A complicated plan had been put into effect aided by her exchange of correspondence with different figures in the Canadian government, few of whom had previously discussed the issue of child immigration or who had agreed a co-ordinated response.

Doubtless Macpherson benefited from Rye having cleared away official obstacles in 1869, but she had, in any case, been quietly preparing to take a large group of boys to Canada in 1870. Dixon became aware of this and duly reported it to

Ottawa;[13] he was told that Macpherson should not bring as many as was planned. Macpherson agreed not to exceed 100 and invited Dixon to visit the Home of Industry and examine the boys who were to go. He reported that they 'were very fine looking well grown lads, and [that] there was nothing apparent to which I could reasonably have raised objection'.[14] On her behalf he asked Taché whether the boys could be transported free once in Canada, pointing out that her scheme was 'purely one of philanthropy' aimed at rescuing lads from abject poverty. The whole tone of Dixon's reports on Macpherson was entirely different from that which he employed when referring to Rye. This was partly because her approach was more circumspect and co-operative. Macpherson had clearly won Dixon's support at the London end. He then went on to smooth the way for her with the Canadian authorities; but she, unlike Rye, was not intending to bring out children from the Poor Law.

Despite Dixon's help Macpherson's first party of boys was distributed without the aid of a reception Home or plans having been made beforehand. However, in Belleville (mid-way between Ottawa and Toronto) the council offered her premises free of charge as long as she located her activities there on a permanent basis.[15] Macpherson accepted the offer and Ellen Bilbrough, who had travelled with the group, was left in charge. Before returning to London Macpherson visited other towns, explaining her intentions and enlisting support as well as promises of homes for any children whom she was able to bring. Two other parties of boys were dispatched in 1870, the last in the charge of Louisa Birt, Macpherson's sister. The following year another distribution Home was established west of Toronto at Galt, also with the aid of the local community. Macpherson repeated her pattern of travelling and addressing various townships in the following year. In 1872 she was invited to establish a third Home at Knowlton in the Protestant area of eastern Québec. This she duly did with the help of local donations and some from Britain.

Whereas Rye approached the task of obtaining Canadian support by tackling senior levels of government, Macpherson relied more on explaining her plans at local meetings and thereby winning the goodwill, and financial support, of leading inhabitants. Nevertheless, she also benefited from the interest and encouragement of influential people in Canada, although they less often occupied positions in the world of politics. As Clara Lowe wrote, Macpherson pleaded 'the cause of her children before many in positions of influence, judges, merchants, lawyers, and doctors'.[16] She also drew extensively on the sympathy of like-minded Christians who responded to her conviction that child emigration was an opportunity to perform God's work, and no doubt also to add to the meagre supply of agricultural and domestic labour.

It is tempting to interpret the prominence of these two women in the child emigration movement in terms of their personalities, their experiences and their motivations. Yet both, in different ways, were the products of particular social and economic influences. In the case of Rye there was the growing pressure for new economic opportunities for women, especially middle-class women. For

Macpherson the revival movement was more important. Nonetheless, both these themes converged in what was, or what could be interpreted as, charitable work. As Prochaska has written, 'if we are to isolate one profession that did more than any other to enlarge the horizons of women in nineteenth-century England it would have to be the profession of charity'.[17] In addition, of course, the intensification of distress in the latter part of the 1860s produced a flood of child casualties, some of whom swelled the pauper ranks while others joined the legion of street-arabs or became an important means of family survival by the addition of their pitiful earnings, won in a variety of marginal and casual occupations. Every major period of economic depression was a time of crisis for the children of the poor, but the recession at the end of the 1860s was particularly devastating, aggravated in east London by the cholera epidemic.

Rye and Macpherson having opened the door to child emigration to Canada, others began to follow. The Reverend Thomas Stephenson (1839-1912) and two colleagues launched the third enduring initiative in London. Stephenson was a Wesleyan Methodist minister who rose to become a leading figure in the Methodist Conference. He had arrived in London in 1868 and, together with Alfred Mager and Francis Horner, acquired a cottage in Lambeth for boys in great need where they received some basic training and education.[18] A second cottage was opened soon after. In 1871 Stephenson was relieved of his ministerial duties in order to become the full-time head of the new venture, which now included a third Home in Bethnal Green. A house and land at Edgeworth, near Bolton, were bequeathed in 1871, which, by the following year, was ready to receive boys to be trained in farming; later, girls were also admitted, but for domestic instruction.[19]

Stephenson was initially encouraged to consider child emigration by a friend and fellow Methodist minister who had spent some time in Toronto. The minister wrote extolling the opportunities that Canada had to offer for trained young people and suggested that Stephenson should visit to see for himself what might be done. He was able to do this in 1872 after he had attended the General Conference of the Methodist Episcopal Church in the US. Crossing into Canada Stephenson saw that there was an enormous demand for agricultural labour. More especially he was impressed by 'the social and religious conditions of the Canadian population', which, he concluded, held out 'a most hopeful prospect' that any child sent out would 'be able to command an honourable and respectable career in life'. Furthermore, Stephenson was convinced that for children from 'the pauper or semi-criminal class' emigration offered the best and 'perhaps the only chance of their rising above the level of their birth'.[20]

A few years later, after further visits, Stephenson described more fully the advantages that he considered Canada had to offer. It was, he wrote, a country where:

> ... the people ... are remarkable, as well for their sobriety as their industry. Public houses are few and far between. Pernicious amusements

such as are common in great towns and cities of this land, are far rarer.… Agricultural employment, affording health to the mind and body, yield their ample remuneration.[21]

There were, of course, other reasons that encouraged Stephenson to embark on his scheme for emigration. He faced the same problem as Macpherson – unless the boys who had been taken into the limited accommodation could later be discharged to a satisfactory future, how could the work with such children in Britain be expanded? He almost certainly had this in mind during his Canadian tour of 1872 and during his discussions there with people like Miss Bilbrough and Miss Barber who ran Macpherson's Homes at Belleville and Knowlton respectively.[22] Indeed, it was clear that he had already decided to launch a similar scheme. While in Hamilton it had been agreed that a subscription would be raised locally for the purchase of a reception Home. The appeal enabled a large house to be bought and refurbished. W.E. Sandford undertook to act as treasurer. Indeed, it was he who donated most of the money needed to establish the Home. Sandford was not only a rich businessman (the fourth largest employer in Ontario) but also a prominent Methodist and an enthusiastic advocate of immigration. In 1887 he became a Conservative senator, in which position he was able not only to argue Stephenson's cause but that of child immigration in general.

From the outset Stephenson's approach to emigration was rather more restrained than that of his contemporaries. For instance, in his annual report for 1872 he had written that emigration was not to be regarded as a 'panacea for social ills' and that he did:

> … not propose to send abroad any child for whom a suitable opening could be found in England, unless there is something in his early life, or in his associations, which renders it specially desirable that he be … severed from old haunts.…[23]

Later, in 1877, it was also explained that no child would be sent to Canada 'against their will, or without the written consent of their legal representatives'.[24] Emigration therefore played a comparatively modest role in the arrangements made by the NCH (National Children's Homes, the name that, by then, Stephenson's organisation had adopted) for children in their care. The proportion being sent to Canada each year illustrates this: typically around six per cent, although there were a few years (particularly in the 1880s) when the figure was larger.

Unlike Rye's and Macpherson's schemes, all Stephenson's child rescue work became constitutionally part of a wider organisation: that of the Methodist Church. None of this is to say that he did not exercise considerable influence; clearly he did. Ultimately, however, he was answerable to (and paid by) the Methodist Conference. Indeed, before embarking on his venture he was obliged to obtain the approval of its president, a post that he was later to occupy himself.

II Liverpool: Nugent and Birt

Much philanthropic activity was concentrated in London, especially in the 1860s and 1870s. Stedman Jones reminds us that the capital was also regarded as the focal point of those social problems that most frequently attracted political and charitable attention. He attributes this to the economic changes that London underwent during these years and which accentuated the problem of intermittent employment. Casual labour raised the spectre of social disorder. The 'mob', the 'dangerous classes' or the 'residuum' were terms variously applied to those who suffered the poverty and uncertainty of an economic order unable to provide them with permanent work; they constituted 'outcast London'.[25]

While London was almost certainly a special case in these and other respects, other cities were comparable, Liverpool not least among them. It too contained its outcast population, created in part by its prominence as a port. Liverpool had an extensive system of casual labour associated with the docks, a considerable loss of men at sea that had left many families fatherless and immigration from Ireland that, although at its peak during the famine years, continued throughout the 1850s and 1860s. The Irish who remained in Liverpool were often the most destitute. This, together with their large families and lack of industrial skills, consigned them to the most wretched areas and denied them and their children a secure foothold in the labour market.

However, although it arose for superficially different reasons, the nature of child suffering in Liverpool hardly differed at all from that witnessed in London. Furthermore, it was equally common for children who were at large on the streets to be regarded as a threat to an orderly and safe society. Similarly, in most middle-class circles it was generally concluded that the children of the under-class were in dire moral peril – on the one hand, from their parents' undesirable influence and on the other, from the social contamination of the areas in which they lived.

Rye had already included Poor Law children from the Liverpool Industrial School at Kirkdale in the party that she took to Canada in 1869. However, her association with the city was fortuitous, the result of having captured the interest of William Rathbone MP in her scheme and of his willingness to recommend it to his fellow guardians. Others, however, were also active in Liverpool, Father Nugent in particular. James Nugent (1822-1903)[26] was born in Liverpool and assumed his first priestly duties there in 1849. He became involved in developing Catholic education, in establishing night shelters for homeless children and, in 1869, with the foundation of a boys' refuge. He was also a prominent figure in the Liverpool Catholic Reformatory Association that, by 1864, had secured and opened the reformatory ship *Clarence*. Earlier, in 1863, Nugent had been appointed Catholic chaplain to Walton gaol in Liverpool, a step made possible by the Borough Prisons Act of that year that permitted justices to pay for the services of chaplains other than those belonging to the Church of England. This was an important and sensitive issue in Liverpool where it was estimated that Catholics constituted some two-thirds of the prison population. However, the willingness of the justices to appoint a Catholic priest to Walton gaol was not matched by a readiness on the part of the guardians to give priests access to Catholic children in their institutions, even though probably half of the children in the large Kirkdale school were Catholics. As in other places, the Liverpool board of guardians contained a sufficient element of anti-Catholic feeling to keep the priesthood at arm's length.

So Catholics like Nugent were not only 'appalled at the sight of the streets overrun by hordes of homeless vagabond children struggling for a precarious existence by theft, begging and street trading',[27] but also concerned that Poor Law children were being denied a Catholic education and, to all intents and purposes, being brought up as Protestants. Throughout the 1860s Cardinal Manning (the head of the Catholic Church in Britain) campaigned nationally to 'rescue' Catholic children from the workhouses and Poor Law schools as well as to gather from the streets 'the tens of thousands of poor Catholic children' who were 'without education or training'.[28] Manning spoke and wrote principally of London but his concerns were widespread. Progress seemed to have been made in 1859 when the Poor Law Board (PLB) issued an Order that prohibited the instruction of Catholic Poor Law children in any other religion and that also instructed guardians to maintain a creed register in all their institutions. However, scant attention seemed to have been paid to these requirements. In 1869 the Order was revised to strengthen the hand of the central PLB in dealing with recalcitrant local boards of guardians. As *The Tablet* argued, this was important since the Catholic struggle had not been with the government but with 'workhouse bigotry'.[29]

The problem for the Catholics was accentuated by their lack of sufficient residential accommodation to be able to admit all the Catholic children in Poor Law schools, let alone the 'street children' as well. However, as the number of Catholic Homes and industrial schools increased in the second half of the 1860s, Catholics became better placed to urge that Poor Law children be transferred. They were helped in this by the 1869 Order since it empowered the PLB to order that such transfers be made on the application of a child's parent or next of kin. There were two results. First, Manning called for a concerted effort to identify the parents of Catholic children in the care of guardians and then for them to be encouraged to apply for their children to be removed to a Catholic institution. Second, since, when this was achieved, the PLB's Order specified that boards of guardians should pay six shillings a week as a maintenance fee, many of them were prepared to settle for transfers without the involvement of parents if a lower fee could be negotiated. However, these developments only began to gather momentum from about 1870. Many Catholic children remained in the Poor Law schools where it was believed by Catholics that they were being exposed to Protestant indoctrination. Thus, despite the 1869 Order, such misgivings continued to alarm the Catholic Church, an alarm that was exacerbated by more general anxiety about the so-called 'leakage' from the faith.[30] For both reasons the Catholic hierarchy attached great importance to ensuring the Catholic upbringing of Catholic children.

It is against this background that Nugent's initiatives for the encouragement of child emigration must be seen. Emigration to Canada under Catholic auspices not only offered to save Catholic children from the moral and physical hazards of city life and from parental neglect but also from the clutches of a predominantly Protestant Poor Law system, and to do so without placing impossible demands on the limited amount of Catholic residential provision. Furthermore, it promised an upbringing in Catholic families often living in identifiable Catholic communities, particularly in Québec. Over and above these considerations it also had a defensive aspect. Nugent had seen Rye, an outspoken anti-Catholic, begin to assemble children for emigration from the Liverpool guardians. The possibility that Catholic children might be included, either by accident or design, had to be forestalled.

Like Macpherson, Nugent took his first party of children to Canada in 1870. Half of them came from the Kirkdale school. That done he stayed on and embarked on a lecturing tour that, over the following nine months, enabled him to travel widely in Canada and the US.[31] This led to new plans, particularly for taking children to the US as well as to Canada. In 1871 Nugent attended a meeting of the board of guardians in Liverpool and explained that he had made arrangements for a number of Catholic girls to go to Maryland and that he would be willing to include some for whom they were responsible. However, this came to the attention of the US Ambassador who wrote to the Foreign Secretary protesting about the plan, pointing out that such an undertaking 'would be regarded in no other light than as a violation of the amity which ever ought to characterise the intercourse of Nations'.[32]

The matter was duly referred to the President of the Local Government Board (LGB) (James Stansfeld) for his observations.[33] As a result instructions were issued that nothing further should be done without the LGB's permission. The clerk to the guardians replied that because the cost of the children's emigration was not to be met from the poor rate he did not consider that such permission was required. However, the LGB insisted that it was.[34] And on this note the correspondence ceased and no children went to the US; attention turned firmly towards Canada.

In London Louisa Birt had been assisting her sister Annie Macpherson in her missionary social work. During 1872 their work came to the attention of Alexander Balfour, a Liverpool merchant and ship-owner who was already involved in the establishment of the Liverpool Seaman's Orphanage. He now proposed that something similar to what Macpherson was doing in London should be done in his city. Louisa was persuaded to undertake the commission. Balfour, together with Samuel Smith, the Liverpool MP, then set about forming a committee of businessmen and other notables to finance and manage the new initiative. Premises were acquired rent free and opened as the Liverpool Sheltering Homes in 1873.

However, no arrangements had yet been made for the reception of the children from these Homes who were to be sent to Canada. So when J. W. Laurie, a farmer of means from Nova Scotia (NS), wrote suggesting that he should oversee the placement and supervision of any children she cared to bring to the province, Birt willingly accepted the offer. Laurie had heard of the Liverpool development from several sources, but he also had an established link with the Royal Philanthropic School, from which he had been receiving several boys a year on his estate. His offer to extend his activities to children from the Liverpool Sheltering Homes allowed Birt to begin her emigration work at once. Initially, accommodation was to be provided at the boys' industrial school in Halifax and at the Protestant girls' Home. Later, Laurie was to use a house on his estate for receiving the children and for taking back those whose placements had broken down. This was run by J.C. Arnold, a lay preacher, whose appointment was financed by the Halifax branch of the Colonial and Continental Church Society.[35]

The government of Nova Scotia was anxious to encourage the immigration of boys and girls. Laurie had established that it would grant a passage subsidy of $10 for children over the age of 14 and $5 for the younger children. There would also be a Dominion subsidy of $2 a head. Furthermore, all expenses were to be met until the children were distributed and if they had to be returned to Laurie's estate. No charge was to be made for transport within the province.[36] These were generous terms that, together with the free services of Laurie and Arnold, effectively relieved Birt of most of her emigration expenses. She had a strong incentive to choose Nova Scotia as the destination for some of the Liverpool Sheltering Homes' children.

However, these arrangements did not last. Laurie bowed out in 1876, ostensibly because of ill health but there were also charges that some of the children whom he had placed had been abused. Clay, the Dominion immigration agent at Halifax, discovered the case of Emma Daniel,[37] and John Walter of Truro, NS, raised deep concerns about the practice of child immigration in general and about Laurie's involvement in it in particular. He wrote a series of letters to the Colonial Secretary in London, the outcome of which was that Laurie was asked to give an account of what had been happening.[38] Soon after this Laurie left for Europe and disassociated himself from Birt's activities.[39] However, the government of Nova Scotia was not prepared to assume the responsibilities that he had taken upon himself, at least not beyond a temporary arrangement. Furthermore, the province withdrew the financial support that it had previously provided. It was at this point (1877) that Annie Macpherson offered Birt her distribution Home at Knowlton in Québec.[40] This was accepted and henceforth the Home became the centre from which the Liverpool Sheltering Homes operated, although later, when the government of Québec declined to support her financially, Birt endeavoured to move everything back to Nova Scotia with that government's renewed help; but she was told firmly that they would offer her no such assistance.[41]

III Quarrier and Glasgow

Conditions in Glasgow in the 1860s were as dire for the poor, and especially for their children, as they were in London or Liverpool. Indeed, in at least one respect they were worse. In Scotland, unlike in England, the able-bodied were not eligible for poor relief, neither in the poorhouses nor in their own homes. The children of the destitute obtained what they could on the streets, to help support their families or to survive alone if they no longer had a family. Some were orphaned, some were homeless and many suffered illness and disease, especially tuberculosis. It was the plight of these street-children that first captured the attention of William Quarrier (1829-1903), a successful young businessman and fervent evangelist.[42] In 1871 he used the columns of the *Glasgow Herald* and the *North British Daily Mail*[43] to enlist financial support for the purchase of a house that was to be a Home for 'orphan and destitute' boys and to serve as a centre in which some of them could be prepared for emigration to Canada. All this was achieved before the end of the year, to be followed soon afterwards by a similar Home for girls. Three other Glasgow Homes followed in 1872, eventually to replace the first two. People such as bible-women, medical missionaries, pastors, Poor Law officers and concerned private individuals referred children to Quarrier.

Quarrier's commitment to emigration was made explicit from the outset. He referred to it in his 1871 letters to the press, having been much influenced by Annie Macpherson. It seems that he met her first on a visit to London, but he subsequently discussed the venture with her when she visited Glasgow, at which time she promised him her collaboration, in particular by offering him the use of her distribution Homes in Canada.[44] The principal link between Quarrier and Macpherson was undoubtedly a shared evangelical conviction and a sense of calling, but also Quarrier clearly had a special admiration for Macpherson and her work. Indeed, he named his last, but short-lived, daughter Annie Macpherson Quarrier. However, unlike virtually all of his leading contemporaries in philanthropic child saving and child welfare Quarrier had grown up the son of a poor (but not destitute) widowed mother. He was apprenticed very young as a shoemaker and, by the age of 23, had established himself as a boot and shoe retailer with the first of three shops. He had no formal education; but he had married the well-educated daughter of his last (and prosperous) employer.

The first party of 64 children to be assembled by Quarrier for Canada sailed in July 1872, helped, he records, by Macpherson's sister Louisa Birt.[45] However, not all in this first party were drawn from his Homes – nearly half had come from other institutions, in particular from Mrs Blaikie's Home in Edinburgh and from the Maryhill girls' industrial school in Glasgow. There were clearly contacts here too; indeed, for a number of years there was a small but steady stream of children joining Quarrier's emigration parties from the Blaikie Home.

Despite the nature of the referrals, efforts appear to have been made to obtain the parents' or relatives' consent to a child's departure, although the relatives could sometimes be brothers and sisters who were little older than the child in question. Others who had shouldered the responsibility for looking after an orphaned nephew or niece signed willingly, faced with poverty and often having large enough families of their own. Nonetheless, where consents were refused the decisions seem to have been respected. In 1875, for example, the annual report recorded that several children had to be excluded from the emigration party because their relatives 'were unwilling to let them go'.[46] Relatives were not always easy to trace, however.

Unlike Rye, Macpherson, Stephenson, Birt or Nugent, Quarrier was not well travelled. Indeed, he did not visit Canada until 1878. Hence the reports and letters that he received from those who had, or who worked in Canada on his behalf, were particularly important in sustaining his enthusiasm for child emigration. They gave glowing accounts of the success of the scheme, a success confirmed in his eyes by his subsequent visits. After the 1878 journey he concluded that 'we can do nothing here [in Scotland] for the class of children we help that will at all compare with what can be done here in Canada'[47] and after the following year's visit he wrote that 'we have come back more than ever impressed', resolving to send yet larger parties in subsequent years.[48]

One curious aspect of Quarrier's work was that no consideration appears to have been given to boarding out in Scotland those children who were sent to Canada. Yet the Scottish Poor Law system had for a long time boarded out a majority of the children for whom it was responsible, many in the highlands and islands with crofters and cottars. Indeed, as the chairman of the Board of Supervision (the central Poor Law authority in Scotland) explained before the Select Committee on the Poor Laws (Scotland) in 1869, 'the rule requiring all deserted or orphan children to be boarded out is almost universal'.[49] Precise figures were not available until 1890, but in that year 87 per cent of the children chargeable to the parishes were boarded out, 40 per cent of them with relatives.[50] Given this well-established tradition it might have been expected that Quarrier would have followed the same path. However, he explained his policy in the following way:

> The boarding-out system adopted by the Parochial Boards of Scotland is much superior to that of the English workhouses, but even it is surpassed in usefulness by our emigration scheme, which … places them [the children] out in the homes of well-to-do farmers, who receive them not as paupers, but as children to be loved and cared for as their own.[51]

This may well have reflected his deeply held belief that, if at all possible, children should be prevented from having to be cared for by the Poor Law. In the light of this it is somewhat surprising that, unlike Rye and some of the other emigrationists, Quarrier appears not to have taken many children to Canada from the parochial boards, possibly because, given the tradition and availability of boarding out, these bodies saw no good reason for their children to be sent overseas.[52] Indeed, placing children with crofters or cottars who had little money was somewhat similar to taking children to Canada and placing them on small family farms. In both cases there was a need for extra hands but limited means with which to pay for them.

IV Middlemore in Birmingham

Although not a port, and with a different industrial base to the other cities that saw an early establishment of child emigration, Birmingham's poor also suffered from uncertain employment and widespread destitution. Again, however, it was one individual who seized on the idea of emigration as at least a partial remedy for the child suffering that this brought in its wake. That individual was John Middlemore (1844-1924). He belonged to a well-established and prosperous Birmingham family engaged in manufacture and holding to strict Baptist principles.[53] When Middlemore was 20 he was sent to work in an uncle's business in Boston, soon enrolling at the University of Brunswick (Maine) to study medicine and, although qualifying, he never practised. While in North America he travelled widely, including to Canada. He returned to Britain in 1868 and became concerned about the condition of children in Birmingham. Having seen what he considered to be splendid opportunities in Canada, Middlemore determined to launch a scheme for the emigration of the most endangered of these children. However, unlike Barnardo, Quarrier, Stephenson and others, he restricted his child-saving activities to emigration. He did not seek to provide 'general' child care facilities; in this, of course, he followed in Rye's footsteps. Nonetheless, a reception Home was needed into which children could be admitted and given some preparation prior to their departure. Two small establishments (one for boys and one for girls) were acquired in 1872 with the aid of funds collected from the influential Birmingham network of which he was part. Indeed, Middlemore was a leading figure in the city, becoming a member of its council in 1883. Seven years later he was elected to Parliament as the Unionist member for Birmingham North, a seat that he occupied for the next 19 years.

The first group to be emigrated from the Birmingham Emigration Homes (as they were called) consisted of 29 boys who sailed in May 1873. Middlemore accompanied them (as he was to do frequently thereafter) but, as he admitted, he had made no prior arrangements for their reception or placement on arrival. He wrote later that he 'had not a single friend in Canada, and did not know what to do with my children when I arrived there'.[54] However, he 'had heard of' a George Allan and a Professor Wilson in Toronto, both of whom he telegraphed just before his departure seeking their help. Allan approached the immigration agent in Toronto in order to obtain temporary accommodation for the children but was offered only the immigration sheds. He considered that these were unacceptable and went on to persuade three charitable institutions in the city to accept the young immigrants.[55] Such an arrangement could be no more than temporary, and in the first year of his Canadian venture Middlemore obtained a reception and distribution Home of his own in London, Ontario. This was provided rent-free by the city council.[56] However, it was closed in 1890 because, as it was explained, Middlemore was not in good health and because 'certain points in the management have been so unsatisfactory'. The manager was dismissed but claimed that the closure was due to the loss of local support. A temporary arrangement was made with Annie Macpherson to take over the work while Middlemore sought to re-establish his activities in the Maritimes.[57] By 1893 he was again taking parties of children to Canada and placing them in Nova Scotia, New Brunswick and Prince Edward Island but using Emma Stirling's Home for their reception.[58] (We shall learn more about her activities in chapter 7.) It was not until 1896 that work began on the construction of a new Home in the suburbs of Halifax,[59] which seems not to have opened until 1898.[60] This development followed the insistence of the Department of the Interior that each society should have its own reception Home.[61]

The rationale for Middlemore's emigration scheme was set out in various early annual reports. For example, children were not to be sent to Canada simply because they were poor but because it was necessary 'to ensure the permanence and completeness of [their] ... reformation'. Since they were rescued 'more from their bad associations than from their own vice', the work, it was explained, 'would be incomplete' if they remained in Birmingham.[62] However, in a later report the emphasis switched somewhat to 'leading criminal children out of temptation'.[63] Thus, like all the other individuals and agencies who sent children to Canada, the primary reason for doing so was severance combined with the notion of a new start. Nevertheless, emigration was only to be used 'with extreme cases' because, Middlemore explained, 'expatriation is too strong a remedy for cases of ordinary misfortune'.[64] These were quite stringent criteria for admission to the emigration Homes that, if strictly interpreted, enabled the size of the intake to be rather carefully regulated. Despite his enthusiasm for emigration Middlemore seems to have recognised more clearly than most of his fellow emigrationists the terrible wrench and trauma that it imposed. For instance, in 1882 it was reported that the parents of the 'little emigrants' had been invited to tea a couple of days before departure in order that they could 'meet their children once again, and ... bid them a life-long farewell'. Middlemore described the occasion as one:

> ... when mothers and children were meeting for the last time on earth,
> [it] was as pathetic as life could present. After tea had been served, and
> a few simple speeches had been made, the parents and children were
> left for a short time together ... farewell kisses were exchanged, and
> the life-long separation was at length effected.

Young as the children were, 'they were about to turn their backs forever on the crime and drunkenness amid which they had been nurtured – to leave kith, kin and country, to cross the Atlantic and to face a new future in a new world'.[65]

Middlemore made no provision for the care of children in Birmingham itself, except by way of their preparation for emigration. And there were three further respects in which he stood out from the other emigrationists. First, although a firm Baptist Middlemore did not express the vehement anti-Catholicism that characterised many of his evangelical contemporaries, perhaps because his forebears had been staunch Catholics. Second, he was to become a prominent local and national politician and the only head of a nineteenth-century children's society to be knighted. Third, he established a strong friendship with John Lowe, the Deputy Minister in the Canadian Department of Agriculture,[66] a relationship that was to serve the cause of his emigration activities well until the transfer of responsibility for immigration to the Department of the Interior in the early 1890s.

V The Networks

Thus, Birmingham became the fourth centre of the early initiatives in child emigration. While there are differences in the histories of these various developments, their general features are remarkably similar. Apart from the common social conditions in which they evolved, the intricacies of the prevailing networks are noteworthy. Each of the people discussed cultivated and benefited from complex networks of influence, of power, of information and of money. These networks extended across the Atlantic and between different parts of Britain. Many reflected particular religious affiliations and sympathies. Others overlapped into boards of guardians, included government officials, or MPs in both Britain and Canada. As businessmen, Quarrier and Middlemore enjoyed networks that spanned both commerce and evangelism. Some people who were prominent in one network reappeared in others, figures like Shaftesbury, Rathbone and Smith for instance.

These early initiatives in child emigration (and also later ones) were widely advertised; news of such work travelled rapidly. To a large extent, of course, communications followed the lines of the prevailing networks on a word-of-mouth basis; but this is not the whole story – three other factors stand out. Newspapers were important, especially their correspondence columns. Rye used *The Times* extensively and Quarrier the *Glasgow Herald*, the *North British Daily Mail* and, later, *The Christian*. Macpherson relied on the readership of the evangelical paper the *Revivalist*. Stephenson turned to the *Methodist Recorder*. *The Tablet* was important for Catholics.

Then there were the meetings. Some were specially arranged public gatherings like those to which Macpherson spoke in Canada; and there were private house meetings such as the ones that Birt addressed in Liverpool, which Macpherson arranged in London and which both Quarrier and Macpherson attended in Glasgow. There were also meetings to which Nugent and Rye were invited (separately) in order to explain their schemes; and, not least, there were the meetings of particular societies like the National Association for the Promotion of Social Science, of which Rye was a member and to whose proceedings she contributed. She was also a member of the so-called Langham Place Group, a group working for improvement in the rights of women and for a widening of their employment opportunities.[67]

Personal correspondence was also a prominent feature of the communicating networks. Rye and Birt were energetic letter-writers and were prepared to introduce themselves and their work directly in this way, often with the additional help of the printed circulars or annual reports that they enclosed. Extensive correspondence served to establish contacts and to maintain those that already existed. Much influenced by the style and approach of George Müller (in Bristol) Quarrier repeatedly claimed that he never asked for financial support for his work; prayer was all that was necessary. Even so, he did make known his aspirations in both private and public letters, usually adding what it would cost to put his plans into practice.

Important parts of the networks, and of the communications that they fostered, were also created and sustained by travel. Five of the early emigrationists had travelled extensively, both abroad and at home. They were, in the terms of a later sociology, 'cosmopolitans' rather than 'locals'. Yet, in their transactions with bodies like the guardians they were dealing with people who were usually 'local' rather than 'cosmopolitan'. That sometimes gave them an important edge. And many contacts were made in Canada. Father Nugent, for example, was invited to attend the first federal-provincial ministers' conference on immigration while he was in the country in 1869. The possibility of extensive travel was also increased for those who combined it with evangelical preaching. Indeed, the importance of the national and international links that were secured through the various branches of the evangelical movement cannot be over-emphasised. The links that they created penetrated virtually all walks of life and could be called on for assistance, the more so where the cause was rescuing children.

Together with the importance of networks and communications for an understanding of these early initiatives in child emigration, there was also the freedom enjoyed by individuals to conduct such ventures largely unhindered by any governmental regulation or, at the start (with the exception of Birt and Stephenson) any committee of management. For some these were to come later, and were often reluctantly accepted. Of course, when they received children from the guardians the emigrationists had to satisfy the boards and the boards, in their turn, were supposed to observe the legal requirements. But for most of the nineteenth century there was no registration, no inspection and no formal public scrutiny of what they did. Only when they infringed major governmental sensitivities (as in the case of the objections of the US) or when serious shortcomings were suspected was their scope curtailed. This was partly because government regulation of such matters was in general undeveloped (especially in Canada) and the means of imposing it often wanting.

One final observation must be added. Both the opportunity to engage in such work as child emigration, and also the time and resources to attend to the necessary networks and communications on which it relied, depended on a measure of financial security and the ability to detach oneself from other responsibilities. Quarrier, for instance, sold first one of his shops and then another in order to devote himself more fully to his child-saving activities. While there are no detailed records of the domestic circumstances of the seven figures who appear prominently in this chapter,[68] we do know that all except Quarrier came from relatively secure middle-class backgrounds. Even Nugent, one of nine children of an Irish immigrant family, had a father in business as a fruiterer and poultry dealer. Birt's case, in particular, is of some interest. She was a married woman with four children and an ailing husband. It must be presumed that their care was entrusted to a variety of servants, governesses or nurses. All the other emigrationists, except Quarrier, were without such extensive family responsibilities, but Quarrier gradually involved several of his adult children in his child-saving mission. For example, his daughter Agnes took several parties of children to Canada, helped to distribute them and eventually, together with her husband Alexander Burges, stayed to manage his reception Home in Canada. Later Burges' brother, James, became one of their Canadian-based visitors and then succeeded his brother as head of Quarrier's Canadian Home. Quarrier's wife too, appears to have provided much support, travelling with him on most of his Canadian visits.

Lastly, it must be emphasised that all these schemes for sending children to Canada evolved within a particular economic and social climate, the most important elements of which were the state of the actual or expected demand for labour; fears about the threat to the social order that the poor and the dispossessed were believed to pose, and widespread and deeply held religious convictions among a sizeable section of the population together with a desire to see these beliefs manifested in some form of social action. Superimposed on all these factors was the suffering of poor children, albeit compounded with disquiet about their uncontrollability.

Part II
Setbacks and Anxieties

THREE

Checks and Balances

I Orphans, Waifs, Strays and the Deserted

It will have become apparent by now that the Local Government Board (LGB) (the successor to the Poor Law Board [PLB] in 1871) was responsible for the oversight and regulation of the activities of local boards of guardians and that this included the emigration of children in their charge. In particular the central authority was required to approve the departure of each child individually. As a result important questions arose, especially about the proper interpretation and application of the law as well as about how policy should be framed.

In sharp contrast, the activities of the private bodies and individuals having taken children into their care were not subject to any comparable regulation or scrutiny, except when they fell foul of certain general laws such as the law of *habeus corpus*. Nevertheless, many of the questions that surfaced in connection with the emigration of Poor Law children were equally pertinent in the case of the trans-shipment of those who were the responsibility of private agencies. For this reason the way in which the issues confronting the LGB were dealt with has a wider relevance than would be suggested by the fact that eventually the majority of children sent to Canada were drawn from private organisations.

At the outset the Local Government Board wrestled with the problem of which Poor Law children were eligible for emigration. The current legislation only permitted those who were orphans or who had been deserted to be included.[1] But who exactly was an orphan and who had been deserted? Orphan status was not a settled matter. For example, in 1870 the Wareham-Purbeck union wrote to the PLB telling them that they were considering sending a few 'orphan girls' to Canada with Maria Rye. Shortly after, however, their clerk wrote again to explain that they were not taking matters further because 'the parents of the children in question don't at present … seem inclined to let them go out'.[2] These children were obviously not orphans, but the correspondence reflected the fact that the term 'orphan' was commonly used to refer to many children who happened to be separated from living parents. Sometimes the phrase 'orphaned in one parent' was used.

Despite the continuation of this imprecise usage the LGB gradually paid less attention to the issue unless it was patently obvious that a child had a living parent who was readily identifiable. Likewise, the private organisations often used the term 'orphan' whether or not that was actually the case. This served a number of purposes. It enlisted public sympathy for the 'cause' and that often translated into more generous donations. Perhaps for similar reasons many institutions for children were called orphanages, both formally and informally, although they rarely contained even a majority of true orphans. Other descriptions of children as foundlings, waifs or strays were liable to confuse matters even further, but served equally well to attract Victorian sympathy. In fact the casual use of the term 'orphan' was not often challenged, even though one of the consequences was that it enabled living parents to be ignored when key decisions about their offspring were being taken. This not only minimised the possibility of protest and the delay that was likely to follow, but also made it easier for agencies to secure the permanent severance of children from parents who were considered to be unfit to care for them. Emigration, of course, achieved a virtually irreversible separation.

As well as the interpretation of the term 'orphan' the LGB also faced problems when it came to deciding whether or not a Poor Law child had been deserted. For example, there are letters from various boards of guardians that mention – usually by way of support for the proposed emigration – that a child's parent or parents had given their consent. Indeed, parents (who could be workhouse inmates or in prison) were sometimes asked to sign a document indicating their agreement in the presence of a witness. In a number of instances guardians explained to the central Board that certain children proposed for emigration had not gone before justices to give their consent because their parents' consent had already been obtained.[3] Under these circumstances could the children be considered to have been deserted? In some instances the answer was no. For example, with respect to a party of 38 children from Stepney, an assistant secretary at the Board concluded that because parental consent had been obtained for six of the children they could not be considered to have been deserted and were, therefore, ineligible for emigration.[4] In another case, however, the question of desertion was glossed over. In 1871 the Brighton guardians proposed to send 33 children to Canada. However, the justices refused to hear the consents of two of them because parents had given their consent beforehand. That being so, they argued, the children had clearly not been deserted. The clerk sought the guidance of the LGB and was told that approval would be forthcoming as long as the children's consents were properly obtained and, in the cases where there were living and known parents, that their consent was *also* furnished.[5] However, this was not a legal requirement until much later, and nor was a private individual or organisation obliged to obtain a parent's consent to the emigration of a child in their care.

The issue of parental consent aside, children were often assumed to have been deserted simply because a parent, usually the mother, was no longer in contact. Yet for many whose child had been admitted to the Poor Law or to a private institution it was difficult to sustain that contact, especially for widows who were still looking after other children, or unmarried mothers who were obliged to enter domestic service where not only were their children unwelcome but where little free time was allowed. Furthermore, it was not uncommon for parental visiting to be severely restricted and for a failure to keep up financial contributions to be interpreted as a loss of interest. In circumstances such as these, desertion could rather easily be claimed and children then proposed for emigration.

II Asking the Children

Despite inconsistencies in the interpretation of 'orphan' and 'desertion', however, one thing that the LGB always insisted on was the child's consent to being emigrated be given before magistrates. It is not possible, of course, to reconstruct what happened during these appearances. As a number of children were usually assembled from the same institution prior to joining the larger parties that those like Maria Rye or Annie Macpherson booked on a particular sailing, they generally all came before the justices at the same time, and some would know each other. This may have exercised an important influence on a child's decision. One bold or leading member of the party might encourage the others one way or another, and brothers and sisters usually wanted to stay together. Certainly when children refused to be emigrated they sometimes did so in fairly large numbers and on the same occasion. In 1872 nine children from the ages of 10-12 in a party of 39 from Islington all declined to go to Canada.[6] Indeed, there seems to have been a small but steady stream of children whose names were deleted from the prepared lists and 'child declined' written in the margins. The correspondence that has been inspected suggests that the overall refusal rate might have been between five and ten per cent. Surprisingly perhaps, it seems to have been the younger children who were more likely to refuse to be emigrated, possibly because the justices took special care to establish their wishes or perhaps because young children were more anxious about the uncertainties that lay ahead.

What went on before a child arrived in front of the magistrates must also have been important. How was the idea of emigration first put? By whom? With what options or information? Could the children really understand what emigration to Canada meant? Did they actually know where Canada *was*? There are occasional glimpses of what might have happened from the correspondence that resulted when relatives or others protested about the intended emigration. Two letters exist, for example, about a Roman Catholic boy, 11-year-old Charles Cox of Islington, whom the guardians had planned to send to Canada in 1872.[7] The first is from his aunt who wrote to her priest as follows:

> I have seen my niece Charlotte Cox today and she tells me that they are going to send her little brother Charles out to Canada ... but Sir I do not wish him to go, or his Grandmother either, for it seems they are going to send him to Canada without letting either of us know anything about it as it was by chance that his sister heard about it. Sir I should feel very much obliged to you if you could do anything to prevent them from sending him to Canada because he is to [sic] young but they have been praising the country to him yet he has no idea what sort of place it is or how far it is they want him to go to

> or what they are going to do with him and I think it is a very wrong thing to intice [sic] a young child like that to go out of the country without letting his relatives know a word about it and poor Charlotte is fretting very much about it.

The priest's assistant saw the boy and wrote to the Reverend Thomas Seddon, the secretary of the newly formed Catholic Emigration Society, who, in turn, sent all the material to the LGB, asking it to intercede. The letter to Seddon is similar to the aunt's, but adds to our picture of the circumstances in which the idea of emigration might have been presented to children:

> The authorities of the Workhouse School … from time to time send children to Canada. Hitherto they have left the Catholic children alone; but I find from the enclosed letter that they are going to send Charles Cox about eleven to Canada next month. On questioning the lad I find that they simply asked him whether he would like to go and he answered, ignorant of the destination, and of what they were going to do with him there, that he would....

Notwithstanding this correspondence, however, Charles Cox appeared on the next Islington list of children for emigration, but any intervention that the LGB might have contemplated was rendered unnecessary because, when asked by the justices whether he wanted to go to Canada, Charles reversed his earlier decision and said 'no'.

Whether or not they were the responsibility of the Poor Law the question of how, if at all, the wishes of children were (or could be) established remains. One can sympathise with an assistant secretary at the LGB who, in 1875, expressed the view that taking a five-year-old child before justices in order to obtain her consent was 'a farce', although the required certificate was in fact signed and accepted.[8] On another occasion four infants between the ages of four and six were included in the 1870 party that the Bristol guardians proposed to send to Canada with Rye. It was explained to the central Board, however, that the justices would not take the consents of children of such tender ages, although the guardians were satisfied 'that it would be very much to the advantage of these little creatures to be sent to Canada where they would be adopted and in all possibility better provided for in every respect than many of the older children'.[9] The clerk of the Bristol board of guardians asked how this might be achieved without a certificate from the justices. The PLB replied firmly that it could not be dispensed with; without it the children could not go to Canada.[10] Their names were duly removed from the list. Where older brothers or sisters were involved very young children were sometimes included for emigration in order that they should not be left behind. Some justices seem to have considered this a reasonable ground for accepting the consents of four-, five- or six-year-olds.

We learn little about the reasons for the selection of particular children as candidates for emigration, although several factors are suggested by the correspondence. First, it is plain that the LGB steadfastly refused to issue general sanctions, for example, 'for a party of thirteen boys'. It was also adamant that responsibility for selection lay with the guardians, not with the emigration agents. Nevertheless, the agents seem to have wished to choose the children they took and there is more than a suggestion that they were able to do so. On the standard Poor Law form entitled 'List and Description of the Persons Desirous of Emigration' the clerk of the Cheltenham board of guardians wrote in 1871: 'these boys are especially selected by Miss Macpherson to place with people who will adopt them as their own children'.[11] Thus, in some cases in this early period Rye and Macpherson (or their helpers) actually visited the children and were directly involved in the processes of explanation, persuasion and selection. Of course, there are similar questions about how children were selected for Canada who were in privately run institutions, some answers to which will emerge in later chapters.

III The Pros and Cons of Emigration

Despite the ability of central government to regulate the emigration of Poor Law children the primary level of control rested with local boards of guardians. They enlisted the aid of particular emigrationists or responded to their overtures. We have already described the various considerations that the Wolverhampton guardians took into account when reaching their decision about whether or not to emigrate pauper girls and, having decided to do so, what arguments prevailed about who should be selected. Members of that local board, it will be recalled, were not unanimous and one imagines that there were similar differences of opinion in other unions. Matters often turned on whether the likes of Rye or Macpherson were successful in capturing the interest and support of a prominent member of a local board. However, that notwithstanding, some Poor Law unions actively opposed the idea of child emigration, particularly those that were located in the cotton–manufacturing areas of Lancashire. In 1877, for instance, the guardians of the Stockport union submitted a petition to the LGB pleading *against* the encouragement of such emigration, especially through the offices of Rye, whose circular letter they had recently received. They objected because:

> ... in Lancashire and Cheshire, and in the manufacturing districts generally, there is a great dearth of young girls for domestic service; and ... the expenditure of money in assisting Miss Rye to take such girls to Canada to place them chiefly in places of domestic service ... is a waste of public money.[12]

It is interesting to see that the principal reason for the Stockport union raising objections to the emigration of pauper girls was the chronic shortage of domestic servants in that part of the country, not that the labour of these girls was required in the mills. This was because the widespread employment of women in the textile industry seriously reduced the supply of domestic servants. Neither women nor girls could be spared for emigration if there were to be enough factory labour *and* enough hands available for domestic service.

Elsewhere, however, there were guardians who were eager to use the services of the emigrationists. For example, in explaining the reasons for their first venture into child emigration in 1870 the Cheltenham board wrote:

> … there are some eight to ten orphan boys of from fourteen to sixteen years of age now in the Union School for whom no satisfactory apprenticeship can be found and who, if not speedily got out of the House will lapse into confirmed Pauperism. [We] consider [it] desirable to enable these boys to emigrate to Canada….[13]

Other unions saw the length of time that a child had already been their responsibility as of prime importance. In Windsor, for instance, the clerk noted that only children who had spent at least three years in the Poor Law school were to be considered for emigration, although it was unclear whether this was because they were especially well trained or because they were becoming a long-term liability. Nevertheless, guardians frequently favoured emigration because they considered that it would break the cycle of pauperism. Beyond that, however, emigration was undoubtedly regarded as an effective means of saving a child once and for all from the clutches of cruel or immoral parents. The problem, of course, was that evil parental influences were seen in all kinds of situations, some of which were simply the consequences of abject poverty.

It would be misleading, therefore, to conclude that guardians were only concerned with the economic aspects of child emigration, either in terms of the needs of the local labour market or of reducing the call on the rates. Indeed, in the short run these were contradictory objectives, and other matters also intruded – such as the actual composition of the local boards. Shopkeepers, mill owners, local landowners or clergymen had different interests, although in one respect they shared a common experience as employers of domestic servants. Where these were scarce the emigration of girls was likely to be opposed, except if they were believed to be in moral danger.

IV Growing Anxieties

With the weight of its president behind the policy the PLB had swung round in 1869 to giving qualified support to child emigration. By 1872, however, its successor, the LGB, had begun to examine certain aspects of Rye's operations more closely. Early in 1872 the Windsor guardians had sought the approval of the LGB to send a party of boys to Canada with her. However, Rye's circular offering her services had explained that her scheme was for the emigration of girls. The

Board therefore queried whether her arrangements were suitable for boys as well. In addition the proposed expenditure of £12 a head was questioned because, in earlier cases, it had been only £10. Because of this all permissions for children to be emigrated were withheld.[14] No doubt concern was increased when, a few days after the Windsor request, the Board received similar proposals from Islington and from Chelsea.[15] At much the same time the Kensington board of guardians was pressing the LGB to conduct a general enquiry into the emigration of Poor Law children so that they and others could be reassured about the wisdom of sending children abroad.[16] The Board then decided that until it had more information the emigration of Poor Law children should be suspended.

Eventually, over three months later, Rye wrote to the LGB, explaining the reason for the increase in her charge. This, it transpired, was caused by the need to switch from sailing ships to steamers. Despite an inadequate answer to the enquiry about her arrangements for boys, her reply was considered to be satisfactory and, from June 1872, approvals for the emigration of pauper children were again issued.[17] However, the moratorium, in practice, had been selective. Applications from those boards of guardians using Macpherson's services continued to be sanctioned as, for example, in the case of Nottingham.[18] Even taking this into account, the ease with which the central Board accepted Rye's explanations was surprising in the light of other enquiries that they had been making. They noted that Macpherson's charge was only £6.6.0d, the adult fare to Canada from Liverpool. Furthermore, it was confirmed that children under the age of eight sailed at half price.[19]

Thus, seeds of doubt about Rye's activities had been sown at the LGB. During the following year there were also signs of a growing unease among more guardians about the arrangements for child emigration. The reassurance that Kensington had sought from the LGB has already been mentioned, and a number of other similar requests had also been received. That prepared by the East Preston union on the south coast was typical. They wrote that they united 'with those other Boards who have sent out children with Miss Rye to Canada in urging the Local Government Board to institute an official enquiry into the working of the Emigration movement under Miss Rye's auspices'.[20]

However, it was another event two years later that led to the imposition of a second moratorium on the emigration of pauper children. This time it was to last for nine years. The LGB was almost certainly obliged to prohibit further child emigration – at least pending inquiries – because of the accusations levelled against Rye by Allerdale Grainger. Grainger, as Wagner points out, 'had married a Miss Martin, a girl once in Miss Rye's service in Canada but who had been discharged by her, and Maria made it clear that there was no love lost between them'.[21] Grainger had written to at least one newspaper in Canada claiming that Rye had a pecuniary interest in the immigration of British children.[22] In the early part of 1874 he also wrote to both the chairman and the clerk of the Islington guardians, drawing their attention to the ill-usage that might befall children sent to Canada. He was especially critical of Rye. Both letters were submitted to a full meeting of the guardians in March 1874.[23] It was agreed to defer the matter until the next meeting however; but, in the meantime, it was decided to invite Grainger and Rye to be present. Both duly arrived for the rearranged meeting. Grainger was accompanied by Alsager Hay Hill of the Labour News Office and Rye by a much larger party comprising the Reverend Weller (Sub-Dean of St Paul's Cathedral), the Honourable William MacDougall from Canada[24] and four others, including her honorary accountant, Antrobus, who was also a magistrate.[25] First, Grainger made his statement, then Rye delivered hers. Grainger concluded by asking that the guardians request the LGB to send some 'proper person to Canada to report truthfully on the workings of the whole system', while Antrobus characterised Grainger's speech as 'an insult not only to Miss Rye but also to the Earl of Shaftesbury ... and other Magistrates and Gentlemen who assisted her in her movement'.

Having listened to the contending statements the Islington guardians deferred further consideration until their next meeting. By then there were further letters from both Grainger and Rye to be considered. Grainger's merely offered to attend, whereas Rye's struck a pre-emptive blow at the objectivity of Grainger's evidence by explaining, as the minutes record, that his wife before her marriage (Miss Martin)

> ... went with her [Rye] to Canada as an Assistant in October 1870, and that she had to discharge her for untruthfulness and deceit in February 1871, since which she had circulated slanderous reports ... which were then refuted in Canada, and should the Guardians pass a vote of confidence in her the matter cannot stand where it does as she [Rye] shall demand an enquiry from the Local Government Board.[26]

The committee also heard extracts read from the LGB's annual report of 1870-71 that had encouraged guardians to employ the services of Rye and Macpherson in sending children to Canada, as well as a passage from the *Local Government Chronicle* reporting the satisfactory outcome of that board's enquiries of the Canadian government the previous year.[27] Fortified by these submissions the guardians passed a vote of confidence in Rye by nine to one. At their next meeting another letter from Grainger was read that deplored the guardians' vote of confidence. However, 'next business' was moved without discussion.[28]

Not being convinced that the Islington guardians would take any further action Grainger sent a long letter to the LGB cataloguing Rye's misdemeanours and describing the shortcomings of her system.[29] It was dealt with personally by John Lambert, who was effectively the permanent head of the department. Grainger was promised that his complaints would receive proper attention. One of the complaints was that some of the children whom Rye had brought out had been placed in the US, where it was impossible for the Dominion government 'to pronounce' on them. Another was that Rye had failed to prosecute, or to take any action against, people who were known to have ill-treated children placed in their care. Furthermore, he claimed, she was insensitive and harsh towards those in her care. He described in particular the case of Annie Thompson, aged 10, who, he claimed, had been placed in solitary confinement and given only bread and water for several days on being returned to Rye's Home at Niagara. Rye, he contended, had also beaten the child with the back of a brush and, when she escaped, had allowed her to 'remain out all night during one of the coldest nights in a Canadian winter'. Fortunately, the girl had been sheltered at a nearby house where she had sought refuge. Thereupon, according to Grainger's account, Rye 'ordered the child to be arrested and confined in the Public Lock up during her pleasure, which was done and this little child was confined in a cell…'. But soon, Grainger went on, 'public opinion became so strong that the Mayor allowed the Constable to take the child … to his [house] where it remained … until a situation was found for it'. Such treatment, Grainger protested, was both illegal and inhuman and an indictment of Rye's character and fitness to be entrusted with children.

Grainger further charged that the system of relying on local references was worthless, since it would 'go hard' with anyone who 'gave his neighbour a character that would prevent his successful application for one of Miss Rye's girls'. He also maintained that the diet at the Niagara Home was inadequate and gave details of the sparsity of the meals. Next it was argued that there was no supervision of the children once they had been placed. If the girls Rye took to Canada were too young for the 'home market' there was, Grainger contended, no justification for placing them at such a distance, bereft of safeguards and entirely dependent on their employers for protection and instruction. Lastly, he returned to the issue of Rye's pecuniary interest. He claimed that her accounts were inadequate. Grainger completed his onslaught by saying that should the LGB refuse to institute a proper inquiry he would feel constrained 'to give free lectures throughout the country on behalf of the orphan'.[30]

If only some of these accusations were true Lambert would have been gravely disturbed, for he was a man for whom administrative correctness was of the utmost importance. Rye's style of activities, her incomplete accounts, together with her casual approach to administrative niceties, would have been anathema to him. His namesake, Royston Lambert, provides an insight into the permanent secretary's character. He recounts how 'his mastery of figures and organising ability had early brought him special assignments of importance' and how his command of detail allowed him to exercise considerable influence over his political masters.[31] The Webbs formed the same opinion[32] as did Lambert's contemporary, the inspector Preston-Thomas, who wrote that:

> Accuracy and precision were qualities which he rated most highly, and a blunder in a statistical table distressed him as much as if he had played a false note in one of the string quartettes [sic] in which it had been his delight to take part with Cardinal Newman and two other friends.[33]

When Grainger's letter arrived Lambert called for a detailed report. Bauke, the principal clerk responsible for emigration, undertook the work and provided an account of events surrounding the emigration of Poor Law children to Canada from 1869. This was submitted to Lambert and then passed to the President. It provides a particularly valuable resumé of developments up to 1874.[34]

Among other things it pointed out that the first direct complaint about Rye that the Board had received was in January 1874 (before Grainger took his initiative). This came from a Mrs Barclay, then living in New York. She had drawn attention to a report in a Canadian paper that a woman with whom one of the girls had been placed had been fined $40 for beating her. She went on to add that she had paid two visits (together with two other ladies) to the Niagara Home. Rye was absent but the matron showed them around. 'Everything we saw caused great pain and with me indignation, when I remembered how displeased the English people would be at knowing how these helpless young creatures were situated.'[35] At the LGB it was decided to send a copy of the letter to Rye for her observations. She replied that:

> The facts of the case are these. A child named Constance Branch from Lambeth Union was placed by me about a year ago with a Mr and Mrs Switzer ... the people being recommended to me by the very Magistrate who tried the case.... In a fit of ungovernable temper Mrs Switzer ... beat the child very cruelly and unnecessarily for which we had her up tried and fined ... after which the Child went back with me to the Home at Niagara....[36]

James Stansfeld, the President of the LGB, considered the explanation satisfactory and a copy was sent to Mrs Barclay. At about the same time Rye had a meeting at the Board and was asked to provide a list of children returned to her Home or removed from their placements over the past four years. It showed that they comprised 22 per cent of the 786 children taken out.[37]

Barclay's accusation against Rye had, therefore, already set the scene for Grainger's charges. Evidence was mounting and could not be dismissed. Furthermore, the rather ineffectual George Sclater-Booth had now replaced Stansfeld as President. This was important since not only did it shift power towards Lambert, the permanent secretary, but removed a man who had given his personal and political support to Rye and who had been responsible for having a favourable paragraph inserted in the Board's 1870-71 annual report. While Stansfeld remained at the head of the LGB his earlier commitment to child emigration through Rye and Macpherson made it unlikely that he would be easily convinced that he had made an error of judgement. It is also probable that the problem was accentuated because Stansfeld's support had been expressed publicly as the Board's policy, contrary to the advice of his senior civil servants. Grainger's accusations against Rye, unlike Barclay's, reached the LGB just after Stansfeld had left and when Sclater-Booth had only just arrived.

V The Doyle Inquiry and the Moratorium

In the light of these various disquieting representations the LGB decided, in 1874, to instigate its own enquiries in Canada. To this end it commissioned Andrew Doyle, one of its most senior inspectors, to undertake a full investigation.[38] He may well have been chosen because of his vast experience, his skill in making reports on visits overseas, and because he was approaching retirement (he died in 1888). Doyle also shared much in common with Lambert, the permanent secretary. They were both precise and thorough men, intolerant of inefficiency as they saw it, and scrupulous in their attention to detail. Both were lawyers by training and both were Catholics. Indeed, Lambert was a prominent Catholic. He was, as we have seen, a friend of Cardinal Newman. As a practising Catholic he was likely to have viewed Rye's anti-Catholicism with considerable disfavour. Likewise, Doyle's religion caused his impartiality to be questioned. For example, the *Globe* newspaper in Canada felt able to claim that the appointment of a Catholic to examine the work 'of ladies who have not only all along avowed themselves ... Protestant but who, in order to avoid the very appearance of proselytism, have always taken out the children of Protestants only ... was, to say the least of it unfortunate'.[39]

However, as well as being a Catholic Doyle was regarded as one of the ablest inspectors.[40] He was convinced of the value of indoor relief (that is, in a Poor Law institution) both as a means of reducing the poor rate and as a means of ensuring high standards. He was also extremely dubious about boarding out Poor Law children, fearing for their exploitation, especially if they were placed with paupers. In January 1874 he had submitted a detailed and critical account of the use of boarding out in the Swansea union, part of his area of responsibility as the inspector covering most of Wales. He reported that the children:

> ... are not as a rule regularly visited nor is there any systematic supervision of them. There are I am happy to say but very few Unions in the District in which the condition of the indoor children would not contrast favourably in all essential respects with the children who are placed out.[41]

In a letter to the chairman of the Swansea guardians in 1875, Doyle also referred to the likelihood of children who were placed in rural areas being kept away from school and neglected in other ways. He pointed out that many children were 'placed in lonely districts far away from any existing schools; they have a long walk to go over rough and hilly roads; they are often scantily clad, and in bad weather they cannot attend with perfect regularity ... *they have no advocate to tell of what they endure*' (original emphasis).[42] Doyle may also have been encouraged to stress the advantages of residential provision for children as a result of his visits the previous year to continental schools at Mettray (now Mettrai), Dusseltal, Rouen and Brussels, reporting on some of the new developments.[43] This, and the inspector's concern about the boarding out of Poor Law children in rural

Wales, would have predisposed him to look with an especially critical eye at the condition of the children placed out in Canada.

Doyle's report on his investigation in Canada, where he saw not only the key figures but also visited several hundred children (both pauper and other), was completed in December 1874 and laid before the House of Commons the following February.[44] It is an impressive document that demonstrates the inspector's ability to marshal and present the diverse facts and impressions that he had assembled while in Canada. He recorded many misgivings about the emigration of British children as conducted by Rye and Macpherson. He was concerned about the lack of care with which the placements were made and about the lack of information concerning the applicants and the children. He connected this with the fact that both Rye and Macpherson sought to have the children 'off their hands immediately upon their arrival'.[45] However, it was the failure to ensure adequate subsequent supervision that most worried him. The children had no legal or official protection from ill-treatment and harsh working conditions, and were frequently lost sight of when they moved from place to place (as they often did). In any case, he found many cases of incorrect addresses, a reflection of the poor standard of the records. When the children were returned to the Homes, for whatever reason, proper arrangements were not made for their care and, in Rye's case, they were sometimes punished excessively for alleged or actual misdemeanours.

Doyle's report conveys a genuine concern for the well-being of the children: a concern about their loneliness and the fracture of past ties and attachments, about their not always being sent to school, about the risk of their stigmatisation when they, or their parents, were described in a dismissive or pejorative fashion (as they often were) and about the likelihood of their being cast adrift 'without friends or advisors, and, as a rule, without associations that attach them to families or to neighbourhoods in which they are known'.[46] In short, the inspector's view was that children sent out as emigrants stood 'in an altogether exceptional position, and should not be deprived of that help in distress that the law would have given them had they not been removed from their own country'.[47] He did not deny that some placements were satisfactory (particularly where very young children were adopted rather than being put to work under the guise of adoption), but in too many instances it simply could not be known how the children were faring in situations where the risks of mistreatment or unhappiness were patently clear. Doyle also investigated the financial side of Rye and Macpherson's activities. Although he said that they could not provide him with adequate records he calculated that 'there could be a clear gain of £5 per head upon every pauper child taken by these ladies to Canada'.[48] In particular, he criticised Macpherson's practice of asking the children for the repayment of their passage money in order to enable yet more children to be emigrated.

There can be little doubt that such a forceful report, prepared by a well-trusted inspector, would have convinced Lambert that the emigration of Poor Law children should be prohibited unless and until radical improvements had been made in their supervision and protection in Canada, and in the way in which the emigrationists conducted their affairs.

While Doyle was pursuing his inquiry in Canada the issue of the emigration of Poor Law children was kept before the LGB by another letter from Mrs Barclay that recounted the sad story of Charlotte Williams, now a girl of 17, whom Rye had brought to Canada some three years earlier. She was placed with a wealthy farmer where she was:

> … employed in rough work for 3 years & 2 months when she was discovered to be enceinte, the girl said she had been seduced by Mr F's son a lad of 19 … the mistress & Miss Rye … threatened they would put her in the Penitentiary for life, if she said so, the simple and ignorant girl believed it, & made a confession which she retracted whenever the pressure was withdrawn, she was then dismissed, without money or help of any kind – In the neighbour [sic] lives a most respectable coloured woman … and this person kindly took her in, & kept her for a fortnight.…

Rye's riposte, addressed to Mrs Barclay's husband, was vigorous and dismissive. 'Are you aware', she wrote, 'that your wife is constantly interfering & annoying me with absurd letters – concerning matters about which she really knows nothing', adding that the girl had confessed to having had 'connections' with three men, 'one of them coloured and we presume the father of the child'.[49] In the event the child born to Charlotte was white.

Whatever the truth of the matter the receipt of such correspondence at the LGB would have done nothing to reduce the concerns that had prompted Doyle's dispatch to Canada or those confirmed by his report. His major recommendation, that the emigration of Poor Law children be prohibited unless and until adequate safeguards were provided, especially through Canadian government inspection,[50] led to the provisional moratorium that had been announced prior to his departure now becoming LGB policy, a policy that was to run until 1883.

Nevertheless, several exceptions were made during the period of the embargo, usually to allow a younger child to join an older brother or sister who was already in Canada, although they rarely found themselves living together. Although the Board required an undertaking to be given that the child would be placed in 'the same neighbourhood',[51] it is hard to say whether or not this happened (or for how long). There were also a few cases where boards of guardians arranged for certain children to go to Canada without having obtained the necessary permission, either through ignorance of what was required or by design.[52]

During the years of the moratorium there were attempts to reverse the LGB's policy. For example, in 1877 Sclater–Booth (the President) received a deputation from the St George's union in London that pressed for a relaxation of the prohibition on the emigration of Poor Law children. *The Times* reported that Sclater–Booth had said that when he had discovered that upwards of 1,000 children from the workhouses had been sent out under the direct authority and responsibility of the Government, without any regard to their official inspection, or any Report coming home as to how they were getting on, it seemed to him that the time had arrived when an inquiry should be made.

Furthermore, he was reported as saying that

> as a responsible Minister of the Crown, he did not feel that he should be justified in continuing the system of emigration to Canada.... There was something very objectionable about shiploads of children being sent over with no security as to what became of them.[53]

Rye's hand can be seen behind the St George's initiative but also Doyle and Lambert's influence behind Sclater–Booth's response. The bitter controversy that raged between Doyle and Rye in the press and elsewhere during 1877 seems to have been extended to this encounter in which neither took part directly. However, as we shall see, it was not until 1883 that the LGB lifted its ban on the emigration of Poor Law children, largely as a result of the agreement of the Canadian government to provide for their regular inspection. It must be emphasised, however, that both the moratorium and the subsequent Canadian system of inspection applied *only* to children who were in the care of the Poor Law. Other children, who were the responsibility of the emerging voluntary children's organisations, were not subject to these restrictions and regulations. Nonetheless, the LGB's obvious disquiet about child emigration influenced a variety of decisions that were made by these bodies and by freelancing individuals. In the first place they were unable to recruit children from the Poor Law for their emigration enterprises during the moratorium and, second, the knowledge that central government entertained grave misgivings about the propriety and wisdom of expatriating separated children led some to proceed with more caution than might otherwise have been the case. The fact that Poor Law children could not be sent abroad for so many years may well have contributed to the emigrationists turning their attention to other children whom they assumed needed to be separated from dangerous influences or offered a fresh start in life. In doing so they forwent the fees that the guardians would have paid although continuing to receive the *per capita* subsidies provided by the Dominion and by the government of Ontario.

FOUR

The Issue of Inspection

I The Canadian Answer to Doyle's Report

Andrew Doyle's report was sent to the Governor-General of Canada with a request that the Canadian government consider it. As its House of Commons' Select Committee on Immigration and Colonisation was sitting at the time, the matter was referred to them. When John Lowe, the Deputy Minister in the Department of Agriculture, appeared before the Committee he was asked how Doyle's allegations should be met. His view was that a general statement about the condition of the children would be insufficient. What was needed, he believed, was 'a detailed report based upon a full inspection'.[1] It was agreed that an enquiry should be conducted in order to collect information in much the same way that Doyle had done. This would enable his conclusions to be checked. Nevertheless, the commencement of the work waited on the outcome of discussions about whether it should be carried out by the Dominion or by the provincial governments. Without waiting for the enquiry to be started Charles Pelletier, the Minister of Agriculture, told the Privy Council that the 'testimony which has been adduced from different parts of the Dominion ... is sufficient to lead to the conclusion that the work ... has been generally beneficial and particularly to the children themselves'. In justification of this view he referred to what Mr Justice Dunkin (the former Minister of Agriculture and supporter of Louisa Birt's work) had told the Select Committee. This was that:

> ... covert cruelty to, or ill-treatment of children or young people to any extent, merely cannot be ... Canadian social habits are such as to make it morally certain, that some neighbour or other, if not the whole neighbourhood will protect any child from wrong.[2]

Despite such a confident assertion five of the Dominion's immigration agents were commissioned to undertake the recommended enquiry. Parr provides a disturbing account of how this was carried out. Among other things 'the Homes were informed in advance of the inspector's approach' and 'representatives of the agencies were allowed to substitute their own reports for submission by government inspectors'.[3]

It is not surprising therefore that the final report of the inspections concluded that, with a few exceptions, the children were well and comfortably settled and that the work of Rye and Macpherson was to be applauded. Even so, at the beginning of 1878 the Privy Council in Ottawa approved a proposal that, in future, immigration officers would inspect all Poor Law children once a year. Parr argues that the Canadian government had been stung into making this concession as a result of the critical comments that had been made by Sclater-Booth (the President of the Local Government Board [LBG]) and which, as we have seen, had been reported in *The Times*.[4] Certainly, apart from having Doyle's report before it, the Dominion government was aware of a more widespread disquiet in Britain about the lack of a proper surveillance of Poor Law and indeed other children sent to Canada. It was assumed, however, that the new arrangements that were being offered would serve to temper these criticisms and encourage the LGB to lift its moratorium.

II The Response of the Local Government Board

When the report of the Canadian Privy Council was received at the LGB it was considered to be 'very meagre as to the method of carrying out the inspection and of preventing any wrong being done to the children'.[5] It was decided that Doyle should be asked for his observations on the Canadian offer to carry out an annual inspection of Poor Law children. An extract from his letter warrants a rather full reproduction. In it he said he did not believe that:

> ... officers connected with the Immigration Department would ... be proper persons to report as to the success of a scheme in which, as immigration agents, they are much interested ... as between the interests of immigration and the interests of these children they are not and cannot be disinterested.... Can you believe that visits to children from men engaged in such work is the sort of supervision with which the LGB ought to be satisfied?

Why not, Doyle continued, place the inspection in the hands of the school inspectors in Canada? Although they might not provide very full information about the children at least they would be reasonably dispassionate. In any case, why should the LGB be satisfied 'with arrangements for visiting ... so far short of what you properly insist upon for England ... depend upon it ... these children need better protection ... and to your Board they have to look for it'?[6]

Despite further correspondence with the Canadian authorities the LGB remained unconvinced that Doyle's criticisms had been answered satisfactorily; but the final report of the Canadian 'house-to-house' inspection had not yet been received in London. When it did arrive, later in 1878, it did little to reassure the Board, even though Pelletier, the Dominion Minister of Agriculture, maintained that it showed that due care was being taken in placing the children and that most of them were doing well.[7] However, the statistics in the report caused a good deal of concern, especially the fact that 31 per cent of the children who had been placed by Rye had not been able to be traced. In the case of those for whom Macpherson was responsible the figure was a less worrying 13 per cent.

However, the Canadians claimed that being 'lost sight of' did not necessarily imply that children had 'entered into evil courses'. On the contrary, it indicated that having benefited from the training that they had received on the farms, they were then ready to move on in order to seek better opportunities.[8] This explanation did not convince the LGB. Nor did the synopsis of the individual visits that the report contained. Too many were considered to be unsatisfactory; for example, Mary Bury was only 'in a fair home'; Mary Neal was in 'a poor home and badly clothed'; and Martha Barnes 'got into the employment of a scoundrel and was seduced'.[9] Such reports were, as the Canadian authorities pointed out, a small proportion of the total, but together with the number who were not traced, they were sufficient to sustain the profound unease at the LGB that had been aroused by Doyle's initial report and by his subsequent opinions.

Of course, none of this touched on the question of how those children who were not from the Poor Law system fared in Canada, and yet their position could be just as vulnerable and uncertain. There was no more reliable inspection of their placements and, as we shall see, this was to become a common criticism of the practices of those who were responsible for their emigration. Hence, in certain respects the steps being taken by the LGB to ensure at least a modicum of protection for Poor Law children in Canada had begun to acknowledge that the interests of *all* children sent to Canada needed to be better safeguarded.

III A Second Canadian Offer

There matters rested until the beginning of 1883 when the Colonial Office was informed that the Canadian Department of Agriculture would undertake an annual inspection of Poor Law children and forward reports.[10] In fact the proposal differed little from that which had been made five years earlier. However, once it became known that there was a renewed offer moves were set afoot in order to persuade the LGB that the emigration of Poor Law children should now be resumed. A conference on emigration was convened in London under the auspices of the Charity Organisation Society (COS) and chaired by James Stansfeld, the former President of the LGB. Among several decisions that it took was one to send a deputation to see Sir Charles Dilke (the then President of the LGB in Gladstone's second administration and sympathetic to the development of emigration) and to put before him the case for allowing child emigration to resume. The Board also received requests to be heard on the subject from two London boards of guardians: St George's Hanover Square[11] and St Pancras[12] as well as from the Metropolitan Poor Law Guardians' Association.[13] Clearly this was an orchestrated initiative and in the event all the bodies appeared before the President together.

In the notes that Dilke prepared in readiness for the meeting he wrote that in the light of the Canadian offer he did 'not feel disposed' to prohibit boards of guardians from arranging the emigration of youngsters in their care, but they had to be entirely satisfied that good homes would be found for them.[14] He met the enlarged delegation in April 1883 and presumably made his points; the representatives also seem to have confirmed his existing inclination to allow child emigration to be resumed, although he only promised to review the matter at that stage.[15] By the beginning of May, however, the LGB circulated a memorandum specifying the conditions upon which it would approve the emigration of pauper children.[16] It was a very cautious document and could hardly be regarded as opening the floodgates to such emigration, principally because it imposed several important restrictions. As a general rule girls were not to be sent abroad above the age of 10 and never over the age of 12, except in very special circumstances. The children had to have received at least six months' instruction in a workhouse or district school and be certified as medically fit. The person taking a child to Canada had to provide the Department of Agriculture in Ottawa with details about them as well as about those with whom they were placed, in particular their full address. Children had to go to families of the same religion. Before it was decided that a child be sent to Canada the guardians had to obtain satisfactory evidence that the people to whom the emigration was entrusted had a reasonable prospect of finding them a suitable home. Over and above these requirements the total number of Poor Law children who were to be allowed to be emigrated was not to exceed 300, at least in the first year. In fact only 131 children were sent, but from 25 Poor Law unions.[17]

By May 1884 none of the promised reports from the Dominion government had been received. It was felt that the LGB should enquire in particular about how many children the Canadian authorities could actually manage to inspect each year.[18] Hugh (later Sir Hugh) Owen (the newly promoted permanent secretary to the Board) and the President agreed, but no reply was received and months passed without a single report having arrived. By November 1884 an assistant secretary at the Board asked Owen whether it was wise to give any further approvals until satisfactory information had been obtained from the Canadian authorities 'as to the results of previous emigration?'.[19] In turn Owen wrote to the President proposing that:

> ... the Board should decline to sanction the emigration of any more children to Canada until the Board have been furnished with reports....
> At present the Board have no evidence whatever that the Canadian Government are fulfilling the conditions on which the Board assented to the emigration of these children.[20]

On the basis of this the Canadian government was informed that no further emigration of Poor Law children would be sanctioned until the Board had 'accurate and trustworthy' information about the circumstances of the children who had already been sent.

IV A Particular Case

In addition to the fact that the Board had not received the promised reports, there were at least two other factors that concerned them. The first was that the emigration 'season' would soon be starting and it was known that several unions would be submitting proposals for approval. Second, the Board was also conscious that not all was well with child emigrants in Canada. This was highlighted by one particularly sad case that was drawn to their attention at the end of 1883, although it did not involve a Poor Law child.

In November 1883 the Colonial Office forwarded a letter to the LGB that they had received from a Mrs Gee complaining about the treatment of her two daughters, Alice and Anna, who had gone to Canada with Rye. Mrs Gee had written to the Colonial Secretary as follows:

> You will please excuse the liberty I take in writing to you, but I am in very great trouble on account of two of my children I had the misfortune to send to Canada under the charge of Miss Rye – I sent them on conditions that they should be well cared for and have some good education, but she, Miss Rye, has not done one thing or the other for one of them – the eldest is in hospital in Ontario in a dying state brought on by ill usage, and I enclose a letter to you Sir to prove to you what I write, and the youngest which I sent out on conditions as the woman that sent them out told me that they should be kept together as much as possible but as soon as they landed there they were parted, and have not seen or heard from one or the other since, and as for school Sir, you can see for yourself what schooling she has had for I send you the last letter I received from her – she could write better three years ago when she left home.... Sir, why I write to you now is to know if you can give me permission to have her home again if she is still alive, as I am in very great doubt whether she is not in a worse state than her sister for I cannot get any tidings from her so you must know Sir I am very anxious to hear from her and I pray you will help me to find out if she is still alive and if she is so to know if I can get her home again – her sister I never expect to see again.[21]

The letter Mrs Gee mentioned also warrants quotation. It was from Sophia Dangerfield:

> It is your daughter Alice's request that I write to you. She has been living with us for three weeks. When she lived with Mrs Whaley she never had the privilege of writing to you without their knowing everything she wrote. On that account she never told you her circumstances, which I know of a certainty were not very good. Mrs Whaley did not use her well from the first. Last winter she had to work

out-doors feeding cows and suchlike before the weather was warm she had to go about on her bare feet, through hard work and exposure she has become lame. There is a stiffness in the cords of her right leg, they did not take her to a doctor for six or seven weeks after the lameness troubled her first, and then they did not follow his directions. I am afraid it will never be all right again although it seems to be getting some better. When she was the very worst she had to milk cows and churn. She was kept on her feet continually which was against the doctors orders.... My brother worked Mr Whaley's farm last year; it was through that that she knew of this place. Mrs Whaley got in a rage at Alice for a very trifling affair and took the liberty to strike her. It was on that account that she left ... and came here.[22]

It was suggested that the Colonial Office write to Mrs Gee for further information, especially as to whether or not her two daughters had been emigrated by the guardians. Mrs Gee replied, explaining that she had agreed to her elder daughter going to Canada because she was rather beyond her control and she thought that 'if she could get her away for a year or two from her old companions she would be a better girl', but because Alice (the elder girl) would not go by herself she had let the younger daughter Anna go as well. Since her first letter to the Colonial Secretary Alice had died in hospital from, as Mrs Gee claimed, her ill-treatment. She now wanted Anna back. Finally, she explained that the girls had not been in the care of the Poor Law and that she herself had never received any parish relief.[23]

Along with her reply Mrs Gee enclosed a letter that she had received from Maria Matlock, 'the lady that was the means of sending my children out to Canada'.[24] Matlock had introduced Mrs Gee to Rye and paid for the girls' emigration. Mrs Gee had contacted her in order to find out what had happened to Anna but despite having made various enquiries Matlock had been unable to obtain any information about Anna's whereabouts or her well-being. At the age of 15, three years after her arrival, she had disappeared 'without trace' after several changes of address.

These long extracts are important for several reasons – first, for what they tell us about the destinies of at least two children who went to Canada. Second, because they show the extent to which parents and others thought that they were constrained by some kind of legal (and therefore binding) undertaking that prevented them recovering their children. This, superimposed on the near impossibility of poor parents actually being able to overcome the practicalities of getting a child back from Canada without the help of those who had organised the emigration, meant that reunification was highly unlikely. Third, and most importantly, the case illustrates that there was no protection or redress (except through the courts) for children who were neither from the Poor Law nor from industrial schools. For children like Alice and Anna no public body, either in Britain or Canada, bore any responsibility. Indeed, once it became clear that

Mrs Gee's daughters had not been subject to the care of the guardians, the LGB – and thereby the British government – concluded that there were no grounds to interfere. These, indeed, were the terms in which the Board wrote to the Colonial Office at the close of 1883.[25]

Thus, while waiting for the Dominion government to furnish the promised reports on Poor Law children in Canada, the LGB also had 'case' evidence such as this that all was not well with at least some of the children sent out. This did nothing to allay the misgivings that had already been aroused by the Canadian inspection report of 1878 and by Doyle's earlier submission. The outcome of all this was that it was decided that the earlier moratorium should be re-imposed.

V Eventually Something is Heard of the Children

At the end of March 1885 reports on 20 children were received from Canada, although it transpired that five of the children were not the responsibility of Poor Law guardians. However, the LGB seems to have been satisfied with them and, assuming that the remainder would now be forthcoming, they wrote to the Colonial Office asking them to tell the Canadian authorities that they would no longer withhold permission for children to be emigrated. Yet by August 1885 no more reports had arrived and a reminder was sent. The year passed, still without the required reports. Another reminder was dispatched at the end of January 1886. In desperation Owen, the permanent secretary, wrote to the President of the Board in February 1886 to the effect that if no further information were received from Canada they should 'revert to their previous practice'.[26] 'Bring up in six weeks', replied the President, but by April there were still no reports, and guardians in Liverpool had applied for permission to send 50 children to Canada. However, in view of the absence of reports the Board did not consider that they were justified in giving their approval, and this decision was duly communicated to the Canadian government.

At last, at the end of April 1886, three years after the relaxation of the LGB's first prohibition, an explanation for the delays was forthcoming from Canada together with another 20 reports. The Minister of Agriculture protested that only 40 names and addresses had so far been made available to him and that, in any case, it was difficult to distinguish Poor Law children from the other children.[27] This, of course, implied that the agencies taking the children to Canada had failed to abide by one of the conditions of the 1883 memorandum in the great majority of cases. Parr, however, also points out that 'in Ottawa, placement addresses filed by the Homes were lost, ignored or left unrecorded'.[28]

Despite these explanations and the additional reports the view of the Board was that consents should continue to be withheld until more information was received.[29] In the meantime, however, a list of the names and addresses of all the Poor Law children known to have been emigrated was sent to Canada.[30] At much the same time the Canadian High Commissioner's Office in London was alerted to a passage in the *Liverpool Mercury* that reported that the Birkenhead guardians had not been allowed to emigrate children in their care because the Canadian government had not carried out the agreed inspections.[31] The Commissioner promptly wrote to the Colonial Secretary drawing his attention to an order-in-council (Canada) that indicated that enquiries had been made about all the Poor Law children whose details had been given to the Department of Agriculture. The LGB must, therefore, he felt sure, be under a misapprehension.[32] They were not under any misapprehension, replied the Board. There had been long delays in obtaining any information, there were still only 40 reports to hand, and the Canadian government had had as full a list of children as could be provided. Their policy remained firm: Poor Law children were not to be sent to Canada.

However, as might have been expected, many of those who advocated child emigration or acted as agents were dissatisfied with the continuing prohibition. A campaign was mounted – encouraged perhaps by the change of government – to persuade the Board to relax its policy. The secretary of the Howard Association, for example, wrote to Charles Ritchie (now President of the LGB with the fall of Gladstone's third Liberal administration), pressing him to revoke the moratorium, having earlier written to *The Times* on the matter.[33] The Association's letter to Ritchie stressed the relativities:

> But the *worst* of Colonial life is more free from temptation and abuses than the *ordinary* life of English city *slums*. The poor girls, especially, in British slums, are far *worse* off, as to supervision and temptations than they would be in Canadian homes, even if there were no formal official supervision[34] (original emphases).

Another letter to *The Times* from Samuel Smith, the Liverpool MP,[35] followed soon after and was supported on the same day by a sympathetic leader.[36] Smith began by outlining the work of the Liverpool Sheltering Homes (of which he was a patron) and then went on to ask why such an admirable system could not be applied to 'the number of children brought up by the State'. Then he launched a forthright attack on the LGB in the following terms:

> Any one who reads this letter … will marvel what fog has clouded the eyes of our officials to this splendid opening … the Local Government Board has put such obstacles in the way of emigrating these children that hardly anything has been accomplished.

However, Smith maintained that the organisations and individuals with whom Poor Law guardians had arranged to take their children to Canada were inspecting them to the satisfaction of the Dominion government. Official intervention was therefore unnecessary. Nevertheless, he suggested that a meeting with the heads of the emigration agencies be arranged by the Board in order to try to 'devise some working scheme that will be free from danger of abuse, but not so strait-laced as to close the door of emigration to the great army of State-supported children'. The two main reasons for encouraging such emigration were, he argued, to relieve the 'burdened ratepayers' and to deal with the threat of social unrest. This he attributed to the 'enormous number of the unemployed and destitute [that was] becoming a positive danger to the State'. The evidence for this was, he contended, to be seen in 'the alarming growth of Socialism in London of late years'.

This groundswell of pressure made it increasingly urgent for the LGB to clarify the position with the Canadian government, in particular to establish whether or not any more reports would be forthcoming. A further reminder was sent at the beginning of January 1887 and another mid-way through February. At last 348 reports of visits of inspection were received.[37] These were carefully analysed, after which it was concluded that 'on the whole' they could be regarded as satisfactory and emigration could be allowed to be resumed, albeit that detailed information about the whereabouts of the children should always be provided.[38] This requirement was one of the recommendations that had accompanied the last batch of reports from Canada in which it was pointed out yet again that there had been great difficulty in locating the children because of the inadequacy of the addresses provided.

However, an underlying unease was still evident among the LGB's officials. For example, although agreeing that emigration could be resumed Owen, the permanent secretary, still felt that:

> ... the proportion of failures is larger than one would have expected. It is certainly not satisfactory to learn of boys of 9, 10 & 11 years of age running away, & all traces of them being lost & the reports as to some of the girls are very unfavourable.[39]

He recommended that the relevant Poor Law guardians should be asked for more precise information about the children who had not been contacted, that reports should be submitted to the guardians by the people with whom the children had been sent out and that all the societies involved should be asked whether they had a reception Home to which, if necessary, children could be returned and what arrangements they had for obtaining their own reports. The President added his own note to the effect that in future all unfavourable reports should be identified together with details of the agency concerned and the ages of the children. All these recommendations were duly agreed on. With these provisos therefore the emigration of Poor Law children was resumed without further hindrance as from the 'season' of 1887. By April 1888 a revised *Memorandum of Conditions* had been issued. Although its provisions followed fairly closely those contained in the 1883 memorandum greater emphasis was placed on those taking a Poor Law child to Canada providing the Department of Agriculture in Ottawa *immediately* with the child's name and age, as well as the name and address of the person with whom they were placed (specifying the nearest post office, the lot or concession number and the township). The guardians were to obtain an undertaking in writing that this would be done. In addition they were instructed to see that one of their own medical officers inspected each child proposed for emigration. A copy of his report and a certificate confirming that the child was fit for emigration had then to be forwarded to the LGB.[40] The restriction as to age (that was, no girls over 10, or in exceptional circumstances, 12) remained in force, as did those concerning religion and the necessity for guardians to have satisfied themselves that the agencies to whom they entrusted a child had 'a reasonable prospect of finding a suitable home' for them.

Thus, the relaxation of the moratorium in 1887 owed something to the receipt of a reasonably large number of reports from Canada but also to mounting pressure on the LGB not to impede the emigration of Poor Law children. That, of course, has to be seen in the context of a renewed enthusiasm for emigration generally that was fuelled by rising levels of unemployment and the fear of consequent social unrest. However, although the moratorium had been lifted there was no rush on the part of local guardians to take advantage of the opportunity that that presented. After a brief surge in 1888 – possibly reflecting the fact that some guardians who had wished to send children before had been prevented from doing so – the annual rate for emigration was about 300.[41]

Thus, throughout the period 1876-87 the emigration of Poor Law children made halting progress. The central issue was the lack of adequate inspection once the children were in Canada. A picture emerges of considerable unease and scepticism among officials at the LGB, doubts that were primarily about the welfare and protection of such children. Indeed, even when the Board's prohibition was eventually lifted it was with some misgiving on the part of senior civil servants. The attitudes of the political heads of the Board – the presidents – were mixed. The avowed 'emigrationists' such as the Liberal Stansfeld favoured child emigration, albeit recognising some of its shortcomings. Others, like the Conservatives Sclater-Booth and Ritchie, were less committed. In Canada inspection was only reluctantly accepted as the price that had to be paid for the immigration of more children. This reluctance derived partly from concerns about the cost of conducting the inspections but also from the practical difficulties involved. There was a limited number of officers available who, in any case, had other duties, it could be a time-consuming business to trace the children, especially when they had moved and the distances to be covered in order to make a single visit were often considerable, with roads sometimes impassable.

The eventual resolution of the inspection dispute should not obscure the fact that what was offered and finally agreed on was just one visit a year. However thoughtfully these were done much could change in a year and, in any case, would a child feel secure and confident enough to tell a strange inspector how they were being treated and what might be troubling them? Admittedly, some of the Poor Law children were being visited by representatives of the agencies that had taken them to Canada, but such visits, when they occurred, were usually not made more than once a year either. Thus, even the precautions being insisted on by the LGB were unlikely to have done much to ensure better protection for Poor Law children. But the years of prohibition did affect the work of the early child emigrationists in one important respect – namely, that in the period between 1876 and 1887 they were severely limited in being able to recruit children from the Poor Law. However, by the late 1880s other individuals and organisations were appearing on the scene and gathering children for emigration from elsewhere than the Poor Law although not ignoring that source. It is to the emergence of these new ventures that we now turn.

Part III
The Field Expands

FIVE

The Second Wave of Organised Protestant Child Emigration

I Enter Barnardo

More has been written about Thomas John Barnardo (1845–1905) and his organisation than about any other child welfare society in Britain.[1] It is therefore unnecessary to dwell on his biographical details or the rather tempestuous history of the organisation in the nineteenth century. However, Barnardos sent more children to Canada than any other agency – altogether 24,854 children (70 per cent of them boys) were reportedly emigrated under its auspices between 1882 and 1915, the peak years being after the turn of the century.[2] Given the size of the organisation's contribution to juvenile emigration to Canada it is important to appreciate what led to its prominent position and, indeed, to understand what prevented an even greater number of children being sent across the Atlantic.

The roots of Barnardo's child welfare activities lay in evangelism, as did those of so many other philanthropic enterprises of the period. By the time Barnardo arrived in London from Ireland in 1866 he had already embraced the precepts of the Brethren movement and although he later rejected some of its stricter injunctions, its influence remained important throughout his life. He believed that he was divinely called to the work of child salvation and this conviction merged with his autocratic and ambitious personality to create an abiding sense of self-righteousness, a resistance to criticism, an often reckless disregard of the law and a desire to occupy the foremost position in the field of child welfare. He also harboured an antagonism towards Catholicism that, among other things, drew him into lengthy and costly litigation.[3]

In 1866 Barnardo's evangelism had taken him to London's East End as a preacher and it was there that he established his juvenile mission two years later. Although this provided some shelter and some training it was primarily concerned with the propagation of the Gospel; but the need for accommodation led to the opening of the first Home in 1870, to be followed by others soon afterwards. At the time of his death in 1905 there were 37 Homes as well as many other different kinds of centres.[4] Yet how had all this been possible for a man who was not wealthy? There are two principal explanations. One lies in Barnardo's relentless drive and expansionist vision. The other, equally if not more important, is to be found in the financial and other support that he was able to mobilise through his evangelical associations.

However, financial aid was not the only asset on which Barnardo's evangelical connections enabled him to call: they also gave him access to prominent people in public life. For example, Lord Cairns (Lord Chancellor briefly in 1868 and then in Disraeli's second administration from 1874 until 1880) became the first president of the organisation in 1877 after it was no longer possible for Barnardo to continue without trustees, a committee and a treasurer.[5] Cairns was followed by the Marquis of Lorne (a former Governor-General of Canada) and then by a succession of influential peers. Royalty was also drawn into the network of supporters – for instance, Princess Alexandra (later Queen Alexandra) became a patron.

Barnardo's flair for advertisement also helped to ensure that his schemes were launched and mostly prospered despite arousing hostility in some quarters. Furthermore, he secured considerable support as a result of his widely distributed vivid and somewhat sentimental writings and the use of the evangelical press. He was a frequent contributor to the *Revival* (later *The Christian*). As well as these means of engaging the evangelical community there were also numerous private and public meetings. Some involved prayer and missionary preaching while others, like his annual meetings, provided Barnardo with an opportunity to lobby the great and the good among the many who attended.

However, his introduction to child emigration came through his acquaintance with fellow evangelist, Annie Macpherson. As we have seen, Macpherson began to send boys to Canada in 1869 and once Barnardo had established his juvenile mission, and later his Homes, he arranged for 200 boys to accompany her. It was not until 1882 that he decided to organise his own scheme of emigration, encouraged by a generous donation for the purpose from Samuel Smith, the Liverpool MP.[6] The interesting question is why he waited so long. Wagner offers three explanations.[7] First, she points out that Barnardo was clearly aware of the unfavourable report that Doyle had submitted to the Local Government Board (LGB) in 1875 and foresaw the danger of adverse publicity were he to embark on child emigration without adequate safeguards. Second, Barnardo was disinclined to follow anyone else's lead. Finally, during the latter half of the 1870s, the economy had been recovering and it became easier to place older children (especially boys) in work at home.

By the early 1880s, however, economic recession had struck again and this, combined with the rapidly increasing number of children for whom Barnardo was responsible, called for new ways of placing them out. This became more urgent once Barnardo had adopted and proclaimed his slogan: 'no destitute child ever refused admission'. In today's organisational language he now faced a problem of rationing[8] or, put another way, the Homes threatened to silt-up unless he could accelerate the throughput, expand their capacity or abandon his cherished slogan. As he favoured expansion Barnardo chose the first two options, the first becoming an important rationale for his aspirations for child emigration. 'To be a life-giving force', he wrote, his organisation had to have 'its *outlets* as well as its *tributaries*', and in order to secure 'the *open door in front*' it had to 'maintain its *exit door* at the rear' (original emphases).[9] 'It may safely be said', he explained, 'that but for the invaluable outlet offered by the Colonies ... our work must have been greatly hampered and retarded in its development.'[10]

As well as permitting the front door to be kept open Barnardo argued that juvenile emigration would relieve the pressure of population at home; that it would help to forestall the much-feared growth of civil disorder; that it would avoid the return of children to dangerous parents or criminal associations; and that it would contribute to the economic growth of Canada and thereby to strengthening the Empire.[11] Furthermore, Barnardo maintained that emigration would secure a better life for the children, especially since they had 'few ties to bind them to the mother country' and adapted easily to new situations.[12] Placed in rural areas with abstemious and God-fearing Canadian families he saw them being protected from the pernicious influences of city life and brought up in ways that would strengthen their faith. In short, Barnardo regarded emigration as 'the best and most practical remedy for many of the evils of which child misery and destitution are prominent symptoms'.[13] He ensured that he had a largely free hand in promoting this remedy by adding an emigration clause to the admission forms that parents were required to sign. This provided for children's emigration if it were considered to be in their best interests.

One therefore sees several factors working together to move Barnardo towards his programme of emigration. In policy terms it gave every appearance of a truly economical solution to a range of problems. Only in Canada did he foresee the likelihood of opposition, primarily from the emergent trade union movement, but he took steps to neutralise it as far as he could by enlisting official and unofficial support from the Dominion government and by giving an undertaking that he would 'bring back to the mother country any lad or girl who brings disgrace on the Colony, to the Homes, or to themselves by grave moral delinquency'.[14]

It was possible for Barnardo's first party of boys to be sent to Canada in 1882 without the prior acquisition of a reception Home because the Rev. Thomas Stephenson (of the National Children's Homes) had offered to make his establishment at Hamilton available. Having accompanied the boys the Rev. Fielder (governor of the boys' Home at Stepney) wrote to John Lowe, the Deputy Minister at the Department of Agriculture, explaining that Barnardo's intentions could not be realised without the assistance of the Dominion government in providing free rail travel from Québec. He also asked for passes for the subsequent distribution of the children, as well as for himself and his wife so that he could assess the possibilities and finalise arrangements for the future.[15] Lowe replied that the government would offer 'every facility'.[16] Fielder duly reported back that the prospects for further emigration were extremely favourable. Furthermore, it is interesting to see that one of the reasons that he gave for encouraging Barnardo to embark on more emigration was that since admissions to the Homes in Britain were running at about 400 annually, this was the number that it was necessary 'to draft off' each year.[17]

The first group of girls was dispatched in 1883, a year after the boys. Their reception, and that of further parties of boys, was made possible by the gift of a large house (Hazelbrae) at Peterborough. The benefactor was George Cox, mayor of the town but also President of the Midland Railway. Soon after this, other premises were rented in Toronto to accommodate the boys separately from the girls who were to remain at Hazelbrae. At much the same time (1883) Alfred de Brissac Owen was engaged as a visiting officer and was to become Barnardo's representative in Canada.

Meanwhile in Britain Barnardo was planning to extend his emigration activities to the north west of Canada, with the development of the Canadian Pacific Railway (CPR) opening up areas for settlement, having reached Winnipeg in 1882. He wrote to Sir Charles Tupper, the newly appointed Canadian High Commissioner in London,[18] suggesting that he should be granted 3,000–5,000 acres of good land near Winnipeg in order that a farm training school could be established for older boys. They would stay there for a year, working unpaid for their keep, and then be placed out on farms and, if all went well, later be granted land to set up for themselves, aided by a loan from the institution. Of course, he pointed out, he would also need free rail passes from ports of entry to Winnipeg. Rather blatantly he endeavoured to ensure a favourable response by threatening that if the Dominion government did not agree to collaborate then he would look to the US instead.

Tupper's reply was encouraging and he provided Barnardo with a letter of introduction to the Minister of Agriculture, J.H. Pope, suggesting that he contact the president of the CPR about free passes.[19] Barnardo made his first visit to Canada in 1884 and met the minister, although it was explained that land grants were the responsibility of the Department of the Interior;[20] but he was given to understand that his proposal would be well received.[21] Despite this reassurance only 960 acres were provided, although this was substantially augmented soon afterwards by a grant of 2,400 acres from the Manitoba and North West Railway.[22] It was not until 1887, however, that Barnardo returned to Canada to finalise the terms and conditions, to purchase additional land, to arrange for the construction of a building to house 100 boys and to appoint a superintendent.[23] Around 1,500 older boys were sent to what was called the Russell Industrial Farm before its closure in 1905.[24]

As well as the scheme at Russell a reception Home was opened in Winnipeg in 1896 for boys between the ages of 10 and 14. In the first year 400 boys passed through its doors and, by 1911, there were 850 'under supervision'. The majority had been sent to Canada when quite young and boarded out first in Ontario.[25] Parr found that 34 per cent of those who had been placed in this way in the 1890s moved to their first 'wage indentures' in either Manitoba or Saskatchewan, although this proportion fell to six per cent during the first eight years of the new century as enthusiasm for these distant placements waned in the face of Barnardos' increasing debts.[26]

There are no complete details of the ages at which the children were sent to Canada. However, Parr did investigate a sample of 997 of the records of children emigrated by Barnardos between 1882 and 1908. She found that the average age at departure was 15 for the boys and 11 for the girls. Indeed, whereas 26 per cent of the boys were under 13 this proportion rose to 48 per cent for the girls.[27] In my analysis of 40 sailing parties of boys between 1894 and 1905 I found that 23 per cent were under the age of 12. During the shorter period 1901–05, but also including girls, that proportion stood at 21 per cent.[28] Whatever the precise distribution of ages these figures make two things clear. First, that the new century saw no relaxation in the policy (or practice) of sending young children to Canada and, second, that around half of the children dispatched were below the prevailing British school-leaving age of 13.

The involvement of so many young children was partly attributable to the fact that, between 1890 and 1893 Barnardo had inaugurated a scheme for boarding-out children under the age of 11 in Canada, for which an allowance was paid. These children were distinguished from those who, from 11 to 14, or 15 in the case of girls, were expected to work for 'board, clothing and school' and from the older boys and girls who were to be paid wages.[29] Although the boarding-out allowance was intended to protect young children from unreasonable work, to provide that they went to school, and to ensure that they were treated as members of the family,[30] it should be noted that whereas similar payments made by Barnardos in Britain continued until the children were 13, in Canada they ceased at 11 when they were returned to the reception Home to be placed out.

In 1896 Owen, Barnardos' Canadian agent, acknowledged that a considerable number of young children were being sent for boarding out but went on to explain that this was advantageous to the Dominion because 'they had been brought up in English country households, had attended village schools, and become thoroughly familiar with country life'.[31] Clearly, these were children who had been boarded out in Britain. However, such an upheaval, Owen maintained, did not cause the children undue difficulty because they were 'at an age when they have scarcely begun to form habits or personal attachments'.[32] Indeed, in the 1894–1905 sailing parties 67 per cent of the boys under 12 had been removed from British foster homes. The percentage among the girls under 12 who left between 1901 and 1905 stood at 77 per cent.[33]

There are perhaps several reasons for what would seem to have been unnecessary upheavals. First, emigration may have been used to deal with foster home breakdown in Britain instead of bringing children back into residential care. A second reason might have been the need to secure a reasonable rate of turnover of foster home placements. By removing the somewhat older children places could be freed for younger ones and, of course, merely transferring an older child back to a British institution would not have solved the problem of how to keep places there available for newcomers. However, a third and more plausible motive for the emigration of Barnardos' boarded-out children may lie in the intense competition between the child-saving agencies for prestige, financial support and popular acclaim. By the end of the century rivalry was probably at its peak. A sweep through the foster homes may have been one way of enlarging

71

the emigration parties, the size of which had come to be taken as something of a touchstone of success.

There are two further pieces of evidence that point to Barnardo's quest for an increasingly larger number of child emigrants. The first is that a growing proportion of those involved were Poor Law children. From 1899 onwards they comprised around 12 per cent of the boys and a slightly smaller percentage of the girls. Earlier, the overall proportion had hovered around three per cent.[34] Parr found eight per cent in her sample covering the years 1882–1908.[35] A second piece of evidence is a letter from Adam Fowler (head of the Stepney Home in London) to Barnardo in 1905. He wrote to tell him that the next party would not reach the target of 450, and that the director did not appreciate the difficulties involved. He was, he wrote, 'proposing to take all the risks he could' but could not 'permit boys to remain on the list who are manifestly unsuitable'.[36] It seems likely, therefore, that some quite young children who *were* considered to be suitable were uprooted from their British foster homes in order to swell the emigration parties. In any case it must be borne in mind that for a number of years Barnardos had pursued a policy of withdrawing children from foster homes at around the age of 13 in order to return them to the Homes for 'training'.[37] The likely effect on a child who was taken from their foster home in Britain is captured in an account of her emigration given by Daisy Peacock to Gail Corbett, and included in her book *Barnardo Children in Canada*. Daisy had been in her British foster home for eight years before she was removed in order to go to Canada in 1914. 'It broke my heart', she said, 'I cried and cried. I couldn't eat or sleep.'[38] Some who had to leave their Canadian foster homes might well have experienced a similar wrench, perhaps repeating what had happened to them in Britain.

The peak year for the number of children emigrated by Barnardos coincided with the year of the founder's death – 1905. Thereafter the numbers gradually began to fall and were nearly halved between then and 1914. A small party sailed in the following year but that was the last until the movement was resumed after the war, albeit on a much reduced scale.[39] Thus, some of the impetus for the policy of emigration appears to have been lost without Barnardo's presence, but it might also have been partly attributable to improved opportunities for young people in the British labour market, especially for boys. It is impossible, of course, to determine what effect (if any) Barnardo's death had on the pattern of emigration, but he was certainly a keen and forceful advocate of its use, a keenness that his successor William Baker may not have shared to the same extent. Furthermore, as Rose points out, by 1913 concern was being expressed in Barnardos' Council about children being emigrated when they were too young, about inadequate inspection, and about the dangers of the children being overworked.[40] Indeed, other signs of growing unease were evident before then, including disquiet about the objections of parents and about the reluctance of girls to being sent to Canada.[41]

In addition, in 1900 signs of a major scandal began to appear. Rose describes the events in some detail[42] but, in essence, Owen (the superintendent in Canada) was accused of the sexual exploitation of Barnardo girls. However, it was not until

1916 that the secretary at the Toronto headquarters (C.H. Black) made a formal accusation in a detailed letter to McCall, the chairman of Barnardos' Executive Committee, at the same time tendering his resignation because he 'could not condone the offences and irregularities' that he had discovered. In addition to the accusation that Owen was sexually exploiting girls, Black described several of his superior's other misdeeds, among which was that Owen had failed to ensure sufficient protection for girls placed out, thus enabling 'evil men to take advantage of them'. He had also been encouraging under-aged boys to enlist. One other accusation, in a rather lengthy list, was that no appropriate action had been taken when cases of cruelty to the children had been reported. Black informed McCall that these and several others were only a few of the irregularities about which he knew. He called for an urgent investigation, but McCall demurred, claiming that the exigencies of war made it impossible to send anyone senior to Canada to carry out such an inquiry.[43]

It was not until 1919 that John Hobday was sent. This, as Rose explains, was only after Owen had been arrested by the Canadian police and accused of co-habiting with a Barnardo girl.[44] Although confessing his guilt Owen was never convicted, perhaps because Hobday (who became the Canadian manager) had, as he wrote in his report, 'made every endeavour' that there would be 'no grounds for gossip or undue enquiries'.[45] Indeed, until Rose published her book in 1987 this chapter in the account of Barnardos' Canadian activities remained largely closed.

Nevertheless, despite opposition and scandal Barnardos did send around 25,000 children to Canada between 1882 and 1915,[46] many more than any other organisation. This not only made a considerable contribution to the immigrant child population in Canada but also constituted a significant feature of Barnardos' overall arrangements. For instance, until 1907 the children sent to Canada each year represented between 14 per cent and 19 per cent of all those in their care; thereafter the figure stood at 11 per cent up to the outbreak of war.[47] These proportions were larger than the comparable percentages in most of the other societies that were also providing care in Britain *and* emigrating children to Canada. We now turn to the activities of the largest of these.

II Shaw and Manchester

We have seen how systematic child emigration started in London, Liverpool, Glasgow and Birmingham at the beginning of the 1870s. Manchester, however, waited until the 1880s for a similar development to occur. It is not immediately clear why, since various child-saving activities were already established, in particular the Manchester and Salford Boys' and Girls' Refuges and Homes (MSBG – now the Together Trust), which was inaugurated in 1870 by Leonard Shaw (1836–1902) and Richard Taylor. As the organisation's honorary secretary and its public face Shaw's initial caution in embracing the idea of emigration as a remedy for the plight of street-children may have reflected his apprehension about the implications of Doyle's report; but, as we shall see, it seems more likely to have been influenced by the somewhat different structure of Manchester's industries and labour markets.

Shaw was born in Dublin of Protestant parents and was working in a Manchester warehouse by the age of 14. He later became manager of the Scottish Life Assurance agency in the city and in 1884 set up in a similar business of his own.[48] Early on he had become involved with the Ragged School movement and it was through these activities that he became aware of the number of boys sleeping rough in the city. A Ragged School in the daytime was all well and good but it did not meet the need for night-time shelter. It was with this in mind that, together with Taylor (also a Ragged School teacher), he established a boys' refuge in 1870. The establishment of various 'industrial brigades' soon followed and, later, a number of Homes. Then there was a training ship (the *Indefatigable* on the Mersey), a special Home for crippled and incurable children, a police court mission and a remand Home. The Manchester and Salford Society became the largest children's organisation in the north of England, Shaw remaining its honorary secretary until his death.

Unlike certain other initiatives that were launched at about the same time Shaw's was located within a conventional organisational and corporate setting, as well as being carefully connected with the Manchester business community. From the outset trustees were appointed, as well as a committee and a smaller executive committee. John Rylands,[49] the most powerful of the cotton mill owners, chaired the first annual general meeting and continued to be a trustee thereafter.[50] Other notable businessmen contributed in similar ways. By the mid-1880s the committee boasted 67 members and was chaired by the mayor of Manchester with the mayor of Salford as his deputy. The composition of the committee was impressive: there were 12 MPs, 20 justices of the peace; many businessmen and the chief constables of both Manchester and Salford. The relatively small number of clerics was notable although they included the Lord Bishop of Manchester.[51] Incorporating leading business and civic figures into the structure of the organisation achieved two important objectives. One was to establish the *bone fides* of the organisation, and the other (as we have already seen with other schemes) was to create links with potential sources of financial support. Both aims appear to have been met. Indeed, the rapid growth of the Society's activities testifies to the flow of sizeable donations and legacies, many given anonymously.

Thus, although Shaw was religious, evangelical zeal was not a prominent feature of the Society that he founded. It remained non-denominational but essentially Protestant, and although its aims were stated as being 'to reclaim, reform and evangelise homeless and destitute boys' (girls were included in 1878), staff appear to have carried out evangelical work quietly and within the various Homes. Certainly, the monthly journal of the MSGB (which Shaw wrote) was entitled *The Christian Worker* (superseded in 1895 by *The Children's Haven*) and the case records are at pains to note that this or that child 'has found God', or words to that effect.

The Society's approach to the question of emigration was at first tentative. Two boys were sent to Canada with Macpherson in 1871 but, as Shaw wrote in the annual report for that year, it was felt that 'any large scheme …would not find public favour' and, he continued, the Society believed 'that every boy we … train … to become an honest and industrious man at home, is so much added to the strength and stability of our country', even though there would be individual cases 'where the circumstances are such that emigration becomes almost a necessity if the boy is to be saved'.[52] Perhaps the influence of the business community can be detected here. Indeed, in the following year (in which seven boys went to Canada) Shaw wrote that 'living in the midst of a community where the demand for labour seems exceeding [sic] the supply, we have been and are, naturally averse to exporting those hands and minds which should form the strength of the mother country'.[53]

By 1883, however, there was a marked change of emphasis. Emigration was becoming more significant and this was attributed to two changes: first to recession and a downturn in the demand for labour and, second, to a mounting awareness that the population was growing rapidly, prompted perhaps by the report of the 1881 Census.[54] However, two further reasons for Shaw's greater willingness to contemplate the use of emigration emerged. One was that, for the first time, there was a concern to see children removed from Poor Law schools.[55] This may well have been linked to the relaxation of the LGB's moratorium on the emigration of Poor Law children in 1883, although the Society's emigration training Homes were not certified for the reception of such children until 1891. Until then any Poor Law child included in the Manchester sailing parties could only have joined them directly from a Poor Law Home. The second additional reason for favouring a greater use of emigration gradually appeared in the annual reports. These noted the financial savings that could be made by sending children to Canada. Setting a target in 1886 of 100 for each annual emigration party it was recognised that this was '*the cheapest and most efficient way of providing for a homeless and destitute child*'[56] (original emphasis). It was to be undertaken 'from motives of economy as well as philanthropy'.[57]

The first emigration of girls took place in 1883, one group being sent with Rye and another with Birt. Thereafter a special training Home for such girls (Rosen Hallas) was established. Nevertheless, fewer girls than boys were admitted to the Homes and fewer girls were emigrated. The reasons given for sending girls to Canada were similar to those advanced for dispatching boys, but there was an awareness of the widespread opposition to losing girls who might well help to boost the number of domestic servants at home and, perhaps, the future supply of mill hands. Even so, girls were considered to stand in even greater need than boys of being separated from 'degrading', 'vicious' and 'immoral' surroundings.

The size of the emigration groups grew steadily from 1883, the number of girls never exceeding the number of boys and generally being no more than a quarter of any party. From that year until 1914, a total of 2,045 children left for Canada. Up to 1883 the total had hardly reached 50.[58] The children's ages typically ranged between 10 and 14. The inclusion of Poor Law children was gradually acknowledged, but their number was only recorded in three years – in 1905, 1906 and 1907 they comprised 28 per cent, 55 per cent and 39 per cent respectively of the total.[59] Nevertheless, as early as 1884 Shaw was asking: 'Is it not under God's blessing that the removal of children from pauper schools is undertaken?'[60] The ostensible reason was to save them from subsequent pauperism, but it is unclear on what basis they were chosen. It would seem that some Poor Law unions in and around Manchester approached the MSBG with proposals for the emigration of certain of their children who may have been considered to have been at risk of becoming pauperised or of being returned to 'unworthy' parents. The Chorlton union in particular seems to have been enthusiastic about emigration; but it was they who first entertained doubts about its use. Parr has described this change of heart, drawing on reports in the Manchester newspapers.[61] Olga Hertz,[62] who chaired Chorlton's Cottage Homes Committee, visited Canada on behalf of the guardians in 1910 charged with reporting on the circumstances of the children sent by them through the MSBG. She found their school attendance unsatisfactory and was critical of the reports made by the Dominion's inspectors (none of whom, she pointed out, was a woman). Nonetheless, she concluded favourably on the benefits of child emigration. This, however, was not the conclusion reached by her board of guardians, who expressed considerable concern, especially about the younger children, who 'were sent to work for their livelihood at an age which would not be tolerated' in Britain. Furthermore, they found the terms of the indentures 'more like forced labour than free labour contracts'. The attack was spearheaded by socialist members who, among other things, charged that the policy was 'one of economy bought at a fearful price – the price of a child's toil'. As a result of these deliberations the Chorlton board voted to cease sending children to Canada, a step that was followed by several other unions around the country. It is interesting that after this the number of children emigrated by Shaw's organisation fell from 71 in 1910 to 36 in 1914.[63]

Until 1912 the MSBG had no reception and distribution Home of its own in Canada, but in 1886 arrangements had been made to use the Marchmont Home at Belleville.[64] It was to this Home that virtually all the children were sent from 1888 onwards. Its history not only adds to the picture of how the Society organised its emigration but also throws an interesting light on the relationships that existed between some of the societies engaged in the trans-shipment of children to Canada.

Ellen Bilbrough had worked with Macpherson in east London at the end of the 1860s and, as we have seen, she accompanied her to Canada with her first party of boys. However, when the council of the town of Belleville (115 miles east of Toronto) provided a rent-free Home, Bilbrough was left in charge. Although the Home was burnt down twice, it was rebuilt with the aid of local funds and, on the second occasion, given to Macpherson. In the meantime she had established two other Homes (at Galt and at Knowlton) and decided to transfer the Marchmont Home to Quarrier. Nevertheless, Bilbrough remained in charge.[65] In 1882 she married Robert Wallace, a Scottish Baptist minister, and when, in 1888, Quarrier opened a separate Canadian Home, Marchmont passed into the hands of the Wallaces.[66] Thereafter they ran it as their private enterprise. After his wife's death in 1900 Wallace continued in charge until he retired in 1912.

Although there were five trustees (including the Wallaces) there was no management committee at Marchmont and no base in Britain, the work being financed by the fees received from the various societies and Poor Law unions that used their services. Each year, as Wallace explained in 1895 to the Mundella Committee on Poor Law schools, he visited Britain in order to assemble a party of about 100 boys from various sources. His wife did the same later in the year with respect to the girls. In whichever way the children were chosen it remains a fact that the MSBG was an important customer for the Wallaces' services. For example, Wallace also told the Mundella Committee that in the previous year (1894) he and his wife had received 222 children,[67] 108, or 49 per cent, of whom had been sent by Shaw's organisation.[68] However, as the years passed it became the predominant user. In 1906, for instance, 93 per cent of the children arriving at the Marchmont Home came from or via the Manchester organisation.[69] Nonetheless, it is interesting to note that the Canadian inspector of British immigrant children could list the principal societies engaged in juvenile emigration without mentioning the Manchester Society; only Robert Wallace's name appears, and that continued to be the case right up to 1914 and despite his retirement two years earlier.[70]

During their ownership of the Marchmont Home the Wallaces adopted their own practices and these, of course, affected the children sent to them by the MSBG. In his evidence before the Mundella Committee in London in 1895 Wallace described how they worked. The families to whom the children were entrusted were, he explained, first sent a list of questions and rules and were then required to obtain a minister's recommendation.[71] An 'indenture' was then signed, which, among other matters, specified that the child had to go to school for a certain proportion of the year and this was checked, Wallace maintained, by getting the school teacher to verify the number of attendances.[72] The children were visited once a year either by the Wallaces or by one of two inspectors associated with the Home.

As with virtually all the other emigration agencies the MSBG was at pains to stress that *their* children were well trained before they left for Canada. Whereas the training that the girls received as domestic workers might have prepared them for what they would be expected to do when they arrived, the training that the boys were given in work such as carpentry, blacksmithing or printing would not have fitted them for their typical destinies as farm workers. Although this was gradually recognised no farm training establishment was created, despite appeals for funds for that purpose. It is interesting to speculate why, when funds for a range of other projects and Homes seemed relatively easy to attract. Perhaps it reflected a hesitancy about the export of potentially useful labour. Indeed, it is notable that although subscribers to the organisation could nominate the purposes to which their contributions should be put, relatively few specified emigration.[73]

In 1898 there was a significant reduction in the number of children emigrated by the Society. This was almost certainly attributable to its anxieties about the consequences of the Ontario Act to Regulate Juvenile Immigration that was passed in 1897. This imposed more stringent requirements on the organisations arranging the emigration of British children. For example, there had to be four inspections a year, supervision had to continue until the children were 18 and the agencies concerned were to be held financially liable for any child they sent who became dependent on a public body within three years of their arrival.[74] Although eventually made much less exacting, and not thoroughly implemented, this legislation did cause a wave of disquiet among the British child emigration agencies. Some, such as Quarriers, decided to halt their emigration activities altogether; others proceeded cautiously and sought clarification. The MSBG was one of them.[75] Shaw went to Canada in 1897 to see John Kelso (the Ontario inspector of juvenile immigration) and others in order to gauge the implications of what was intended. After these discussions he concluded, however, that the new Act 'merely makes *compulsory* what has been done *voluntarily* by the best conducted agencies ... the Act is fair all round'[76] (original emphases). Nevertheless, the flow of young emigrants was curtailed and this may have reflected a more careful selection of the children in order to meet the conditions specified in the Ontario legislation as well as a particular concern about the financial consequences should some of the children become a charge on Canadian public funds. Furthermore, since the work in that country was carried out by the Wallaces no direct control could be exercised over the choice of placements or the standard of subsequent supervision, despite the visits of the Manchester staff and committee members from time to time. Learning that Robert Wallace was intending to retire, the MSBG bought Marchmont in 1912, installing their own superintendent.[77]

However, the new ownership of the Marchmont Home did not last long. Faced with growing financial problems the MSBG decided to sell the establishment to the Liverpool Sheltering Homes in 1914, at the same time securing an agreement that that organisation would supervise the children who had already been placed out from the Home and that it would receive any subsequent arrivals.[78] But before that could happen any further emigration was halted because of the First World War. In the 1920s Barnardos absorbed the Liverpool Sheltering Homes and thus acquired the Marchmont Home, subsequently selling it for other purposes.[79] Up to that point the history of this particular reception and distribution establishment provides an example of the kind of links (despite certain rivalries) that existed between some of the organisations engaged in child emigration; but it also illustrates the difficulties that could arise for British-based organisations in regulating what actually went on in Canada in their name.

III Fegan's Boys

Although James Fegan (1852–1925) had begun his work with deprived boys in London in 1870, it was not until 1884 that he embarked on the emigration of some of them to Canada. He was born into a strongly evangelical family that embraced the beliefs of the Exclusive Brethren (a division of the Plymouth Brethren). However, the evangelical convictions that he was later to propound as a Baptist lay preacher in open air and tent missions only became evident in his young adulthood. This, and his contact with a Ragged School in London, was what led him to become concerned about the plight of street-boys. At the beginning he rented a cottage in the locality as a night shelter for those who were sleeping rough. In 1872 he opened a non-denominational but Protestant boys' Home in Deptford (south east London), organising the boys into shoe-black and messenger brigades. In 1879 another Home was established at Greenwich and in 1882 the Deptford Home was transferred to Southwark. The following year an orphanage was opened in Ramsgate. Eventually, the Greenwich Home was replaced by a much larger training Home at Stony Stratford in Buckinghamshire.[80] The similarities to the way in which the activities of others developed are striking; for example, the effect of experience in the Ragged School movement and then the establishment of night shelters.

It is not entirely clear how Fegan, who was not a rich man, raised the funds for the expansion of his activities; indeed, in 1874, at the age of 21, he abandoned his employment in a broker's office in order to devote himself to his missionary endeavours. Certainly, later, he was successful in enlisting the financial support of a number of wealthy patrons, prominent among whom was Lord Blantyre, a Scottish landowner and businessman. In his benefactor's obituary, published in Fegan's paper *The Rescue*, he acknowledged the considerable donations that the peer had made, sometimes one-off gifts (as large as £1,000) but also regular contributions, both to the organisation's activities in general and to its emigration work in particular.[81] Indeed, Fegan attributed the start of this work to Blantyre's encouragement and funding for the first party of 10 boys to go to Canada in 1884. Being impressed by the opportunities that he saw there Fegan took another group of 50 later in the same year. Whereas the initial party had been placed in Ontario, 45 of the subsequent batch went to Manitoba, the first young emigrants, it was claimed, to be taken 'to the vast North-West'.[82] On the way, however, the boys were lodged in a new Canadian boys' Home in Toronto that William Gooderham (a rich businessman who had been 'converted to God' in later life) had paid for and in which he took a close interest. However, in 1885 the new Home was still not fully occupied and the next group of 100 Fegan boys was accommodated there prior to being placed out. Nevertheless, the Toronto Boys' Home could not be used on a permanent basis and, with this in mind, Gooderham bought and fully equipped another property in Toronto that he presented to Fegan in 1886.[83]

Thus the impetus for Fegan starting his emigration work was a mixture of opportunity, necessity and conviction. The opportunity was provided by Blantyre's financial support. As with so many others engaged in child saving, the necessity was to create vacancies in his British Homes in order to be able to admit new cases. This had to be done without discharging boys to what were regarded as unsatisfactory conditions. Fegan's belief that emigration was a desirable solution was based on his conviction that Canada offered an excellent prospect for boys' advancement and for the maintenance of their faith.[84] However, like so many of the other emigrationists, Fegan entertained a rather romantic view of how his charges might live in Canada, or at least this was the impression that he endeavoured to convey in the succession of house journals that he wrote and had printed by the boys.[85] In 1905, for instance, he assured his readers that 'for £10 we can transplant a boy from our London slums to the fire-side circle of a Canadian farmhouse…'.[86] Nonetheless, there were several features of Fegan's enterprise that differed from those of his contemporaries, most notably that he took only boys. In any case he did not believe that the emigration of girls was wise. Indeed, he characterised the life of the Canadian farm wife in far from romantic language: 'she has to be wife, mother, dairy-maid, cook, housemaid and washerwoman, not only for her husband and children, but for the hired hands too, without the slightest possibility of female help. Her life is one round of drudgery….'[87] He had no wish, he implied, to see young British girls plunged into such drudgery as 'little helpers'.

A second feature of Fegan's emigration activities was the considerable emphasis that was placed on the boys repaying as much of the cost of their emigration as they could. A roll of honour listing those who had done so was established and their names advertised in his journal *The Rescue* and in its successor publications. Bronze medals were struck and distributed to the honour-list boys. Over the years the sum repatriated mounted. Between 1889 and 1913, for example, 943 boys had repaid a total of £12,809.[88] It is also noticeable that, unlike other emigrationists, Fegan placed less emphasis on the value of emigration as a means of separating children from unworthy parents. Indeed, he foresaw the possibility of an eventual reunification of the family, or part of it, in Canada, assisted by the earnings of the boys already there.

One further unique aspect of Fegan's emigration scheme was the creation (albeit well into the twentieth century) of a replica Canadian farm at Goudhurst in Kent. Its purpose was not only to train boys in the rudiments of farming but also to introduce them to Canadian farming in particular. A large Canadian-style barn was built and Canadian farm machinery obtained (donated by Massey Ferguson). The first batch of boys arrived in 1911. A home was provided on the site for Fegan and his wife, where they lived until his death in 1925.[89]

Certainly, the clear intention was that once in Canada all but the very young boys should be found work on farms. As George Greenaway, the long-serving superintendent of the Toronto distribution Home, wrote in 1900:

> Boys of 10, 11 or 12 years old are sent out on an agreement for 3, 4 or
> 5 years for food, clothes and school in winter (no wages). Older boys of

13 or 14 and upwards are engaged by the year at wages varying from $24 to $54 per year according to size and ability. Clothes of course being provided out of boys' wages.[90]

The agreements for the older boys were re-negotiated each spring and they either remained where they were or sought employment elsewhere, although some who were discontented left during the year. These arrangements underline the boys' status as essentially farm labourers rather than long-term members of the household, even though some stayed on. Those who were under 10 when they arrived were usually classified as 'for adoption', although placements for them were hard to find and they often languished in the distribution Home.

However, apart from these aspects of his emigration activities Fegan trod a similar path to that of most of the other emigrationists. But he did arrange public meetings for what was termed 'the hiving off' at which those destined for Canada were presented. In 1885, for instance, there were three farewell meetings for the same party, at Blackheath, Exeter Hall in central London and at Deptford where the inhabitants

> ... were roused by the stirring tones of the Drum and Fife Band from the Southwark Boys' Home, as at the head of a hundred young emigrants, it marched steadily on to the New Cross Public Hall, where all interested in the welfare of the lads were invited that they might finally bid 'God-Speed' to the youthful pioneers.[91]

These gatherings, as well as the monthly chronicles and penny tracts that Fegan wrote, were a means of bringing his work to the notice of a potentially sympathetic public in order to obtain financial help. So too were his regular contributions to evangelical papers such as *The Christian* and *The Life of Faith*. Even so, despite his successes the organisation found itself in considerable debt from the turn of the century. Rather like Barnardo, Fegan's schemes and aspirations frequently outran the resources that he had available. The minutes of his council's meetings, and more especially those of the finance committee, are peppered with items concerning this. From time to time members resigned (or threatened to do so) in protest at insufficient priority being given to dealing with the growing liabilities.[92] In 1904 there were proposals to curtail the work until an in-road could be made into the accumulating debt, but Fegan countered by launching what he called his 'Million Shilling Fund'. However, this did little to reduce the indebtedness. In 1912, for example, bank loans stood at £10,000 in addition to sundry creditors. Such financial difficulties at home gave additional urgency to the emigration side of the work. Once placed in Canada the boys were no longer a drain on resources. What is not clear is the extent to which Fegan included Poor Law children in his parties and was able, therefore, to be reimbursed by the guardians. Certainly, Poor Law children did join his parties, for in 1915 boys from the West Ham, Aylesbury and Maidstone unions are mentioned.[93]

There appear to have been three phases in Fegan's emigration activities that may have reflected the ups and downs of his finances or variations in the number of boys available from the Homes or from Poor Law guardians. Between 1886 and 1895 around a hundred a year crossed to Canada. Between 1896 and 1908 this fell substantially, dipping to 40 in 1898. The period from 1909 until 1914 again saw the assembly of annual parties of a hundred or more, with a final group of 75 leaving in 1915 before further departures were interrupted by the First World War.[94] Even during the middle years (1896–1908), however, emigration to Canada played an important part in the disposal of the boys from the British Homes. For example, 134 boys were admitted in 1900 and, according to the subsequent entries in the admission register, 40 per cent of them went to Canada. More might have gone had 16 per cent not absconded and another five per cent been expelled. By 1910, however, Canada had become a much more prominent form of disposal. Of the 121 boys admitted that year, 67 per cent were recorded as having left for the Dominion (three to relatives). None was listed as absconding and only two as having been expelled. Significantly more (14 per cent compared with six per cent of the entrants of 1900) were noted as having been restored to a relative or guardian.[95]

Altogether 2,563[96] boys went to Canada under Fegan's auspices between 1884 and 1915, some of them having been taken from other organisations, in particular Mrs Smyly's Home in Dublin. Between 1885 and 1913 it was noted that nine per cent of the young emigrants had returned, or been returned, to England and that six per cent were known to have gone to the US. Indeed, the form of consent to emigration asked those giving that consent to agree to a boy going to Canada *or* to the US, a clause likely to have been at odds with that country's policy. Although these forms were designed to be signed by a relative, some were not, even though the endorsing magistrates or clergymen countersigned that they had witnessed the signature.

Having arrived in the distribution Home the boys, Fegan explained, were rested, their outfits overhauled, and an opportunity provided for them to see Toronto. Then they were allotted 'to what seemed the most suitable places'.[97] This was called 'the scattering', although it was kept within limited distances because, as Fegan claimed in 1914, boys should not be placed 'outside the radius' of convenient visiting.[98] He certainly considered his arrangements in this and in other respects to be superior to those of other emigrationists who were, he complained, flooding areas of Canada

> ... with boys whose physique and character have not commended them as a desirable element in the population, and whose brief training is quite inadequate ... [the effect] of rushing out big parties one after the other ... is an underselling of colonial labour in certain parts, and the necessity of getting rid of the boys by placing them out on such low terms as are unfair to the little fellows....[99]

Furthermore, unlike Quarrier and others, Fegan actively welcomed the Ontario legislation of 1897 that imposed tighter controls on British child emigration agencies. These controls, he argued, 'had done away with a most disreputable traffic in flesh and blood on the part of unscrupulous persons who brought out children and dumped them in the Province without any subsequent protection or supervision'.[100] He was at pains to emphasise that he had never been 'a mere Shipping Agency to transport boys from England to Canada'.[101]

Like most of the other emigrationists Fegan published letters from those who had gone to Canada. Sometimes these were in pamphlet form, for example *A Budget of Letters from 'Our Sons Across the Sea'*,[102] and sometimes in his monthly chronicles. The letters usually struck a thankful and optimistic tone and were obviously made public in order to cast the organisation in as favourable a light as possible. For instance, one boy wrote that he 'did not wish to come to Canada when I first came under your care, but it was the best thing that ever happened to me'. Nevertheless, here and there, small items of information were included that revealed other aspects of the boys' experiences. Another boy explained that he had 'not heard from my mother and father or any of the other children for 9 years, so I write to you. I have nobody to write to but you.' One other letter included this wistful message: 'What wouldn't I give to be back amongst the boys again [at Stony Stratford].'[103] Indeed, one of the interesting features of many of the children's letters to be found in the records of all the organisations is the feeling of nostalgia for the British Homes.

This may have contributed to the feeling of a group identity that seemed to have been created among at least some of the boys. For instance, the Christmas reunions at the Toronto Home were reported to attract 50–60 of the boys. It may be that the honour-list system achieved more than its money-raising function – it may have given those who succeeded in being enrolled a sense of status and achievement. Furthermore, and rather in the later mould of Fairbridge, Fegan referred to the boys as 'pioneers' and 'empire builders', which may also have encouraged some to feel a certain pride. However, their experiences as farm workers were doubtless similar to those of other boys who were sent to Canada by other organisations.

In several ways, therefore, Fegan's emigration scheme differed somewhat from those of his contemporaries. He took only boys; he introduced Canadian-style farm training before they left Britain; he was unapologetic about pressing the boys to repay the cost of their passage and outfit; he did not unduly stress emigration as a means of severance from unsatisfactory parents but rather encouraged reunion in Canada; and he limited the area in which the boys were initially placed in order to make visiting them easier.

IV The Established Church

The last of the agencies to enter the child emigration field in the 1880s was the Church of England Waifs and Strays Society (now The Children's Society). Edward

Rudolf (1852–1933) is credited with its establishment, although he was never identified with its activities as closely as, for example, Stephenson or Barnardo were with the organisations that they founded. Nonetheless, he was instrumental in persuading the Church of England to set up its own child care organisation in 1881 and then to embark on emigration in 1885, by which time he had been appointed honorary secretary to the Society. He eventually retired in 1919, having been ordained in 1907.

Rudolf came from a poor but middle-class background. He received no formal education and began office work at the age of 13. When he was 17 he conducted a 'popular education class' in the East End of London and later became a Sunday school superintendent in Kennington, south of the Thames, a post he held for 10 years.[104] In the meantime he had passed the newly instituted civil service examination (1871) and had entered the Office of Works as a junior clerk. He remained in the same department, with steady promotion, until 1890 when he resigned to become the full-time and paid secretary of the Waifs and Strays Society. The fact that he was able to combine his government duties with being secretary of the organisation and with other activities for so long says much about the leisurely character of the civil service before the 1890s and about the depth of Rudolf's dedication to the causes he espoused. However – returning to his involvement in child welfare – it is noteworthy that in 1874 he had joined the Guild of St Alban, an order of lay brothers committed, among other things, to work with the poor. This, as well as his Sunday school teaching, brought him into contact with destitute children. Nevertheless, it was not until 1880 that, having had to apply for two homeless boys who had attended his Sunday school to be admitted to Barnardos, he came to believe that the Church of England should have its own comparable organisation, at least for the reception of such children. This conviction grew alongside his misgivings about Barnardos. This was not only because of its founder's 'flamboyance, his showmanship, his teetering finances [and] his brushes with the law', but also because of the un-denominational (although Protestant) character of the organisation that he led. In particular, 'there was suspicion about the religious creed which he professed. He was not High Church ... was he Low, was he Latitudinarian, was he *Chapel*?' (original emphasis).[105] Given such doubts it was not surprising that Rudolf should have written that he was:

> ... deeply concerned, that after receiving Church teaching for some years, these little fellows [the boys admitted to Barnardos] should have to be placed where the religious instruction would be of a totally different kind, with the result that they would be lost to the Church of England.[106]

These sentiments emphasise yet again the important part that inter-denominational and sectarian suspicions, distrust and rivalry played in the proliferation of child welfare societies in nineteenth-century Britain and in the emigration to which many subscribed. In order to understand such tensions and the depth of feeling that they aroused, one has to appreciate the extent of the religious turbulence that prevailed throughout the Victorian era, and in particular during its last 40 years.[107] This was to be seen, for example, in the divisions within Methodism, in the Presbyterian wing of the Church of England and in the rising tide of agnosticism and atheism. Yet, as Chadwick has emphasised, it was evangelical fervour that exercised the greatest influence, touching virtually every denomination. 'To many Victorians', he wrote, 'evangelical doctrine was the authentic voice and the scriptural piety of Protestant Reformation. It looked to be the sharpest arrow to pierce the soul of labouring heathen.'[108] Nonetheless, it was because of the pervasiveness and assumed power of evangelical doctrine that it created the potential for schism and passionate affiliation.

Although it was his anxiety about the religious education that Barnardos might provide that was the most immediate reason for Rudolf wishing to see the Church of England establish its own facilities for the care of children in need, what he intended was that there should be a central reception Home from which the children could then be placed in existing private Church of England Homes. Despite considerable doubt within the Church itself as to whether such a development was called for, Rudolf, through persistence and quiet lobbying, overcame objections and eventually won the support of the Archbishop of Canterbury who, in 1881, agreed to become the president of what at first was called the Church of England Central Home for Waifs and Strays. However, the idea of a single national reception Home, albeit separate for boys and girls, was quickly superseded as a variety of Homes around the country, run by local committees, were established or absorbed into what now became the Church's official organisation. Indeed, in 1883 it became its declared policy to have a Home in every diocese from which children could be placed in other approved Homes, boarded out or emigrated. In line with this enlarged objective the organisation's name was changed to the Church of England's Central Society for Providing Homes for Waifs and Strays.[109] Despite this title, as Ward's research makes clear, the admission arrangements were markedly decentralised, with the dioceses and individuals within them proposing and often sponsoring particular children.[110]

In his history of the 'Waifs and Strays' Stroud asks why Rudolf 'with no obvious talent or charisma' was successful in bringing his brainchild to fruition and thereafter sustaining and developing it. He suggested three reasons. The first was Rudolf's humility and sincere faith; second, there was his methodical and painstaking way of working that reassured supporters and potential supporters that the Society was in reliable hands and, third, his 'mildly neurotic drive'.[111] However, the fact that he was working within the established Church whose membership included much of the 'establishment' of the day must be added to these influences. Indeed, the Queen became patron of the Society in 1895 and was succeeded on her death by Edward VII. Furthermore, it also meant, as Stroud points out, that 'the financial resources of a vast congregation could be tapped'.[112]

Although the Society had arranged for a small number of children to go to Canada with Rye and Macpherson in 1882 and 1883, it was not until 1884 that it was decided to form an emigration committee and to establish a reception and distribution Home in Canada. The initial plan appears to have assumed that only girls between the ages of six and 12, or possibly over the age of 16, would be selected. This may have been the result of a letter that Rye had written to Rudolf in 1881, urging him to concentrate on the needs of young girls.[113] That message was certainly reflected in the Society's first venture into emigration on its own account in 1885 that saw a party of girls sent to Canada with the Rev. Bridger of the Society for Promoting Christian Knowledge. It was also to him that Rudolf turned in order to find a suitable property for the Canadian Home, partly no doubt because Bridger had been invited to be a member of the Waifs and Strays' emigration committee and because he was a regular visitor to the Dominion. His advice that a house at Sherbrooke in eastern Québec should be purchased was accepted and an appeal launched for the £1,000 that this required.[114] In the event over a quarter of that sum was given by members of the Gibbs family, three of whom sat on the emigration committee and whose gift was acknowledged in the Home being named after them.

The 'girls only' policy, however, was soon abandoned and a second building at Sherbrooke was constructed to permit boys and girls to be accommodated separately. Later, in 1896, Rye transferred both her London and Canadian Homes to the Waifs and Strays. After this the Society used her Niagara establishment for the reception of its girls and the Sherbrooke Home for the boys. Rye's Peckham Home in south London continued to operate as a preparation centre for girls destined for Canada. The preparation of the boys was generally longer and mostly took place at the farm Homes that the Society gradually established, but in particular at the Standon Farm School, opened in 1885 and registered as an industrial school.[115]

Between 1885 and 1914 the Waifs and Strays Society sent 2,240 children to Canada and despite the early preference for sending girls 60 per cent were boys.[116] The principal purpose of this emigration, as Rudolf described it, was to separate children 'entirely from their former dangerous surroundings, to which they might return after leaving the Homes if they remained in the Mother Country'.[117] Nevertheless, by comparison with most other societies the Waifs and Strays sent a smaller proportion of their children to Canada. During the years covered by her impressive study (1887–94), Ward found that, although 19 per cent of her sample (400) of all children in the Society's care were *considered* for emigration, only slightly over half of them went. The most common reason for this erosion was the refusal of the parents (and sometimes of the children) to give their permission. Unlike Barnardos the application form for a child's admission to the Waifs and Strays did not oblige the parents to agree to the possibility of emigration, although there was such a clause to which they could agree. In fact, Ward found that a third of them had refused to endorse this option. However, although the Society's policy was not to emigrate a child without the parents' permission, Ward concluded that its local agents 'had little compunction as to the means by which consent might be reached. A number were', she found, 'prepared to use every means at their disposal to persuade relatives to drop what they saw as misguided opposition to an unprecedented opportunity.'[118] Furthermore, she estimated that during her study years '12% of the … young emigrants left the country precipitately in order to present vacillating parents with a *fait accompli*'.[119]

The children who could be emigrated without the Society having to take their parents' anxiety into account were, of course, the true orphans, or those whose parents' whereabouts were unknown. Indeed, some two-thirds of the children in Ward's sample who went to Canada fell into one or other of these categories although, as she found from the case records, there was little evidence that strenuous efforts were made to trace parents whose addresses were not immediately known.[120] Apart from the refusal of parents to give consent to their child's emigration some children proposed for Canada did not go for other reasons. For example, in 1910 those not passed for emigration suffered from 'excega', poor eyesight, or a heart condition. Others were excluded because they were not strong enough, were too small, or 'not suitable for outside work'. Then there were those who were not to be trusted, who were educationally 'backward' or incontinent.[121] These were specific reasons for children not being emigrated; but the Waifs and Strays appear to have been somewhat more cautious than some of the other societies about who should be selected and when. For example, in 1888 it was decided that no child should be sent to Canada without first having spent at least three months in one of the Society's Homes.[122] The state of the labour market in Britain also seems to have been taken into account. When it was easy to find employment for children at home emigration was only considered, so the 1910 annual report maintained, 'in cases of urgency', that was, when there was a danger that children would return to 'bad homes', thereby 'undoing all the good that [had] been done'.[123] Much, of course, turned on the assessment of a home as bad or surroundings as prejudicial, and this was usually based on reports from local committees.

Another reason why the Waifs and Strays exercised a measure of restraint about emigration, particularly in the 1890s, was their concern not to fall foul of the 1893 Ontario Children's Protection Act and, later, the province's Act of 1897 to Regulate Juvenile Immigration.[124] For example, in 1893 the Society's annual report explained that so few children had been emigrated (just 18) because the implications of the Ontario legislation were unclear as to how they affected the immigration and settlement of British young people. However, it was also maintained that the reduction also reflected a growing reluctance of local committees 'to sever themselves entirely from the children who have conducted themselves well in the Homes'.[125] Later, bearing in mind the requirements of the 1897 Act, it was decided that although children might be considered to have 'unsatisfactory antecedents', they could be sent to Canada as long as they had spent at least a year in a Home in Britain and that they had shown 'no moral or physical defect'.[126]

As well as these reasons for restricting the number of children being sent to Canada there was the 1909 policy decision concerning girls. Initially the girls were usually younger than the boys when they sailed,[127] but it was now decided not to emigrate them until they were 14. This may have been the result of an earlier unsuccessful experiment in sending young girls to Winnipeg. The idea for this scheme seems to have arisen as a result of a visit that Rudolf made to Manitoba in 1906, although the reasoning behind it is obscure. Nevertheless, a group of infant girls did go to Winnipeg in the following year,[128] but there was no reception Home from which they could be placed out or to which they could return if necessary.

It is unclear how many infant girls arrived in Winnipeg, but by 1910 the general secretary of the Associated Charities of Winnipeg (Falk) expressed his misgivings.[129] Rudolf had approached him in search of reception accommodation, but nothing was available except the immigrant sheds, and these were dismissed as unacceptable.[130] Would it be acceptable, Rudolf asked the Superintendent of Immigration in Ottawa, if either the Young Women's Christian Association (YWCA) hostel or the Girls' Friendly Society Lodge were used instead?[131] The reply was that this might be considered satisfactory.[132] However, it seems likely that negotiations with these organisations foundered since a Babies' Home for girls as well as boys up to the age of five was in fact established in Winnipeg, but survived only briefly. The Society's evidence to the recent House of Commons' Select Committee on *The Welfare of Former British Child Migrants* claimed that the venture lasted from 1909 to 1911, but the Canadian archival material indicates a rather later opening date.[133] Either way, since the Winnipeg Babies' Home was for girls and boys its creation would appear to have been at odds with the 1909 policy not to send girls under the age of 14 to Canada. It is also surprising that Rudolf makes no mention of the Winnipeg Babies' Home in his history of the Society.[134]

However, the question of the Society making satisfactory arrangements in Winnipeg was not the only matter to concern the Canadian authorities. The most prominent was the absence of effective visiting and supervision. In 1901 Bogue Smart (the Dominion's inspector of British immigrant children) had already noted that no regular visits were being made to the children placed out,[135] and by 1905 he was writing formally to Rudolf to emphasise the necessity for a permanent visitor to be appointed.[136] The following year Smart wrote again, but more sharply, saying that the absence of systematic visiting appeared to show 'a lack of individual interest in the child'.[137] Rudolf replied that he would call on the inspector when he was next in Canada, but that in the meantime he would try to make arrangements for better supervision.[138]

Some improvements were made over the next year or two since, by 1912, there was a female visitor[139] and a male inspector, although he was also referred to as the superintendent of the Sherbrooke Home.[140] There were at least three factors, over and above the usual difficulties of travel and 'lost' children, that had made visiting such a hit-and-miss affair. One was that until 1912 the Society had relied on either the staff of their Home or local volunteers to do the inspections. The latter in particular were not easily recruited or, if they were, they were difficult to retain or hold accountable. The second reason for the failure to ensure regular visiting arose from the practice of relying on reports from ministers and neighbours as to the welfare of the children.[141] Such a reliance was doubtless connected with a third reason for the Society failing to secure proper supervision. This was the fact that children were only placed with Church of England families who were vouched for by their local minister. This appears to have created a false sense of confidence that no harm would come to the child and that subsequent oversight was hardly needed.

One explanation for why the lack of adequate inspection and other shortcomings were not fully appreciated by the Society until attention was drawn to them by the Canadian authorities[142] was that those who visited Canada and reported back gave such glowing accounts of what they had seen and heard. These were often reported in the Society's journal, *Our Waifs and Strays*. For example, in 1887 the Rev. Barrett and the Hon. J. Abercromby (the Society's honorary secretary for emigration) were asked to report on the work in Canada. Although they reported favourably on all the placements that they visited they were critical of what others were doing.[143] They castigated the 'philanthropic enthusiasts' who seemed 'to have an unreasoning faith in the instantaneous conversion of a nature by the mere change of environment', adding that 'till the public can discriminate between the various organisations, and learn to repose confidence in us, every care should be taken to emigrate only suitable children...'.[144] However, as with all the other emigrationists, the emphasis in this was on the suitability of the children and not on the suitability of their placements.

Thus, a somewhat mixed picture of the emigration activities of the Waifs and Strays Society emerges. On the one hand, Rudolf and his committee appear to have approached the emigration of the children in their care with rather more caution than many of the other organisations and, in principle, accorded more respect to the wishes of the parents. However, much of the impetus for the emigration of particular children, and the information on which this drew, originated at a local level and had to be taken at face value. The practice of personal sponsorship of individual children by local people complicated the implementation of any policy. Nevertheless, these features apart, the Waifs and Strays had much in common with what was done (or not done) by the other societies. The principal rationale for sending children to Canada was their severance from what were regarded as contaminating influences at home. The supervision there was inadequate but the reports that filtered through were almost universally favourable, except certain communications from the Department of the Interior. Such criticisms as these contained were not acted on swiftly, probably because of insufficient staff in Canada.

★ ★ ★ ★ ★

Thus, by 1885 the number of Protestant agencies engaged in the emigration of children to Canada had increased considerably. However, alongside these activities the 1880s also saw a rapid expansion of Catholic initiatives, not to mention a variety of other ventures launched by individuals who continued without any, or with very little, formal organisation. We turn to the Catholics next and then to those 'unorganised' agencies.

SIX

The Catholic Response

I The Context

We have seen in chapter 2 that Father Nugent's early initiatives in the emigration of Catholic children from Liverpool sprang not only from a concern to save them from the 'ravages of destitution' but also from an anxiety about a 'leakage from the faith'. One of the reasons why this was considered difficult to withstand was because of the Church's limited resources. On the one hand, there were heavy concentrations of poor Catholics in the densely populated urban areas and on the other, there was the class composition of Catholicism in Britain. At the lowest end of the social scale there was a huge army of unskilled poor and at the top a group of old aristocracy. What was missing were the middle and artisan classes, precisely the groups from which the Protestants recruited so many of their lay supporters and among whom much evangelical fervour was to be found.[1]

However, when Henry Edward Manning (1808-92) became Archbishop of Westminster in 1865 various initiatives were launched to stem this loss of the faithful. These mostly originated from a programme set out in 1866[2] in which the creation of a special fund to increase the number of Catholic schools occupied a prominent position.[3] It was felt that too many Catholic children were insufficiently educated or not educated at all, and yet it was to the allegiance of the children that the Church had to look if the future of the faith were to be secured. The widespread and excessive consumption of alcohol was also seen as a major cause of the poor abandoning their faith, which in turn led to their failure to pass on that faith to the next generation. In an attempt to combat this and to safeguard the children, Manning founded the Total Abstinence League of the Cross in 1872, but it had only limited success. The importance attached to securing the children's faith was also to be seen in the attempts that were made to reduce the number of Catholics marrying non-Catholics, a practice that had become increasingly common. Steps were taken, in particular by the local priesthood, to discourage such unions or, if that were unsuccessful, to persuade the non-Catholic partner to convert or give assurances that their children would be raised as Catholics.

A further factor to which Catholic losses were attributed preoccupied the Church until the end of the 1880s – this was the likelihood that the children of the destitute Catholic poor would be admitted to Poor Law or philanthropic institutions where Protestantism prevailed and where 'the power of assimilation', as Manning put it, 'was silently irresistible'.[4] However, in order to extricate Catholic children from such institutions and to avoid their being admitted in the first place, additional Catholic facilities had to be made available. However, this was not the only problem. First, Catholic children had to be actually identified. This should have been possible for those in Poor Law institutions by consulting the Creed Registers that boards of guardians had been required to maintain since 1859. In actual fact, some unions had failed to establish a register while others did not keep it up to date. Gradually, however, under increasing pressure from the Local Government Board (LGB), the guardians were forced to comply.

Yet even when Catholic children were identified, many boards of guardians were reluctant to transfer them to certified Catholic Homes or schools, sometimes arguing that there was no evidence that a child was a Catholic, sometimes that they had adopted a Protestant faith,[5] and sometimes that the local rate-payers would not countenance paying for children in any but those institutions under the control of elected representatives. After 1869, however, it was possible for the LGB to order that a Catholic child be transferred, albeit on the application of a parent or next of kin. This led to a flurry of activity on the part of many priests in order to locate parents and then to encourage them to make the relevant application.

Nevertheless, such arrangements did not extend to the voluntary Homes, and even when Catholic parents asked that their children be transferred from them their request could be blocked in various ways – sometimes by the pre-emptive emigration of the child to Canada. Towards the end of the 1880s, however, the campaign to have Catholic children transferred to Catholic facilities had largely been won, particularly as the strength of anti-Catholic feeling began to subside. As the number of transfers increased, the pressure on Catholic institutions mounted, added to which the desire to prevent admissions to the Poor Law system or to Protestant agencies led to an increasing number of children being received directly into Catholic establishments.

Even with the steady addition of extra places it still remained necessary to seek ways of increasing the turnover of children in order to accommodate the stream of new entrants. As Edward St John explained, one important solution was emigration, not least because if the children were 'voluntary' cases (that is, not transferred from the Poor Law) no financial assistance would be forthcoming.[6] However, once they were in Canada this ceased to be a problem because the cost of their maintenance no longer fell on the diocese; moreover, there was the *per capita* subsidy paid by the Dominion for each non-Poor Law child emigrated. In effect, therefore, the desire of the Catholic Church to prevent their children being admitted to Poor Law institutions meant that it had to create what almost amounted to a parallel Poor Law system and that, together with its resolve not to have Catholic children brought up by philanthropic organisations with either an explicit or implicit Protestant commitment, placed a great strain on its resources. Relief was found by sending some children to Canada.

Since throughout most of the second half of the nineteenth century children were seen as the key to preserving the Catholic faith, it is in this context that the emergence and pattern of Catholic child emigration has to be set. It is also important to appreciate the administrative complexity of the Catholic agencies that were involved. There were at least two reasons for this. First, although the various societies were subject to the overall authority of the Church each developed within their separate dioceses where they answered to their respective bishops. The different and changing titles given to the organisations created a second source of confusion, not least as a result of the various amalgamations. As has already been explained in relation to other societies this made it difficult for officials, especially those in Canada, to know with whom they were dealing. Thus, in order to keep matters as clear as possible each of the four principal organisations is dealt with separately in the rest of this chapter, but the different, although overlapping, themes are also illustrated. In addition, there is an account of the case of a Catholic 'outsider' – J.H. Boyd – that adds a further dimension.

II Liverpool: Preserving the Faith

The Liverpool Catholic Children's Protection Society (LCCPS, now Nugent Care) was founded in 1881 through the efforts of Father Nugent and Bishop O'Reilly. O'Reilly had:

> ... called together the Clergy of Liverpool and others interested in the welfare of the poor, to consider what could be done for the protection of Catholic children, who were, it was known, being accepted by other than Catholic agencies.[7]

This remained a recurrent theme. For example, the Society's annual report of 1892, explained that there were:

> ... always numbers of poor Catholic children drifting towards pauperism and crime, and if these are not taken in hand by Catholics, there are other agencies ready to look after their worldly welfare, but it will be at the cost of the faith of the children.[8]

One way in which Catholic children could be 'protected' in their religion and from destitution was, as the Society's constitution stated, 'by means of emigration'.[9] To this end it assembled a special committee with Nugent as administrator, a post that he held for 10 years. In 1882 a house was rented where children awaiting emigration could be accommodated. A superintendent was appointed and it was she and her successor who accompanied the children to Canada. Some of them were received in a hostel in Montreal before being allocated; others were placed with the assistance of various orders. In some cases parish priests assumed the responsibility. However, by 1894 (or perhaps even earlier) the Society, together with other diocesan emigration societies, was using the Catholic Protection and Rescue Home (St Vincent's) in Montreal.

The LCCPS emigrated a wide age range of children, although the average ages hovered around 12–13. Boys and girls were sent in fairly equal numbers.

Between 1881 and 1902 (after which, as we shall see, the Society operated under the umbrella of the Catholic Emigration Association) 2,400 children were taken to Canada.[10] The exact number is elusive not least because, in 1893, Father Berry's Homes in Liverpool (which had been independently established two years earlier by the Society of St Vincent de Paul) were taken over by the LCCPS, although in the official Canadian records the children being emigrated were sometimes still listed separately.

Whatever the precise number of the LCCPS's young emigrants between 1881 and 1902 (and those sent by Nugent earlier), it is plain that there was a desire to see a regular increase. This largely derived from ongoing concern about the spiritual welfare of Catholic children admitted to Poor Law institutions. Indeed, a common plea was for them to be 'rescued' from such Protestant-dominated environments. In Liverpool this was seen as a particularly urgent matter. In the first place there was a large poor Catholic population, but there was also a very large Poor Law school (Kirkdale) serving several unions and that accommodated between 1,200 and 1,500 children, a good many of whom were Catholics. The LCCPS was anxious to see these young people removed to situations where they could be brought up under a proper Catholic influence. Yet, as has been explained, there were insufficient Catholic residential provisions and boarding out in Catholic homes hardly existed. Canada seemed to offer a solution to the problem for, as Nugent had pointed out, the Dominion, with 'its strong Catholic population, especially in the French Canadian and Scottish settlements where the colonists had come over as a community with their priests', offered the religious influence that was being sought. There was less enthusiasm for placing children with English or Irish Catholics since they had 'just filtered in without any organisation' and had often settled miles from a church and priest and were, in consequence, considered to be in danger of losing the faith themselves.[11] Until the early twentieth century, therefore, children tended to be placed in French and Scottish Catholic communities in Québec and eastern Ontario, albeit sometimes small communities but ministered to by a resident or nearby priest. Indeed, until the 1902 amalgamation the various forms of agreement that had to be signed by those receiving the children were written in both English and French.

Thus, after 1883, with the relaxation of the LGB's prohibition on the emigration of Poor Law children, a substantial proportion of the young people sent to Canada by the LCCPS were drawn from the Kirkdale institution. This concentration on Poor Law children was made more possible because the various guardians met the cost of the children's passage as well as their outfit. There were also additional special payments; for example, to the sisters who arranged some of the placements.[12]

However, the 'rescue' of children from Poor Law institutions was not the LCCPS's only concern; it was also anxious to recover those in non-Catholic industrial schools.[13] In addition, a close watch was kept on the activities of the various Protestant child emigration agencies and in particular on the children embarking at Liverpool. As the 1895 annual report explained: 'The names and appearances of the children sent out by the Protestant Agencies testify that the necessity for this Society is as urgent as ever.' Clearly the LCCPS was still convinced that Catholic children were being included in Protestant groups and then placed in Canada without regard to their Catholic faith.

As with most of the other societies, there were questions about the adequacy of visiting, although those brought out by the LCCPS from the Poor Law were (if they could be found) inspected annually by the Canadian authorities. However, in 1900 George Bogue Smart (the Canadian inspector of British immigrant children) reported that visits were being made once a year by the superintendent of the Liverpool Home or by the matron of the Home being used in Montreal (Agnes Brennan), but more often if a complaint were received.[14] How these were dealt with varied, however. For example, in 1898, Pereira, the assistant secretary in the Department of the Interior, wrote to Brennan concerning Louis Bohinne who, he understood, had been 'constantly ill-used' and was 'fearful of receiving greater ill-treatment'. Brennan was asked to investigate, but after no reply was received for four months, a reminder was sent.[15] Brennan, it was recorded, 'called and said she did not wish to press the case'.[16] The next year she received a similar letter about Ian McDermott who was found wandering and who, during his four-and-a-half years in Canada, had lived with at least 10 different families. The *Ottawa Journal*[17] reported that he had been placed in a police cell to keep him from the cold. In another case a government inspector reported that he had seen a boy aged six from the West Derby union (Liverpool) whose body and hands were covered in sores and with matter running from his nose continually. He recommended that he be returned to Liverpool. Although taken to the Home in Montreal there is no record of what eventually befell the child.[18]

Sometimes neighbours sounded the alarm. John Pearl wrote to Brennan in 1902:

> The little boy by the name of John O'Grady who you gave to a man in Caledonia ... is really abused. He has run away three times and come to my place. One of his big toes was very badly frozen ... so I done all in my power to cure the toe. Now it is almost well, the child is not clad for this cold weather.... Please come as soon as convenient.

Brennan replied that she could not go but arranged for the immigration agent's assistant in Montreal to visit instead. He did so, but not until 12 days later;[19] there is no record of subsequent events. Perhaps because of these and other similar cases the LCCPS decided that they would no longer send children to be placed out from Brennan's fee-paying Home in Montreal. However, by then their emigration activities had already been substantially curtailed. In 1900, for example, only 43 children were sent to Canada by comparison with 150 a year between 1895 and 1898. There is no record of any child being emigrated in 1901 or in the first part of 1902 before the Society was merged with the newly formed Catholic Emigration Association (CEA). Thereafter, children were again sent to Canada by the LCCPS but sailed under the banner of the CEA and were accommodated on their arrival in its reception Home.

Thus, the Liverpool Catholic agency was drawn into child emigration by a mixture of considerations, but foremost among them was a concern to extricate Catholic children from Protestant institutions, particularly those run by the local Poor Law guardians. This increased the demand on limited Catholic provisions, a demand that could be eased by sending some children to Canada. Nevertheless, despite the attraction of Catholic communities in French Canada, emigration was not embraced as enthusiastically as it was, for example, by Barnardo. This was partly because of anxieties about the 'moral vulnerability' of girls and disquieting reports about the treatment of some of the boys. This (as with a number of the other organisations) emphasised the unreliability of leaving the placement and any subsequent supervision of the children to Canadian-based agents over whom the Liverpool-based Society exercised little or no control.

III Westminster and the French Connection

The first exploration of the possibilities of emigration by the Westminster diocese seems to have occurred in 1880 when one of Cardinal Manning's priests visited Canada and arranged with the Archbishop of Toronto 'to receive and dispose of Catholic children who might be sent out'. The hope was that others would follow suit as, in fact, the Archbishop of Montreal did.[20] It is unclear, however, when the first party of children arrived, but probably in 1881 with Father Thomas Seddon who was Cardinal Manning's secretary and who became the secretary of the emigration committee that was set up to select and send children across the Atlantic. However, the children assembled by the Westminster society (called the Canadian Catholic Emigration Society) were drawn from several sources: from the Poor Law, from independent Catholic institutions as well as from rescue and protection societies in a number of other dioceses. Even within Westminster there was the separate Society of the Crusade of Rescue and Homes for Destitute Catholic Children[21] as well as the Westminster Diocese Fund for the Poor (later the Westminster Diocese Education Fund) that, among its other activities, supported a number of Homes run by religious orders. It is not easy therefore to determine the contribution that each made to Westminster's emigration parties. Clearly, however, the emigration of children by the Westminster diocese was already under way by 1883, for Seddon wrote to John Lowe, the Deputy Minister in the Canadian Department of Agriculture, at the end of that year to say that during his visit several cases of hardship among the children had come to his notice and that this had 'strengthened [his] resolution … to abandon the work unless some more efficient means of carrying it on could be found'.[22]

The emigration may have begun, but this correspondence suggests that there were doubts (at least on Seddon's part) about the wisdom of continuing unless there were better safeguards for the children. To these uncertainties were added financial and other problems. In 1887 Seddon wrote to the Canadian High

Commissioner's Office in London to say that the withdrawal of the concessionary railway fares, the increase in the cost of the sea passage and the ending of the Dominion's capitation grant for Poor Law children, together with 'the thousand worries and the thankless trouble' involved, had cooled his enthusiasm for emigration.[23] At the same time he wrote to various guardians to tell them that Westminster had decided not to send girls to Canada 'except in very rare instances, and then only by pre-arrangement, by reason of the grave dangers to which they are exposed'.[24] How long this policy lasted is unclear, but girls were sent in later years, although boys predominated throughout.

One of the features of Seddon's work was his meticulous recording – of who was sent, to whom and where – and his scrupulous accounting. These printed statements provide valuable information. For example, 57 per cent of a party of 75 emigrated in 1890 were Poor Law children; 80 per cent were boys; most of the children were 13 or 14 years old. Only six found themselves in English-speaking families. About half were placed in or around Montreal and only five were located outside the province of Québec, all of them in or near Ottawa. Seven were placed in obviously remote areas. Two went to live with relatives in the US. It was also noted that all the non-Poor Law children were paid for by 'friends or benefactors'.[25] A similar analysis of a party leaving in 1893 reveals much the same picture although on this occasion all but one of the group were placed in Québec and every child went to an identifiably French-speaking household. A fifth of the party was placed in Montreal itself or very close by. Only three went to live in remote areas.[26]

The impression that these details convey is that placement with French Canadian families was common. The impact that this was likely to have had on English children was captured by the *Montreal Witness* in an article published in 1891. Under the heading 'English Immigrant Boys' the newspaper pointed out that:

> They have never heard a syllable of the French language…. The environment is strange and circumstances distressing. The master speaks no English. The boy speaks no French. The fellowship of a common tongue is lost. The boy is torn from companions, often from brothers and sisters who understood and loved him. The *habitant* takes the boy or girl for what he can make out of him or her. Sometimes they are passably kind. Often they are cruel. Frequently, the children run away.[27]

The following day Antoine Robert, the Society's agent in Canada and financial secretary to the Archbishop of Montreal, wrote to rebut these accusations. He rejected the idea that there was suffering. He insisted that every care was exercised and that, in any case, the children soon picked up the language. Brothers and sisters were not separated (although from the lists of addresses this was only sometimes the case). A priest, he said, came from England every six months to visit the children and gave them writing material and stamped envelopes so that they could tell him how they were getting on.[28] Much of this may have been true but it did not properly address the issue of children being placed in strange circumstances surrounded by an unknown language. However, not all the children were placed with French Canadians in Québec. There were exceptions. For example, 80 per cent of a party leaving in 1888 were placed in Ontario, mostly in and around Ottawa with people bearing obviously British (often Scottish) names.[29] However, wherever they went each party was, it seems, placed in broad clusters. The effect may have been that some children were able to keep in contact with others nearby and that the task of visiting was made somewhat easier. However, there were later disruptions that could have altered the picture.

As we have noted, it is difficult to determine how many children the Westminster committee sent to Canada prior to the amalgamation of its emigration activities with other dioceses in 1903. However, there are fairly firm figures from 1893 onwards. In those 10 years about 600 left for the Dominion, although some came from other dioceses.[30] Given that the Westminster Society covered a large metropolitan area this seems a rather modest total. It may have reflected the rather cautious approach adopted by Seddon (the organising secretary), or it may have been because, by the end of the century, the diocese ran or oversaw many more orphanages, industrial schools and reformatories, making it less necessary for children to be sent to Canada. Furthermore, the Crusade of Rescue, which provided some of the children for the emigration parties, tended to discharge a fairly high proportion of those in its care to their relatives (38 per cent in 1904 rising to 64 per cent in 1912) and supported some others at home. They also began to develop boarding out and by 1909, for example, 19 per cent of their charges were placed in this way, although the proportion fell somewhat thereafter.[31]

There are therefore several features of the activities of the Westminster Canadian Catholic Emigration Society that should be emphasised. Relatively small proportions of the children for whom the diocese was (or became) responsible went to Canada. Substantial proportions of those who did, however, had been in the care of the Poor Law. The majority were boys of around the age of 13. Most of the children were placed in Québec, often with French-speaking families because of the wish to see them settled within a community with a resident priest *as well as* with a Catholic family.

IV Southwark and Different Policies for Girls and Boys

It is unclear exactly when the Southwark Catholic Emigration Society (SCES) was formed, partly because, initially, it sent children from its diocese to Canada under arrangements with the neighbouring Westminster scheme. However, the first report of the arrival of Southwark children in Canada is to be found in 1893 when 45 boys landed at Québec. The following year there were 17 more. Over the next three years a further 84 boys were sent, taken either by the Rev. Edward St John or by the Rev. Lord Archibald Douglas, the joint secretaries overseeing the emigration.[32] A reception Home (New Orpington Lodge) was rented in Ottawa and later purchased. The involvement of Douglas is interesting because, between 1874 and 1887, he had been the priest in charge of the St Vincent's Home for boys in Paddington, London.[33] While there he had arranged for some of them to be emigrated and in 1882 had accompanied a party of 40 to Manitoba.

One noteworthy feature of the Southwark scheme was that, until 1897, only boys under the age of 16 were emigrated. As in Westminster there was a concern that the moral welfare of girls could be endangered were they to be sent to Canada. St John explained this to the LGB as follows: 'the wholesale emigration of small girls into farmhouses or to become little white slaves at nine and ten in village shops, [is] not desirable, morally or as a matter of common humanity'. Furthermore, he continued:

> ... arrangements which are good for boys do not apply to girls, thus – a farming district is good for boys ... while the placing of girls in farmhouses has led ... to the most grievous results: and this may be easily understood. Not even a child of nine ought to be left, in an isolated farm, at the mercy of and subject to the chance of rough shanty men and farm labourers.[34]

These views had been conveyed to the LGB in 1897 because the Society now felt that it was safe to emigrate girls as long as they were aged 14 or more and were placed in towns in Québec. As things stood, however, it would be prevented from doing so with respect to those supported by boards of guardians because, as we have seen, the central Board had recently adopted regulations that prohibited any girls of 14 or over being sent abroad. Each saw their policies as protecting vulnerable girls, but interpreted the age of greatest vulnerability differently. Furthermore, the SCES believed that they should only emigrate girls over school age (14, at the time) who had been trained to be capable of earning their own living, and this meant training in domestic service at the diocese's Home in Sussex.

The reception of the girls in Canada was to be catered for through an arrangement with a Canadian institution: the Women's Protective Immigration Society Home in Montreal. Miss Procter from the Southwark diocese had visited and lived there for three weeks in order to satisfy herself that it was an appropriate place for the girls to be received and to return to if necessary. Furthermore, the local priest was to be consulted before any girl was placed out and all of them were to have individual visitors reporting to the Society's agent in Canada. This would now be Miss Procter who was also to join the committee of the Home. The visitors were to be drawn from 'a confraternity [sic] of ladies in Montreal numbering over 300'.[35] In the light of these assurances the LGB gave its approval to the scheme despite its new regulations, but on condition that, at the end of a year, a report on the venture would be submitted, on the basis of which it would decide whether or not approval would be renewed. The required report on the scheme must have been satisfactory because older Poor Law girls were allowed to be emigrated beyond the trial year. In the meantime boys continued to be sent to Canada and visited from time to time by staff from the New Orpington Lodge.

The addition of girls to the Society's emigration parties may have accounted for the sharp rise in the 1898 figure (120). Thereafter, however, it becomes difficult to determine just how many boys and girls from Southwark went to Canada each year because in 1899 it amalgamated its emigration activities with those of the Westminster diocese, being content also to share its neighbour's name (the Canadian Catholic Emigration Society). As well as the change of policy towards girls, the end of the century witnessed a new development with respect to the boys. Like several other emigration agencies, the SCES saw new possibilities in Manitoba as land began to be allocated and occupied. A site was acquired at Makinac in 1895 in order to establish a farm school where boys of between 16 and 20 could be trained, much along the lines of Barnardo's venture at Russell. It was to be called the New Southwark Farm and, as well as admitting the older boys from Britain, the intention was that those who had been placed for some time in Québec or Ontario would be given the opportunity to be introduced to farming in the north west and then perhaps obtain a holding of their own through the land grant system. Lord Archibald Douglas who, as we have seen, had already taken boys to Manitoba in the 1880s, spent six months conducting the negotiations and overseeing the development, the first party arriving in 1897. The plan was that henceforth all boys of 16 or more who were emigrated by the Society should go to the New Southwark Farm and this appears to have been the case, although it is unclear how long the scheme lasted.

There are several aspects of the history of Southwark's child emigration venture that should be emphasised. As in Liverpool and in Westminster it appears to have been approached with a good deal of caution. In particular, there was concern about the vulnerability of girls and at first none were sent. Only from 1897 were some of those aged 14 or more included. Linked to this was a clear assumption that different arrangements should be made for boys and girls. Boys were destined for the farms and the older ones for the north west. In any case, they were to be steered away from towns and cities. Girls, on the other hand, were considered to be safer in the towns employed in domestic service. Furthermore, in the urban areas there was a pool of potential female visitors on which to draw.

V Salford Records the Details but Soon Withdraws

As well as the initiatives in Liverpool and London there was also Catholic emigration activity in Manchester. This began formally in 1889, although some children from its Protection and Rescue Society had been sent to Canada before with Westminster parties. The Salford scheme was initiated and run by the Rev. Robert Rossall and from the outset he made detailed reports to the executive committee of the parent Society. In the second of these, submitted in 1890, he explained that in the first two years of its operation 144 children had been taken to Canada (80 of whom were from Poor Law unions – 55 per cent). The arrangements for their reception were made by Antoine Robert who, as has been noted, also acted for the Westminster diocese. All the children were placed in Québec 'in batches of from four to ten or twelve in a parish', all of whom Rossall reported having visited.

The advantages of placements being made exclusively in this part of Canada derived, Rossall explained, from the fact that Québec was a Catholic province in which 'the people are ... religious in every sense of the word. They are remarkable as being a peaceful, honest, sober, and industrious race, simple and frugal in their habits of life, sincere and devout'. Furthermore, he continued, 'each parish has generally its three, six, or nine schools' where the education 'is based on religious teaching and the Roman Catholic Catechism'.[36] Rossall's report also provides an illuminating description of the manner in which the children were placed:

> A few months before my departure with an emigrant party ... the agent, will visit a few country parishes and address a meeting of the farmers, previously convened by the Parish Priest. He will explain ... that a number of orphan and deserted children are about to arrive ... for the purpose of being placed with or adopted by French-Canadian farmers, and after telling them something of the history of those about to come will take a list of names of those ... who would like to take a boy or girl. This list is submitted to the Parish Priest for his approval or rejection.... A Parish Priest in Canada is a person of great local importance and influence.[37]

If a child were ill-treated or over-worked, Rossall maintained, it would be sure to come to the priest's notice. There was, however, a danger that the opportunities for the placement of the children would decline because of their conduct. Bed-wetting, he reported, was a particular problem, the more so because it was commonly regarded 'as evidence of bad moral lives on the part of the child's parents', as a result of which 'people are unwilling to become responsible for the physical and religious moral conduct of such children'.[38]

The details in Rossall's reports enable us to gain a picture of some of the children's characteristics. For example, in the first two years the 80 Poor Law children who were included came from nine unions, most from Chorlton (26) and from Manchester (17). Seven others came from three industrial schools and five were listed as 'private'. The rest (36 per cent) came from the Protection and Rescue Society itself. We have information about the age and gender of the 150 in the first, second and fourth emigration parties. Sixty-seven per cent were boys, 21 per cent of the whole group were under the age of 10, 42 per cent were aged 10–12, 27 per cent 13 or 14 and 10 per cent between 15 and 17. Thus, two-thirds were less than 13 years old.[39] There was not much difference between the ages of the boys and the girls. In the first two parties about two-thirds of the children (mostly boys) were placed on farms, the rest in various forms of domestic service, although in nine cases 'adoption' was mentioned, but 'adoption for domestic service' and 'adoption by Sisters for future farm work'. The details of the second party noted the occupations of those with whom the children were placed and although half were listed as 'farmer' most of the others included a wide range of trades such as shopkeeper, tinsmith, carpenter, confectioner, dressmaker and butcher. A sprinkling of professions also made an appearance: doctor, notary and lawyer. These were the children's first placements, of course, and their subsequent movement may have altered the pattern. Although the most common placements were on a farm or in domestic service, those who went to artisans may have had a chance to learn a trade.

In 1893 the Salford Society emigrated its largest number of children (138) but thereafter numbers rapidly declined: to 31 in 1894 and to 24 in 1895.[40] There is no evidence of any further child emigration after 1895, but some were sent to Canada later under the auspices of other societies, making about 600 altogether between 1888 and 1908.[41] It is not entirely clear why the Society did not persevere in its individual child emigration activities, but it may have been linked to Bishop Vaughan's departure to Westminster in 1892, first to become Archbishop and then Cardinal. Another possible explanation may be found in the growing number of Catholic Homes available in the diocese that made it less necessary to resort to emigration.[42] However, there are certain important points to be noted about its brief venture into this field. At least at the outset full and detailed printed reports (as at Westminster) were submitted to the executive committee explaining why and how the children were placed in Canada. Reports on visits were also included. The scheme relied heavily on the collaboration of the local priesthood and on the goodwill of the Archbishop of Montreal. This may have been what enabled the Society to operate without a Canadian reception and distribution Home despite the requirement that there should be one. As with other Catholic societies, the children were placed (at least initially) in clusters based on the various parishes. Details of the children's ages (where they are given) suggest that the Society sent younger children to Canada than other Catholic agencies, and that all the children appear to have been placed in Québec with French-speaking families.

VI The Amalgamation and New Policies

In 1902 the Rev. Emanuel Bans (secretary of the Westminster Diocese Crusade of Rescue) and Arthur Chilton Thomas (barrister, and manager of the Father Berry's Homes in Liverpool) were asked by Cardinal Vaughan (who had succeeded Manning on his death in 1892) to review the work of Catholic child emigration and to make recommendations.[43] They visited Canada during that year and remained for three months, interviewing key figures and visiting many of the children in the homes in which they had been placed. On their return they presented their findings in a report entitled *Catholic Child Emigration to Canada*,[44] one of the recommendations of which was that the activities of the various diocesan societies should be merged in order to achieve a consistently high standard and the pooling of information.[45] The Canadian Catholic Emigration

Society (which, by then, covered both Westminster and Southwark) declined to abandon its independence.[46] In the event, only the Liverpool Catholic Children's Protection Society and Father Berry's Homes joined forces in 1903, sharing the new name of the Catholic Emigrating Association. Bans (who became its president) and Thomas argued that this should be regarded as a prelude to an across-the-board integration. To that end a Canadian agent and manager was appointed (Cecil Arden) and a second visit made to the Dominion in 1904 in order to gather additional evidence for the amalgamation. This was set out in *Further Notes on Catholic Child Emigration*.[47]

The second report seems to have overcome the previous reluctance to form a common body and in November 1904 the Catholic Emigration Association was formed to oversee the emigration activities of all the dioceses. St George's Home in Ottawa (previously Southwark's New Orpington Lodge) was chosen as the Canadian headquarters and as the centre for the reception of the children. The work of the new Association was placed under the control of the rescue societies of the dioceses of Westminster, Southwark, Liverpool and Birmingham. Birmingham's emergence probably reflected the enthusiasm of George Hudson, founder and manager of the Father Hudson's Homes in the city.[48] In fact, he became secretary of the newly formed Association.

However, it was not only the organisation of Catholic child emigration that was changed in the early years of the twentieth century but also some of its policies. First, although Bans and Thomas had argued that the children were, in the main, better treated by the French than by the English, and that it was 'certainly of great advantage for a girl to be placed with the French on account of the extra refinement that she acquires', nonetheless the dominance of placements in French Canada was to be reduced. This was not, as might have been expected, because of the difference of language but because of what was felt to be a strong prejudice in Britain against such placements,[49] perhaps reflecting concerns about the growing influx of non-British immigrants to English-speaking Canada and the threat that this was thought to pose to the continuation of a British majority. However, the Association could not afford to ignore Catholic French Canada. The new approach was to give preference to English-speaking applicants without refusing to place children with those who spoke French. Nonetheless, it was still felt that French families made the child 'one of themselves' more often than English families of a similar standing and were more likely to give them a thorough grounding in the faith.[50] There was, Arden (the Association's Canadian agent) declared, a greater likelihood of children losing their faith in Ontario than in Québec because of their 'contact with so many varying forms of Protestantism'.[51]

The second shift of policy, or its re-affirmation in the case of some of the member societies, was with regard to where the children were placed. Girls were not to be placed on farms where they would learn few domestic skills and where they were exposed to 'danger' because of isolated locations. Nor were the big cities thought to be appropriate. Preferred placements for the girls were in the country towns where those who took them were considered more likely to treat them as members of the family and teach them the skills of domestic service. In the case of boys it was acknowledged that not all were suited to farm work and that others might, in fact, resent it. If placed in country towns they were more likely to be able to learn a trade instead.[52]

A third shift of policy that accompanied the 1902-04 shake-up concerned the ages of the children to be emigrated. Bans and Thomas recommended that children who were placed in what amounted to employment should be at least 12 years old and preferably 13 or older, rather than 10 as had been a common practice. No child under 12 should be sent to Canada, they argued, unless specifically asked for by the agent or unless there were a guarantee that they would be maintained in a Catholic institution until of an age when they could be placed out. Broadly speaking, therefore, the emigration of young children was to be discouraged, even though it was believed that they settled more readily and fully than older children.[53]

We have already mentioned the appointment in 1903 of Arden as the Association's agent in Canada and this reflected a fourth aspect of the changes introduced at that time – namely, the creation of a more formal administration. In 1904, for example, an assistant agent was appointed as well as two visitors in order to ensure that the children were seen more regularly. Indeed, during 1903 Arden reported that 950 visits had been made and that most had found the children satisfactorily placed; it was considered that it was their behaviour that was largely responsible for the problems that did arise. Indeed, only one offence against a child was noted during the agent's first year in office: the rape of a 13-year-old girl for which the offender (a neighbour) was sentenced to four months imprisonment;[54] others came to light later. For instance, Arden brought a case against the employer of Benjamin Hill (aged 14) in 1905, although the magistrate dismissed it 'for lack of sufficient evidence'. Nonetheless, it was agreed that the boy had been 'most cruelly beaten by some person'. In explaining to the Canadian inspector of British children what had happened Arden wrote that the magistrate was:

> ... only a local JP [justice of the peace], and never doubting that he would be obliged to commit the accused for trial we brought no evidence, other than the boy's own story, and the exhibition of the wounds in the court.... It was a case of the man's sworn denial against the boy's sworn testimony. The boy, as is usual ... being proved to be the liar.[55]

Although cases like these appear only intermittently in the archival material there is evidence that many children experienced a great deal of movement from one place to the next. Of the boys emigrated in 1902, for example, 41 per cent had been 'returned' at least once by 1904 and 74 per cent of the girls 'returned'. For those arriving in 1903 the proportions were 48 per cent and 63 per cent respectively, and for the 1904 party 26 per cent and 25 per cent.[56] Such frequent moves reflected in part the policy of the Association that required agreements either to be renewed or annulled each May. This did not apply, however, in the case of young children taken for 'adoption'.

Yet the idealised view of the benefits that accrued to a child from emigration was hardly compatible with the reality. For example, in 1905 Chilton Thomas wrote in his *Wise Imperialism* that in being sent to Canada a child would:

> ... begin to live ... life again, one of a family, loving and loved in turn, with a consciousness, a proud confidence, that he belongs to someone and someone belongs to him: that a mutual affection binds him to others and others to him; that human beings take a deep interest in his welfare....[57]

This was, of course, for public consumption. More privately he and other senior colleagues were expressing certain anxieties about the adequacy of the visiting and therefore about the proper protection of the children. For example, in the same year as his publication Thomas wrote to the Canadian inspector of British children to suggest that Dominion government inspectors should visit all young British immigrants and not only those sent by boards of guardians, at the same time proposing that the societies should be charged a fee to offset the costs involved;[58] but the Department of the Interior stoutly resisted any enlargement of its responsibilities.

Including the interim year of 1903 the Catholic Emigration Association sent 3,646 children to Canada[59]. Before 1903 Waugh calculated that 5,000 Catholic children had gone to the Dominion through the different diocesan societies,[60] making a total of more than 8,500, or around one in ten of all the unaccompanied British children who were dispatched to Canada in the years between 1867 and 1917. Inevitably, these figures are best estimates because of the complexity and overlapping activities of the various societies that eventually formed the Catholic Emigration Association. Moreover, as with the Protestants, some emigration of Catholic children was organised by 'unattached' individuals. One such was J.H. Boyd, the account of whose activities and the reaction to them throw additional light on the issues of control and regulation, and hence on the safeguarding of children's well-being.

VII The Disapproved

John Boyd was a prominent figure in the revitalisation of the campaign for state-assisted emigration at the start of the 1880s. However, he was, it was claimed, 'a person of uncertain antecedents and possibly interested motives'.[61] In 1884 he became involved in the emigration of Catholic children through what he called his Catholic Colonisation Fund. This venture may have been a consequence of his having been ousted from his post as secretary of the Central Emigration Society (which, by amalgamation, had become the National Association for Promoting State-Directed Emigration and Colonisation). His dismissal was partly due to his uncompromising commitment to his own particular land grant scheme[62] but also, as Malchow has pointed out, because of the rumours of self-gain that began to circulate in the press.[63]

Boyd claimed that his Catholic Colonisation Fund had the approval of Cardinal Manning and of the Archbishop of Glasgow and that it enjoyed the patronage of the Archbishops of Halifax, Québec and Toronto, as well as the Department of Agriculture in Ottawa. The children were to be taken first to a Home at Rimouski in Québec, a small town located on the southern bank of the St Lawrence River. The Homes, one for boys and one for girls, were run by the Sisters of Charity. Conveniently, the Allan line steamers made a mail stop at Rimouski before they reached Québec. In order to promote his scheme Boyd circulated all boards of guardians with the details.[64] Several responded – for example, Lanchester (Durham), Auckland (also Durham) and Toxteth Park (Liverpool). The Lanchester union asked the Local Government Board (LGB) for permission to send five children to Canada with Boyd in 1884.[65] However, it was noted that the £4 10s. listed for 'other expenses' was unsatisfactory. As a result a fuller explanation was sought, but all that the clerk was able to report was that 'Mr Boyd says that it is impossible to say how it will be spent until after the arrival of the child in Canada'.[66] Notwithstanding this rather vague explanation permission was eventually granted.

Not long after this, however, the LGB received similar requests for approval to be given for the emigration with Boyd of Poor Law children from the Auckland and Toxteth Park unions. Each developed differently. The Auckland application was refused because the quota of 300 (that had been imposed when the moratorium on the emigration of Poor Law children had been lifted) had been reached and because the question of allowable costs was in 'an unsatisfactory state'.[67] However, it was discovered that six children *had* been sent to Canada with Boyd because of a 'misunderstanding'.[68] The district auditor duly imposed a surcharge[69] (that was later remitted) but the children remained in Canada.

The Toxteth Park case, however, took a different course. On receiving the application from the guardians to send 10 children to Canada with Boyd[70] the LGB asked whether September was not too late in the year for children to be going.[71] The query was referred to the Canadian High Commissioner in London. All this gave time for the Toxteth case to be considered alongside those of Lanchester and Auckland, the matter being referred to Sir Charles Dilke, the President, with the suggestion that he should consult Cardinal Manning.[72] Having done so Dilke noted that the Cardinal had said that he thought that Boyd had 'a craze for emigration and is not quite generally sound of mind' and that, in any case 'the LGB should summon him … to give an account of the way in which the children are to be cared for'. Finally, he had asked what authority Boyd had for the use of several Archbishops' names in his circular.[73] As a result Dilke proposed that, henceforth, northern guardians intending to use Boyd's scheme should check the plan with the secretary of the Liverpool Catholic Children's Protection Society. Seddon (the Secretary of the Westminster scheme) made a similar suggestion in writing to the LGB on behalf of Cardinal Manning. The Cardinal, he explained, wished to say 'that he cannot and does not in any way sanction or approve of Mr Boyd's scheme ... [and] that the L.G.Board should warn the Guardians to require more than Mr Boyd's assurance ... [furthermore] that as regards the Metropolitan area he cannot allow Mr Boyd to interfere with the long established work of this [his] committee'.[74]

The Board sent a cautionary letter reflecting these misgivings to all unions in October 1884.[75] Among other things it emphasised that whereas at first Cardinal Manning had agreed to be a patron of Boyd's scheme he had now changed his mind. Furthermore, the circular drew attention to the fact that the placement of children in Canadian homes was entrusted to an agent (yet again, Antoine Robert) who lived in Montreal 320 miles away from Rimouski. Without actually prohibiting guardians from using Boyd's scheme the central Board asked them to consider these facts as well as the nature of the indenture that the children were asked to sign. This bound them to Boyd until they were 17 and entitled him to receive 'any portion of the pocket money, salary or wages' that they were paid.

Only two days after dispatching its circular the LGB received a letter of protest about Boyd's activities from the Bishop of Liverpool.[76] This emphasised that the Liverpool Catholic Children's Protection Society had no confidence in Boyd and that some children who had been sent with him 'were put on board with no attendant or protector – with no outfit whatever – without a blanket or towel – that on arriving in Rimouski there was no one to receive the children'. The letter ended by requesting the LGB to withhold its permission for the proposed emigration of Catholic children from Toxteth with Boyd. The burden of all this was conveyed to Boyd, whereupon he immediately bombarded the LGB with 'evidence' of the propriety of his scheme.[77] In the meantime, however, enquiries were being made in Canada about the enforceability of Boyd's indenture, the upshot of which was that it had no legal standing. But without waiting for this reply the LGB decided that they would no longer sanction the emigration of Poor Law children with Boyd because of the unspecified nature of the expenditures and the requirement that children should give him all or part of their wages.[78]

Several important conclusions may be drawn from the Boyd episode. Some opposition from the Catholic Church may have reflected a desire to retain control of child emigration within the confines of the respective dioceses. Nevertheless, Boyd did at first win the support of Cardinal Manning as well as a number of bishops in Britain, but as doubts about his activities grew these endorsements were progressively withdrawn. Initially, perhaps, the full implications of his scheme had not been appreciated, or it had been thought that he could be brought within the scope of a diocesan organisation. In Canada Boyd mobilised the support of various Catholic dignitaries, doubtless because of Manning's original approval but also because of a desire on their part to add to the Catholic population and to the population in general.

Although Boyd's indenture attracted the critical attention of the LGB it is probably true that had other indentures or agreements drawn up by other individuals and societies been subjected to the same scrutiny they too would have been shown to be equally unacceptable and unenforceable. Yet it was the question of the children's wages being siphoned off to Boyd that raised sufficient concern that eventually curbed his activities. It is also important to appreciate the connections in the wider environment within which some of the child emigrationists were active. Cardinal Manning, for example, although involved with the emigration of Catholics, was also a member of the National Association for Promoting State-Assisted Emigration and would have been aware of the growing suspicions about Boyd within that organisation.

Once again this particular episode in the history of child emigration emphasises that it was matters other than the immediate well-being of the children that were likely to trigger disquiet. Even then, however, action was slow to be taken and, in any case, one has to ask what happened to the children when schemes such as Boyd's collapsed? There should have been annual visits from the Canadian government's inspectors for the Poor Law children; but the inadequacy of Boyd's records may have made this difficult. Were local priests involved? Did Antoine Robert continue to feel responsible? Or was no subsequent provision made for the children's support and protection?

VIII The Main Features

What is evident from these various accounts is that the organisation of Catholic child emigration was closely associated with the prevailing structure and concerns of the Catholic Church. Cardinal Manning, as its head (and later Cardinal Vaughan), not only took a special interest in the spiritual and material welfare of children but also exercised a considerable influence over the associated policies and practices. Nevertheless, there was a strong diocesan system in which each Bishop brought his particular interests to bear. The hierarchy in Canada played a somewhat similar role, although generally welcoming any scheme that brought in more Catholic children. Moreover, the priests in the areas where such children were placed were usually expected to vet the placements and ensure the subsequent well-being of the children. How well they discharged these duties doubtless varied from priest to priest.

As we have seen, the Church's concern with the fate of Catholic children was closely connected with its concern about the 'leakage from the faith'. While lapsed adults were usually regarded as something of a lost cause, children's faith was seen as capable of being preserved and strengthened. One way of achieving this was by their placement in strong Catholic communities, of which residential Homes were one type. Another means to this end was emigration to predominantly Catholic locations: Québec fitted the bill admirably despite being French-speaking.

Indeed, it was the Church's sense of its vulnerability in a largely Protestant British society that helped to encourage Catholic child emigration. The fear that Catholic children were being included in emigration parties assembled by the likes of Rye or Barnardo was one reason for what might be regarded as its initial defensive entry into the field. Likewise, the need, as it was seen, to extricate Catholic children from a predominantly Protestant Poor Law system also strengthened the case for emigration. Nevertheless, there were apprehensions about certain of its aspects. For example, there was persistent concern about the moral dangers that beset girls, and although this anxiety is to be found in the deliberations of the non-Catholic societies it appears to have been more prominent among the Catholics. In particular, there was an unwillingness to see girls placed on farms away from centres of greater settlement and thus beyond the immediate surveillance of a parish priest. There were therefore both differences and similarities with respect to the organisation and practices of the Catholic societies compared with those of their Protestant counterparts. Boyd's case illustrates some of these, but, as will become apparent in the next chapter, interesting conclusions may also be drawn from the individualistic excursions into child emigration among those with Protestant affiliations.

SEVEN

The 'Unorganised' Emigrationists

I The Examples

Sooner or later most of the child emigration ventures became organisations in the sense that their conduct was subject to a measure of control by a management committee, their finances were scrutinised and certain formal posts created. That said, however, their founders frequently continued to exercise considerable influence and tended only reluctantly to relinquish the reins of power. Nevertheless, there was a clear evolution from individual initiative to incorporated agency and thus to the continuation of the organisation after the retirement or death of the originator. However, there were some schemes that did not follow this course and which, until they disintegrated or were absorbed by established organisations, remained essentially 'unorganised'; that is to say, they operated without any formal structure and hence without a superordinate authority to which, in the last resort, they were answerable. Maria Rye and Annie Macpherson fall into this category, as does the Catholic John Boyd; there were also others who worked independently of an administrative framework. Although having this in common their histories vary; yet each illustrates the pitfalls and dangers to which such individualistic enterprises exposed the children who were emigrated. Three lesser-known examples are considered here: Emma Stirling, W.J. Pady and, paradoxically, given its name, the Bristol Emigration Society (BES).

II Emma Stirling Confronts the Law

Emma Stirling (1828-1907) was a Scottish spinster whose wealth enabled her to finance various schemes for child protection. In 1877 she established a day nursery in Edinburgh for the care of the children of working mothers. This was followed soon afterwards by a shelter for homeless children and then by a number of Homes. At first these establishments were simply called 'Miss Stirling's Homes', but following the appointment of a committee in 1884 the enterprise became known as the Edinburgh and Leith Children's Aid and Refuge Society,[1] a body that, having merged with a similar Glasgow Society in 1885, is generally regarded as a forerunner of the Scottish Society for the Prevention of Cruelty to Children. However, in 1887 Stirling resigned from the organisation and thereafter pursued her schemes independently.

In 1882 she visited Canada to explore the possibilities of child emigration. The account that she wrote, however, was extremely critical of what she had seen. The *Glasgow Herald*[2] built on her report, arguing that in too many instances the children were 'to all intents and purposes in the position of white slaves' and that 'unless those who receive them … make complaint and return them, they are left to themselves, are overlooked or forgotten'. Child emigration, the *Glasgow Herald* concluded, had to be put on a proper footing and made subject to official supervision. Quarrier interpreted this as an attack on his activities but made no public response. Rye did, however – she wrote angrily to the paper to defend the work of child emigration that she and her 'imitators', as she called them, were undertaking.[3]

In the light of her visit to Canada Stirling decided not to use existing agencies for the emigration of certain children in her Homes. However, she did not abandon the idea of emigration as 'a favourable outlet', for the older boys in particular. She made another journey to Canada in 1883 and had encouraging discussions with the Secretary for Agriculture in Nova Scotia. Liberal grants were offered and she resolved to acquire a farm in the province in order 'to teach lads farming and to be independent'.[4] The following year she rented a farm and took out two parties of children. Although the original reason for her scheme had been to provide for older boys these parties comprised much younger boys and girls. As she wrote in one of her pamphlets her first group included many 'under 8 years old, four below 4 years and a baby of 2'.[5] Furthermore, the plan that the farm (Stirling bought another in 1887 to replace the first) should be for agricultural training was soon abandoned and the children were quickly placed out.[6]

Despite having resigned from the Edinburgh and Leith Children's Aid and Refuge organisation Stirling soon found herself embroiled in legal proceedings that turned on their respective responsibilities for decisions about what had or should happen to the children. In 1887 John Markey applied to the Court of Sessions for the recovery of his son (also called John) who had been admitted to one of Stirling's Homes from the Children's Aid and Refuge and then taken to Nova Scotia.[7] The Court ordered that the parents should be visited and a report submitted. The police found them living in one room without furniture except for a straw-covered bed. Both parents were said to have been drunk. Despite this adverse report the Court ordered young John Markey to be returned to Scotland and for the parents to be given the opportunity to see him, but not to resume his custody. He was duly brought back and boarded out in Dumfries. The parents said that it was impossible for them to visit him there and asked that he be placed in Edinburgh. Stirling, now in Scotland, refused, whereupon the parents submitted another petition that prompted the Court to require a second home visit. However, the police found everything as it had been before. The Court denied the petition and the child remained where he was in the care of the Children's Aid and Refuge. Its directors breathed a sigh of relief. 'For the first time', they wrote, 'the Courts of Law have justified an Institution like this in retaining the custody of a neglected child, as against the parents whose incapacity to care for the child's moral or physical welfare has been duly ascertained.'[8] Although relieved at the outcome of the hearing the directors were concerned about their future accountability for what Stirling might or might not have done. They wanted a clear understanding about the return of children and pressed her to meet the costs that they had incurred in defending the petition, the Court having held them and not Stirling responsible for John's emigration. She agreed to pay and signed an undertaking to return children if ordered to do so by a Court of Law. Nevertheless, relations between Stirling and the Children's Aid and Refuge had become strained and the directors resolved that no children should be emigrated unless they were complete orphans; unless their parents had signed a written agreement; or unless the children were old enough to have made the choice for themselves.[9] In the meantime, however, another much more serious petition for the return of children had been lodged with the Court of Sessions.

Arthur Delaney's wife died, leaving him with three young children. At the end of 1882, through the intercession of a bible-woman, loosely connected with the Children's Aid and Refuge, the children, James (4), Annie (2) and Robina (a few months), had been admitted to one of Stirling's Homes, but prior to Stirling's resignation from the organisation. Subsequently, Delaney claimed that he had sought the children's return on numerous occasions but had been refused. In 1887 he filed a petition with the help of a Catholic priest. This suggests that, as elsewhere, the Catholic Church was anxious to see Catholic children extricated from what it regarded as proselytising Protestant environments.

However, Stirling had taken the children to Nova Scotia in 1886.[10] The directors, who were again held responsible, claimed (relying on Stirling's information) that the father had deserted his children and that it followed that they ought not to be returned. The father countered that he had not deserted his children, that he had visited them often when they were in the Home, as had his mother and sister. He admitted that he had not been up to date with his contributions but argued that he had paid what he could, having been faced with periods of unemployment and part-time work. Furthermore, he had remarried and now had a home to offer his children. The Court found in his favour and ordered the children to be restored to him. The directors duly asked Stirling (in Canada) to do so, but she refused. Thereafter the story becomes confused; Stirling subsequently maintained that the children had been returned to Scotland. However, Delaney was denied information concerning their whereabouts – they were not in the Homes. It was later claimed that they had been taken back to Nova Scotia because their father was not continuing to press his case in the Court. The father argued that he was now without the resources to do so. Nevertheless, he was successful in being registered on the Poors Roll that, in Scotland, was an early form of legal aid. This enabled him to return to the Court to demand that its order be obeyed. The directors were duly instructed to show what steps they had taken, or were intending to take, to see that this was done.

Accordingly they renewed their demand that Stirling comply with the Court order unless she were able to provide them with compelling evidence why she should not.[11] She wrote saying that the children 'were a considerable time ago located in excellent homes in Canada, and therefore, having been away from my Home, and beyond my control entirely, I can hold out no prospect of restoring them to the old country'.[12] She reiterated that she would not comply with the Scottish Court's order. The Children's Aid and Refuge now faced a dilemma. The Court demanded to know why they were not acting in accordance with its instruction and then ordered them to take legal action against Stirling. The directors thereon applied to the Supreme Court of Nova Scotia for a writ of *habeas corpus*. Although this was issued Stirling still did not produce the children and consequently was called to appear before that Court. Her statement there was the first clear indication that she had no idea where the Delaney children were and that all the prevarication that had gone before was no more than an attempt to disguise this fact which, in the light of her earlier charges against fellow emigrationists, was deeply embarrassing and reflected unfavourably on her activities. The judge said that he could not believe that Stirling had allowed a boy of 12 'to run away from the person with whom he was placed without making inquiries about him, or endeavouring to trace him in any way, particularly when such a thing happened within a few miles of her residence'.[13]

Stirling was found to be in contempt of Court because, having been served with the writ, she was considered not to have done enough to locate and recover the children.[14] However, she did not give up and appealed against the judgment. Her appeal was upheld on a majority decision on the grounds that she *had* done what could reasonably have been expected to comply with the writ.[15] But this did not satisfy the Edinburgh Court of Sessions nor, of course, the father. The directors of the Children's Aid and Refuge were now instructed to make further efforts to recover the children by engaging a private detective to trace them or, it was suggested, assist Delaney to go to Canada in order to search for the children himself. They declined to do this, but they did commission a Halifax detective to mount a search. He reported to the Court[16] that despite considerable effort it had been impossible to find the children. All had been moved, or had run away from, their placements. For example, Robina (then aged 8 or 9) had been 'taken away by a man who came for her in the company of her brother'. Annie, the detective found, had moved to Grand Metis, a French settlement in Québec, where she had lived with a married couple with no family, but a man had come for her representing himself as her uncle. She had been unwilling to go with him but the couple with whom she was living were threatened and felt unable to resist.

The only further document in the case is a transcript of Stirling's 'witness statement' taken before the British Consul in Pau, France, in March 1893. She appears to have lived there since February 1892 and presumably had abandoned her activities in Canada although why a statement was being required is unclear. The Delaney children were not recovered and the Court's order was therefore not enforced even though, by then, Delaney had been fighting for their return for more than six years.

What conclusions are to be drawn from these aspects of Emma Stirling's excursion into child emigration? First, like so many other philanthropists at the time, she launched and undertook her activities completely unregulated by any official body. That freedom was made possible by her wealth. Second, she regarded emigration as a necessary outlet for her Edinburgh Homes as more children came to be admitted. Canada represented a 'safe' destination for children who might otherwise fall back into the hands of those who had maltreated them or into undesirable associations. However, once started, emigration gradually became more of an end in itself. A third conclusion to be drawn from this account is that as the Canadian venture grew so did the practical problems of providing adequate supervision of the children's placements. At first, Stirling visited the children herself, but with her declining health and with mounting numbers of children thus placed, this became impossible. It also became impossible to keep track of all the movements that the children experienced, the more so as these multiplied with the passage of time. What must have seemed a simple and straightforward activity at the beginning became a complicated and demanding undertaking that eventually proved to be beyond her resources.

One other conclusion concerns the pressures placed on the Edinburgh and Leith Society once Stirling had resigned. Children for whom they had assumed responsibility had been placed in her Homes and hence in her custody. But the directors were still held to be responsible for what happened to the children. Their corporate accountability had to be acknowledged and to that end a constitution was adopted. Furthermore, because the respective responsibilities of the Society and Stirling were confused even the most persistent parents faced grave difficulty in recovering their children. Finally, in all of this, and most importantly, the protection and well-being of a child taken to Canada by a freelancing individual such as Stirling could be at particular risk.

III The Pady Scandal

The shadowy figure of W.J. Pady emerged onto the child emigration scene in the last decade of the nineteenth century. Pady, sometimes wrongly referred to as a Baptist minister, first took children to Canada in 1890, later claiming that he had done so because he understood that Barnardo was no longer including those from the Poor Law in his parties.[17] Over the next four years he took about 200 children to the Dominion. He worked by distributing circulars informing those who wished to send children to Canada that he was organising parties to sail on particular dates. He then collected those who were nominated; but it is unclear where or how they awaited their departure. Before he arrived in the Dominion Pady notified local papers and invited farmers or others who wanted children to meet the group at a specified place and to make their choice. Some boys were sent to Winnipeg where one of his settler sons placed them with neighbouring farmers.[18] In both cases those who took them were only asked to sign a rudimentary form. There was no reception or distribution Home (although, as we shall see, Pady falsely claimed to have one in Manitoba), nor was there any subsequent supervision.

Yet the full extent of these serious shortcomings and the consequent dangers to which the children were exposed only gradually came to light, and even then official steps to curb Pady's activities were unco-ordinated and painfully slow. In the first place this confusion and delay sprang from the failure of both the British and Canadian governments to have established a sufficiently robust system for regulating the emigration entrepreneurs. Second, it illustrated the fact that there was in any case no adequate system on either side of the Atlantic for collecting the information that would have enabled this to have been done. Third, just when Pady was busy bringing children into Canada responsibility for immigration was transferred from the Department of Agriculture to the Department of the Interior (in 1892), a department with no previous experience of dealing with emigrationists. Finally, and perhaps as important as anything else, Pady evinced all the outward signs of a devout and responsible philanthropist. He appeared, it was reported, 'to be very religious ... and sanctimonious, going about carrying a bible and seeming full of religious zeal ...'.[19] He wrote on notepaper headed 'The Canadian Emigration Bureau' with an address in London and called himself its manager; but he employed no staff, had no committee and no facilities for the care of children.

The first evidence of Pady's intended activities emerged early in 1890 following a request to the Local Government Board (LGB) from the Chichester board of guardians that three of their children be permitted to accompany him to Canada. The LGB sought the advice of the High Commissioner in London who in turn referred the matter to the Minister of Agriculture in Ottawa, explaining that Pady did not seem to have a distribution Home and querying whether, therefore, he should be allowed to bring the children.[20] The Minister replied that since there appeared to be an arrangement with the immigration agent (Smith) at Hamilton to receive and place the children on Pady's behalf, permission could be granted.[21] Having been informed of this the LGB gave their somewhat reluctant approval, but asked for more details about Pady's arrangements.[22] Lowe, the Deputy Minister at the Department of Agriculture in Ottawa, turned to the Hamilton agent to provide this. He replied that

> ... the children ... are placed with the farmers on arrival. Mr Pady has no Home in Canada. After the children are placed he returns to London, but I have instructions to see after them and to incur any necessary expenditure for their protection and assistance....[23]

This appears to have been a private arrangement between Pady and Smith, and the instructions referred to were obviously Pady's. The fact that one of the Dominion's officers was prepared to assume responsibility for the young immigrants appears to have reassured officialdom, but so did the fact that, at least at first, just the three Chichester children seemed to be involved; but that was only the start. Having obtained 'clearance' for them Pady then increased his party to 16, the other boards of guardians involved also having gained the approval of the LGB.

Thus, it soon became apparent that Pady was planning a more extensive and regular scheme of juvenile emigration, not least because he enquired about the possibility of being granted land in Manitoba to establish a Home for boys.[24] However, he was told that under the Dominion Lands Act it was not possible for a grant to be made for such a purpose.[25] Despite this setback he continued to take children to Canada without any attempt on the part of either the British or Dominion administrations to stop him. For example, in 1893 he landed with 54 boys and 8 girls.[26] Indeed, it was not until that year that further evidence of official disquiet began to surface. Thomas Bennett (probably an employee of the Dominion Lands Agency) submitted a report to the Commissioner of Dominion Lands in Winnipeg. He had been asked to provide a list of the names and ages of the boys brought to the province by 'the Rev. Mr Pady'. However, he did more, maintaining that the children in question were 'too small, and much too young to be sent to obtain a living in so rigorous a climate' and that many were 'fit subjects for a nursery or children's home'.[27] Furthermore, it was explained that Pady had been told the previous year (presumably by the Dominion Lands Agency) not to bring such young children but that he had ignored this and, if anything, had now gathered 'a smaller sized lot'. All these observations were sent to the Canadian Department of the Interior and thence to the High Commissioner in London. A couple of months later a senior figure (signature missing) wrote to the Department in Ottawa from Québec saying that the Dominion immigration agent there (Doyle) had been asked to prepare a special report on Pady:

> ... whose scalp you are after. Look out for it [the report] and take the necessary action when received. So far as I can learn, Mr Pady does not conform to the requirements as he has no 'Home' or Institution of any kind in Canada and his boys are not subjected to any medical examination. He is a mere adventurer, and unworthy of any sort of encouragement – therefore 'sit on him if you can'.[28]

The Department of the Interior thereupon wrote to Pady asking him why he was bringing children to Manitoba who were too young. They also wrote to their agent at Québec instructing him to 'look out for Pady's arrival' and to 'take especial notice of the children and report exhaustively'.[29] But the next party to arrive was escorted by Pady's daughter, Bertha. Upon inspection the immigration agent found two of the 16 children to be 'undesirable'. Miss Pady contended that all the children had been medically examined before leaving and insisted that there *was* a reception Home at Emerson near Winnipeg run by her brother. She promised to place the two 'unfit' children in a Montreal hospital and then to take them back to Britain with her on her return journey, which she failed to do.[30]

At much the same time the Department of the Interior received a reply from Pady explaining that he thought it best to choose younger boys for emigration because they would not yet have acquired 'farming habits that would hinder them'. He was also at pains to reassure the Department that his daughter had stayed on to see the children settled in the placements that her brother had arranged.[31] However, the Department wrote to the Commissioner of the

Dominion Lands Board in Winnipeg asking him to find out whether Pady had a Home at Emerson.[32] Clearly disquiet was mounting, but little or no firm action was taken. Furthermore, the principal concern of the Canadian authorities was whether the children Pady was bringing were 'suitable'. There was also concern about who would foot the bill for their return if they were not. At this point two British organisations stepped into the picture. First, Gretton, the secretary of the East End Emigration Fund, wrote to the Canadian High Commissioner's office in 1893 to say that he had important information concerning Pady.[33] There is no record of what exactly was passed on, but when Gretton later gave evidence before the Poor Law Schools Committee in 1896 much of it was devoted to a bitter indictment of Pady and his operations. Although he was only referred to as 'Mr A' there is no doubt about his identity. Much of what was said before that Committee probably reflected what had been conveyed to the Canadian authorities earlier. Indeed, while in Montreal that year, Gretton explained that he had been greeted 'by a chorus of complaints about a professional workhouse child importer' who 'places them anyhow … leaving no one to adequately represent him, and the children [to] drift about anywhere'. For example, he said that he had found three small boys (brought by Pady from the Sutton and the Great Yarmouth unions) in 'a common lodging-house for men in which [they] sleep 70 or 80 to a room together on stretchers'. Officials in the Immigration Department had, he stated, entreated him 'to work them up a good case' to assist them in stopping what he described as 'this iniquitous traffic in children'.[34]

On his return Gretton took steps to fulfil this commission through his membership of the Council of the Charity Organisation Society (COS). As a result, A.H. Paterson (a district secretary of the COS) was appointed to undertake a full investigation of Pady's activities, both in Britain and Canada.[35] In Canada he twice interviewed Pady's daughter, although describing himself to her as a reporter from the *Daily Graphic*. She admitted that she had heard serious complaints about her father's work but 'professed herself to be nearly distracted in consequence, and in great distress'. She also maintained that she knew nothing about her father's so-called 'Bureau' in London. Paterson also saw officials in the Department of the Interior, several immigration agents and the staff of three children's Homes in Montreal. One manager insisted that Pady brought out 'gutter-children of the lowest type', while another found them to be 'criminals as a rule, or slightly imbecile, or diseased'. Furthermore, he felt sure, he added, that there was cruelty to the children since they were 'too often taken to be made slaves of'. The staff of these Homes felt able to express such opinions for two reasons: first, because Pady sometimes persuaded Canadian Homes and asylums to admit his children on their arrival if he could not quickly place them out and, second, because children who were placed but who left for one reason or another gravitated to the city where they were liable to be picked up by the police or by charity workers and taken to those establishments.

Later, Paterson had a long interview with Pady himself, the details of which were sent, together with the main report, to the Canadian High Commissioner.

Pady was described as a 'slimy scoundrel' and it was concluded that he made a profit from the various grants that he received from boards of guardians and others. This helped to explain, it was maintained, why he included such young children in his parties: if they were under 12 the passage fare was only half.[36]

Soon afterwards, and belatedly, the report that the Department of the Interior had asked the Dominion Lands Agency in Winnipeg to make on Pady's arrangements in Manitoba was submitted. This added yet more evidence of the disreputable nature of what he was doing. His son had been summoned to be interviewed by the inspector of homesteads and had confirmed that he placed children with farmers for his father, but denied that he received any remuneration: he did it, he said, 'for Christ's sake'. Despite these Christian sentiments he was not, the report concluded, 'a proper person to be entrusted with the care of such children'. He was a single man in his early twenties 'without any accommodation or female help' and was, in any case, 'from his manner', not suitable.[37] Later, the homestead inspector visited Pady's son at home which was, he wrote, 'much worse than I at first thought: cold, filthy and only a small board shanty'.[38]

An indication of the mounting indignation about Pady in and around Winnipeg was also to be found in articles carried by the local press. For example, under the headline 'Cruel Case of Desertion', the *Winnipeg Tribune* reported that three young boys (in other reports six) whom Pady had been unable to place had been given 50 cents each and told to 'look out for themselves', perhaps as bootblacks. The youngest had eventually gone to the Protestant orphanage and asked to be admitted; but when it was learned that he was a Catholic he was taken instead to a Catholic institution.[39]

In the light of the reports from the COS in London and from the Dominion Lands Agency in Winnipeg the Department of the Interior finally acted. The High Commissioner was instructed that Pady was not fit to conduct juvenile emigration and that the LGB should be informed accordingly.[40] They were, and Pady was told that he would no longer be allowed to take children to Canada.[41] He had, by then, however, set off with another group of 16 'workhouse boys'. On arrival at Québec he insisted to the immigration agent that he did have a distribution Home in Manitoba, and the boys, said the agent, had all passed the immigration medical examination. The Québec immigration officer was at a loss to know what to do and sought guidance from Ottawa.[42] There is no record of the reply, but the boys were permitted to enter. Doubtless encouraged by this Pady wrote to reassure the Department of the Interior that he *had* visited many of the children and that he was happy with what he had found. Furthermore, he was, he explained, negotiating to buy properties in order to establish Homes in both Montreal and Manitoba and was forming a committee in Winnipeg 'to act as guardians' of the boys in that area.[43] Despite all that it already knew the Department of the Interior took the trouble to ask the Winnipeg Commissioner of Dominion Lands to find out whether the man whom Pady claimed was assembling his committee for him was a fit and responsible person. 'Yes' came the answer, 'he's a Baptist.'[44] Even so, the *coup de grâce* was at last delivered: it was confirmed that the decision not to allow Pady to bring any more children into Canada was final and no further correspondence with him was to be countenanced.[45]

What, then, is to be learned from this wretched story? First, it is clear that many of the children whom Pady brought to Canada suffered greatly. Yet, in many ways, the grave deficiencies that eventually emerged were also to be found in other child emigration agencies, albeit not necessarily in so blatant and exaggerated a form. Indeed, in his evidence before the Mundella Committee Gretton had claimed that there were two or three other people involved in this work whose record was little, if at all, better than Pady's. Even by the 1890s the lack of adequate inspection and support for the children was widespread, too much reliance being placed on adult goodwill.

Second, the four years during which Pady was allowed to continue his activities produced ample evidence of his disreputable character, evidence that should have been more than sufficient for the authorities, both British and Canadian, to have realised that he had to be stopped. The LGB could have done so by refusing to give their approval to the emigration of the Poor Law children. The immigration authorities in Canada could have prevented Pady from landing and obliged him to return the children, but once they had arrived it was difficult for their agents to do so unless, on inspection, they were found to be 'unfit'.

The Pady scandal also illustrates the ease with which such people could set up an apparently philanthropic enterprise under the guise of religious zeal. There was no obligation for any 'Bureau', 'Society' or 'Mission' to be registered, for their accounts to be audited, or for their *bona fides* to be checked. The subsidy arrangements and deals with the shipping companies, together with the lure of free or cheap land in Canada, made enterprises of the kind that Pady engineered potentially financially rewarding. Indeed, several other agencies also came under strong suspicion for their accounting improprieties. Furthermore, there were so many bodies and individuals involved in the field of juvenile emigration that it was difficult for governments to keep track of who was who and who was doing what. For example, in 1893 the Department of the Interior recorded 23 different individuals and organisations bringing children into Canada.

It must also be recognised that those who entrusted the children for whom they were responsible to the mercy of people like Pady rarely took steps to verify their standing or to establish how exactly the welfare of the young people would be assured once they were in Canada. In the case of Pady it is interesting to see which boards of guardians he was able to hoodwink. Several (such as Wolverhampton) had a history of favouring child emigration; others perhaps had little experience on which to draw in deciding how to respond to his invitations.

One other notable feature of this case was the important intervention of the COS.[46] We have seen elsewhere that it entertained misgivings about Barnardo and that internal reports about his activities were produced. However, it was only when it came to Pady that the COS intervened more publicly, perhaps because the evidence against him was so compelling and because he was a single individual without the weight of an organisation or powerful sponsors behind him. Finally, it is unclear who was responsible for the children after Pady ceased his activities. Although the Canadian government was inspecting Poor Law children once a year there would have been few if any records from which they could identify these young people and obtain their addresses. Mostly they would have been left to fend for themselves as best they could.

IV Confusion: the Bristol Emigration Society

It may seem odd that a 'society' be included among the examples of the 'unorganised' emigrationists. However, the adoption of a corporate title did not mean that any formal organisation existed even though, in this case, there was an honorary secretary. In fact, the BES appears to have been no more than a loosely bound group of individuals, the most prominent among whom were Mark Whitwill (1826-1903) and Mary Clifford (1842-1919).[47] Whitwill was a non-conformist ship-owner, a ship and insurance broker, a shipping agent, a justice of the peace (JP) and a manager of the Park Row and the Clifton industrial schools for boys as well as the Carlton House industrial school for girls. In addition he was chairman of the Bristol School Board, a Bristol city councillor and a supporter of the women's suffrage movement.[48] He was clearly a man who played a variety of interlocking roles and who had similarly interlocking interests, among which was the encouragement of emigration. Indeed, he appeared to have been the driving force behind the Bristol initiative, concentrating first (from about 1880) on the emigration of children from the industrial schools with which he was involved but later (from 1883) encouraging the inclusion of Poor Law children, not least by bearing part of the cost. This, the *Bristol Mercury* maintained, was 'to stop any opposition on the grounds of expense'.[49] Moreover, as a magistrate, some of the children may well have appeared before him in order to give or withhold their consents to being sent to Canada.

Whitwill's enthusiasm for child emigration was shared by Mary Clifford. She was one of the first women to be elected to a board of guardians (in 1882), in this case to the Barton Regis union.[50] Deeply Christian, she concerned herself in particular with the plight of the women, older people and children in the workhouses.[51] Being aware of the emigration that Whitwill was arranging she sought to extend the opportunity, as she saw it, to some of the children in the care of her union, particularly those who needed to be protected from the 'baleful influence' of their families. Indeed, as Hollis points out, 'she was quite ruthless about denying parental rights. She went to immense trouble to ensure that the parents should have no clues' as to their children's whereabouts.[52] Obviously, Canada provided the perfect solution.

Clifford's endeavours were aided by a Margaret Forster who, although from time to time described as the 'agent' for the BES, dealt only with the Poor Law children, children who were gradually assembled from nearby unions as well as from Barton Regis. For his part Whitwill only regarded himself as being responsible for the children sent from the industrial schools. The majority of the children selected for emigration from both sources were sent to New Brunswick (NB). A few went to Québec and to Nova Scotia. From 1880 to 1906 an average of 40 a year were involved – something over 1,000 altogether.[53]

Even so, the 'organisation' of the BES remained extremely vague. Certainly, on several occasions Canadian officials confessed themselves perplexed about who was responsible for which children. However, in 1903 a committee from the locality was formed with the Lord Bishop of Bristol as its president.[54] This coincided with Whitwill's death in the same year. Notwithstanding this move towards a greater formalisation the Society's activities were brought to an end in 1906 when the last group of 72 children left for Canada.[55] Thus, unlike agencies such as Barnardos or Fegans the BES did not become formalised during the lifetime of its principal activist.

The history of the BES and of the children who were emigrated is in many ways similar but less dire than that which unfolded around Pady's activities. Nevertheless, no comparable outcry was heard about its shortcomings even though a few Canadian officials expressed their concern. What may well account for the different responses in the two cases is the social class of those involved. However, one of the similarities was that both Pady and the BES had engineered private agreements with Dominion immigration agents to receive and place out the children they sent – Smith in Hamilton and Gardner in St John, NB. In neither case was the Department of Agriculture consulted, but once the arrangement was known it appears to have reassured the authorities in Ottawa that all was well. For example, it was not until 1894 (again after the transfer of responsibility to the Department of the Interior and the introduction of more stringent regulations) that Gardner was asked to explain his role as agent for the BES. 'There should be', it was impressed upon him, 'some responsible person ... who will look after the children sent out by the Society and to whom they could be returned should a necessity arise.' If he were willing to assume such a responsibility the Department was willing for him to do so but it was, they insisted, a matter for him to decide.[56] Gardner replied that he accepted 'all the obligation that is required of the BES in connection with the Barton Regis or other workhouses from whom the agents of this Society send to my care and have done ... for the past 14 years'. All the children he received, he added, looked on him as their guardian and he did all that was necessary in that capacity.[57] The Department of the Interior was satisfied, although it should be noted that the first part of Gardner's reply only mentioned 'workhouse' children, not those from the industrial schools. 'No organisation of any kind can work better than our arrangement with Mr Gardner' wrote Whitwill in repudiating certain criticisms that the acting immigration agent at Liverpool had sent to the High Commission in London.[58]

From time to time the Department of the Interior reminded Gardner of the responsibilities that he had assumed. For example, in 1898 there was a complaint about a boy from the Park Row industrial school because he was enuretic. It had to be understood, Gardner was told, that he was regarded as the accredited agent for the BES and, as such, that he had to take responsibility for the boy. He was to see him returned to his care and if he were found to be 'incurable', he was to arrange for him to be sent back to Bristol.[59] Gardner agreed to do what was required.[60]

However, some time between 1900 and 1902 Gardner retired and was replaced by Lantalum. Thereon the BES made it clear that they would not continue to send children to be placed by him because he was a Catholic; in any case, he did not wish to act for them.[61] Lantalum confirmed this and told the Department of the Interior that he considered the BES to be an unsatisfactory organisation. They did not have a Home in New Brunswick (or anywhere else for that matter) and they left the immigration agent to bear any expenses that arose. Furthermore, were he to follow in Gardner's footsteps he considered that it would be in conflict with his Dominion responsibilities. However, he said that he would carry on if he were instructed to do so.[62] Whether he was instructed to do so or not, he did, in the event, take up where Gardiner had left off.

What is surprising is that the BES was allowed to continue its activities without a distribution Home, certainly in view of the fact that it was partly on that ground that Pady was eventually prohibited from engaging in juvenile emigration and that Middlemore was obliged to establish such a Home as a condition of his continuing with emigration. It may have been the involvement of a Dominion officer that tipped the balance although two other people were also named as the BES's agents. One was the Rev. Renaud (superintendent of a Protestant Home in Montreal) and the other the shadowy figure of a Mr Walters of New Glasgow in Nova Scotia.

The general lack of clarity that pervaded the activities of the BES confused the Canadian authorities. Thus, in 1896, L.C. Pereira (the assistant secretary in the Department of the Interior) was impelled to write to Gardner at St John about the matter:

> A great deal of confusion is caused by using the names of people instead of Societies and this leads to endless confusion when one person is, for the sake of convenience, acting for two or more organisations. Thus, Mr Whitwill has been writing as the representative of the Park Row Industrial School, as the representative of the Carlton House Industrial School, as a Justice of the Peace certifying ... affidavits and as a Shipping Agent.[63]

Apart from such confusion and the lack of a distribution Home, three other shortcomings of the BES's activities were the subjects of uneasy correspondence but never satisfactorily resolved. One was the fact that some groups of children were sent without an escort and with no provisions for their onward journeys. A second complaint was that the 'Society' often failed to submit the documentation demanded by the Canadian immigration authorities.[64] A third misgiving about the way in which the BES conducted its work concerned the almost total absence of any subsequent supervision, inspection or assistance once the children had arrived in Canada. These deficiencies were briefly spelt out in a note that Bogue Smart (the inspector of British immigrant children) prepared for William Scott (the new Dominion Inspector of Immigration) in 1903. This was sent on to the High Commission in London.[65] There the Commissioner of Immigration (W.T. Preston) asked Mrs Forster (the so-called agent of the BES in Bristol) to call. Following the interview (of which there is no record) she wrote back, sending an agreement form that she claimed was used by the BES when placing children (no copy) and maintaining that whenever she accompanied parties to Canada she visited as many of those already placed as she could.[66] These details were sent back to Ottawa where Smart advised that although her letter was rather evasive he thought 'the fact of ... having written [to her] will have good results in the future'. For that reason he felt that 'it would be just as well to drop the matter for the present'.[67] And that seems to have been what happened.

In 1904, however, one of Smart's assistant inspectors, F.C. Blair, reported more strongly on the unsatisfactory state of the BES's activities in New Brunswick. There were several aspects that disturbed him. Since there was no Home, a child who had to be removed and replaced had to remain for some time in the old situation. Most of the children placed by the BES were never visited, except by the government's inspectors, and they did not visit non-union children. For both these reasons Blair maintained that 'if difficulties arise they [the children] must go on while the employer takes advantage of [them] or the child leaves.... In a number of instances the children plainly told me that no person cared for them after they landed in the farmhouse.' Blair had three further complaints. First, the majority of the Bristol children were placed without any written agreement, as a result of which 'employers sometimes give them to one another or simply turn them adrift'. Second, little regard was paid to the fact that children under the age of 14 should be going to school for certain periods each year. The picture was the same, Blair maintained, with respect to church attendance. His third complaint was the failure of employers to pay appropriate, or indeed any, wages. This, he concluded, was responsible for the children 'running about from place to place'.[68]

Certainly, the only indication of anyone from the BES visiting the children in the Dominion is a note that Forster went to Canada in 1896 to take back a lame boy and to visit children from the Barton Regis union.[69] Later, Whitwill wrote to Gardner that it was only these children with whom she dealt: 'she has nothing to do with our industrial school boys or girls. I am on the committees of these schools and [they] ... leave all the arrangements about them entirely to me.'[70] There is no evidence, however, that these children were visited by anyone.

Why, it must be asked, was the BES permitted to continue its activities for so long? Several reasons have already been suggested, but one further reason was connected with the fact that most of the placements were made in New Brunswick, a province that, because of its location, tended to be weakly placed for capturing new immigrants. Indeed, the unsatisfied demand for child labour there was probably as great as anywhere in Canada, aggravated by the loss of workers (in particular from the west of the Province) to the US. The authorities (both Dominion and Provincial) may have been hesitant therefore before halting this modest but still important stream of child immigrants to that part of Canada. Nevertheless, it must be stressed again how little protection the BES children ever received, not least once the Society abandoned its activities after 1906. As Bogue Smart wrote in a report for the Department of the Interior, it then became difficult to find some of the children, and it did 'not speak well for the Society that brought them to Canada and is now allowing them to wander around, to look after their own salvation'.[71]

Several conclusions emerge from this account of the activities of the BES. First, like so many of the other enterprises, the enthusiasm and drive of individuals were important in launching the project. As with Stirling, Whitwill's wealth enabled things to get started; but that very factor, probably inhibited the enterprise's formalisation. Although the BES did adopt a more corporate identity in 1903 it seems to have been too late to survive Whitwill's death and Mary Clifford's retirement from public life. A second conclusion also follows from the *ad hoc* nature of the BES throughout most of its life. This is that the various agreements and arrangements (for example, with the Canadian immigration agent) were negotiated on an entirely personal basis and thus had no clear contractual foundation. That also happened with other 'organised' ventures, of course, but in their name and usually with a record of what had been agreed and by whom. Third, it must be noted that the election of women to boards of guardians had mixed results in terms of the history of child emigration. In the early years they often encouraged the dispatch of children to Canada to save them, as they saw it, from poverty or maltreatment. Later, from about the 1890s, more of them became convinced that this trans-shipment should cease, particularly for the girls.

Finally, as has been pointed out already, the lack of organisation and of continuity meant that the children were provided with few or no safeguards and that it was impossible to determine who actually had responsibility for their well-being. Did it reside with Whitwill, with Clifford, with Forster, with the respective industrial schools, with the boards of guardians of origin, with the LGB or Home Office in London, with the Canadian federal government, with one of its immigration agents or with one or more of the provincial governments?

V The General Pattern

The distinction that has been drawn between the organised and the 'unorganised' nature of the emigrationists' activities is somewhat arbitrary. Nevertheless, there are grounds for making it. Furthermore, the 'unorganised' serve to highlight some of the shortcomings to be found in many of the more formalised bodies. In particular, one sees the ease with which any individual (or group of individuals) could set themselves up as emigration agents without any kind of official sanction, vetting, or subsequent regulation. Some limited control was introduced in Canada at the end of the nineteenth century but in Britain the only hurdles to be surmounted were the need to obtain the permission of the LGB where Poor Law children were concerned or the Home Secretary's consent for the emigration of those from industrial schools or reformatories. If neither group were involved the emigrationists enjoyed a completely free hand.

Another aspect of the activities of the 'unorganised' interventions that is to be seen in the more organised as well is the heavy reliance on a range of informal arrangements and personal agreements, both of which by-passed the official bodies, particularly in Canada. It was only when serious deficiencies were exposed that such authorities took steps (rarely speedily) to apply administrative sanctions or to commence legal proceedings. The 'unorganised' initiatives also serve to highlight the uncritical trust that was generally placed in the good faith of those involved, especially when it was believed that they acted from the best of motives (which some did), when they enjoyed a prominent social standing or when (as was usually the case) they professed strong religious convictions. Nevertheless, none of these attributes ensured that those who arranged the emigration would provide for the proper care and protection of children once they were in Canada.

Part IV
The Canadian Dimension

EIGHT

Canadian Demand for Child Labour

I The Farm Family

There was considerable Canadian demand for British child immigrants throughout the 50 years after Confederation, and it remained at a high level even during periods of economic recession. In order to appreciate why these demands were so insistent it is necessary to explore the nature of the Canadian farm family economy.

Most British immigrant children were placed in rural areas and overwhelmingly on farms. This is explained by the persistent shortages of farm labour that were endlessly reported by the immigration agents stationed across the country. What most farmers wanted was a ready supply of cheap casual labour that could be hired and fired according to the tempo of the year's work. Short growing seasons made it uneconomical to retain people on a permanent footing, especially on small farms. Indeed, the relatively small size of Canadian farms was a major factor that shaped this demand for casual labour. In its turn the size of farms was much influenced by the land grant systems.[1] While the overriding aim was to encourage settlement, there were limits to what an individual settler family could be expected to do, especially those with little or no capital. The size of allocations was fixed accordingly – typically less than 200 acres. Families were granted what they could manage by dint of hard work and some occasional help. Additional land was acquired when farms prospered and other plots were bought and sold, but the initial and pervasive influence on the size of farms in the older provinces was the point of physical exhaustion of the family unit.

Table 1 shows the percentage distribution of farm sizes between 1871 and 1921. Not until the 1911 Census were more than half of Canadian farms recorded as being larger than 100 acres. In the earlier years there was little difference in the size of holdings in the various provinces but, as the west was developed, pronounced differences began to emerge. In the prairies farms were significantly larger and became larger still, whereas in the more established areas they generally remained small. The enlarged scale of western farming was facilitated by mechanisation and also by the importation of more capital and by various forms of co-operative enterprise. Table 2 illustrates these differences and changes.

Not only did most of the British immigrant children go to the rural areas but most went to Ontario, the Maritimes and Québec, even after the westward developments. In the old provinces work on the smaller farms still depended on unpaid family help, but when this proved insufficient, particularly at times of

Table 1: Distribution of farm sizes (%), Canada, 1871-1921[2]

Acreage	1871	1881	1891	1901	1911	1921
Under 10	11.0	16.2	30.9	11.3	10.0	6.2
10-50	21.4	20.1	14.2	15.9	13.0	11.6
51-100	38.4	33.8	25.4	30.7	24.1	22.3
101-200	22.3	22.0	21.0	29.5	33.4	32.3
Over 200	6.9	7.9	8.5	12.6	19.5	27.6
Total	**100.0**	**100.0**	**100.0**	**100.0**	**100.0**	**100.0**

greatest activity, extra hands were needed. Whether or not they were forthcoming depended on local availability and on what farmers could afford. The result was that only a limited use was made of wage labour. This can be seen from the special returns contained in the 1901 Census. In Canada the average amount of hired labour on farms during that year generally corresponded to nine weeks' work. The average total amount paid by farmers in wages was $51.

There were, however, marked provincial differences. Little labour was employed in the Maritimes, rather more in Québec and somewhat above the average in Ontario. Proportionately, most wage labour was utilised in British Columbia with its more benevolent climate and longer growing season. Table 3 (overleaf) summarises the data.

Table 2: Size of occupied holdings (acreage):[3] percentages by Canadian provinces, 1881-1921

		50 or fewer	51-100	Over 100	Total
Ontario	1881	37	36	27	100
	1901	30	37	33	100
	1921	25	38	37	100
Québec	1881	32	35	33	100
	1901	24	33	43	100
	1921	20	32	48	100
Nova Scotia	1881	46	26	28	100
	1901	46	26	28	100
	1921	42	26	32	100
New Brunswick	1881	37	36	27	100
	1901	30	35	35	100
	1921	29	36	35	100
Manitoba Saskatchewan Alberta }	1901	2	2	96	100
	1921	3	3	94	100

Table 3: Hired farm labour, Canada, 1901[4]

	Weeks of hired labour		Value of hired labour	
	000s	Average per farm	$000s	Average per farm, $
Canada	4,465	9	24,173	51
Nova Scotia	178	4	939	20
New Brunswick	158	5	841	24
Québec	895	7	4,513	35
Ontario	2,358	13	12,141	65
Manitoba	419	13	2,615	82
British Columbia	134	23	1,213	204

These data, however, only related to farms of five acres or more. Smaller holdings were classified as 'lots'. To all intents and purposes their owners did not employ labour. On the farms that were not 'lots' but that were nevertheless small, the demand for labour was chiefly determined by the composition of farm families. Wives and older children played a crucial role; without them other help was needed. Yet from the mid-nineteenth century onwards several forces converged to siphon off the labour of sons and daughters. The 1871 Census reported that 80 per cent of the population lived in rural areas. However, at each successive census until 1911 the balance shifted by about six per cent towards urban locations. By that year only 56 per cent of the population was classed as rural. The processes of urbanisation and industrialisation inevitably drew people away from the rural areas, especially young adults. In 1898 Kelso, the newly appointed superintendent of neglected and deprived children in Ontario, explained the incessant demand for British children:

> There is not an agency engaged in the work that does not receive more applications than they have children. Each party of fifty, seventy-five or one hundred children is almost completely disposed of within two weeks after arrival, and the requests for children seem to increase rather than diminish as time goes on....The reason for this would appear to be that small families prevail as a rule in the agricultural districts, and when there are four or five sons and daughters it is seldom more than one or two remain on the farm. They go off to the colleges, professions, to the city shops and factories, to be typewriters or conductors on street cars, and as help is imperatively needed on the farms the boys and girls from the Old Country take the places of sons and daughters.[5]

The development and improvement of transport facilitated such internal migration. At Confederation in 1867 there were only 2,250 miles of railway in

Canada. This figure doubled within 10 years and doubled again in the decade after that. The construction of railways (and also the canals) absorbed a good deal of immigrant labour, but it also attracted labour away from the farms. In 1875 (the first year for which there are figures) 2,270 miles of track were being laid, a figure only surpassed in the early 1880s at the height of activity in building the Canadian Pacific line across Canada. Table 4 illustrates the pattern of railway construction between 1875 and 1895.

Table 4: Miles of first main railway line under construction in Canada[6]

	Miles
1875	2,276
1879	945
1882	3,189
1885	812
1889	416
1892	210
1895	225

The Canadian Pacific Railway (CPR) across Canada was completed in 1881[7] and laid the foundation for the development and exploitation of the west. A vast number of immigrants from all over Europe, as well as from the US, were settled on the new lands; but the promise and opportunities of the west also attracted people from elsewhere within Canada, again, young adults in particular. In his report for 1882, for example, the Hamilton immigration agent drew attention to the fact that farmers' sons were leaving for the north west and that this was leading to an upsurge in the demand for labour to replace them.[8] Table 5 shows the general pattern and scale of this internal migration.

The most pronounced migration, in absolute terms, was from Ontario. It is impossible to determine exactly how much the rural areas contributed to this

Table 5: Estimates of the net internal migration of the 'native-born' population in Canada, 1881-91 to 1901-11[9]

	000s		
	1881-91	1891-1901	1901-11
The Maritimes	−7.3	−7.7	−27.0
Québec	−10.2	−4.5	−24.0
Ontario	−45.6	−51.7	−147.3
Manitoba	+22.2	+18.5	−16.0
Saskatchewan and Alberta	+23.8	+22.3	+184.9
British Columbia	+17.0	+18.9	+41.1

westward flow, but it is reasonable to assume that farm people would be especially excited by the prospects that the new free or cheap lands offered. Corroborative evidence is to be found in the census reports from 1891 onwards in which analyses of the composition of the male agricultural labour force were published. Table 6 summarises these data for Ontario and Québec.

Table 6: Composition of the male workforce in agriculture, 1891-1921: Ontario and Québec[10]

	'Operators'* (%)	Other family workers (%)	Wage earners (%)	All workers (000s)	Total (%)
Ontario					
1891	54	34	12	332	100
1901	59	27	14	303	100
1911	70	11	19	301	100
1921	61	20	19	290	100
Québec					
1891	58	35	7	205	100
1901	61	31	8	194	100
1911	72	17	11	202	100
1921	56	32	12	217	100

Note: * 'Operators' were the owners or tenants.

The dramatic reduction in both the relative and absolute number of male 'family workers' in the period after 1901 is evident, but there were also more farms and more smaller farms (see Table 2), which accounts for the increase in the proportion of 'operators' by 1911. Although some of the losses of family workers were made good by the employment of more wage labour, its contribution remained comparatively small. More farms had to be worked with fewer farmers' sons – and daughters too, although no mention was made of them in the censuses. The erosion of family labour on the farms of the older provinces was exacerbated, of course, by the enlistment of young men during and after 1914 – altogether, between 1914 and 1918, 615,000 men joined the non-commissioned ranks of the Canadian Expeditionary Force.[11]

Even on farms that had the benefit of the unpaid labour of older offspring it is plain, certainly from the 1911 Census report, that the availability of this help did not last long. With the increased popularity of education and, in Ontario at least, with the implementation of more effective legislation to secure attendance after 1891, fewer sons under the age of 14 (the statutory upper age for compulsory education) were automatically available for farm labour. Alongside these changes in education and the new opportunities in the west there were the attractions of the cities. Together these changes meant that fewer adult sons and daughters remained on the farms. The limited time that a son's labour (no mention of daughters') was available is vividly demonstrated in Table 7.

Thus, throughout the second half of the nineteenth century and the early part of the twentieth, there was a general shortage of agricultural labour, especially cheap labour that could be engaged on a seasonal basis; and the shortage was most pronounced in the longer settled areas. British children, and boys most notably, partly met that shortfall. They were *replacement* labourers, but replacement labourers who were more akin to unpaid family workers than to hired workers, even though many had indentures of apprenticeship drawn up for them. Some idea of the scale and importance of this boy-labour can be gained from the fact that between 1901 and 1911, 49,000 male family workers (farmers' sons) were lost to the farms of Ontario. During the same period, over 13,000 British boys were placed in the province, almost all of them on farms. That represented a replacement rate of some 27 per cent. If, alternatively, these boys are regarded as wage labour instead of family workers, they could be reckoned to have constituted 80 per cent of the growth in male wage labourers on Ontario farms during the same time.[13] In whichever way they were actually enumerated for census purposes, the conclusion that they provided a crucial and significant addition to the agricultural labour force is inescapable. However, it would be misleading to suggest either that all the children were placed in the old provinces or that there was no demand for them in the north west. Indeed, in 1897 Owen (Barnardo's agent in Canada) reported that in Manitoba the demand for boys aged 12-14 was 'practically unlimited'.[14]

Table 7: Farmers' sons enumerated in the census of the male agricultural workforce, 1911 Census[12]

Ages	Number
10-14	612
15-24	100,668
25+	1,794
Total	103,074

The extent of the demand for British children is tellingly illustrated by the figures showing the difference between the number emigrated and the number of applications for their services recorded by the Department of the Interior in the early years of the twentieth century (Table 8 overleaf).

One of the other indications of the considerable demand that existed for child labour on the farms was the fact that the market was also anxious to absorb *Canadian* children from institutions in their own country. The danger of any 'competition' between the 'claims' of British and Canadian children was repeatedly discounted – there was room for all. 'So far', wrote Kelso in 1893, 'there has been no clashing.'[16] In the following year he observed, in relation to 'homeless' Canadian children, that 'especially when old enough to be made useful [they] are often bandied about and traded off like cattle, compelled to work far beyond their strength, and shut off from education and the usual social pleasures of childhood'.[17] In a report of the proceedings of an Ontario conference on child saving held in 1894 the head of a Canadian industrial school told the audience that there was 'a greater demand for boys from our ... school than we can supply....

Table 8: The supply of and demand for British child immigrants, 1900-01 to 1913-14 (financial years)[15]

	Children emigrated	Applications received	Ratio of applications to children available
1900-01	977	5,783	5.9
1901-02	1,540	8,587	5.6
1902-03	1,979	14,219	7.2
1903-04	2,212	16,573	7.5
1904-05	2,808	17,833	6.3
1905-06	3,264	19,374	5.9
1906-07	1,455	15,800	10.9
1907-08	2,375	17,239	7.3
1908-09	2,424	15,417	6.4
1909-10	2,422	18,477	7.6
1910-11	2,524	21,778	8.6
1911-12	2,689	31,040	11.5
1912-13	2,642	32,417	12.3
1913-14	1,899	30,854	16.2
Total	**31,210**	**265,391**	**8.5**

I hear the same from all the institutions in the country ... we do not find that these English children displace any of ours; we find that there is demand enough for both classes on the farm.'[18]

Although in 1896 the Ontario Children's Aid Societies (CAS) placed as many as 500 Canadian children on farms,[19] the number remained small by comparison with the influx of British children. There were two reasons for this. First and foremost, there was a smaller population on which to draw. Although the 1901 Census classified 44,000 children as living in institutions throughout Canada, more than 30,000 of them were in convents, the majority in Québec.[20] Some were very young and others were there only temporarily during spells of parental adversity. It is impossible to say exactly how many children from Canadian institutions were available for farm placement at any time, but it probably never exceeded 5,000 scattered across the country and fewer in the earlier years.

Nevertheless, there was a second reason why so few of the Canadian children were offered for placement. Kelso summed it up in 1896 when he wrote that:

> Long established custom and usage have placed the orphan asylum on a high pinnacle of Christian veneration; all the passages of Scripture bearing upon the care of the young have been construed as commands to build and enlarge Institutions, and any one calling in question the aims or methods pursued is apt to be regarded with suspicion and

distrust. Each Institution is managed by from 40 to 60 ladies occupying the highest social position, and he would be brave, indeed, who would willingly antagonise such powerful combinations.[21]

Although supported by people such as Kelso, the boarding out of Canadian children was unpopular with those who ran the voluntary orphanages and Homes. Places needed to be kept full to encourage subscriptions and thus to enable such visible charitable activities to continue, despite the fact that, as Kelso reported in 1899, the demand for Canadian children '... for adoption and apprenticeship continues to be one of the most notable features of our work'.[22] There was no unique demand for *British* children, therefore; rather, the demand could not be met from Canadian institutions.

II Girls as Domestic Servants

As with agricultural labour there was a severe and persistent shortage of domestic servants throughout Canada. The various census reports indicate that they constituted a relatively small proportion of the labour force. Certainly, by comparison with Britain, the percentage was extremely low. This can be seen from Table 9.

Agents throughout the country continually reported a dire shortage of female domestic servants in almost identical terms to the accounts that they gave of the need for boys as agricultural labourers. In 1870, for instance, the Toronto immigration agent was recommending that it was 'most desirable that some system should be adopted whereby a large number of domestic servants could be induced to come to Canada; the demand for this class of people increases every year ...'.[24] Few

Table 9: The number and percentage of the Canadian labour force classified as 'domestic servants'[23]

Census	Number	%
1881	62,813	4.6
1891	96,280	6.8
1901	91,994	5.2
1911	122,451	4.5

'who are not brought into contact with the problem', wrote Kelso 35 years later, 'can realise the great demand there is through the country for the services of young girls from 12 years and upwards'.[25]

In her analysis of the demand for female domestics in Ontario between 1870 and 1930, Barber emphasised that:

> The servant girl problem ...was a dominant concern of many Ontario women ... the province suffered from a chronic shortage of domestic servants. Servants were employed not simply by the rich, but also by the wives of professional and small business men in towns and villages as well as cities. In addition, there was a strong unsatisfied demand for household help on the farms....[26]

While the general shortage of domestic servants created the context in which young British girls were so much sought after, the majority went to the farm households that Barber identified as but one of the elements in this overall demand. Why were so many dispatched to the countryside rather than being placed in urban areas where there was also a pressing demand? There were at least two reasons. First, the few adult women who were employed in domestic service sought the best conditions and the best wages. This usually meant that they found positions in the larger towns and cities. Increasingly, servants also chose living-out arrangements and these were more often available (and more feasible) in urban areas. The particular shortage of domestic help in rural areas was further exacerbated by the fact that young Canadian girls in the localities were required to work for their own farm family and were usually not available for other positions. Furthermore, older single women and girls in the rural areas were increasingly drawn to factory or service employments in the cities.

The second reason for the reluctance of female domestics to go to the rural areas was the nature of the work. Young women were required who could undertake a range of chores, both inside and outside the house, alongside the other women of the household. It was, therefore, typically general work that was demanded, albeit with a domestic emphasis. This was at the lower end of the hierarchy of domestic employment. Not only was it low status work, but also frequently done in a household where no other help was kept and also likely to be in remote places. Hours were usually not fixed and when free time was available there was little by way of diversion, companionship or entertainment.

There was therefore a particular and large gap in the availability of domestic labour in rural areas, a shortage that persisted even during those periods when demand in the towns slackened. Unaccompanied immigrant girls could be directed towards this section of the labour market since they were young, unable to exercise any choice and, in any case, were almost certainly unaware of the different opportunities that were open to them. But why, given the extra expense of making rural placements and the parallel demand in the cities, did so many of the societies choose to make farm placements their policy for girls? An important answer is to be found in their concern for child saving. Rural areas were considered to present less temptation and threaten less moral danger. Having been saved from the evils of British cities, young girls, it was argued, should not be placed in similar jeopardy in Canada. However, the policy was not followed in all cases. By the early years of the twentieth century more British immigrant girls were being placed in urban areas. Although this may have been the outcome of strong informal middle-class pressure, it was also connected with the growing concern about the quality of supervision that it was possible to provide in the rural areas. The Catholic organisations in particular switched their policy from rural to urban placements for young girls in domestic service so that female visitors could maintain a closer and more regular oversight of their welfare.

Despite the apparently similar level of demand for British boys and girls, only about one girl for every two boys was sent to Canada during the period

1867-1917. In order to explain this it is necessary to appreciate the position in Britain. In the first place, as we have seen, the Local Government Board's (LGB's) policy throughout most of the latter part of the nineteenth century prohibited the emigration of pauper girls over the age of 14 unless there were special circumstances. That policy did not apply to girls who were in the care of the voluntary societies and they, it must be noted, emigrated boys and girls in more equal numbers, not least because of their characteristic concern with child rescue and moral salvation. Even placed in service in Britain, they argued, girls could not be adequately protected from vicious or unscrupulous relatives and friends or from dangerous urban environments. The prospect of factory employment was regarded with even more disquiet, the moral dangers being seen as particularly great.[27] Even so, the other major explanation for the greater number of boys than girls being sent to Canada was the persistent demand for girls for domestic work in Britain. In 1900, for example, the Ontario emigration agent in Liverpool could still report that 'complaints are often heard from people who cannot get servants that it is a shame to send so many trained girls out of the country when they are so much wanted here'.[28] By contrast, the demand for the labour of boys was more erratic, concentrated as it was in marginal occupations that, in any case, were regarded as unsuitable and dead-end.

III Ages and Wages

The demand for children was heavily concentrated between the ages of 12 and 16. However, girls were both demanded and supplied at younger ages than boys, presumably because they were considered to be useful around the house and in minding children even at quite tender years. In her study of Barnardo children Parr found that in the period 1888-92 the mean age of placement was 15 for boys and 11 for girls. Even so, there were many young children – 26 per cent of the boys and 48 per cent of the girls in her sample were under the age of 13.[29]

Generally speaking, children seem to have been offered at somewhat younger ages than farmers would have liked but, as Kelso explained in his report for 1903, because of the general scarcity of agricultural labour and the particular dearth of adolescent children there was a ready demand for those 'who were nearly of serviceable age'.[30] Up to a point farmers were willing to accept younger children, especially if they looked well developed for their age. In any case, as Lowe, the Deputy Minister in the Department of Agriculture, told *The Toronto Mail* in 1887, 'it costs so very little to keep a child which very soon begins to be useful and earns much more than it costs'.[31] Certainly, on a mixed farm producing much of its own food, the marginal cost of an eight- or nine-year-old was small. Yet, especially in the case of boys, much dissatisfaction was expressed when they were found to be too weak or too small to undertake the work that was demanded of them. They were returned to the distribution Homes as unsuitable and a stronger replacement requested. Indeed, the agencies frequently reported that they found it difficult to place the very young children, who often remained on their hands well after their older compatriots had left for the farms. Here, for example, is Merry of Macpherson's Home reporting on the fortunes of an 1888 party of British children: 'we are glad to say that all of them with the exception of thirty little ones, have been satisfactorily placed out'.[32] Similar difficulties were also encountered in placing out young children from Canadian institutions. In 1893 Kelso bemoaned the fact that:

> In all the institutions there are many intelligent, good-looking and healthy children from infancy up to 8 years of age, for whom foster homes would be very acceptable.... But they are not sought after as they might be and are consequently compelled to lead a somewhat artificial existence *until ready for the market*[33] (emphasis added).

It was probably difficulties such as these that encouraged Barnardos, and later some of the Catholic organisations, to introduce boarding-out systems in which, up to a certain age, a fee was paid. Barnardos began these payments in 1890 for boys and three years later for girls. The fact that it began with boys is not without its significance — all along, girls had been taken at younger ages than boys and young boys were more difficult to place. However, in Parr's study, the average age for both boys and girls at boarding out for a fee was nine, although some were placed as young as five.[34] The argument for the boarding-out system was that by providing payment the child would be protected from premature demands on their labour and would be free to attend school. From her scrutiny of the Barnardo case records Parr concluded that for many children the boarding-out fees did succeed in these respects.[35]

Nonetheless, the Canadian authorities did not approve of the immigration of young children because they were seen as competing with young children from Canadian institutions for boarding-out places. Kelso summed this up when he wrote in his 1907 Ontario report that 'it is not our policy to encourage the bringing over of very young children since it is our object and policy to place our own native born children in any homes that may offer'.[36] In the light of this, and of the other difficulties, it is rather surprising that the emigrationists persisted in including children of such tender years in their sailing parties. Even more surprising, as we have seen, is the fact that Barnardos, and probably some of the other agencies, removed children from British foster homes in order to board them out in Canada. There are three possible explanations for this: organisational, economic and 'child-saving'.

Organisations may have been forced to include younger children in their emigration parties in order to sustain the flow that would enable them to continue to admit other children. Barnardo certainly wrote about his emigration activities in these terms. It may have been that the problem of 'silting-up' was exacerbated by the presence of young children who remained a responsibility for much longer than those who were admitted in adolescence. Furthermore, by the turn of the century it seemed to be becoming difficult to assemble enough older children for the annual emigration parties. However, little children in the Homes were more likely to be available, not least because they could not contribute as much to the daily routines and work of the institutions. Younger children were organisationally less valuable because they were more dependent; but that explanation can only really be applied to general children's organisations such as Barnardos or the Waifs and Strays. People such as Rye or Middlemore who were *only* concerned with emigration also brought some very young children to Canada.

Another explanation for the inclusion of very young children might be found in the economics of the child emigration movement. Subsidies were paid by the federal government and by some of the provincial governments. These did not vary according to the child's age and nor did the amounts paid by British Poor Law guardians to those who arranged to take children from them to Canada. However, the cost of the sea passage did vary. Those under eight (at other times under 10) were carried at substantially lower rates. In crude financial terms, therefore, the emigration of the very young cost less than the emigration of older children, at least as long as they could be placed out reasonably quickly.

There was also the question of 'child saving'. In Britain the emigrationists frequently justified their activities by claiming that in sending children abroad they were rescuing them from abuse or destitution. This was certainly an important public image and one that attracted donations and other forms of support. However, although children of all ages could be at risk the youngest were considered to be especially vulnerable. Were they to be denied the chance that emigration was claimed to offer, the case for emigration would thereby be weakened. Indeed, some of the emigrationists subscribed to the view that in the worst circumstances this was the *only* form of long-term protection that could be offered.

The question of children's ages was closely linked to the question of what and when they should be paid for their labours. Boys and girls were often treated differently. For example, when Barnardos' Canadian boarding-out system was extended to girls in 1893 it was linked with an intermediate status that was not applied to the boys; namely, agreements that after the expiry of the boarding-out arrangement girls were to work for 'board, clothes and schooling' but no wages. Only later, as they grew older, did they progress to a wage agreement. The different 'indentures' that were devised for boys and girls yet again reflect the rather precise calculation of their respective value. The domestic work that was typically undertaken by the girls (albeit combined with outside work as well) was considered to be more susceptible to gradation although that was not always the case in practice. When boys were put to work, especially on small farms, it was often assumed that they would do the kind of work that men did. Work in the fields could not easily be altered to suit a child's more limited strength – when sheaves had to be stacked or when ploughing needed to be done there was little scope for making the labour less hard. The only way that adjustments could be made was by reducing the hours to be worked, but in the short Canadian seasons the household routines (rising, eating and sleeping) were arranged around long working days and these were not likely to be modified to take account of the lesser strength of a boy or, indeed, of a girl. That notwithstanding, boys were usually thought to be entitled to a wage at an earlier age than girls. What, in the event, either was paid is another matter.

It is somewhat misleading to relate these kinds of calculations only to a child's chronological age for, as Bogue Smart (the inspector of British immigrant children) explained: 'Industry, snap, intelligence, physique and weight reckon more than years in estimating a boy's usefulness and the value of his labour'.[37] Such concern about the children's physical attributes was vividly illustrated in one of the regular reports submitted by the government inspectors who eventually visited Poor Law children in their Canadian placements. Assistant Inspector Herbert wrote of his 1894 tour:

> I am pleased to state that I found 68 of the 71 children in a most healthy condition, and fully up to the physical standards of their respective ages. Measurements of their heads showed them to be of the ordinary size, and evenly, and well shaped. Heights and measurements of boys' chests showed them to be fully up to the standard.[38]

The parallels with the physical requirements demanded for boys to be admitted to the armed services did not pass unnoticed. The standard required in a juvenile immigrant should be 'similar to that for the Imperial Army or Navy. Those with the slightest suspicion of physical weakness or mental defect should be rejected out of kindness to themselves.'[39]

Evidence that older boys – and to a lesser extent girls – were increasingly acknowledged as wage labourers is to be found in the growing use that was made of annual engagements. For example, all the boys brought to Canada by Fegans' Homes were placed out on yearly indentures.[40] Such indentures (which could usually be terminated at a month's notice) were, as Parr observes, also regarded by many Canadian employers as a 'suitable definition of their relationship with a British child'.[41] Nevertheless, annual indentures did not necessarily lead to a change of employer when they were re-negotiated. For instance, the system used by the National Children's Homes was described in 1908 as follows: '... boys are only placed out for one year and at the end of this period if agreeable to all concerned, a new and different agreement is entered into providing for wages according to the boy's actual earning power'.[42]

This is how Bogue Smart summarised the general position in 1911:

> In the month of April, indentures and apprenticeships expire, consequently many of these young farm labourers change situations. For boys who have passed the school attendance period, yearly indentures are more advantageous than those extending over a period of two or three years, in that it gives them an increased wage, proportionate to their advancement in efficiency and knowledge of

farm work. Experience and close observation have convinced me that after a reasonable period of service a change of employer is more often beneficial than otherwise. The child thereby varies his experience, and knowledge of life and work is expanded.[43]

Any ideas of permanence or of ensuring the security that family life might offer children took second place to considerations that derived from the arithmetic of a child's labour value. Indeed, by the end of the century many of the societies when speaking on the Canadian side of the Atlantic made no bones about the matter. They saw themselves as pursuing the child's best interests by securing good terms within the fine gradations of the agricultural labour market. However, they had not always described their activities in such a frank manner. Certainly, in the earlier years of child emigration much was made of the claim that even older children were being placed to be brought up *in* families rather than *with* families for their labour. This was especially true when the organisations described their work for British audiences where the benefits of family placement were given precedence. Where the child's labour was mentioned, if at all, it was typically described as an incidental feature. Even in Canada as late as 1904 Kelso was still painting a picture of children who worked but who enjoyed the benefits of being accepted into a family circle on a permanent basis:

> All the children are expected to work and this is very largely the motive that prompts the application for them. At the same time this is not a serious objection if there are compensating advantages. The essential thing is that the children should be given good food, comfortable clothing, sleeping room, and should have all the social advantages of the home and neighbourhood. In the great majority of cases children enjoy these privileges, and they do not mind the *incidental* work of the farm, which is participated in by all alike – by the master and mistress, the hired help, or the boy and girl whom they have *taken to 'raise'*[44] (emphases added).

Children did, of course, go to farm families but in comparatively few cases were they regarded as members of those families, or adopted in the full sense of the term; and even then it may have been after several previous placements in which they were not. Indeed, it was misleading, Bogue Smart pointed out, to refer to them as 'Home' children. It was more appropriate to describe them as 'hired' boys and girls.[45] When challenged the emigrationists admitted that the children were expected to work but argued, as Kelso and other Canadians did, that this was beneficial to them and that it enabled them to become a normal member of the family group. Yet the evidence is overwhelming that in most cases their labour did not qualify children for family membership. Their impermanence was one important disqualification. And there were other reasons why they were unlikely to enjoy the benefits of family life, even on a temporary basis. First, they usually found themselves in a decidedly inferior position to that which would have been occupied by a son or a daughter of a similar age. Second, as Parr and others have made plain, girls in particular were not protected from sexual abuse by the taboos that usually accompanied family membership. Third, children were often rejected because they failed to provide satisfactory labour rather than for other shortcomings in their behaviour although, of course, the two reasons often became confused. Lastly, the question of wages remained a bone of contention throughout the period, not only the level at which they were to be paid but also, in some cases, the fact that agreed wages were not paid, not paid in full or were withheld until later.

IV The School Lottery

In Canada responsibility for education was devolved to the provinces and each developed its own legislation at its own pace. Nevertheless, they all accorded a good deal of autonomy to the school districts, and thereby to the local managers or trustees. In particular, rural areas were usually allowed to decide whether or not they would do those things that they were empowered to do. Much less choice was made available to the urban authorities. In 1871 Ontario required that all children between the ages of seven and 12 should attend school for at least four months a year. This was later raised to 100 days. By 1891 attendance was made compulsory for all children between eight and 14 throughout the school year. In other provinces such developments occurred later and entailed different requirements. Manitoba followed broadly in Ontario's footsteps in 1876. Legislation was not enacted in Nova Scotia until 1883 and then it only permitted compulsory education for children between seven and 12 if there were a two-thirds majority in favour in any section (a local district based on land divisions); in any case, children who lived more than two miles away from a public school could be exempted. Compulsory schooling was not introduced in New Brunswick until 1905 and in Québec it was not finally endorsed until 1942.[46] Even when and where legislation for compulsory education existed its actual requirements were commonly ignored throughout the nineteenth century, especially in the rural areas – the problem was enforcement. Although Ontario permitted municipalities to appoint enforcement officers in the 1880s and obliged urban areas to do so in 1891, the rural authorities were allowed to decide the matter for themselves until the 1919 School Attendance Act. Other provinces trailed behind.

As a social problem truancy was defined almost entirely in urban terms, despite the fact that irregular or non-attendance was more prevalent in the countryside. By the end of the 1880s, for instance, the average daily attendance of those listed on school rolls stood at 62 per cent in the cities, 60 per cent in the towns, but at only 46 per cent in the rural localities.[47] 'It was', wrote Stamp, 'the city environment that had made truancy visible and created the pressure for government action.'[48] The problem was, as an official inquiry in 1860 entitled its report, one of *'Truancy and Juvenile Crime in the Cities'*.[49] The same diagnosis was to be heard 30 or 40 years later.[50] In fact, the impetus for Ontario's compulsory education legislation of 1871 seems to have originated largely in the mounting anxiety about the street-arabs who were to be found in Toronto and in towns like Hamilton. Given such preoccupations it is not surprising to find Ontario, the most urbanised and industrialised province, leading the way with compulsory schooling while at the same time exempting its rural areas from the rigours of enforcement.

'Idle' city children were regarded with alarm. Those on the farms were not only thought to be out of the reach of temptation but also busily engaged in the wholesome work that had to be done. Admittedly, there were geographical reasons why the enforcement of school attendance in the countryside was difficult, especially in scattered communities with poor roads and winter conditions, but the principal reason for the lax attitude towards rural attendance lay in the essential role that children played in the economy of the farm family. They were too valuable a part of the labour force for locally chosen school managers to insist on the strict observation of the law, and certainly too valuable on the farms for the appointment of an enforcement officer to be made until it had to be.

In short, if parents were not keen to send their children to school in the country districts there was little likelihood that they would be obliged to do so. Admittedly, farming parents were gradually encouraged to send their sons (and later their daughters) to school, but less through the machinery of enforcement than through the introduction of a 'more relevant' curriculum.[51] It is noticeable that agricultural education (particularly that associated with the new mechanisation and with the 'scientific' approach) played an important part in late nineteenth-century Canadian educational planning, especially at college level. Haythorne and Marsh, writing of conditions in the 1920s and 1930s, drew attention to the relationship between the content of the curriculum, the needs of practical farming and non-attendance in the case of Québec. They argued that:

> The absence of any compulsory school law in Québec has its greatest effects in the rural areas, not only because children can be kept at home to help on the farm at the least pretext, but because the advantages of education are easily discounted by the 'practical' farmer. The strong emphasis upon the classical curriculum in Québec education bears some share of responsibility.[52]

It is almost impossible to establish the scale of non-attendance in rural Canada during the latter part of the nineteenth century; but there are some indications of its extent more generally, bearing in mind two cautionary observations. First, although there are figures about enrolment not all children were enrolled. Second, there are data about the attendance of those who were listed on the rolls but they deal with average daily attendances. Table 10 shows the proportion of Canadian children aged between five and 14 who were enrolled at the time of the censuses from 1871 to 1911. Table 11 shows, for Ontario only, the average

Table 10: The child population aged 5 to 14 and school enrolment, Canada, 1871-1911[53]

Census	Child population aged 5 to 14 (000s)	% enrolled
1871	995	78
1881	1,075	79
1891	1,186	79
1901	1,201	91
1911	1,487	91

daily attendance as a proportion of the enrolled populations at five-yearly intervals from Confederation onwards.

Thus, by the turn of the century the Canadian enrolment rate stood at about 90 per cent, but since the figures included five- and six-year-olds (who were not obliged to go to school) the proportion within the compulsory age band was almost certainly higher. Nonetheless, significant improvement in attendance did not occur until the 1890s, and even by 1905 the Ontario data in Table 11 indicate that average daily attendance was still only a little over half of the enrolment figure.

The accepted view is that the norm was for irregular attendance rather than complete non–attendance, but this may need to be qualified. Those who were not enrolled never went to school, but there is some evidence among the others to suggest that those who attended comprised a high proportion of regular attenders at least by the turn of the century. For example, the 1901 Census shows that of those children who went to school, most attended for most of the year. In Canada as a whole 55 per cent of those who went to school were there for 10 months of the year or more, and nearly 82 per cent went for six months or more. Only six per cent attended for less than the four months statutory minimum.[55] The conclusion would seem to be that many of the enrolled did not go to school after, perhaps, they had spent their early years in attendance. Older children did not become irregular attenders; they simply stopped going to school.[56]

Table 11: Daily attendance as a percentage of those enrolled in publicly controlled elementary and secondary schools in Ontario, 1867-1915[54]

1867	42.8
1870	41.9
1875	39.4
1880	45.8
1885	48.1
1890	50.9
1895	55.2
1900	55.7
1905	57.8
1910	58.7
1915	64.4

Such then, was the general educational background against which the fortunes of the British immigrant child must be viewed. Although the emigrating agencies gradually included clauses about schooling in their agreements and indentures it is clear from much of the correspondence, as well as from annual statements and the government inspectors' reports, that schooling for such children was at best erratic and at worst non-existent. Child labour was too useful for its contribution to be lessened by school attendance.

It is noteworthy how often Canadian government inspectors and others remarked on the comparatively high educational standards of the British immigrant children when they did go to school. For instance, in 1902 Bogue Smart wrote in his annual report that 'on the whole they are bright and intelligent, and of those who are attending school not a few are regarded by their teachers as amongst their cleverest pupils'.[57] The various processes of selection may well have led to the children who arrived in Canada being not only a superior group in terms of their physical health and development by comparison with their fellows who were not emigrated but better educated as well. For example, this is part of a letter that Andrew Doyle received (during his inspection tour in Canada) from a girl who had been in the Southampton workhouse for four years before being emigrated:

> I write to tell you that I would very much like to see you on Wednesday, but no, I cannot any more have the heart to go to Marchmont, for it has never been a home for me, although it was told to me and all the rest, that when we came to Canada it was to be a home. But, sir, I have known the time when I would have been glad for a bit to eat and a bed to lie on....[58]

The circumstances that are described are obviously important, but what also impresses the reader is the child's literacy. The letter may, of course, have been edited before publication, although Doyle implies that these are the girl's own words. Nonetheless, she was able to write and express clearly what she wished to convey.

How many opportunities for British children to build on an existing educational basis were lost for want of Canadian schooling remains a matter of speculation. Immigrant children would not have attended school as much as their Canadian fellows, not least because, as education gradually became more valued by parents in rural areas, the presence of an 'orphan' child in the household provided an opportunity for some farmers to free their own children from farm labour in order for them to benefit from education. Certainly Canadian farmers had no incentives to send their 'hired' child to school, and the emigration societies did little if anything to enforce even the limited conditions of their agreements. The inspectors visited too infrequently (if at all) to be able to make proper checks, and more often than not they accepted what they were told.[59] Even when the societies were informed that their agreements were not being adhered to they were inclined to turn a blind eye. To start with they had no means of enforcement short of moving the child to another farm where, in all likelihood, the same thing would happen. Furthermore, they sensed correctly that too much insistence on schooling would undermine the demand for their children.

Thus, neither the farmers nor the societies were inclined to see that the British children went to school. To make matters worse the federal immigration authority that ultimately became responsible for the inspection of pauper children was not prepared to assume responsibility for educational matters since these were seen as the preserve of the provinces. But the provinces, in their turn, were not insisting on school attendance in the rural areas in any case: a matter about which those concerned with the promotion of education commented despairingly.

Despite such a generally unfavourable picture Kelso reported in 1908 that there had been a steady improvement in the amount of schooling received by the *Canadian* children who were boarded out by the CASs. He went on to explain that 'in the early days it was exceedingly difficult to keep people up to the mark, but now a boy or girl who does not get at least four months' attendance at a district school is the great exception'.[60] Of course, he had every reason to play down the size of the problem, committed as he was to the encouragement of placements in foster homes. Others, however, continued to be more openly sceptical. In 1911 the CASs held a special conference on children in rural districts.[61] When he came to address the conference a Mr Goodwill declared that in the rural communities children were simply not sent to school. He found, he said, 'case after case, not foster parents, but parents of the child, who keep boys home to do "chores"…. What I find is this, people are keeping their own children home from school, and if so, what can you expect when they adopt children?' Referring still to the Canadian children who were placed in foster homes by the CASs, a Mr Miller told the conference that 'people said they did not want a boy that had to go to school all the time, as they could get an immigrant boy who only had to go to school for four months'. Kelso pointed out, however, that since the Ontario legislation of 1897[62] the British children's societies were obliged to issue agreements that required the children they placed to attend school according to the law of the province. Nonetheless, the reported *belief* that lower standards were permitted for British 'orphans' suggests that even less supervision was exercised over them than over the Canadian children who were similarly placed by the CASs. Indeed, even in 1907 the Barnardo boy's indenture specified the number of years during which he had to be sent to school for 'at least four months'.[63]

The CASs' conference probably had its eye on the new legislation that was to reach the Ontario statute book later in 1911. The School Attendance Act not only obliged all authorities to appoint attendance inspectors but also made it quite clear, for the first time, that every society, agent or person having the custody of any child brought into the province was *entitled* to send that child to a school in the municipality or section in which the child lived. Previously some local school authorities had excluded British immigrant 'orphans' from their schools. The issue had been brought to a head in 1896 when Barnardos initiated an action against the school trustees of Stisted for refusing admission to one of their boys. He, and other such boys, had been turned away after the trustees had been obliged to reduce the number of pupils accommodated in the school from 46 to 32 in order to conform with the education department's space regulations. The implication was that they had to provide extra accommodation. There were, at that time, 15 boys from Barnardos on the roll and they were excluded rather than Stisted incur the additional expenditure. The initial judgment found that since the man with whom the boy in question was placed was not his guardian the boy had no right to local schooling on the grounds of residence. Furthermore, the judgment made plain that under the prevailing Ontario legislation the trustees were only required to provide places for two-thirds of the number of children between the ages of five and 16 whose parents or guardians lived in the section. This was based on 'an estimate or conjecture that in all probability not more than two-thirds ... would be in attendance at any one time'.[64] On both counts, therefore, the judge found that the school trustees had not acted unlawfully, a conclusion that was upheld on appeal.[65]

This continued to be the position in Ontario until the 1911 Education Act although, of course, what actually happened could vary from place to place depending on the view of the local trustees. However, the new legislation made it plain that those who had the custody of British children were not exempt from the requirements respecting school attendance; but progress was slow and excuses continued to be offered for why they could not attend. Assistant Inspector Henry, writing of his tour of inspection of British Poor Law children in 1911, reported that:

> ... the plea for non-attendance was the great distance to walk, in some cases two or three miles, and that being chiefly in the winter months.... I would respectfully suggest that a boy or girl during school age should not, no matter how good the home may appear, be placed in such a position.[66]

It was from about this time that some of the British societies began to deal with the problem more firmly. For example, in giving an account of their work in 1913 Quarriers noted that the year had been 'especially marked by the effort we have made to get nine months schooling for all our children under 14. This has involved much work and many removals; but we have felt it to be a very necessary work. *It has caused a decline in applications for younger children*' (emphasis added).[67] Despite such efforts it is probably true that at the outbreak of war in 1914 many immigrant British children (particularly outside Ontario) who should have been at school were not and that those who did attend still went only on an irregular basis when it was felt that they could be spared – this, of course, was likely to be in the winter when weather conditions could make it difficult for a child to get to school in any case.

In economic terms young British children were sought by Canadian farmers not only because they offered cheap labour but because the extent of that labour was largely unconstrained by the necessity of having to send them to school.

Furthermore, the British immigrant 'orphan' was probably the last category of child in the rural areas to be brought fully within the scope of the increasingly effective provisions for compelling attendance at school.

It is tempting to conclude that the British children who were sent to Canada found themselves confronted by an entirely different educational system, and one that allowed their employers to keep them away from school if they chose to do so. However, that would be too simple a view. In fact the schooling requirements imposed on urban Canadian parents and their children were similar to those exacted in Britain. The crucial difference was in the extent to which Canada remained a rural country. In the towns and cities of Canada, just as in Britain, children became increasingly marginal to the industrial workforce, but in rural Canada children continued to play a key part in agricultural labour. There they were by no means marginal. Thus, Canadian educational law and regulation had to marry the need to incorporate the urban child into a universal school system while, at the same time, allowing for the rural child not to be fully incorporated. Local discretion and lax enforcement provided both the opportunity and the justification for such inconsistency, an inconsistency that bore heavily on the British immigrant children. As a result not only did their education suffer, but because of their absence from school, they remained less visible and therefore less likely to have any ill-usage noticed.

NINE

Canadian Opposition to Child Immigration

I The Setting

Throughout the first half of the nineteenth century there had been an undercurrent of opposition in Canada to certain classes of immigrants. Soon after Confederation, however, legislation specified particular categories that could be denied entry altogether. They were: the dependent, the criminal, the diseased, and those, like confirmed paupers, who were expected to become a liability. Unaccompanied children constituted an interesting group in this respect since although the younger ones were dependent on arrival their dependency could be expected to decline. In fact they could be regarded as an investment, both nationally and by individual employers. However, from the 1880s until the turn of the century in particular, their immigration was opposed for three main reasons: economic, eugenic and political.

There was a conviction on the part of organised labour and some communities that as low-paid or unpaid servants the children prejudiced employment opportunities and, in general, depressed the level of wages. Other fears could easily be aroused, particularly that because of their deprived backgrounds in British slums the children carried with them the threat of contamination, a contamination that was thought to be of a congenital nature and therefore not to be eradicated by benign Canadian influences. There was believed to be the risk of diseases like syphilis or tuberculosis, as well as the risk of genetic deterioration as a result of inter-marriage or promiscuous relationships. There was also the fear that Canadian youth might be exposed to the immoral or criminal influences that the British immigrant children were supposed to exercise. Opposition also derived from the assumption that, sooner or later, at least some of these children would become social liabilities rather than economic assets. The girls might produce illegitimate children, while the boys could swell the prison population. Coming as they did from 'poor stock', both the boys and the girls might become sick or 'mentally disordered' or cease to be able to earn their living for other reasons. Since they had no family on which to call in times of trouble, and since those who had arranged their immigration would not usually assume continuous responsibility for them, they were particularly liable to become a charge on charitable or public funds. Resort could be made to deportation, but usually only within two years of the children's arrival. It was as much the fear of what the children might *become* as what they *were* that occasioned the misgivings to be heard in various sectors of Canadian society. Furthermore, should their public dependency materialise there were both economic and political consequences, not least the pressure to which they would thereby contribute for the expansion of welfare provision.

All these fears tended to become further exaggerated from the 1880s onwards with the increasing scale of child immigration and with every sign that it would continue to grow. In particular, the appearance of Barnardo, with his flair for publicity and drive for a large-scale operation, magnified the threat in the popular mind. This was influenced by the fact that the children were identifiable and identified, for example, by being generally referred to as 'Home children'. Given these fears and apprehensions about British immigrant children (which, it must be said, reflected those more generally heard with respect to certain other groups of immigrants such as Chinese labourers), it is not surprising that the main sources of consistent opposition sprang from the trade unions, from the civic leadership of the principal towns, from urban charitable bodies, from some medical quarters and from some sections of the press. It is more surprising to discover a period of active opposition on the part of farmers. However, it should not be assumed that each of these groups kept to the kinds of arguments against child immigration that their particular interests may have suggested. Eugenic considerations, for instance, seem to have provided a rather generalised basis for all of them. The children could also fill the role of scapegoats – they could readily be blamed for a variety of ills. Their language, their background, their status and sometimes their clothing distinguished them as outsiders, and outsiders without either the protection of a family or a community of other outsiders placed in similar circumstances.

Thus, although Canadian governments generally supported and encouraged child immigration as a source of cheap additional labour for which there was ample demand, neither they nor the emigrationists could ignore the opposition. Steps were taken to manage the discontent. Chapter 10 explores how this was done. Here the main centres of opposition are described and explained.

II Organised Labour Takes a Stand

Some of the most forthright and persistent opposition to child immigration came from the emergent Canadian trade union movement and, in particular, from the Toronto Trades and Labor Council where D.J. O'Donoghue (regarded by many as 'the father of the Canadian labour movement'[1]) exercised considerable influence after his arrival in the city in 1880. He had previously been elected from Ottawa as the first 'working man's' member of the Ontario legislature, a seat that he held from 1874 until 1879.[2]

Although the Canadian trade union movement had begun to establish itself in the 1870s it was not until the 1880s, with the acceleration of industrialisation and the recovery from the economic depression in the latter part of the previous decade, that it became significant in the political arena. Separate and fragmented craft unions began to be brought together in regional and national federations such as the Canadian Trades and Labor Congress (founded in 1883), while increasing support was mobilised for the cause of general unionism, especially through the Knights of Labor.[3] This organisation, which originated in the US, aspired to an all-inclusive membership of working people (especially the unskilled and women). Indeed, it was the Knights of Labor in particular who attracted the wrath of the British emigrationists as well as the concern of Canadian officials.[4]

It was not so much the immigration of experienced agricultural labourers or other workers against which O'Donoghue and his colleagues railed but rather what they characterised as the 'abuses' of Canadian immigration policy. Foremost among these was the payment of various subsidies to encourage immigration and, linked with this, the entry of what were frequently referred to as 'the pauper and indigent classes'.[5] Both concerns embraced child immigrants from Britain since the emigrationists received considerable formal and informal financial help from the various Canadian governments and many of the children were (or had been) paupers, while some had been resident in industrial schools or reformatories.

Canadian trade union opposition to child immigration focused in particular on Barnardo's activities, partly because, by the mid-1880s he was bringing more and more young people to Canada and partly because of his prominent publicity. For example, in 1885 he arranged for the distribution (in Canada and Britain) of a circular asking for donations to help him in his work of bringing 'a rich stream of new blood' into Canada. The Toronto Trades and Labor Council responded angrily that it did not 'believe in "the rich stream of new blood" either figuratively or in fact ...'. Indeed, it went on to recommend that restrictions should be imposed on the immigration of British juveniles, but added that there was 'in any case an absolute necessity for strict Government supervision of the children on both sides of the Atlantic'.[6]

By 1888 the opposition of the Toronto Trades and Labor Council (largely orchestrated by O'Donoghue) had become increasingly forceful, with repeated calls for a complete prohibition to be placed on the entry of pauper and orphan children. The attacks on Barnardo became increasingly vituperative, questioning his financial probity and claiming that he, and others like him, were 'down on' the Canadian trade unions because 'they laid bare the reasons why such leeches should no longer be allowed to impose on Canada's generosity'.[7]

The pressure on the government from organised labour to curb immigration continued throughout the difficult winter of 1888 and into 1889. A stream of reports and resolutions bombarded John Carling, the Minister of Agriculture, and every opportunity was found to publicise this opposition in both the Canadian and British press. Descriptions of the 'ample' supply of agricultural labourers already in the country were relayed as well as information about the amount of distress (especially in Toronto) and about the number who had to be assisted in different ways, many of whom, it was pointed out, were recent immigrants.[8] Particular examples were seized on, not least from a combing of the British press. For instance, it had been reported that the Thanet board of guardians was intending to send 14 children to Canada, but first they were to be transferred to a Barnardo Home pending their departure.[9] The Toronto Trades and Labor Council charged that, as a result, they would gain entry to Canada under the 'specious guise' of a philanthropic organisation.

However, it was not only the Toronto Trades and Labor Council that so vigorously attacked the arrival of immigrants in the 1880s. At each of the annual conferences held by the Dominion Trades and Labor Council from 1886 to 1889 resolutions were passed deploring all forms of assisted immigration.[10] In 1889, for instance, a motion was adopted to the effect that:

> ... the continued and systematic expenditure of large sums of money in encouraging to this country paupers, indigents and orphans from abroad, is a gross injustice to the people of Canada, and in particular to the working classes; therefore ... it is the imperative duty of the Government to ... abolish the existing immigration system.[11]

However, frequent and clamorous though the trade union protests were they won no official concessions. Indeed, each particular charge was fended off and the general thrust of the criticism rebutted. Attempts were made, therefore, to increase the pressure. For example, the Toronto Trades and Labor Council issued a circular in 1890 entitled *To Organised Labour*. It began:

> The wage-earners of Canada do not, nor have they in the past, opposed the immigration to Canada of those who out of their own means and of their free will paid their way to Canada. The fight is against a system ... through which a host of officials and parasites of the usual philanthropic stamp live and fatten thereon ... and in doing so help to keep congested an over-supply in this country.[12]

In 1889 the Canadian Royal Commission on the Relationship between Capital and Labour had published its report that painted a grim picture of conditions in the proliferating factories and workshops of the emergent industrial age.[13] Such evidence was seized on by the trade union movement in its campaign for better protection against accidents and disease in the workplace, for reduced hours of work, and for various prohibitions to be placed on the employment of children. In this respect, at least, O'Donoghue and his colleagues did concern themselves with the well-being of juvenile workers rather than concentrating on the threat that their employment posed to the achievement of secure employment and fair wages for adults.

At the same time every opportunity was taken to highlight the scourge of unrestricted immigration. In 1890, for example, the Ontario Prison Reform Commission of Inquiry heard evidence from organised labour. Although O'Donoghue was its principal witness the commission did include A.F. Jury who was also a member of the Toronto Trades and Labor Council. When it came to the issue of child immigration he was the most persistent questioner – of O'Donoghue, Barnardo, Kelso and Stark (of the Toronto police).[14] O'Donoghue endeavoured to connect policies of assisted immigration with the growing burden of criminality, by claiming that there were large proportions of 'foreign-born' (that is, recent immigrants) in prisons and semi-penal institutions. He further maintained that immigrant children contributed to this burden, an opinion substantiated by Inspector Stark. In short, British orphan and pauper children were being 'dumped' in Canada as cheap labour, cheap labour that was likely to end up in its prisons and reformatories. O'Donoghue must have regarded as something of a victory the commission's conclusion that:

> The importation of children taken from the reformatories, refuges and workhouses of the old world [is] … fraught with much danger and … unless conducted with the utmost care and prudence [will] … swell the ranks of the criminal classes of this country.[15]

There was another opportunity for the trade union movement to put forward its views in 1894 at a conference on child saving that had been organised by Kelso who had been appointed the previous year to be superintendent of neglected and dependent children under the Ontario Children's Protection Act. One of the most controversial matters at the conference was the immigration of British children. O'Donoghue was a participant and reiterated the unions' opposition, but, on this occasion, he also maintained that many of those in the labour movement had been brought to Canada as British waifs and that 'their stories of the treatment they received in the country places before they reached the age of manhood are of a character to make an ordinary Christian's blood curdle'.[16] Such remarks were seized on eagerly by the press.

Thus, throughout the 1890s in these and other ways O'Donoghue and his colleagues were able to keep the issue of immigration policy, including child immigration, at the forefront of their lobbying. For example, the regular reports of the Select Standing Committee on Agriculture and Colonisation provided an opportunity for the trade unionists to scrutinise the evidence of witnesses and, where this aided their cause, to exploit it. In 1895, for instance, Alexander Burgess, the Deputy Minister in the Department of the Interior (which had assumed responsibility for immigration in 1892), told the committee that 85 per cent of Barnardo children sent to Canada had, in adulthood, succeeded in managing or owning their own farms. O'Donoghue promptly wrote to the Minister of the Interior asking for evidence of this claim.[17] The figure had been provided by Owen (Barnardo's Canadian agent) who was therefore invited to reply. His deputy wrote that the figure had been a 'best estimate'.[18] However, it was later maintained that Owen's original report to Burgess had been 'mis-quoted'. Owen had written: '… fully eighty-five per cent are permanently and definitely established on the land'.[19]

At the same time that this mis-quotation was being exposed by the Toronto Trades and Labor Council the sad case of 16-year-old George Green became the subject of extensive press coverage. George, who had been emigrated by

Barnardos, died while placed on the farm of Helen Findlay. She was charged with his manslaughter but was later acquitted.[20] Neighbours bore witness that the boy had been badly beaten and neglected and that he was 'lame, knock-kneed, hump-backed and cross-eyed; that his mouth was crooked and [that] he was short-sighted and of weak intellect'.[21] The Toronto Trades and Labor Council sent its views on the case to Prime Minister Mackenzie Bowell. It said little about the terrible fate of George Green but concentrated instead (as much other public commentary did) on the question of why a boy with such impairments had been selected for Canada. How was it possible, O'Donoghue asked, that he had passed Barnardos' medical examinations in Britain as well as those of the Dominion immigration service? The obvious lack of rigour, it was argued, provided yet further proof that the $2 subsidy should be abolished and 'the importation of children ... as carried out by Dr Barnardo and others prohibited'.[22]

Although none of these attacks persuaded the government to change its policy, they did contribute to the growing weight of criticism and outright opposition to child immigration and served to keep the administration on the defensive. However, in 1896 the Conservative government was defeated. Laurier's Liberal Party assumed power (which it was to hold until 1911) and Clifford Sifton became the new Minister of the Interior. Not only was he more sympathetic to the labour movement than his predecessors but he had (as O'Donoghue reminded him) been recorded as saying that 'the whole question of immigration had to be studied anew, from top to bottom, and a radical change made'.[23] Indeed, he had already said that juvenile immigration was 'one of the most objectionable features of the system pursued by the late Government'.[24] As if to underline his sympathy for trade union views he appointed Jury to be Dominion immigration agent in Liverpool, charging him, among other things, to look into the operation of the British societies concerned with child emigration.

O'Donoghue and his colleagues became more willing to co-operate and to compromise with government, not least because, as Parr points out, Sifton sought to draw a distinction between the immigration of wage labourers and that of so-called 'agriculturalists' who would settle the 'new' lands in the west and become self-employed proprietors.[25] Furthermore, if they were to be successful such people were likely to come from essentially 'peasant' backgrounds rather than from urban Britain. A second reason for the reduction of the labour movement's opposition to immigration was, as Parr also notes, that by 1896 men such as O'Donoghue and Jury aspired to a 'place in the councils of power and patronage of the Liberal Party'.[26] In the language of modern political analysis they were 'co-opted' by the Laurier government, in effect becoming 'Lib-Labs' in the terminology of the time. Jury, as we have seen, accepted a post in Liverpool and in 1900 O'Donoghue was appointed as Canada's first fair-wage officer in the new Department of Labour.

The decline of union antagonism towards child immigration as the nineteenth century drew to its close was also related to the establishment of the first legislation aimed at safeguarding children from harm and exploitation. In 1893 the province of Ontario passed the Children's Protection Act, with other provinces following suit soon afterwards. Kelso, the new superintendent of neglected and dependent children under the Act, began to press for the 'government inspection of immigration agencies; guarantees by the agencies that only normal and healthy children would be brought into the country, and the employment of sufficient staff to supervise the children in their new homes'.[27] These and other proposals were adopted in the 1897 Ontario Act to Regulate Juvenile Immigration. Kelso's responsibilities were extended to include the inspection of juvenile immigrants and, by the end of 1897, he had produced a comprehensive report on the subject[28] in which he contended that if the Act were carefully operated (which by and large it was not), most of the objections, like those of latent criminality that O'Donoghue had employed to strengthen his case, would disappear. The important point was that Kelso appeared, at least in part, to acknowledge the case articulated by organised labour. Furthermore, as we have seen, in 1900 the Dominion government eventually appointed an inspector of child immigration (Bogue Smart) who, as well as giving oversight to the well-being of British Poor Law children, collected information and reported on the whole enterprise. Furthermore, as Kelso maintained in his first report as superintendent of juvenile immigration, with the new Ontario Act it would 'be possible to remedy some of the abuses complained of in the past'; he also maintained that public opinion was 'so much against these children that all sorts of iniquities against them are prevalent, and the Homes have practically abandoned the attempt to secure convictions in the courts'.[29]

Finally, confronted with the mass emigration to Canada from all over Europe that gathered momentum around the turn of the century, but particularly between 1903 and 1913,[30] the proportion of child immigrants sank to relative insignificance. At the same time the economic depression was lifting. In the Toronto area, for instance, although wages continued to fall during the first part of the 1890s they had recovered to regain their 1891 level by 1902.[31]

Thus, the opposition of organised labour to child immigration was concentrated in the years from about 1888 to 1895. Thereafter it began to wane. But how influential was it in the politics of child emigration during the earlier period? There are three points to be made. First, trade union opposition was combined with opposition from other quarters in Canada to cause governments to be cautious about the outward appearances of their policies towards child immigration. Time and again both federal and provincial governments were at pains to explain that they played no *official* role in the organisation of this immigration. Faced with any criticism they fell back on the fact that it was the work of independent and charitable bodies. It might be argued, therefore, that because of the particular form that it took, the opposition that the labour movement spearheaded gave the government every incentive *not* to develop any forms of official regulation or control.

The second point to be noted is that the opposition of organised labour also made bodies like Barnardos extremely sensitive to criticism. They were at pains to present their work as almost faultless and, whenever there was an accusation of malpractice, rather than giving it serious attention, which might have resulted in improvements in the condition of the children, it was played down. Similarly, because of the opposition there appears to have been a good deal of collusion between the agencies and the Dominion government for mutual defence. For example, the emigrationists all readily gave undertakings that any 'troublesome' child would be repatriated. Furthermore, in order to combat criticism of the system there was a heavy concentration on all sides on whether or not the children were 'giving satisfaction'. Given that emphasis the feelings, anxieties or dangers to which the children were prey became of secondary importance. In short, because the criticisms levelled by opponents such as the labour movement were not usually centred on the welfare of the children, the steps taken to counteract them were equally lacking in that respect.

The third point about the political influence of the trade union movement on child immigration turns on the state of organised labour at the time. Even by 1911 union membership in Canada only amounted to about five per cent of those gainfully employed in that year.[32] Admittedly, proportions were higher in the cities – especially Toronto and in industrial towns like Hamilton – but as a national political force to be reckoned with union influence was of only limited importance. That was not necessarily true in the sphere of local and city politics in areas where the unions had established themselves more firmly. Nor was it irrelevant that there was fear in the commercial and political establishments that the power of organised labour would grow, unless restrained. Furthermore, in order to understand the attitude of the labour movement in the 1880s it is important to appreciate the role of children's employment in the preceding years as a retarding influence on the development of a Canadian working-class movement. In the printing trade, for example, the unionists spoke of 'the Monster evil – the bane and curse of every printer ... the indiscriminate employment of apprentices'.[33] It is not without significance, of course, that both O'Donoghue and Jury were printers by trade and had been involved in the Ottawa printers' strikes in the early 1870s. During that time the *Ottawa Citizen* managed to publish a shortened paper in which it blatantly advertised for 'untrained boys' and 'bright girls' to replace its striking workforce.[34] Such strike-breaking devices would not have been forgotten.

III The Disquiet of the Civic Authorities and the Charities

We have seen that in the early years of child immigration the emigrationists were able to enlist considerable support from certain local communities. Reception Homes were provided, either rent-free or at a considerably reduced cost. Prominent citizens were persuaded to act as supervisors, albeit at a superficial level. Some local newspapers lent their active support, and donations were forthcoming. However, such goodwill and inducements were mainly to be found in the vicinity of smaller towns. The reaction of the more industrialised areas and the cities was less favourable, and became openly hostile from the 1880s onwards, especially in Toronto. Some of the reasons why Toronto so vigorously opposed the immigration of 'pauper and orphan children' echoed those voiced by the trade union movement, not least because of the influence that it had gained within the city council. For example, E.F. Clarke (who had been arrested as one of the members of the printers' strike committee in 1872) became mayor in 1883. However, even before Clarke's arrival as mayor there had been regular letters from the Mayor's office to the Minister of Agriculture exhorting the government to prevent 'infirm and useless people being sent out'.[35] This reflected serious concerns about where responsibility for indigent immigrants lay. When they were unable to find work, fell sick or committed offences, on whom should the cost of dealing with them fall? The city's view was that the Dominion should foot the bill since, it was argued, 'they' had been instrumental in assisting poor or otherwise inadequate people to come to Canada. Typically, central government's response was to deny any such responsibility, particularly by drawing attention to the decision of the 1871 Dominion–Provincial conference on immigration that, once they had landed, immigrants became the responsibility of the provincial governments.[36] That being the case, the city argued, it was high time that a halt was called to all *assisted* immigration since this was what brought to Canada the class of people which, it believed, swelled the population of its hospitals and penal institutions as well as being a drain on its public and charitable resources; and this 'class' certainly included child immigrants. The question at issue was how far those who, in one way or another, became dependent on the cities *were* immigrants, and pauper immigrants at that. Furthermore, to what extent did immigrant children contribute to the problem? But such questions were only gradually asked and, even then, not adequately answered.

The fact that so much city opposition focused on the immigration of paupers sprang, in large part, from the widespread contemporary assumption that a close relationship existed between an inability to find work, fecklessness, disease and criminality, and for congenital reasons the children were believed to harbour these ingrained predispositions, predispositions which, even if not at first apparent, would become so later. Furthermore, there was little acknowledgement that most of them were not placed in the cities where such social problems were greatest, although there was a belief that they, like so many other young people, were liable to be drawn towards such centres. Certainly in the 1880s immigrants (although hardly the immigrant children) contributed to the problems of casual labour and unemployment in cities like Toronto, but that had no necessary connection with the claim that they also contributed disproportionately to criminality, although their poverty may well have meant that they were more often sick and were forced to seek various forms of relief. That these connections *were* made in such an indiscriminate fashion is surely part of the history of the stigmatisation that newcomers and the poor everywhere are liable to encounter, especially in times of economic depression.

Although Toronto spearheaded the civic opposition to pauper and 'orphan' immigration, it was not alone. For instance, in his first report as superintendent of British immigrant children in 1898, Kelso recorded that 'numerous petitions' had been received from county councils demanding the prohibition of child immigration or, at least, strict regulations 'guarding against [the] indiscriminate shipment' of those who were 'sickly or vicious'.[37] However, such opposition to child immigrants has to be seen in the context of the undeveloped nature of Canada's welfare services at the time and particularly in the light of fear that, sooner or later, the demands on them would outstrip the available resources or impose an increasingly heavy burden of taxation.

Similar apprehensions were also evident among charitable organisations, and they too contributed to the groundswell of opposition to child immigration. Like the trade union movement and the city authorities they mainly referred to the matter in connection with the more generalised issue of the arrival of paupers and other 'unfit' people. Similarly, the bulk of the opposition emanated from those organisations that were active in the cities, in particular Toronto and Montreal. For example, at meetings of the combined city charities of Toronto in 1883 and 1884 critical resolutions were passed and duly sent to J.H. Pope, the Minister in Ottawa. J.E. Pell appears to have been the moving force behind some of these initiatives as well as Goldwin Smith.[38] Pell was the secretary of the St George's Society in Toronto that worked to help English immigrants on their arrival (there was a comparable St Andrew's Society for the Scots). In May 1884, after a bad winter, he wrote, in some desperation, to Lowe (the Deputy Minister in the Department of Agriculture) to say that: 'We are now being overrun with destitute Emigrants.... What is to be done? ... *It is certain something must be done at once*'[39] (original emphasis). Lowe thanked him for the Society's efforts on behalf of the immigrants but held fast to the position that any help must come from the provincial government since the people in question had already arrived.[40]

Pell's fellow secretary in the sister Society in Montreal, Hollis, had already written to the minister in a similar vein at the end of February 1884. He complained that English immigrants were coming out at precisely the wrong time of year when labour was not in demand and when 'our own resident population are more than ordinarily dependent upon charity. The result has been to throw many indigent strangers upon our Society, which is ill able to bear the strain'. Hollis asked that the issue should be referred to the Colonisation and Immigration Committee of the House of Commons.[41] Cruikshank, the secretary of the Montreal Protestant House of Industry and Refuge, also wrote to the minister soon afterwards expressing similar sentiments and likewise asking what he should do about the problem. He too contended that responsibility for destitute immigrants should devolve on the Dominion government rather than the provinces.[42]

Undoubtedly, the winter of 1883–84 was something of a turning point in terms of the demands being made on the city charities. Early in 1884 Donaldson, the Toronto immigration agent, had informed Lowe that there were numerous destitute Irish in the city being supported by charity. Many had been laid off from the building industry because of the severe weather. They often had large families and it was common for the children to be sent out to work, particularly, he noted, boys over the age of 14.[43] Later Lowe wrote to Donaldson, indicating that he should use his funds discreetly to encourage as many of the destitute Irish as possible to go south across the border.[44]

At about the same time, in 1884, David Spence, the secretary of the Ontario Immigration Department, wrote to Lowe about the distress in Toronto, especially among pauper immigrants, stressing that 'feeling has been somewhat strongly expressed in the public press ... the people of the cities are afraid of laying the foundations of pauperism'. Because of this Spence told Lowe that the Ontario government had decided that it would 'no longer ... give assistance to any class of workhouse or "union" people, either in the way of meals or railway passes'.[45] Clearly, in such circumstances, the limited resources of the charitable bodies were becoming exceedingly strained but, again, it is difficult to conclude (as they did) that those who called on their services were recent immigrants, although this is certainly possible as they would be the ones most likely to have an uncertain foothold in even the casual labour market.

The opposition of the Canadian charitable bodies to child immigration was not only a reflection of the additional demands that were being placed on them. There were, as with the Toronto Trades and Labor Council and the city authorities, complaints about the *quality* of the immigrants. The Canadian Girls' Friendly Society provides an example. Towards the end of 1885 a resolution was forwarded to Carling, the minister, explaining that 'through our connections with the Parent Society in England we were induced to take up the work [of female emigration, including girls]' but, it was stressed, the Society had withdrawn from the work completely since it was 'utterly unworthy' of their support until it was taken out of the hands of '*irresponsible* individuals'[46] (original emphasis). The individuals were irresponsible, it was asserted, because the women and girls whom they brought out were of such poor quality and because, as a result, Canada was being used as a 'dumping ground', the phrase repeatedly used in all manner of criticisms of the prevailing 'system' of immigration.

It should not be concluded from these few examples, however, that there was a well-orchestrated opposition from Canadian charities to child immigration – at least not until much later.[47] Their opposition was usually unco-ordinated and, in any case, it did not focus so clearly on children in the way that the trade unionists did. That, presumably, was because until the 1890s, with the formation of the Children's Aid Societies (CASs), *children's* charities in particular were few and far between, that is apart from the various Homes, often with particular religious affiliations.

IV The Doctors Express Alarm

Parr attributes some importance to the opposition of Canadian doctors to child immigration, although most of her evidence is drawn from the 1888 report of the proceedings of the Select Standing Committee on Agriculture and Colonisation.[48] This certainly provides quite a remarkable testimony to the way in which a few doctors, who were also members of parliament, indulged in a veritable orgy of wild and unsubstantiated invective against child immigrants. How far they actually believed what they said and how far they were reflecting the fears and apprehensions of their constituents or fellow doctors is unclear. But because they were doctors their views were likely to have carried weight, claiming, as they did, to speak of medical matters from their own direct experience. In fact there were five doctor MPs on this particular select committee but only three of them spoke in unqualified condemnation of the physical and mental condition of the children. The leading voice was that of Dr Ferguson, a conservative from Welland. During the 1888 sitting of the committee, it was he who first introduced the topic of the children brought to Canada. In his opinion the country:

> ... might just as well import the virus of disease and spread surgeons among our people and inoculate them with the disease [syphilis].... The majority of these children are the offal of the most depraved characters in the cities of the old country.[49]

Three other members, including Laurie (whom we met in connection with Birt's scheme in Nova Scotia, but who was now an MP) immediately intervened to say that in their experience the great majority of the children were healthy and did well; they were certainly in great demand. Dr Wilson, a liberal from Elgin, thereon sprang to the defence of Ferguson's view. He contended that the children brought to Canada:

> ... if not already more or less diseased are frequently the offspring of diseased fathers or mothers and nearly the greater proportion of them ... are diseased in the manner that Dr Ferguson has stated, that is tainted with syphillitic [sic] and perhaps may live to 20 or 30 and die of some consumptive disease.... I do not think that because a farmer desires to get hold of a half grown child without bearing the expense of raising that child, that they should endanger the future welfare of the country.[50]

The way in which medical status was employed to neutralise contrary evidence was exemplified when Dr Wilson said that he could understand how another member, not being a doctor, was unable to understand the dangers that the child immigrants posed, pointing out that:

> Any family would be extremely careless and injudicious to allow one of these little waifs to come into the family, because we know that the syphillitic [sic] taint, although the child may appear healthy, may

be carried to the other children of the family playing with them and they become diseased in the same manner.[51]

Ferguson then drew attention to the link between disease, in particular syphilis, and illegitimacy. They were, he maintained, inextricably related. Since the children were the products of 'illegitimate transactions' they were 'more or less mentally diseased and unfit to go among the people of this country'.[52]

Both the chairman of the committee (White of Renfrew) and Lowe (who was appearing for the Department of Agriculture) pressed Ferguson and Wilson to quantify their claims. Wilson would go no further than saying that the 'great majority' of the children were tainted, but implied that it took time for the full consequences to emerge: 'as mother and father so daughter and son ... you must expect the natural tendency of these children to be transplanted if they mix ... or if they raise children of their own'.[53] Ferguson maintained that the 'vast majority' were as he described and by way of substantiation claimed that the only criminal cases in the court at Welland the previous year were 'these girls blackmailing men and prosecuting them for rape'. He had, he said, attended two children of 'these girls', both of whom died in infancy from the effects of syphilis.[54]

At this point another member suggested that since the doctors could so readily diagnose the disease in their patients all that was required was an obligatory medical examination before the children landed. Yes, said Ferguson, but 'the mental disease you cannot see'. Roome, one of the other doctors, intervened to say that although he agreed with much of what his colleagues had said, he had seen no signs of 'the disease', although he too had had a good deal to do with immigrant children. He knew many who were growing up 'to be smart, active young men and women, and show no signs of disease'. Nevertheless, he conceded that 'it may be running in the blood and may come out in future generations'.[55] Then Dr MacDonald (a liberal from Huron) added his voice to the views of Ferguson and Wilson, even though he admitted to having had little experience of the British children, but in his community he had met 'quite a number' afflicted with chronic skin diseases and 'a syphillitic [sic] tendency in their system'.[56] It was, he admitted, a very difficult question because:

> Unless it has developed in some way, it would be very hard for a medical man to say whether the child was inoculated or not. Perhaps ten years after coming to this country it may manifest itself. If, however ... these children are brought from those districts where immorality, crime and syphillitic [sic] disease prevail, we may rest assured that most of them will be tainted by the same poisons when brought out here.[57]

Dr Sproule (the fifth medical member of the select committee) made a more considered contribution. He granted that a few of the children might be affected by congenital syphilis, but no more than about one in 100 in his experience, and, in any case, the need for population was urgent. Most of the children had turned out to be desirable settlers and 'farmers have felt the benefit of them'.[58] He considered that the answer to the problem was the introduction of more rigorous medical examinations.

The views of the three most critical doctors on the committee were widely reported and may well have added extra weight to the wilder press statements about the condition of British children. However, they were not lone voices within the medical profession at the time and later. Many articles on the general theme of the 'hereditarian' threat posed by the immigration of those 'of degraded and depraved parentage' appeared regularly in such journals as the *Canadian Lancet*, the *Canadian Journal of Medicine and Surgery* and the *Public Health Journal*, as McLaren has pointed out.[59] However, Ferguson at least may have been silenced for future occasions because, as Rye triumphantly reported to Lowe,[60] his wife had applied for one of her girls and, shrewd tactician that she was, she had acceded to the request. Perhaps because of this the doctors adopted a more restrained tone when the Select Standing Committee on Agriculture and Colonisation met again the following year (1889), choosing to emphasise the need for prospective child immigrants to be given more thorough medical examinations.[61] They also turned their attention to criticising the government for allowing into Canada children brought from British reformatories.[62]

As continuing members of the Select Committee on Agriculture and Colonisation sitting in 1894,[63] Drs MacDonald and Roome were still urging the instigation of rigorous medical inspections. They argued that although the children were medically inspected in Britain, the doctors by whom the inspections were conducted were not responsible to the Canadian government. Furthermore, even if there were doubt about their certificates being in order when children were examined at Québec it was impossible, MacDonald claimed, to determine their physical condition by a superficial examination.[64]

When pressed by Burgess, the Deputy Minister of the Interior, for evidence of this, MacDonald reverted to citing claims that many of the children 'turned out badly'. This was, Burgess believed, an exaggeration fed by a few isolated but newsworthy cases that contributed to a 'pretty strong sentiment, almost amounting to prejudice, growing up in the minds of the Canadian people in regard to this class of immigration'. Nevertheless, he was sure that it was 'both right and proper that the farmer and his wife should be more than particular about the antecedents of the persons whose contact with their children must be so close, and whose influence upon their life and character must be so great'.[65]

Although the doctors on the select committee did mention syphilis by name as the disease about which they were mainly concerned, more often than not it was referred to in a veiled fashion. That should not disguise the profound concern in the medical profession and elsewhere about its threat to public health and national degeneration, not least because of the sense of powerlessness to control its spread. Indeed, it was not until 1905 that the causal organism of the disease was identified, and only in the following year that its diagnosis became possible with the availability of the Wasserman test. Furthermore, until the discovery of salvasan in 1910, treatment (with mercury, for example) was largely ineffective and certainly dangerous, but the new treatment was expensive, long drawn-out and unpleasant. It was only with the introduction of penicillin in the 1940s that the disease could be treated successfully and cheaply.[66]

It is against this background that the extent of medical anxiety about the spread of syphilis during the 1880s and 1890s has to be understood. Indeed, it was a concern widely expressed in other countries as well. However, why was there such alarm about the threat posed by British immigrant children? There are several explanations. In the first place the disease was linked to all forms of migration. Beyond this, as Davidson and Hall have emphasised, there was a deep anxiety about the congenital nature of syphilis.[67] In addition to all this there was a widespread conviction that the 'distasteful disease' was due to promiscuity and that that arose from 'a sub-normality of intelligence'.[68] Consequently, illegitimacy was not only regarded as the result of promiscuity but also as a sign of inherited low intelligence and probably of syphilis and other deficiencies as well.

The fact that the British immigrant children were thought likely to be illegitimate, or at least the offspring of 'poor stock', made them targets for the prevailing fears about the dreaded effects of syphilis. It is perhaps difficult today to appreciate the magnitude of these fears, not only in Canada but elsewhere too. For example, in Britain a Royal Commission on the subject was appointed in 1913, the findings of which, published three years later, did little to dispel anxieties.[69] Among other things it reported that in the London Poor Law infirmaries of Shoreditch, Westminster and Paddington 20 per cent of the patients had had a positive reaction to the Wasserman test[70] and that in the Feltham borstal the same proportion of boys was considered to have shown one or more signs of congenital syphilis.[71]

The contemporary political and social significance of syphilis was increased by its obvious relationship with eugenic concerns. As the British Royal Commission's report put it, not only did the disease have 'grave and far-reaching' effects for the individual but for 'the race' as well.[72] If syphilis (and other venereal diseases) could not be controlled the *quality* of the population would suffer. There would be a decline in intelligence, exacerbated by the propensity of the 'sub-normal' to reproduce excessively.

Of course, there was little or no evidence that British immigrant children manifested syphilitic symptoms, but that did not quell fears about them; the disease could be latent. In this, of course, what the outspoken doctors on the various select committees of the 1880s and 1890s had to say about diagnosis was contradictory. On the one hand, they maintained that because of its latency it could not be readily detected while, on the other, they called for more rigorous medical examinations to prevent infected children entering Canada. One of the complicating factors was that the consequences of poverty and early malnutrition (such as stunted growth and eye or ear disorders) could be mistaken for syphilitic symptoms. Finally, as Hall has pointed out, fears about venereal disease and its effects on a whole population were always likely to be focused on the assumed culpability of marginal groups such as the British immigrant children.[73]

V Opposition in the Press

It is clear that the press, in Toronto particularly, both reflected and moulded public opinion about the immigration of 'paupers and orphans' during the 1880s and on into the 1890s. By and large the coverage was critical and disparaging, sometimes echoing the grosser prejudices and wilder generalisations about the children that were expressed elsewhere.

The most comprehensive study of the press and child immigration is that undertaken by Turner.[74] However, he dealt only with the reception by the Ontario papers of Doyle's critical report in 1875. Their response to it was entirely hostile: no fault could be found, it was maintained, with the activities of either Rye or Macpherson. Turner interpreted this as being primarily an example of 'provincial patriotism', although considerations of economic self-interest were not absent. It was also his view that the government's reaction to the Doyle report was reinforced by what the Ontario press had to say.[75] For example, *The Toronto Globe* wished 'Miss Rye, and all such practical workers for the good of the helpless, every success in their work of faith and labour of love'.[76] This was a far cry from the sentiments towards pauper and child immigration that were being expressed by the 1880s, and suggests that economic conditions had had their effect on public opinion. Wagner points out, for example, that 'by the time Barnardo arrived in Canada [in 1882] the campaign against child emigration had already begun'.[77] She notes the kind of attack on child immigration that was being sustained in papers like *The Toronto News*. In May 1884 it carried an editorial saying that Canada had enough orphan and abandoned children in its own streets and castigated the 'impudence of a large class of pseudo-philanthropists who make a trade of shipping outcast children from England'.[78] *The Toronto News* was followed some time afterwards by *The Toronto Globe* that warned against the unselective importation of British children, maintaining that 'street waifs and inmates of reformatories, refuges and lodging houses ... are not the classes with which to build up a strong nationality'.[79] This kind of opposition to the 'importation' of British children became a familiar feature of press reporting throughout the 1880s and into the twentieth century. Whenever one of them was involved in a crime or a scandal the event was seized on by the city-based papers as evidence of the undesirability of allowing such children into the country, although outside the main cities the response of provincial publications was more mixed and tended to reflect the pattern of local economic interests in the employment of the young immigrants. However, it is noteworthy that in whichever newspaper hostile reports appeared they usually attacked those who brought the children to Canada rather than the children themselves. The 'impudent philanthropists' were not Canadian and were suspected of exploiting the opportunities that the country offered for their own ends. Barnardo, in particular, attracted much criticism. For instance, *The Toronto*

World reported in 1891 that 'early this month Dr Barnardo sent a shipment of criminal pauperism to Canada ... the good Doctor appears on the horizon and wins the applause of an admiring world by exporting them to Canada'.[80] It is difficult to judge how far such press comment served to inflame antagonism towards child immigration or whether it did little more than reflect prevailing attitudes. Either way it seems likely that what appeared in the principal newspapers from the 1880s onwards, but not initially, helped to sustain the various anxieties that surrounded the arrival of British children.

VI Needed but not Wanted?

There is no doubt that Canadian farmers needed the help of young British immigrants. Nevertheless, they often complained that the children were not up to doing what was expected of them. In the frequently used phase of the time, they 'did not give satisfaction'. Indeed, as Parr has pointed out, 'even amongst those groups in rural and small town Ontario whose economic interests the British children served, there was considerable distrust and distaste for youngsters regarded as the discarded offspring of British slums'.[81] An opportunity to air such views was provided by the system of local farmer-correspondents that the Ontario Department of Agriculture had established and whose reports on local matters were published in its regular *Bulletins*: that for June 1895 was particularly full of opinions about the children.[82] Extracts from the reports from various places in the province provide a sense of the kind of feelings that were harboured towards the children, such as: 'We would rather do without domestic servants than introduce some of these imported English girls, as they are too often detrimental to the morals of the community'; 'There is a demand for experienced farm servants who are willing to work, but there is a surplus of boys arriving from England ... without experience of farming [they] are often a hindrance rather than a help during harvest'; 'If the Government would encourage the importation of good servant girls and do away with the pauper trash, it would be better all round'; 'We need more good men, but have no room for the criminal classes or their offspring'; 'There are too many useless boys from the Homes'. There was only one report that suggested that more boys and girls – especially girls – would be welcome. It is difficult to say how representative these outbursts were. Nonetheless, they were widely publicised in the press.[83] It was this that doubtless led to the matter coming to the attention of Burgess, the Deputy Minister in the Department of the Interior,[84] who became concerned that so many of these statements were 'decidedly unfavourable ... in regard to the general policy of child immigration'. For that reason he asked for the names and addresses of the informants.[85] The list was duly supplied and letters sent asking on what grounds they had made their comments.[86] Several of the replies remain on file. Whether others did not reply or their letters were lost is not clear. Three are sufficiently interesting to quote at some length. The first was from one McPhee, who wrote that:

... the farmers in this section are practising the greatest economy in view of the poor prospect their crop is presenting, or holding fast. One outcome ... is the employing of boys for low wages who are expected to perform men's work....The selection of boys is not made through the scarcity of men, for in this immediate locality 10 men are unemployed ... and in search of work – and good men at that. And in the face of the fact that many of our sons and daughters have to seek employment in the States & such are brought from the slums of London to do work on farms and demoralize our youth. There is no need whatever for importing [them].

He went on to give an example of the boys' faults. On another farm a boy was

... employed in milking cows in the yard [–] he was annoyed at the cows switching their tails to protect themselves from the flies. This picture of depravity cut the tails off at the root.... His employer and this lad engaged in a combat and one of the results was that the latter left.[87]

This letter exemplifies, on the one hand, a sober analysis of the general problem that was broadly sympathetic to the boys, while on the other, it turns to emphasise their 'depravity'. The theme of cruelty to animals is interesting, since it reappears on several occasions in farmers' criticisms of the boys they employed.

Another letter from a farmer–correspondent was less literate and more vitriolic. Farmer Amos wrote to tell Burgess that he had had three orphan boys but that he found them 'lazey saucey stupid Greatly lacking in ordinary intelligence. Immoral swearing very disobedient Liars of the first water also thieving'.[88] However, some farmers made a distinction between the boys they employed and those whom they had heard about. Farmer White, for instance, wrote that he had an excellent boy, but found

... the great majority ... indolent, impertinent, and not to be depended upon. They will skulk in your absence every time. I am surprised the Minister of the Interior is not better informed about these Homes boys. There are plenty of Canadian boys who have practically no home. If the Government would place these boys in an available position for the Farmers of Canada to reach they would be doing something that would not jeopardise this fair country in years to come.[89]

There is no direct evidence to indicate what impact these replies had on the Department's general view of child immigration, but there was yet another outburst in the reports submitted to the 1898 *Bulletins*. Although these were similar to the earlier ones the competitive theme between the Homes' children and local young people was emphasised rather more. On this occasion, however, the

Department of the Interior not only wrote to the correspondents but instructed Doyle, its immigration agent stationed at Québec, to visit some of the farmers who had reported most unfavourably on the children in order to obtain their views directly. As Pereira, the assistant secretary, explained to him, this was necessary because great weight was being attached to the reports by the public, largely via the press.[90] Doyle submitted detailed reports on his visits.[91] Farmer Altan wanted to stop the immigration for the children's sake, 'as many to his knowledge are not kindly treated and overworked by the farmers'. Doyle went on to report that in Altan's view 'farmers without children take them to work for little or no wages, thereby cutting out many poor boys and men of their own villages from gaining a living at home who have to go elsewhere for work'. Further, he added, 'the children as a rule are not willing to learn farming, hard to manage and not worth any wages, – in fact not worth their keep ...'. Having said all this, however, Altan was at pains to explain that the boy he had had for six years was an exception, faithful and trustworthy.

Another farmer called Shiers sounded a similar note. The Homes' children, he said, 'seriously interfere with the prospects of native children in obtaining employment in their own villages'. Elsewhere Doyle only saw his farmer namesake's wife. Mrs Doyle reported that 'her husband formed his opinion ... from the newspapers of their [the children] not doing well'. They had had a boy for 14 years and he was very good. Another farmer's wife, Mrs Twiss, maintained that she 'would not take another Home child, the trouble in teaching them and the responsibility of bringing them up is too great'.

In general the substance of most of the complaints turned on five shortcomings in the children: namely, that they would not be taught, that they were disobedient, that they were untruthful, that they were unreliable (for instance in feeding the cattle), and that they were liable to ill-treat the animals or damage property. In a few other cases there was reference to the bad influence that they exercised on the farmers' own children, or to boys who allegedly interfered sexually with young daughters of the family.

These *Bulletin* reports, and the letters and interviews that sprang from them, serve to illustrate several things about the nature of the opposition, albeit paradoxical, of Ontario farmers to child immigration during the 1890s. Contradictory forces were at work. On the one hand, faced with depression and falling prices for their produce, farmers looked even more keenly for the cheap (or free) labour that the children could supply. They expected this replacement labour to undertake the work that, in some instances, had previously been performed by an adult. The children often lacked both the skill and the strength to match up to these demands. The work did not get done properly and in some instances mistakes – or what the farmers tended to regard as negligence – imposed extra costs on them. The circumstances seemed to be ready-made to cause frustration, anger, resentment and abuse. Farmers almost certainly wished that they could have had better help but felt that they could not afford it. Added to this was the growing concern in rural communities about the movement of their younger population to the cities.

Immigrant children, it was felt, aggravated this situation, because they undercut wages and took the jobs that the local youth might otherwise have secured.

However, as well as the criticisms that many farmers made of the calibre of the British children, there was also an organised Ontario farming lobby that orchestrated a more direct opposition to assisted immigration, including the British children. This was the Patrons of Industry, an organisation founded in 1889 and which, four years later, boasted 100,000 members and 2,000 local clubs. As Shortt has explained, this rapid growth 'was a reflection of the precarious state of Ontario agriculture in the early 1890s'.[92] The Patrons' mouthpiece was *The Farmers' Sun*. Among other things it claimed that the surge of immigration that had helped to open up the west had thereby jeopardised the interests of Ontario farmers. Therefore, it demanded that a stop be put to 'trumping up immigration out of the dissatisfied and the n'er-do-well class ...'.[93] Surprisingly perhaps, these sentiments spilled over to include the children, probably reflecting an unresolved tension between individual necessity and the view that the depressed economic conditions of the 1890s arose in large part because of the flood of immigrants.

Despite having 17 successful candidates in the Ontario election of 1893, the Patrons movement had collapsed by the early years of the new century, largely as a result of an improvement in the economy. One of the effects of these associated developments was that the upsurge in the opposition of the farmers of Ontario to child immigration subsided. The children continued to be absorbed as cheap additions to the farm labour force, but without too many more outcries about their origins or baleful influence. What effect the intervention of the Patrons of Industry had on the demand for juvenile immigrants is difficult to judge. However, there was a marked decline in the number of applications for the children after 1897 but then a very significant increase between 1901–02 and 1902–03 (see Table 8 in chapter 8). Likewise, it is uncertain how far the other centres of opposition that have been described succeeded in lessening the number of British children being sent to Canada, but they did have two other effects. First, as Parr has concluded, the result was that 'Home children' were 'left with a heavier burden to carry'.[94] Second, because the opposition provoked defensive responses from both the emigrationists and the Dominion government they may have hindered proper attention being paid to the welfare of the children and indeed to the justification for sending them to Canada in the first place.

TEN

The Management of the Opposition in Canada

I May and June 1888

While it is difficult to follow the different ways in which the Canadian government and the emigration societies dealt with the growing volume of opposition to child immigration that developed during the 1880s and 1890s, the nature of these responses becomes more apparent if the pattern is reconstructed for a limited period when the opposition was at its height, namely, during the months of May and June 1888.

The Select Standing Committee on Agriculture and Colonisation, whose deliberations were discussed in chapter 9, met at the beginning of May 1888. It was inevitable that the sensational character of some of the assertions made during the hearing should be widely reported in the press. *The Toronto Mail*, in particular, devoted considerable space to the matter. The hostile nature of its report prompted Rye to write at length to the editor in defence of her work and in particular regarding the health of the children whom she brought to Canada. If, she argued, 'it has taken twenty years to discover such a deplorable state of affairs, surely the matter cannot be very apparent'.[1] She also wrote to Lowe (the Deputy Minister) at the Department of Agriculture in order to draw his attention to her letter. Did he approve? 'Certainly', she told him, 'no one has been here, no one has even written me – the whole attack is from the Knights of Labour – we curse the "lazy louts". '[2] Lowe replied saying that he had seen her letter and 'found the points to be very good. In fact I have cut the letter out as a *pièce pour servir*.... I quite agree with you also that the whole of this attack comes from the Knights of Labour.'[3]

In its response *The Toronto Mail* maintained that Rye had misunderstood the nature of the complaint. It was not that the children in the Homes were diseased or even that they became diseased when placed out; rather their point, and that of the doctors on the select committee, was that:

> There are other 'diseases' than those which at once manifest their presence in the body....There are diseases of the mind and of the moral nature which, inherited from parents whose lives have been spent in vice and debauchery, often fail to show themselves in the young, but develop in time into at least mental and moral weaknesses, which are transmitted to other generations.

The editorial also pointed out that there was now greater cause for concern since the Poor Law guardians in Britain were adopting emigration with greater energy in order 'to get paupers off their hands in the cheapest possible manner'.

A week later there was a debate on pauper immigration in the Canadian Senate on a motion moved by Senator McInnes, a Liberal and another doctor.[4] His motion was that 'the importation of Pauper Children and adults from the Emigration Homes and Poor Law Unions should be discouraged', and that the immigration 'of inmates of workhouses and reformatory schools should be absolutely prohibited'. He explained that he had been prompted to move the motion by what had been said about the diseased condition of British immigrant children two weeks before in the Select Standing Committee on Agriculture and Colonisation.[5]

The day before the Senate debate Senator Sanford (a Conservative from Hamilton) and manager of Stephenson's Home wrote to Lowe at the Department of Agriculture asking him to provide 'any facts coming under your notice favourable to this work [of child immigration] which I may use'.[6] Lowe sent him a copy of a memorandum that he had prepared on the advantages of child immigration that appears to have been drawn up specifically with the Senate resolution in mind. First, it set out the facts about the nature and extent of child emigration. Then it dealt with the main points of criticism that had recently been emerging. It pointed out that most of the children 'were eagerly received by the farmers', and that those about whom complaints were made were ascertained to constitute only between five per cent and seven per cent of the total.[7] Other senators who were sympathetic towards child immigration were similarly briefed. As a result a spirited and informed opposition to McInnes' motion was able to be mounted. This was made somewhat easier by the extreme nature of his claims. For example, he had maintained that it was

> ... just as reasonable to take from our forests a common wolf and try to domesticate him in a few months, and eradicate his wild and savage nature and make a serviceable dog of him, as to expect that we can go amongst the slums of London and take the offspring of crime, with the vices of generations ingrained in them, and convert them in a few months in Reformatory Schools in England into honest, virtuous and industrious people.[8]

Sanford retorted that he had not supposed that the Senate 'were to be favoured by a series of sensational articles cut from the daily journals, which in many instances are written in the interests of party'.[9] He charged McInnes with reporting the views of the select committee in a biased fashion by omitting any reference to the evidence that contradicted the views of the doctors, contradictory evidence, he was at pains to add, offered by members of McInnes' own Liberal Party. Sanford went on to point out that in Stephenson's organisation only five boys out of the 800 children brought out over a period of 13 years had been sent to gaol and only six or eight girls had been 'led astray'. When children did rebel, he felt, said Sanford, that there was often good cause. Furthermore, he informed the Senate that throughout his long association with child immigration he had never heard of any evidence of 'the loathsome disease' (syphilis) complained of by certain doctors. Any child who became 'handicapped' or permanently ill or, in the case of girls, became pregnant, was shipped back to Britain. He explained that Britain was not anxious to emigrate large numbers of children to Canada because 'they want to retain this class of boys and girls ... we have very great difficulty in getting from them as large a number as we have had up to the present time'.[10] Other senators lent their support to these views, one contending that the criticism came from those who wanted 'to make labor so scarce that they can control the price of it, and do not want immigrants to come into the country'.[11]

The tide of the debate was flowing strongly in favour of Sanford and his supporters, and thus of the Conservative government. The debate thereupon began to develop on party lines. It is clear that the attack had been mounted partly as an indictment of the government's 'national policy'. This aimed at strengthening the Canadian state both as a political and as an economic entity, particularly in relation to its powerful neighbour across the border. To this end part of the policy involved imposing higher customs tariffs; there were also two other central objectives. One was a drive to see the completion of the trans-Canada railway and the other to capture as much capital investment as possible. However, economic development, especially in the west, depended on rapid demographic growth, and that meant the encouragement of immigration. Indeed, Macdonald's Conservative government had sought to persuade the British government to provide financial support to what was referred to as 'state-aided emigration', albeit unsuccessfully.

Against such a background it is therefore unsurprising to find the Conservative government disposed towards the immigration of British children. In this Senate debate they were in a strong position to defend such immigration against the charges of the Liberal opposition. This was not only because of the unsubstantiated nature of the accusations but because those senators who had direct experience of child immigration were to be found predominantly in the government ranks. McInnes' position became increasingly vulnerable and something of a party liability. Senator Scott, Leader of the Opposition, entered the debate in order to recover lost ground. There had been a misconception, he claimed: McInnes was not attacking the institutions at Hamilton and Belleville, or Barnardo's work, or that of Rye. What was causing public alarm was the 'dumping' of large numbers of paupers in the last two years.[12] Nonetheless, despite his conciliatory intervention Scott wanted children such as the waifs and strays who had been 'picked up' in the East End of London returned to Britain.[13] As a result his contribution did little to stem the onslaught on McInnes. Clemow (Conservative of Ottawa) thought that the motion was 'exceedingly unfortunate' since it was likely to have an adverse effect on immigration in general, immigration that was much needed. In his view it was particularly deplorable that statements such as those made by

McInnes should emanate from the Senate, for they would certainly be reported in London the next day.

Senator Abbott (Leader of the House) added further weight to the assault on the motion by the Opposition. He struck a moral note, confessing that he was shocked by McInnes' 'blindness to the kind of principle which he was advocating'. He could not believe that he had 'a heart so black as to refuse to a poor helpless child the chance of growing up in honesty and virtue, which is denied to it in its own country'. Instead of relying on newspaper reports he would, he said, furnish the House with the facts as collected by the Department of Agriculture (Lowe's memorandum). For example, only 12 children had been brought out from reformatories during the past year. Surely, he argued, the first-hand experience of those who had spoken in the debate was superior to the limited experience of the doctors on the select committee. The children were a useful class of immigrants and their supply nowhere matched demand.[14]

As the debate drew to a close McInnes sprang to his own defence, largely by way of an attack on Abbott who, he asserted, had introduced gross misrepresentations. But he did back down from the terms of his motion and modified some of the remarks that he had made in his opening address. The observations that concerned the physical and moral character of immigrants were, he maintained, 'entirely directed to and intended for the criminal classes shipped from the workhouses, reformatories and prisons'.[15] He was perfectly satisfied that the children brought to Canada were, until two or three years ago, of a fairly good class. Nevertheless, before the motion was finally withdrawn McInnes discharged a few parting shots. He characterised Sanford's address as 'a nice Sunday school speech'. It was 'better to go to the wilds of Africa and bring out the savages ... than to import the ingrained criminals of London'. In any case, the doctors knew more about 'the disease' than those who had spoken against the motion – the 'virus' referred to could be 'transmitted, is transmitted, and unfortunately the sins of the parents very often are visited on the third and fourth generations'.[16]

Several things stand out from this episode of attack and defence. First, the supporters of child immigration were well organised and several of them had direct links with the emigration organisations. Second, the attack on child immigration displayed certain features that suggested that it was forming part of the Liberal opposition's general offensive against the Macdonald government's national policy. Third, the government, through its Leader in the Senate, made it clear that child immigration was to be encouraged rather than discouraged. Finally, the need for child immigration could be advocated on several grounds. There was an urgent need for more people (especially in the light of the presumed losses of young people to the US); there was a readily available moral argument, with strong overtones of Christian charity; there was the fact that the children were young and therefore more likely to be adaptable than adults; and last, but not least, there was the growing reference to statistics of rates of success. Precisely how these figures were obtained, or how reliable they were, is largely beside the point. They gave the appearance of quantitative precision and, in any case, nobody else had alternative figures with which they could be challenged. The character of the debate was thus shifted from anecdote and sensational individual cases to categories – an important political development.

Under these circumstances it was not surprising that the Senate motion was so effectively defeated (although technically withdrawn). Nevertheless, the extra-parliamentary opposition to child immigration was not quelled. Furthermore, *The Toronto Mail's* editorial in particular found its way to London and the British press.[17] In its turn the Canadian High Commissioner's office in London took steps to minimise the possible damage that this might do to the flow of emigrants. A suitable press statement was issued and the Colonial Office informed of the exaggerated nature of the charges being made. The British government and public were to be reassured that such reports were unduly sensational and that any problems that did exist were of a temporary nature.

In Canada Rye was not going to allow the initiative to slip through her hands. A fortnight after her first letter to the *Mail* she wrote again. In doing so she remarked on the fact that the doctors on the select committee had not visited her or contacted her in any way; nor had they taken up her challenge to name 20 of her children who were morally or physically inferior to the average Canadian child. She also took issue with another *Mail* editorial a few days earlier that had maintained that there were 169 children in Canadian orphan asylums who were 'immigrants and foreigners'.[18] She went on to say that Canada need not be alarmed at the workhouses sending out too many children for it had taken the chairman of one union and herself a year 'to get four children out of one school'. Then she suggested that wider damage to Canadian interests could be inflicted by the campaign that the *Mail* was conducting. Might not their articles have a deleterious effect on the London money market and Canadian prospects there more generally? 'Reading between the lines, John Bull will have to come to the conclusion that all that he has previously been told of this great country is a delusion and a snare, and that a country the size of Europe cannot support a population equal to London.'[19] The *Mail* endeavoured to counter Rye's letter in yet another editorial in the same issue. They wanted to make a distinction between paupers and others; they were especially concerned that English Poor Law guardians had been exceedingly active in building up a 'new export business'. Canada could support millions more, but not those sent only as a 'riddance'.

While Rye was confronting the opposition in the press Annie Macpherson was responding quite differently to the attacks that had been ventilated in the select committee and elsewhere, and particularly to the charges that the immigrant children were diseased. Towards the end of May 1888 she sent a telegram to Stafford, the chief immigration agent at Québec, asking him to engage a doctor at her expense to inspect the party of children that was on its way to Canada. Stafford promptly wrote to Lowe at the Department of Agriculture. 'Her object', he suggested, 'is no doubt ... to satisfy the Minister and the public here that her children are healthy and free from apparent disease.' Although the discussions in Parliament and in the press would have caused the emigrationists 'to be more careful in their selections', he doubted whether a medical inspection on arrival 'would give us more security, and the Doctor's certificate might be used to show that any disease developed in future was contracted in this country'.[20] Nevertheless, Lowe instructed him that medical inspections were to be arranged as Macpherson had requested. Furthermore, he was to send the results to the Department and, since it was Macpherson's wish that the inspections should be publicised, Stafford was told that there was no objection to the local newspapers being informed.[21] Macpherson's children were duly inspected and all of them given a clean bill of health.[22] Macpherson followed up her telegram with a letter to Lowe in which she said that she was pleased to learn that the examinations had been satisfactory but that now she was 'waiting to hear how you publicly reported the fact that they were just lovely rosy cheeked healthy little lassies – all well trained in thrifty domestic habits...', adding that she had 'nothing to do with pauper union or workhouse children'. Furthermore, she claimed that the hundreds of photographs that she possessed showed 'what capital labourers on the land they [the children] become'. She enclosed a few as examples, but, if there were doubts, all the children could be examined when they landed and the 'diseased' immediately sent back at the cost of the senders.[23] Lowe replied as follows:

> Report of the fact of perfect healthfulness of the children has ... been published in the newspapers, and I think it is well you took the step....
> I was very glad to see the photographs you sent me. They tell the story very plainly in the most convincing mode.[24]

The use of photographs as a device for combating the criticisms about the children's condition was not exclusive to Macpherson. At the end of May 1888 Rye had also sent Lowe a photograph of five boys from the Salford workhouse in order to show what sturdy lads she was bringing to Canada. Lowe's reply is illuminating. 'I have shown the photo to the Minister ... I am only sorry that you did not send it to me in time for the Immigration Committee, as I might have made it do better service there.'[25] Indeed, it is interesting, as we shall see, that at the next meeting of the Select Committee on Agriculture and Colonisation the following year (1889) Lowe did pass around another photograph of six of Rye's children with the comment that the committee would see 'that they have a very good appearance'.[26] Macpherson also continued to send photographs to Lowe.[27]

In the meantime *The Toronto Mail* was maintaining its campaign against pauper and child immigration. In June 1888, for example, it carried both an editorial and a report on the issue.[28] The report was of a 'mass' public meeting, described as a gathering of over a thousand working men. The principal speakers were Goldwin Smith, Senator McInnes and Alfred Jury (the trade unionist). All protested against government assistance to immigration although only Jury referred specifically to the children issue. Nevertheless, Rye immediately seized the opportunity that Smith's speech at the meeting offered to draw Lowe's attention to the fact that his wife had asked for one of her girls.[29] She also told him that her assistant had visited the Sunderland union to see the children intended for emigration but that she had not thought much of them and had refused at least a dozen. In replying Lowe said that he would like to see Mrs Smith's letter and 'if you do not consider it confidential, it might be a good joke to use it publicly'.[30] Rye duly sent it, adding that she did 'not think it would be wise to print it – we can do just as much with it & indeed more – by privately passing it round'.[31]

Later that year Dr Ferguson, as we have seen, fell into the same trap. In September 1888 he applied for and was allocated one of Rye's girls.[32] By November Rye could write again to Lowe: 'And what do you think has happened here today? Why Dr Ferguson ... has actually sent his housekeeper ... for a second young woman!!!'.[33] 'Wonders will never cease', replied Lowe. Although he understood that her letter was confidential he asked her permission to show it to the minister.[34] Rye readily agreed.[35]

Thus, a number of measures were employed in order to counteract and manage the opposition to child immigration that came to a head in the spring and summer of 1888. In Parliament there were excellent grounds on which to build defences. The government itself was in favour of the schemes and within the ruling Conservative Party there were influential members who had had direct experience of either the children or the organisations, or both, and who were well disposed to the whole enterprise. They, in turn, could be supported by information supplied by the Department of Agriculture. This was material to which the opposition did not have access. In addition steps were taken to collect medical evidence of the good health of the immigrant children. As early as July 1888 Carling, the Minister of Agriculture, was writing to Tupper, the Commissioner in London, to advise him that a medical examination should be arranged for all the children for whom the $2 bonus was to be paid.[36] In the press, Rye in particular threw down challenges for the production of proof of the allegations which it was almost certain that the critics were unable to produce, since their attacks were of a generalised and polemical character. Furthermore, it is noteworthy that where the opportunity arose, the integrity of the opponents was undermined within a semi-private network. Ferguson and Goldwin Smith in particular made themselves extremely vulnerable to charges of hypocrisy.

II Developments after 1888

The opposition to child immigration did not, of course, cease in 1888 as a result of these manoeuvres. It still had to be reckoned with and managed. At least two opportunities arose for continuing a public attack in 1889. One was the publication of the reports of the Royal Commission on the Relations of Labour and Capital (the so-called Labour Commission). Throughout 1888 and the early part of 1889 evidence was heard across Canada and its two reports (a majority and a minority) were published in 1889. The minority (or 'employers') report appeared in February and among its many recommendations it included one to the effect that:

> ... the sending to Canada of inmates of poorhouses and reformatories should be prohibited. Strict medical examination should be made at the ports of landing and persons likely to become the objects of charity and those having incurable diseases should be forbidden to land....[37]

The majority (or labour faction) report followed shortly after. Its conclusions on immigration were similar to those arrived at by the employers' group, although couched in stronger terms. They did, however, add that they thought children were not suitable immigrants to be brought to Canada at all and that the $2 bonus system should be abolished. The recommendations of the commission were widely reported (although none of the proposals was actually adopted, except that to set up a Bureau of Labour Statistics). It is clear that people like Rye were conscious of its significance for their work. For instance, she wrote to Lowe early in 1889, observing that the commission was still sitting and sending him further photographs of her children and reports of the success of those who had now reached adulthood. 'I think', she told him, 'that in my old age I shall have to begin blowing my own trumpet!'[38]

The emigrationists were also aware of the important deliberations of the Select Committee on Agriculture and Colonialisation, which was reconvened in February 1889. Like Rye and Macpherson, Birt was also anxious about the harmful effect of the medical criticism on her work. The day before the committee was due to meet she wrote to Laurie (her initial patron and now an MP) to tell him that she would be bringing another party of children,

> ... a very fine band of lads, and a very pretty set of little girls.... The words that were raised last session in your House of Parliament about unsuitable emigrants being brought out to the Dominion do not in the least apply to us, or to our Institution for from the beginning we have been most careful about those we undertake to bring out.... Each and all are medically examined, and those our doctor cannot pronounce 'sound' are rejected.... Our Dr Williams examines as thoroughly as if he was doing it for a life insurance policy ... asking for a continuance of your prayers for this blessed and Christ like work.[39]

As well as her letter Birt enclosed a memorandum about the work. This is interesting because it firmly switched the emphasis towards the extent of orphanhood among her children, conscious presumably of the Canadian fears about the origins of those who were sent. 'In Liverpool', she wrote, 'we have a mass of children every year *orphaned by the sea*. Three thousand men, on an average are drowned yearly ... and the majority of these hail from Liverpool' (original emphasis).[40] The children were, it was implied, the victims of misfortune rather than of parental depravity, neglect or transmitted disease. Perhaps she should come to Ottawa to make this clear before the select committee? Lowe, however, advised Laurie to dissuade her. 'It would be of very doubtful expediency for her to come ... at the present time ... I think ... she would ... excite the hostility of the committee instead of getting a favourable expression....' [41] Birt was also seeking a grant to assist the work, but Lowe cautioned her that it would be unwise to ask. He added, however, that it would help if she could get her county MP to support her as he had made 'a pretty bitter speech against all such things when our estimates were passing through the House last session, but please do not give him any hint that I have written you this'. [42]

In the event, as we saw in chapter 9, the 1889 report of the select committee was much less virulent than its predecessor. In particular, the doctor members now switched their attention to the medical inspection of immigrants and to stopping the entry of boys from British reformatories because of their criminal pasts. However, Laurie, with Lowe's assistance, defended the practice while emphasising how few had been admitted into Canada. It seems doubtful whether the committee appreciated the difference between British reformatories and industrial schools or that anyone took steps to enlighten them. Certainly, many more children from the latter institutions were included in the emigration parties and many of them had been young offenders, but they escaped the doctors' disapprobation.

In Britain the Canadian High Commissioner's Office and the immigration agents were at pains to supply the Departure of Agriculture with any evidence of the healthy and good condition of the children that became available. For instance, in 1891, Dyke, the Liverpool agent, sent the minister two clippings from Liverpool papers that dealt with a meeting of the Toxteth guardians. [43] The *Liverpool Daily Post* reported that the board had considered whether any of the 77 children chargeable to them and accommodated in the Kirkdale schools were suitable for emigration. The issue arose because of Samuel Smith's (MP for Liverpool) criticism of the guardians in a speech in the House of Commons for not having taken more energetic steps to send children to Canada. One member of the Toxteth board of guardians pointed out that 'only the healthiest children were admitted to Canada, and that was one of the reasons why the number emigrated was not larger', while another explained that not everyone thought that emigration was desirable because 'they were sending out to Canada the best and the healthiest children and leaving the refuse at home'. [44]

As we have seen, in 1892 responsibility for immigration was transferred from the Department of Agriculture to the Department of the Interior. This was more forcefully bureaucratic in its dealings with the emigrationists. As a result, the informal networks that had been woven around John Lowe were broken. It was obviously hard for people like Rye and Birt to come to terms with the new style of administration and negotiation – instead of corresponding with just one official they now found themselves dealing with several. As well as the deputy minister there was a secretary, an assistant secretary, the head of the Immigration Branch, a commissioner of immigration as well as a superintendent of immigration and, later, an assistant deputy minister. Furthermore, in 1896 a Liberal government was elected with Sifton as its Minister of the Interior, a man on record as being rather critical of child immigration.

One of the first things that happened in 1893 was that the Department of the Interior introduced regulations whereby any person or society engaged in bringing children to Canada had to give the background of each child, and each child had to be medically examined at the port of embarkation and certified by a Canadian agent that they were of a 'desirable class'. Upon landing, the local immigration agent had to make a similar declaration and if he were unable to do so then the child had to be returned to Britain.[45] These more stringent procedures were intended to demonstrate the tight control that was now to be exercised over the *quality* of the child immigrant. This was politically important whether or not the control was as vigorous in practice as the requirements specified.

Faced with new responsibilities and without a long tradition of personal knowledge the Department of the Interior also initiated two enquiries about the agencies involved in child immigration. The first was in 1895 when a questionnaire was sent to all the societies. They were required to give details of their administration, record keeping, inspection and their policy with respect to the removal of children.[46] The survey was probably conducted in readiness for the Select Standing Committee on Agriculture and Colonisation due to meet again that year. In the previous year Burgess, the Deputy Minister, had had to deal with continued criticism of child immigration when he appeared before them. Among the 16 replies to the Department's questionnaire there were some unsatisfactory answers. Many societies made no provision for a signed agreement about the terms on which children would work, others knew little about the children's past history, and some had no systematic arrangements for subsequent inspection. Most sent samples of their forms and their annual reports. For the first time, as a result, the central department possessed a reasonably good picture of how the societies were operating, or at least of how they said they were operating. This information was supplemented in 1899 when Jury (the trade unionist), who had been appointed immigration agent at Liverpool by the Laurier Liberal government, submitted his report on the operation of the child emigration societies in England.[47] He had undertaken a Home-by-Home inspection and provided details of each, as well as a synopsis of the prevailing British legislation. Despite his previous opposition to child emigration his report was generally favourable, although his principal recommendation was that 'a minimum of not less than two years should be established for them [the children] to be under training before being emigrated'. The Canadian immigration agent in Glasgow undertook a similar commission, although his report only dealt with the Quarrier Homes.[48] He also reached generally favourable conclusions about the standard of the children and about the conduct of the organisation.

Thus, by the end of the century the Department of the Interior had begun to gather specific information about child immigration. As we have seen, an inspector of British immigrant children was appointed in 1900 to oversee the whole field and to make annual reports. By 1904 the Department had its own chief medical inspector who was able to deal with the continuing criticism from certain doctors on an equal professional footing. The Department gradually became better equipped to contend with the opposition because it possessed better information. Partly for the same reason it was also able to deal more firmly with the emigration societies. It is interesting to note, however, that from the beginning, with the reluctant introduction of the annual inspection of pauper children, the ability of the central Department to manage and confound the opposition grew in response to each new phase of criticism, but the emigrationists too, particularly Barnardo, had to deal with continuing criticism of their activities.

III A Charge Repudiated

By the end of the 1880s Barnardo had become the leading figure in the child emigration movement and, as such, he had also become a frequent target for its Canadian detractors. Always concerned to safeguard the public image of his activities he took pains to prepare his defences and to respond in detail to criticisms, although in a less combative style than people like Rye. Almost from the start he was careful to emphasise that only healthy, fit and trained children without 'criminal tendencies' were selected for Canada, describing them, in his much used phrase, as the 'flower of the flock'. Furthermore, he gave an undertaking that any of his immigrants who became 'immoral or criminal' would be returned to Britain at his expense. By 1884 these 'principles' had been incorporated in a 'Charter' that was appealed to frequently when charges of the indiscriminate 'dumping' of unsuitable children in Canada were levelled against him.

Unlike many of his contemporaries Barnardo insisted on case records being kept, often supplemented with photographs of the children.[49] Among other things this provided him with a basis for statistical presentations, not least for the purposes of demonstrating the success of the work and also for replying to official enquiries with convincing assurance. Of course, other organisations kept records, albeit of a variable quality, but none seemed to have appreciated their political usefulness as fully as Barnardo. Similarly, like others, he used photographs and the publication of letters from grateful young people to show how successful his child immigrants had been in their new country.[50] Furthermore, he took care to enlist the public support of leading figures, both in Britain and Canada, many of whom, like him, embraced the evangelical cause.

These, and other features of Barnardo's defences, were to be severely tested in 1893 in connection with what became known as the Brandon grand jury case. A youth who had been brought out to the Barnardo farm training school at Russell in Manitoba was charged with indecent assault and tried before what was termed a grand jury. In the event he was convicted of a lesser offence and sentenced to a month's imprisonment.[51] The trial might have passed without much more than local interest had the jury not made a 'presentation' that included damning remarks about the dangers of 'importing' boys from Britain's slums. Even so, it could hardly have been foreseen that such by now familiar accusations would provoke intense and widespread interest. Of course, the event was a newsworthy item and the fact that it was so rapidly distributed may have owed something to the increasing syndication of news. Whatever the reason, the fact is that the jury's statement was reported throughout Canada and also in Britain.

The Department of the Interior was quick to react. Pereira (the assistant secretary) dispatched three letters almost at once. One was sent to H.H. Smith, the secretary of the Dominion Lands Board at Winnipeg, who was told to take immediate steps to make 'a complete report' on the Russell institution.[52] A second letter went to Owen, Barnardo's agent in Canada, requesting copies of all their pamphlets and other information regarding their activities.[53] Hiam, the agent of the Dominion Lands Board at Brandon, received the third letter that instructed him to gather details of all cases brought before the Brandon jury in order to determine what proportion were 'philanthropic immigrants'.[54]

Hiam was the first to reply, but only sent a list of eight boys who were in prison, but he did add that his general impression was 'that the Barnardo boys are on the whole a very desirable class of immigrants'.[55] In the meantime, Smith, the lands agent in Winnipeg, had contacted Struthers, the manager of the Russell Farm School, in order to obtain the sought-after information. Struthers replied that the jury had been under a misapprehension: 'the lads for Manitoba are not from the slums ... but largely from the country and country towns where ... they often leave widowed mothers behind, too poor to help them'. As to the number 'committed for crime', he had enquired at the four penal establishments in Manitoba and consulted his own records and found only 13 (out of 500 coming to Russell since 1886). In order to put the work of the farm school in context Struthers added that in 1893 he had only been able to satisfy some 16 per cent of the demand for boys that he had received.[56]

Before the end of the year Burgess, the Deputy Minister, was seeking 'all possible information' about the Brandon case from his staff in time for the reconvening of Parliament.[57] This certainly reflected how politically sensitive the question of pauper and child immigration remained, and how readily it prompted questions in Parliament, answers to which the responsible department had to be ready to provide for the minister. Early in 1894 Burgess sent all the correspondence and a collection of newspaper cuttings to his minister (Mayne Daly) with an accompanying letter in which he considered whether a full inquiry into the case was warranted.

> There is no doubt, irrespective of what the facts may be, that some concession is due to public opinion, even to public prejudice. The question is whether the adverse opinion or prejudice is sufficiently established in this instance to justify the trouble and expense of a thorough inquiry.[58]

There is no record of the reply, but subsequent events show that the matter was not left there. For example, Pereira wrote to Barnardo inviting his observations on the jury's presentation and asking him about his admission practices as well as the outcomes for his young immigrants.[59] At the same time he wrote again to Hiam, saying that he wanted a complete list of *everyone* who came before the Brandon court, not just the Barnardo boys.[60] Similarly, Smith, the Dominion lands agent, was told to arrange an immediate and full inspection at Russell, detailing its farming methods, its placement policies and the views of the boys' employers.[61] The questions were to be searching and, among other things, aimed at checking the information that Struthers had provided. Such instructions went well beyond the rather relaxed and cursory enquiries that had previously been made by the Department of Agriculture about the activities of the emigrationists.

However, Pereira took further steps to gather information. At the beginning of February 1894 another series of letters was sent to a number of agencies asking them to provide details of various kinds. MacPherson, the immigration agent at Kingston, had to find out how many paupers and children brought out by the philanthropic societies were held in Kingston prison.[62] Rye was asked how many of her children had been in prison and required to state that what she reported was 'bona fide knowledge' and 'not merely ignorance of their careers' after they had been placed out.[63] Similar letters were sent to most of the other individuals and societies engaged in child emigration. Some could not provide the information requested; others were quite precise. Miss E. Meiklejohn of Birt's Home at Knowlton reported that only nine of their children 'had been involved with the law' since 1877.[64] Barnardos returned 40 boys (no mention of girls) who had appeared in court during the previous seven years.[65] Most others listed five to ten children, although the periods over which they had taken their counts varied. Most appeared anxious to co-operate although in doing so they did not always distinguish between offenders and victims, the phrase 'involved with the law' being used to cover both categories. This was true of Rye, for example, whom the Department of the Interior reminded that they only required the number of offenders,[66] an interesting reflection of the Department's balance of concerns. However, the welfare of the children was not overlooked altogether. In her second reply to the Department, for instance, Rye had provided the gratuitous information that Barnardo's activities were in a deplorable state: his finances were in disarray and his Toronto Home 'a pigsty'.[67] Pereira promptly had it inspected 'by surprise', but it was found to be in good order.[68] Clearly, the Department of the Interior was treating its enquiries seriously and taking various steps to assure itself that facts were facts and not unfounded pronouncements. For example, it contacted the North West Mounted Police for information about immigrant child offenders as well as a selection of police magistrates.[69] In the event very few instances were reported, and some of those that were listed as involving 'Barnardo boys' were later found to have had no such connection.

During these official enquiries Struthers, the manager of the Farm School at Russell, had been active on behalf of Barnardos. He had written to the foreman of the Brandon jury asking him to explain why it had been felt necessary to issue the statement that it had. The foreman replied that as well as the boy concerned there was another in gaol, and that there were 'general complaints regarding foreign immigration'. This had persuaded the jury to make their statement in order to ensure the most careful selection of boys for Canada and had not been intended as a general criticism of Barnardo's work. Indeed, he considered it 'most worthy' and, speaking for himself, he had not found the boys 'much inferior to the general run of Canadian youth'.[70] Thereupon Struthers wrote to all the members of the jury asking them whether or not they agreed with their foreman's explanation for their 'presentation', although no record of their replies has survived. All this information was forwarded to Barnardo, who incorporated it in his long and detailed submission to Pereira at the Department of the Interior, attaching at the same time a resolution of the Russell Farmers' Institute criticising the jury's statement.[71]

Barnardo's reply set out the history of his emigration activities, quoted his 'Charter' of undertakings, emphasised the considerable demand for his children and drew on the 'ledger account' of the careers of each boy and girl sent to Canada in order to identify all those who had been convicted of an offence since 1884 – 'less than one per cent' and, in the main, involving only 'trivial offences'. He also provided a comparison of the offence rates for 'his' children with those for the general population of Canada (although not for the same age range), to show that they were *less* likely to be convicted of an offence. He admitted, however, that, apart from the convicted, there were some others whose careers had been unsatisfactory (a shrewd admission) but that most of these had been returned to Britain. Thus, quoting chapter and verse, and employing statistical analysis where possible, Barnardo set out an impressive defence against the 'intemperate language' of the jury, whose utterances had 'inflicted an undeserved and irreparable injury upon a section of the Canadian community who have proved, by the very small number of their offences ... to be amongst the most law-abiding portion of the whole population of the Dominion'. However, as far as the Department of the Interior was concerned, the evidence that the jury's statement had been wildly exaggerated had already been conclusively established. The report of the homestead inspector on the Manitoba Farm School had been entirely favourable.[72] Together with his report the inspector also included favourable statements from the boys' employers whom he had interviewed and a medical report that noted that infectious disease was conspicuous by its absence. Furthermore, the doctor had himself employed several boys at different times and gave a good account of them.

The result of all this was that a successful rebuttal of the charges made by the Brandon jury was achieved, both by Barnardo's organisation and, in a more dispassionate fashion, by the Department of the Interior whose staff foresaw, and then forestalled, an outcry in Parliament by arming themselves with as much factual material as could be gathered in the time. There was also a degree of local defence of the Barnardo boys in Manitoba. As well as the farmers this included the local press. *The Colonist*, for instance, headed its report on the case 'Needless Alarm', and considered the jury's report 'wrong' and 'governed by prejudice and hearsay'.[73]

Certainly, the reputations of the Barnardo boys passing through the Russell Farm School had been vindicated; but throughout the episode it was their criminality that was at issue. With a few notable exceptions the welfare of the boys did not figure in the exchanges or in the kind of evidence that was assembled. Indeed, the 'success' of their immigration was evaluated solely by reference to whether or not they had offended and whether or not they were proving to be competent agricultural workers. How they were treated, what they felt, and how they subsequently fared were not the questions causing public and political disquiet. What becomes clear, however, is that in Manitoba, as in other parts of Canada, the young immigrants provided a convenient focus for the deepening popular anxieties about the threat that the surge of new arrivals was assumed to pose to the established population. But the other side of the coin was that although opposition to child immigration did not disappear after the episodes described, it did begin to subside, being overshadowed by the increasingly large number of other immigrants reaching Canadian shores. Nevertheless, the emigrationists still had to tread carefully, aware that unfavourably reported incidents could quickly spark a new round of popular outcry – not about the welfare of the children but about their 'fitness' to be in Canada.

Many children would have crossed the Atlantic in the S.S. Sardinian, one of the ships of the Allan Line sailing out of Liverpool. It carried mostly emigrants, the great majority travelling steerage, as did the children.

A party of child emigrants from the Quarrier Homes on the ship's deck before leaving Glasgow in 1884. (Courtesy Quarriers, Liverpool University Special Collections and Archives: D.239/J3/3/23.)

Five boys from the Salford workhouse posed for the camera in 1888 prior to going to Canada. Photographs played an increasingly important part in justifying child emigration, in particular by endeavouring to show in Canada how healthy the young immigrants were. (Courtesy the National Archives of Canada: RG 17/585/66101.)

This is the kind of small farm on which some of the children might have found themselves, at least in the early days in Ontario. This one was near Elora some 30 miles west of Hamilton. The date is uncertain. (Courtesy the National Archives of Canada: C 025155.)

A group of children outside their school at Muskoka Lakes, Ontario (no date). When they were allowed to attend some of the British children would have gone to rural schools like this one. (Courtesy the National Archives of Canada: PA 68351.)

A scene on a farm in the Eastern Townships area of Québec (no date). It is important to appreciate the long months of cold winter that the children experienced. (Courtesy the National Archives of Canada: PA 135037.)

A group (mostly boys) photographed on their arrival at the Marchmont reception Home in 1887. Note the 'Welcome Home' (to Canada) sign and the Union Jacks that served to emphasise the British connection. It is not clear which organisation had sent the party. (Courtesy Barnardos and the Liverpool University Special Collections and Archives: D.239/J3/3/23.)

Some of these boys may have been sent to Canada later. Here they are still in the Upton House industrial school for truants at Homerton in east London. It was run by London County Council. The year is 1904. The significance of the photograph is that it illustrates that the emigrationists were probably justified in claiming that boys like these were likely to find themselves in 'dead-end' jobs as boot-blacks working on the streets. Better, they argued, to take them to Canada. (Courtesy the City of London, London Metropolitan Archives: 81/11502.)

Eighty-four girls from Quarrier's Bridge of Weir Home near Glasgow assembled outside his reception Home (Fairknowe) in Brockville, Ontario, in 1905. Note how young some of the girls are. (Courtesy the National Archives of Canada: C 086392.)

A group of boys from the Manchester and Salford Boys' and Girls' Society pictured outside the Manchester Town Hall prior to their emigration (no date). The presence of the Lord Mayor alongside Leonard Shaw (on his right) reflects this organisation's keenness to enlist and retain civic support for their enterprise. Note, again, how young the boys at the front are. (Courtesy the Together Trust and the Liverpool University Special Collections and Archives: D.239/J3/3/23.)

This is a Canadian government vehicle in London (no date) used to encourage emigration. Together with various emigration offices and other advertising it emphasises how important British immigration was considered to be by the Dominion. That climate certainly influenced the development of the child emigration movement. (Courtesy the National Archives of Canada: CO 9671.)

This shows Barnardo's farm school at Russell in Manitoba, to which older boys were sent as 'farming pioneers', often already having been placed in Ontario. (Courtesy the National Archives of Canada: PA 117279.)

These boys were on their way to the St George's Catholic reception Home at Hintonburg, near Ottawa, Ontario (no date). (Courtesy the National Archives of Canada: PA 20907.)

A party of boys before setting out for Canada with the National Children's Homes. There is no date, but it is probably the early years of the twentieth century. (Courtesy the National Children's Homes.)

Boys on arrival at the Marchmont Home sent by Annie Macpherson (no date). (Courtesy the National Archives of Canada: C 34837.)

A group awaiting deportation from Canada (no date). The boy on crutches was probably a British child immigrant. In any case, his being with the group emphasises the Dominion's unwillingness to retain those who became social casualties. (Courtesy the National Archives of Canada: PA 20910.)

Part V
The Ambiguities and Obfuscation

ELEVEN

The Reformatories and Industrial Schools

I The Background

Some of the children who were sent to Canada came from the British reformatories and industrial schools. This was always a sensitive issue since Canadian legislation debarred the entry of anyone with a criminal record, and public opinion could easily be inflamed by the claim that this prohibition had been evaded. In fact, it was only those who had been committed to a reformatory who were specifically precluded from entering the country, but even then there was the disputed question of whether an exception could be made in the case of those who had been fully discharged rather than released on licence. The position of the industrial school children was more ill-defined and less well understood. What was the distinction between these two groups?

Although before the 1850s[1] there had been a number of schemes for the institutional reform and training of young offenders, or for those on the threshold of delinquency, it was the 1854 Reformatory Schools Act, followed three years later by the Industrial Schools Act (and in 1866 by a combined Act) that heralded their rapid expansion. The first piece of legislation enabled courts to send children under the age of 16 (a minimum age of 10 was subsequently introduced) to a reformatory, but only after the expiry of a prison sentence.[2] Such children could be kept in the institutions for between two and five years or until they reached the age of 18 (and later 19). The second Act gave courts the authority to order that children up to the age of 14 be sent to an industrial school and retained there until they were 15 (later 16). The grounds on which such an order could be made were extensive, and further additions were made from time to time. One aim was to combat child vagrancy and begging, but those who were found wandering and destitute, or who were known to frequent the company of thieves, for example, could also be dealt with in this way. So too could those under 14 who were charged by their parents with being beyond their control. Later amendments provided for the children of criminal or drunken parents to be included, as well as girls who lived in brothels or whose fathers had been found guilty of sexually assaulting them.[3] Not least, committal to an industrial school was to become a means of dealing with those who persistently failed to attend school once elementary education had become compulsory. None of these categories of industrial school children therefore had been found guilty of a criminal offence, but those under the age of 12 who had engaged in criminal activity could be sent to such schools which, given that the age of criminal responsibility was seven, could comprise a fairly large group.[4]

Thus, following the classification proposed by Mary Carpenter, one of the strongest advocates of these developments, the reformatories could be considered to be for those from the 'dangerous' class, while the industrial schools were reserved for those of the 'perishing' class.[5] In modern terms the first were for young offenders, the second for those in need of care or protection. In fact, as would often be the case today, the children came from similar backgrounds and shared similar histories. The common threads were those of poverty and deprivation.

Although children from reformatories and industrial schools formed a relatively small proportion (probably some 12 per cent) of all those sent to Canada from Britain, the number was not insignificant. Between 1858 and 1914, for example, the figure stood at 4,131 from the reformatories (44 per cent) and 5,151 from the industrial schools (56 per cent), making 9,282 in all. However, typically, there were far more children in the industrial schools than in the reformatories throughout the period, some three to four times as many – but they were younger. So although more children were sent to Canada from the industrial schools, they represented a smaller proportion of those discharged each year than was the case with the reformatories. It is also notable that between the years 1862 and 1914 only 24 per cent of the emigrants from the industrial schools were girls and just six per cent from the reformatories. These differences only partially reflected the smaller number of girls in both kinds of institutions: fewer girls were sent to Canada relative to their overall number in the schools.[6]

II Rising Unease

Several factors help to explain the rather confusing attitudes towards emigration from the reformatories and industrial schools at the Home Office and among the institutions' managers. There were issues concerned with finance, with the perceived need to separate children from evil influences, with the problems of parental consent, and with the subsequent supervision of those who were sent abroad. In the case of the Home Office there was also a keen sensibility to the views of the Canadian government. Considerable light was shed on these matters during the hearings before the Royal Commission on Reformatory and Industrial Schools that reported in 1884.[7] Its appointment two years earlier had been dictated by a groundswell of disquiet about the conduct of these institutions.

First, the Treasury was facing growing costs in subsidising the increasing number of inmates of these institutions, especially in the case of the industrial schools. Between 1866 and 1882, for example, the total Treasury contribution had risen by 26 per cent in the case of the reformatories but increased more than sixfold with respect to the industrial schools where the resident population had grown from 2,500 to over 17,500 during the same period.[8] A second strong influence on the appointment of the commission lay in the personality and convictions of the new Home Secretary in Gladstone's second administration, formed in 1880. William

Harcourt lost no time in making it clear that he intended to remedy the unduly harsh treatment of young offenders. He wrote to *The Times*[9] on the matter, and asked Queen Victoria to approve the remission of sentences imposed on certain juveniles. By way of explanation, he wrote to her that many of the cases:

> ... were for trifling offences, as, for instance, a boy of nine years old for throwing stones, several boys of eleven and twelve years for damaging grass by running about in the fields; a girl of thirteen for being drunk; several boys of twelve or thirteen for bathing in a canal, and similarly for playing at pitch and toss; a boy of nine for stealing scent; a boy of thirteen for threatening a woman, three boys of eleven for breaking windows; a boy of ten for wilfully damaging timber....[10]

There was, Harcourt maintained, a large number of children in both the reformatories and the industrial schools who should not have been there. He was confirmed in his view that the system should be overhauled by the particular case of James Winch who had died at the St Paul's industrial school in east London from a severe caning.[11]

However, there was a third factor that contributed to the growing unease in central government about the industrial schools in particular. This arose from the implementation of the 1876 Education Act that, among other things, made the local school boards responsible for administering the legislation for the industrial schools. Furthermore, they were charged with seeing that children who were considered to be suitable candidates for such schools were brought before the magistrates. Thus, as Godfrey (later Sir Godfrey) Lushington (the assistant secretary at the Home Office) was at pains to point out, 'whereas formerly [before 1876] it was nobody's business in particular to move to send the children to industrial schools, now it is the business of the local authority'.[12] Nevertheless, alongside this responsibility it remained possible for anyone else to institute proceedings for a child's committal, but the school boards were now obliged to exercise the responsibility in appropriate cases. As a result, Lushington contended, the Acts began to be 'worked to the uttermost'.[13] Clearly, this increased the number of young children in the schools and with it the cost to the Treasury, which was committed to paying *per capita* subsidies.

Another way in which the Elementary Education Acts impinged on the development of the industrial schools arose from the fact that after the mid-1870s most urban school boards adopted bye-laws that made school attendance compulsory for children up to the age of 10. By 1880 this had become a national requirement, although various loopholes were available up to 1918 when all children between the ages of five and 14 were obliged to attend full time. However, once education became compulsory the question of its enforcement had to be confronted. The solution was not only the appointment of attendance committees and truancy officers but also the introduction of attendance orders that could be imposed on those who failed to go to school. If such an order were breached then courts could employ the further sanction of an industrial school order. This, as Lushington explained before the Royal Commission, 'imported into these schools an entirely new class of children'.[14]

Harcourt's first step in instituting an investigation into the issues surrounding the reformatories and industrial schools had been to set up an inter-departmental committee in 1880 to review the matter. Senior figures from the Local Government Board (LGB), the Home Office, the Treasury and Education were enlisted, but although their report was printed it was never published.[15] Nonetheless, it was extremely critical of the prevailing system, particularly of the necessity for a period of imprisonment before a reformatory school order could be made, but also of the lack of less severe alternatives. Many children, it was concluded, might not have been committed to reformatories or industrial schools had there been a tariff of milder penalties or a means of successfully fining parents.

All these factors came together to strengthen Harcourt in his conviction that a further, deeper and more public enquiry was needed. He petitioned the Queen for the appointment of a royal commission, a request that was duly granted. The 11-man team (there were no women) under the chairmanship of Lord Aberdare began its work in 1882.

III The Royal Commission and Child Emigration

The Royal Commission's deliberations covered many matters other than emigration, but emigration was given much attention, thereby providing an insight into the way in which the reformatories and industrial schools fitted into the wider picture of child emigration. In particular, their deliberations illustrated the many cross-currents to which it was subject.

Given the prevailing concern about the rising cost of the institutions, together with unease about discharging children back to their original environments, there would have appeared to have been much in favour of emigration as a mode of 'disposal'. Indeed, its advantages were extolled by many of those who gave evidence, and the commissioners themselves concluded that 'emigration, which is already resorted to by managers for the disposal of children, might be advantageously used to a much greater extent than at present'.[16] Some of the arguments that led them to this conclusion, as well as some of the reasons why it had not been developed as fully as they thought possible, gradually emerged. In the main they revolved around the issues of costs, whether emigration was 'successful' or not, the value of 'severance' from 'depraved' parents, obtaining parental consent, licensing and the adequacy of supervision once a child was in Canada.

The evidence of Trevarthen, secretary to the Redhill Reformatory, provides a useful starting point for examining the influence of costs on the scope for emigration. Trevarthen had been connected with Redhill, the oldest reformatory, for 20 years and recalled that it had 'disposed' of a comparatively large proportion of its boys by way of emigration. Indeed, up to the end of 1881 it had discharged a total of 2,891, of whom 1,302 (45 per cent) had been emigrated.

Nonetheless, emigration was expensive. Between 1872 and 1881 its average cost was £10 12s whereas when the boys were discharged home the cost was only £2 5s. Furthermore, there was no provision in the existing legislation for expenditure incurred in 'disposal' to be met from public monies – whether a boy went home or was emigrated. However, Redhill did accumulate funds for this latter purpose from various sources, although Trevarthen made it plain that it was the institution's financial state that determined whether or not they were devoted to this end. He explained, for example, that 'when our farm was bad in its returns for three or four years we had to cut down our emigration as being one of the most expensive things…'.[17] However, other reformatories and industrial schools were hard pressed all the time. For example, the St Vincent's Industrial School for Roman Catholic boys at Dartford in Kent relied for its income entirely on the Treasury and local government allowances, together with whatever it could earn. There were no voluntary subscriptions. In presenting his evidence the resident manager argued that there were many cases where the Treasury should allow the school a special sum per head to assist emigration. He felt that this would be particularly appropriate where it was known 'from their parentage and friends' that a boy 'would be likely to pursue a vicious course' on his discharge. 'The Treasury', he pointed out, 'has already expended a very large sum … and at the very time that a few pounds would save the boy it withholds its hand.' However, the manager did not consider it appropriate to emigrate boys until they were aged 15 or 16 – close to the expiry date of the committal order – in which case, of course, there would be little saving to the Treasury.[18]

Whitwill, the Bristol magistrate and an influential figure in the Bristol Emigration Society (BES), provided another example of the way in which emigration expenses were met by the institutions. When asked, as a manager of several industrial schools, how the 'considerable expenditure' incurred by a child's emigration was met he explained that, in the case of the Carlton House school for girls, he met the cost out of his own pocket, especially when he felt that children should not be sent back to 'bad homes'.[19] He did this, he said, 'in order to avoid any discussion at the board about the cost of sending these children out'.[20] In some cases the boys contributed to the cost of their emigration from their modest earnings. That happened at the Hertfordshire Industrial School where, in addition, because emigration was considered to be so expensive, it was 'kept as a reward for good conduct'.[21]

So emigration, although favoured as a means of preventing young people from returning to 'vicious' parents on being discharged, was expensive. Any reformatory or industrial school that embarked on such a policy usually had to find the money from its existing budget; no special help was forthcoming, either from the Treasury, via the Home Office or, at that time, from most of the school boards whose children were admitted to the institutions. In addition, an important part of the institutions' income was derived from the labour of the children themselves, either indirectly when, for example, they made the clothes and repaired the boots, or directly through outside contracts. In these enterprises it was the older children whose labour was most valuable. This fact helps to account for the reluctance of managers to release children early on licence, as well as for their reluctance to encourage them to emigrate much before the expiry of the order. Indeed, the commissioners drew particular attention in their report to the dangers of institutions relying too heavily on the income derived from the children's work. In particular, they noted that the managers of reformatories and industrial schools were liable to give preference to the occupations that produced the largest income, work such as wood-chopping, matchbox making and, occasionally, oakum picking or hair-teasing. Although profitable, such activities were condemned; they did not constitute 'industrial training'. Furthermore, the work to which young children were put, and which was classed as 'training', was liable to encroach on the hours of schooling that they were supposed to receive.

It had become evident, therefore, that financial considerations connected with child labour, as well as the structure of the Treasury capitation grants and the declining importance of voluntary donations had, by the 1880s, created a situation in which the interests of central government in the early release of children – whatever the disposition – was at odds with the interests of those institutions where their financial viability depended on the retention of the children for as long as possible and, in parallel, on keeping their establishments full in order to attract the maximum *per capita* grants from the Treasury. Only the better-off reformatories or industrial schools could contemplate emigration on any substantial scale. Such institutions were richer not only because of their private funds but because they had been established before 1872 and, as a result, attracted a higher capitation grant from the Treasury than those that were founded later.

A second issue that exercised the commissioners was the question of whether or not the emigration of reformatory and industrial school children could be considered to be 'successful'. Much of the evidence put forward claimed that it was, or, at least, that it was more successful than other forms of disposal. Typically, success was calculated by reference to rates of reconviction or, in the case of industrial school children, conviction. Understandably, however, the Royal Commission was not convinced that accurate figures could be obtained from abroad. Just how did the reformatories and industrial schools learn about those who subsequently offended? Did not the boys move around a good deal and become difficult to trace? Exactly who was responsible for reporting back to the institutions? How frequently were the reports brought up to date? None of the answers to these queries can have created much confidence in the claims for low relapse rates overseas. Nonetheless, the contention had a common-sense and persuasive ring to it, and although the figures might not have been as accurate as was claimed, neither, of course, were those for children disposed of at home. Also statistics about their successes were probably exaggerated since the institutions that made the returns had a strong interest in giving a favourable impression.

Nevertheless, despite doubts about the credibility of the statistics the general belief that emigration was an effective form of prevention does not seem to have been shaken. What repeatedly emerges from the minutes of evidence to the Royal

Commission is the conviction that removal from evil influences was the surest way to avoid an otherwise irresistible contagion; a criminal contagion that was considered to be most virulent in towns, among children's former associates and, especially, among their vicious or 'depraved' parents. Given the strength of such an interpretation it was hardly likely that the dubious nature of the statistics would dampen the enthusiasm for a policy that offered complete severance.

It was the widespread nature of this enthusiasm among many of those who gave evidence to the Royal Commission that constituted the third theme to shape its deliberations. While committed to a reformatory or an industrial school a child was assumed to be protected from the adverse influences of its former environment. As a result, another reason for managers' reluctance to release children early was added to the financial considerations. In the case of the industrial schools particular concern was expressed about safeguarding the futures of children when they had to be discharged at the age of 16. One course of action that was thought to reduce the risk in the case of boys was to have them enlist or go to sea since that secured their 'more thorough separation ... from the outer world';[22] but there was no guarantee that they would not resume their acquaintances when on leave or at the end of a voyage. In any case, most of the military establishments were located in garrison towns and the ports were full of temptations. Nevertheless, many boys from reformatories and industrial schools did join the army or go to sea, although emigration was usually seen as a preferable means of severance.

For the girls – who were considered to be at special risk if returned to an 'impure house' – domestic service was believed to offer a protected environment. Indeed, this was the most common first employment on release. However, although domestic service provided some degree of insulation from undesirable parents and associates it was by no means complete – employment was often in towns and cities and, in any case, many girls soon left to make their own way.

Thus, for boys and girls, particularly at the 'vulnerable' ages of 15 or 16, emigration appeared to offer a *cordon sanitaire*, more complete, and therefore more effective, than any other protection that could be envisaged. Whitwill of Bristol, for instance, was quite clear that if it were likely to be 'injurious' to return children to their homes they should be sent abroad.[23] He also contended that the children often did not want to be sent back to their parents; in fact, he reported that 'many times boys and girls have said to us at the schools, "do not send us back to our parents or we shall be ruined; we shall be just as bad as we were before". In some cases', he went on, 'parents insist upon their going back.' In these circumstances he considered that managers should get the children to emigrate 'and thus remove them from the influence of those evil parents and friends'.[24] Quarrier took a similar view: he believed that the managers of industrial schools 'should establish a scheme of emigration to dispose of those boys who have criminal surroundings after their discharge'.[25] Indeed, he had already included in his emigration parties children from some Scottish industrial schools.[26]

Not only were many parents assumed to exercise a deplorable influence on their children but also to be exploitative. They wanted them back on their release, it was often claimed, just at the time when they could make a significant contribution to the family income. Given that many reformatory and industrial school children came from what today would be called single-parent families – in particular widows – the desire to benefit from a few years of the child's earnings is hardly surprising. Indeed, that is precisely what the institutions did themselves in their reliance on the children's labour. That particular contradiction seems to have remained unacknowledged.

A fourth matter associated with emigration that began to emerge during the Royal Commission's hearings was that of consent, both of the children and the parents. This was later to assume greater prominence, but in the early 1880s it still remained a relatively low-key issue despite the fact that parental rights were not transferred by the imposition of a reformatory or industrial school order. Thus, legally, it was necessary for managers to obtain parents' consent to their children's emigration or enlistment if they were under the age of 16. A few of the witnesses held that this was a severe impediment to its greater use. Some parents refused to give their permission. However, one wonders to what extent parents were actually consulted and, if they were, what kinds of pressures were brought to bear in order to obtain their agreement. Furthermore, since the children also had to consent to their emigration before justices, their prior agreement must, from time to time, have operated to forestall parental objections. Where emigration was presented as a reward, sometimes linked with early release and sometimes offered as an alternative to enlistment or going to sea, some children would have been ready to go. Others clearly were not. When asked about the prospect of emigration from the Artane Industrial School in Ireland, for instance, the manager told the commissioners that there were 'very few boys leaving the school that would consent'.[27]

In general, the commissioners were more concerned that the schools were not releasing children as early as their progress warranted. This was made clear in their recommendation that:

> ... no consideration as to the comparatively profitable labour of the inmates during the last years of their term, nor the mistaken desire to keep them in leading strings as long as possible, should prevent their restoration at the earliest possible moment to ordinary life.[28]

The point was that the legislation enabled managers, at any time after 18 months of the period of detention, to license a young person 'to live with any trustworthy and respectable person willing to receive and take charge of him';[29] but early licensing had been (and continued to be) little used. This issue heralded yet another theme to emerge from the Royal Commission's deliberation and might have been expected to have led to the official encouragement of licensing whatever the child's destination. However, as we shall see, the Home Office was to issue a circular in 1884 that debarred managers from sending licensed young people abroad.

The commissioners addressed one other question about the emigration of children from the reformatories and industrial schools. This was the extent to which adequate supervision could be provided in Canada. Different witnesses explained their arrangements. The Feltham Industrial School relied on the Dominion immigration agent in Toronto to see that boys 'were properly placed out with responsible employers'.[30] The Royal Philanthropic School at Redhill (a Reformatory), its secretary admitted, had no agents in Canada, but there were 'friends who receive the boys'.[31] Several institutions, such as those in Bristol with which Whitwill was involved, relied on receiving letters from the children themselves for news of how they were faring.[32] Others, like the Hertfordshire Industrial School, spoke vaguely of having 'an agent' in Canada, but also said that they too depended on the children's letters, although the means of encouraging them to communicate was somewhat devious: 'we still hold a little of their savings back, and that induces a boy if he is a little hard up to write to the master and ask for some money'.[33] Thus, despite the assurances given by witnesses about the adequacy of supervision abroad, their evidence could hardly have been reassuring. There was no general system, each reformatory or industrial school made *ad hoc* arrangements, sometimes with employers, sometimes with the societies that included the children in their emigration parties, and sometimes with the local agents of the Dominion government.

IV The Repercussions of the Royal Commission's Report

Although it made several important recommendations for the improvement of the reformatory and industrial school systems, the Royal Commission's report found in favour of the continuation of arrangements along broadly existing lines. It concluded that, with certain reservations, the achievements of the reformatories and industrial schools had been 'very satisfactory'. More specifically, the commissioners wished to see greater encouragement extended to emigration, although they stressed that three main considerations should be borne in mind. First, the attitude of the colonies should be taken into account. Second, it was necessary for children to have undergone prior training in the schools and, third, there needed to be adequate inspection and supervision once they had arrived overseas.[34] However, no recommendations were made about the provision of special Treasury grants for emigration, about how supervision abroad was to be ensured, or about the ages at which children from the schools should be selected for emigration. It was recommended, however, that the managers of the institutions should 'be given full powers of disposing of the child in some employment at home, or at sea, or by arranging for its emigration'.[35] This meant a drastic curtailment of the parents' right to give or withhold their consent to such decisions. There was, furthermore, another recommendation that was closely linked with this – namely, that the period of control that managers exercised over the children should be extended. In the case of industrial school children it was suggested that it should continue until they were 18 instead of 16. For those in the reformatories it was proposed that the duration of the managers' control should be prolonged for two years after the end of the sentence or, if it expired before a young person was 19, until they were 21.[36]

Once the Royal Commission's report had been published a number of bodies communicated their views about its recommendations or omissions to the Home Office. A fairly typical memorandum was submitted by the committee of the Manchester Industrial School that strongly endorsed the need to give managers 'full powers of disposing of the child in some employment at home or at sea or for arranging for its emigration ... without requiring the parents' consent'.[37] Other Manchester views on what should be considered for inclusion in any amendment Bill were submitted by the city's school board. They were particularly concerned about young girls removed from 'houses of ill fame' and committed to industrial schools because, on discharge at 16, their parents would take them back to similar establishments. They felt that the number of such girls was likely to increase because of the operation of an Amendment Act in 1880 that had created new powers for removing young girls from brothels. However, it was their fate at 16 that most concerned the Manchester School Board and, in their opinion, the only means of saving such girls was by emigration; they advocated in particular, therefore, that authority be given to the managers of industrial schools 'to emigrate girls of from 14 to 16 years with their own consent and under proper regulations but without it being necessary to obtain the consent of the parent or parents'.[38]

It was not only the reformatory and industrial school managers who responded to the report, however. The Howard Association's executive committee (composed entirely of magistrates) expressed a similar point of view, contending that the rights of the young person and those of the state 'should be rendered paramount over justly forfeited claims of their various relatives'.[39] Inglis, the chief inspector of reformatories and industrial schools, held a similar opinion. He was, he wrote, 'strongly in favour of giving managers extended powers of disposal'.[40] Despite the weight of these and other responses, as well as the Royal Commission's recommendation, Harcourt, the Home Secretary, profoundly disagreed with any suggestion that the powers of managers should be increased. His reasons were set out in a circular issued in November 1884, in which he informed managers of the schools that

> ... no boy should, under any circumstances whatever, be discharged from a Reformatory or Industrial School for Sea or Coast Service, Emigration or Enlistment in the Army or Navy, without the full knowledge and consent of his parents. The Secretary of State requests that this injunction, which will apply also to the emigration of girls, be strictly observed.[41]

A circular could hardly have been firmer or express more clearly the Home Secretary's grave disquiet about the way in which parental consent to emigration

– and enlistment – had been or might be disregarded. There had been an indication of the way in which Harcourt viewed such matters two years earlier, when another circular on the *Discharge of Boys to Enter the Army or Navy, or for Apprenticeship* had made such disposals dependent on the consent of the Secretary of State.[42] This had already excited vehement objections from many of the reformatories and industrial schools, in particular from those engaged in training boys for service at sea.

The tone of the 1884 circular was likely to have been influenced by a series of 'cases' that had come to Harcourt's notice. He had, he wrote, had to deal with dozens of them. They were instances in which children had been taken away from their parents 'and shipped off they know not where after years of imprisonment, sometimes for the slightest possible offences, sometimes none at all except a single act of truancy'.[43] However, once the 1884 circular had been issued the Home Office was bombarded with protests from the reformatories and industrial schools. One of the most immediate objections was received from Francis Glossop, barrister and chairman of the Middlesex Industrial Schools at Feltham. He had also been a member of the Royal Commission and, naturally enough, launched his protest by pointing out to Harcourt that the circular was contrary to the Royal Commission's recommendations. Glossop was followed by other protestors, not least by Lord Aberdare (chairman of the Royal Commission). His letter does not survive, but Harcourt's reply does. It was a biting indictment of the practices of some institutions; a sense of its tone may be gained from a few of its passages. The reformatories and industrial schools were, the Home Secretary wrote,

> ... intended for hardened and habitually criminal children or for neglected children where the home is bad and the parents are vicious. But in practice these limitations are not at all regarded. Many if not most of the cases in these schools now are those of children who for some petty act of naughtiness (such as our own children commit every day) are seized upon, hauled off by the Police before the Magistrate, who without any enquiry into the character of the home or the parents commits them to Prison and takes them away from good and happy homes for 7 or 8 years and then sends them off to sea or to the Colonies without their parents being even allowed to know where they have gone.
>
> I confess this seems to me the most gross and cruel tyranny practiced [sic] in the name of humanity which would astound me if experience did not show that there is no created thing so barbarous as a Philanthropist and world-betterer run mad.
>
> ... I have found children ... apprenticed to fishing smacks in the North Sea, transported to the Colonies etc etc and that where there was no complaint whatever to be made of the home. This assumption on the part of the State and the Managers to set aside the right of

parents where the parents have done nothing to forfeit it, is in my view absolutely intolerable.[44]

The whole letter was a passionate statement of a point of view that was not common among politicians and civil servants, and certainly not among social reformers or philanthropists. However, held as it was by the Secretary of State, it helps to identify one of the brakes that was applied to child emigration from reformatories and industrial schools – and in particular from the industrial schools.

Nonetheless, the complaints about the circular were forceful and well orchestrated and concentrated on two matters in particular. The first was the explicit requirement that an enquiry be made in each case of proposed emigration to determine whether the parents gave their consent. In the face of the outcry against this injunction senior civil servants counselled the Home Secretary that some compromise would be advisable. Harcourt accepted their advice and agreed that certain revisions would be made in a second circular, eventually issued by his successor in 1888.[45] In the rewording the managers of the institutions were only obliged to *notify* parents that they intended to emigrate their child. If they objected the managers had to present their side of the story in order that the Secretary of State could decide whether the objection should be upheld or dismissed. It was a modest concession, but it may have made it easier for the schools to by-pass obstructive parents who, in any case, were unlikely to have the confidence or skill to lodge an objection.

The second complaint that some managers had about the 1884 circular was its direction that a detainee released early on licence must remain in Britain. However, several reformatories had been licensing those whom they selected for emigration because they had found that if boys (no mention of girls) were discharged unconditionally before the end of their term of detention, and then emigrated, some quickly made their way back, often by working their passage on a cattle ship. The managers were unimpressed with this show of ingenuity and resourcefulness. This is how the chairman of the Redhill reformatory explained the problem when taking issue with the licensing restriction imposed by the circular. It was, he wrote,

> ... becoming a habit with the lads to profess a great desire for emigration and, having been sent abroad at considerable expense, to return to their old haunts in England ... exulting in their cleverness in outwitting the authorities by obtaining an early discharge....[46]

This was why licensing had been preferred to discharge. If a licensed boy returned during the unexpired term of his order he could be recalled to the reformatory. That, it was argued, discouraged a rapid escape from Canada.

At the Home Office the case for emigration on licence made by the Redhill reformatory and, later, by the Birkdale Farm School, a Catholic reformatory in Liverpool, was thought to be convincing. Special permission was given to both institutions for them to emigrate licensed boys. However, perhaps in the expectation that a further batch of similar requests would follow, it was considered wise to send the details to Earl Granville, the Colonial Secretary, for transmission to Sir Charles Tupper, the Canadian High Commissioner. Tupper replied that the Canadian government did not encourage the emigration of people who were 'not of good character'. Although he expressed the hope that 'before long it may be possible to arrange a scheme of emigration ... to apply to Industrial Schools', he felt sure, he wrote, 'that public opinion in Canada would not permit of such a measure being made applicable to Reformatories'.[47] A further letter from Tupper a couple of months later informed the Colonial Office that he had submitted all the material to the Canadian government and that his view had been confirmed.[48]

Once the issue was brought to the attention of the Canadian government, however, it began to escalate. The Privy Council in Ottawa considered it in July 1886. A copy of its report was sent to the Colonial Secretary with a letter saying that it was 'not advisable in any way to encourage the emigration to Canada of boys under licence from the Reformatory Schools', pointing out that it would be contrary to the 1869 Canadian Immigration Act.[49] This clearly raised difficulties for the Home Office, not least because they had already given approval to Redhill and Birkdale to act contrary to the wishes of the Canadian government. It was agreed that the permission of the Secretary of State would be withheld in all future cases. However, what the Home Office foresaw was that having raised the issue of the emigration of reformatory boys on licence the attention of the Canadian government would be drawn to the emigration of other boys who had been discharged and the prohibition extended to them. Their assumption was quickly confirmed in a letter from Tupper that explained that the Canadian government disapproved of the emigration of all reformatory young people, whether they had been discharged or were under licence.[50] In response the Home Office took refuge behind the 'voluntary nature' of such emigration, pointing out that it was neither aided nor encouraged by the British government. It was in the hands of private individuals and organisations. All the Secretary of State could do, it was pleaded, was give or withhold his permission case by case.[51]

Confronted with the Canadian decision the Home Office asked the Colonial Office to write to the Governor-General in Ottawa, to explain that the British government hoped that selected emigration from reformatories would not be discontinued. Would he exercise his influence to see whether the ruling could be relaxed? This he duly did[52] and, as a result, the Canadian Privy Council agreed that as long as children had been discharged, their immigration would not be in contravention of Canadian law. The Home Office agreed to abide by this decision and accordingly included the relevant instructions in a further circular.[53]

Thus, the first Home Office circular (1884) was now revised in order to accommodate the views of the Canadian government and, as we have seen, in other respects in order to meet, in part, the objections of managers of British reformatories and industrial schools concerning the status of parental consent to emigration. However, there was a proposal in play that, if accepted, would have circumvented any parental involvement – provision should be made for an 'emigration order' that would enable magistrates to send certain children to a British colony as an alternative to making an industrial school order.[54] The Liverpool School Board had spearheaded the campaign and mobilised support, including that of the High Commissioner in London. However, the Home Office saw three objections. First, that such an order would give magistrates the extraordinary power to expatriate a child on the grounds of the neglect of its parents; second, that once emigrated the children would be beyond the control of the Secretary of State who would nonetheless be held responsible for any failure or abuse; and third, that although the Canadian government currently seemed willing to countenance (and even to support) such a development, there was no guarantee that they would continue to do so.[55] Although Harcourt agreed to receive the Liverpool delegation it did not alter his view that the proposal was unacceptable.

For the moment any further consideration of such matters, as well as work on the preparation of a draft Bill to deal with various reformatory and industrial school issues, was suspended with the fall of Gladstone's government in June 1885. It was succeeded by Lord Salisbury's Conservative administration in which Sir Richard Cross was appointed Home Secretary, serving until Salisbury's resignation at the end of January 1886. There followed Gladstone's short-lived third administration, with H.C. Childers at the Home Office. With Gladstone's defeat at the polls in July 1886 Salisbury was called on again to form a government, which he led until August 1892. During this period Henry Matthews was Secretary of State for Home Affairs. The rapid succession of governments and Home Secretaries between June 1885 and July 1886 brought developments connected with reformatory and industrial school policy to a halt while secretaries of state were briefed and had time to consider their position. None of them had Harcourt's particular interest in juvenile delinquency or matched him in his abiding mistrust of the magistracy, the managers and the philanthropists. Nevertheless, pressure continued to be applied by those who sought some kind of 'emigration order' and by others who, in a more general sense, sought state aid for child emigration. Despite such agitation none of the proposals found favour, although the issue of child emigration remained on the Home Office agenda, but principally as a result of continuing and growing misgivings about the readiness with which managers of the schools, and indeed, other voluntary organisations, emigrated children without having informed parents or obtained their consent. We shall see in chapter 13 later how this issue gradually unfolded in the late 1880s and the early 1890s.

V Canadian Vacillation

It is not possible to gain an adequate picture of the factors shaping the pattern of emigration from the British reformatories and industrial schools without considering the politics surrounding it in Canada. These politics varied between the two types of institutions and over time. In general, in official Canadian circles immigration from industrial schools was regarded without too many qualms, although it was liable to provoke considerable public opposition in cities like Toronto and Montreal. Elsewhere, for example in the Maritimes, the arrival of such children was broadly welcomed. The Glasgow Juvenile Delinquency Board (responsible for several schools in the city) reported that they had received 'a most cordial invitation from the best men in St John [NB] to send both boys and girls'.[56] In fact, from 1884-89 the Glasgow Board emigrated 53 boys and 73 girls to New Brunswick from its industrial schools. Some other industrial schools elsewhere in Scotland followed suit – notably Fechnay (in Perth) and the United Industrial (in Edinburgh).

The emigration of industrial school children continued steadily throughout the 1890s and into the new century, reaching its peak years between 1905 and 1914. This occurred despite an easily aroused public denunciation of any policy that allowed into Canada any young immigrants with an assumed predisposition to crime. As we have seen, when responsibility for immigration was transferred from the Department of Agriculture to the Department of the Interior in 1892, a sharper sense of concern with the management of such opposition is detectable. For instance, in 1897 Pereira, its assistant secretary, wrote to the High Commission in London to say that:

> It would appear that the authorities of the Reformatories & Industrial Schools are under the impression that because they do not send out large parties of children, do not have them inspected in a similar manner to workhouse children and do not receive any bonus … they are at liberty to send forward their children in an irregular manner.
>
> So far from this being the case, in the present state of public opinion … it is most essential that they should have a perfect practique.[57]

This illustrates two points. First, that even late in the century the reformatories and the industrial schools were likely to be referred to in the same breath, and thus confused. Second, it showed that the number of young immigrants coming from these schools did matter in terms of the management of public hostility. While such young people trickled in, their presence could pass unnoticed. However, were larger shipments to arrive and be 'discovered' they could provide useful ammunition for those opposed to child immigration in general. The conflict that the Canadian authorities faced therefore was that they particularly wanted young men who were trained in farming but they did not want anyone with the taint of criminality. What attitude should they adopt, therefore, towards ex-criminals who had been prepared for farm work? The dilemma, of course, only arose with respect to those sent from the reformatories. We have discussed the way in which the legal prohibition of the immigration of such boys was circumvented by drawing a distinction between those on licence and those who had been discharged. Yet, both before and after the agreement that allowed in the latter but not the former, other devices were used on both sides of the Atlantic that served to obscure the origins of those from the reformatories, and thus avoid probing questions. One was not to mention the word 'reformatory' in giving details of the institution from which the young people were sent. This was not difficult to do as the word could be dropped in favour of such terms as 'training home' or 'farm school' that in any case frequently appeared in the names of the institutions. A few of the reformatories omitted the word 'reformatory' from their formal titles altogether, most notably the Royal Philanthropic at Redhill. Even so, in submitting its views on the Children Bill in 1907 the school asked that, in general, the term 'reformatory' be abandoned, the better to facilitate the emigration of boys to Canada.[58]

There were several other reasons, however, why the origins of those from reformatories were not always recognised. One of these lay in the fact that they were likely to be included in the sailing parties assembled by organisations such as Barnardos, Quarriers and the Catholic Societies.[59] It could easily be assumed therefore that it was from these agencies that they came. Thus, there was, throughout, a degree of obfuscation with regard to reformatory immigrants, largely in order to avoid any public clamour. Nevertheless, despite its shortage of agricultural labour, official Canadian policy remained cautious about receiving such boys well into the years up to 1914. For example, in 1909 Obed Smith, the Dominion commissioner of immigration in London, wrote to his superior Scott, the superintendent of immigration in Ottawa, saying that the more he knew of reformatory boys the more he felt satisfied 'that if he has had a training in one of the farm schools for several years, there is every … chance of his succeeding in Canada'.[60] However, the response was lukewarm to say the least. Scott wrote back that he was 'glad to note that you are not receiving many applications for the emigration of these boys and I think their emigration should be consented to in only rare cases …'.[61]

Certainly, by the time of Obed Smith's letter, official attitudes towards the admission of reformatory school boys had been hardening. Indeed, in his report for 1908 the British inspector of reformatories and industrial schools remarked on the reduction in the number of boys emigrated from the reformatories, explaining that 'special restrictions' had been imposed by the Canadian authorities that amounted 'practically to a prohibition'.[62] However, by the following year these restrictions had been somewhat relaxed, although there was a renewed stiffening of policy in 1910. This appears to have been precipitated by the case of one young man from Redhill, who confirmed on arrival that he wished to be employed in farming but subsequently quickly 'deserted' his situation in order to find work in the city. Refusing to take farm work he was thereupon deported.[63] It was this episode, and perhaps others of a similar nature, that probably led Robertson, the Assistant Superintendent of Immigration, to write that 'no more young men from the institution [Redhill] … should be allowed to enter Canada if they can be legally kept out'.[64] Furthermore, a memorandum and the letter confirming the deportation were sent to all immigration agents both in Canada and the UK. Clearly, discharged reformatory boys were acceptable as long as they could be kept within the agricultural labour force, but they were not if they were likely to switch to employment in the cities where, in any case, opposition to the importation of the 'degenerate and criminal class' was most vociferous.

Notwithstanding the restraints imposed by Canadian 'policy', some of its officers (such as Obed Smith in London) conveyed the impression that the emigration of reformatory boys (nothing was ever said about girls) was welcomed, or at least tolerated. Not only was this the case in London but also in Canada where some of the immigration agents acted virtually in a private capacity as intermediaries to receive and place out such boys. For example, Gardner, the Dominion immigration agent at St John, New Brunswick, worked in this way for several industrial schools and reformatories, as well as with the Bristol Emigration Society. Some of the institutions paid him a premium of so much a head. For instance, the Wellington Reformatory Farm School at Peniwick in Scotland (referred to in Canada simply as the Wellington Farm School) used his 'agency' and paid him ten shillings per boy for his trouble.[65]

VI Uneasy Politics

Although a comparatively small proportion of the children who were sent to Canada came from the reformatories and industrial schools it was not for the want of enthusiasm in many quarters. The Home Office did not, however, share this eagerness, which goes some way to explain why more of the children from these schools did not find themselves in the Dominion. As we have seen, the influence of the Home Office lay in the Secretary of State's overall responsibility for the schools, but also in his power to grant or withhold permission for these children's emigration. In order to appreciate the standpoint of this arm of central government it is important to recognise its strong legal orientation.[66] Several Home Secretaries, such as Harcourt, Mathews and Asquith, were barristers, as were permanent under-secretaries like Lushington and, later, Digby. The legal culture in the Home Office was plainly evident in the treatment of questions such as the consents of children and their parents. Even those who, like Asquith, broadly supported the practice of emigration, were nonetheless unwilling to allow anything that they judged to be contrary to the 'will of Parliament'.

What we see in Canada is a somewhat confused official attitude to the immigration of young people from the reformatories. This reflected the tension that existed between the need for agricultural labour and a desire not to harden a public mood that was generally hostile to any suggestion that criminal or immoral immigrants were being allowed into the country. Of course, there was also support for the movement among those in search of labour; but successive Canadian governments felt themselves vulnerable to damaging criticism should they err too far in the encouragement of 'unworthy' immigrants, whether they were adults or children. Those coming from British reformatories could so easily be tarred with this brush. However, partly because of the less pejorative sound of the name, industrial school children escaped the worst of this opprobrium, especially if the boys were believed to have been well trained in farming and the girls in domestic labour.

On the British side economic considerations were important in determining the scale of emigration from these institutions. The Treasury was anxious to avoid increases in its subventions and had maintained the same level of *per capita* grant throughout. As its value declined, and as voluntary contributions diminished, the financial pressures on certain institutions increased, encouraging them to retain as many children as possible for as long as possible. Matters were not made any easier after 1902 when it became more difficult for them to obtain help from the local authorities, faced as these were by the new demands on their resources created by the requirements of the Education Act of that year.[67] On the other hand, in 1908 the Treasury agreed to provide additional funds for the emigration of those under 14 from industrial schools, partly, it seems, in order to encourage the earlier release of at least some of the children and thus to secure a net reduction in its subsidy bill.[68] This may help to explain the increase in emigration from these schools from then up to the outbreak of war.

Thus, the prevailing culture in the British Home Office, the specific economies of the schools and the political sensitivities in Canada came together to limit what might otherwise have been a considerably larger emigration. This particular combination can be thought of as a convergence of the forces of law, economics and politics – a convergence that stands out more prominently in the case of the reformatories and the industrial schools than in other areas of child emigration.

Part VI
The Children and their Parents

TWELVE

What Befell the Children

I Letters from Canada

Most of the previous chapters have included some details of what happened to certain children. Without repeating these examples it is time to assemble some of the other evidence about what happened to individual children and to draw some conclusions. It must be emphasised, however, that hard evidence is meagre, and much of what there is concerns cases that caused disquiet. As a result it often reflects the worst side of child emigration. Nonetheless, it is likely that for every child about whom such evidence still exists there were others whose circumstances were similar but which were ignored or unknown. Furthermore, the children, their parents, relatives or friends wrote few letters, many of which were lost or destroyed. We start this chapter by looking at extracts from a selection of children's letters that did survive. We cannot know how representative they are, but despite the passage of the years, many do foreshadow what the emigrated children of a later generation have begun to disclose, as will be apparent in chapter 15. The letters that are referred to first are drawn from the archive of the Manchester and Salford Boys' and Girls' Welfare Society (MSBG, but now the Together Trust), not because they are substantially different from what is to be found in other collections but because they were more readily accessible.[1]

These letters reveal recurring themes. The most frequent is the search for information, particularly that concerning the whereabouts of mothers (sometimes fathers), brothers, sisters or friends, especially those with whom the children had lived in the Manchester Homes or who had accompanied them on their journey to Canada. This quest is reflected in what is said about the children in many of the reports of the Society's visitors and in those submitted by the Canadian government officers who inspected children from the Poor Law.[2] The desire to locate relatives and friends and to hear from or about them was present even when the children expressed themselves content with their placement and with having come to Canada. For instance, ER (3215, 1899) wrote to Leonard Shaw to tell him that she has 'a good place – eggs and milk', but that she was anxious to have her brother's address. The children's concern to have addresses was not only because they wanted to write and to be written to, but also because they were worried about what might have befallen relatives or friends and also, in some cases, that they felt responsible for helping them. EB (3222, 1888), writing to Wallace at the Marchmont Home, says:

> I have been thinking it would be as well if we would offer a reward of
> five dollars to find out where my Mother is for I am thinking that I ort
> to help her all I can for I now that she needs it … write and tel me.

Receiving no reply he wrote again, saying that he would try to return to England
to find her. Others wrote in a similar vein. HB (3222, 1886) told Shaw that he did
'not know where any of my fether live or my brother live or my sister … I wish
you would inquire'. Another boy, JB (3223, 1889), sent a letter to his grandparents
on his arrival at the Marchmont Home. He asked them to 'try to get to know
where my mother and father is send me my mothers address and tell her where
I am. Give my Brothers and Sisters my best love … please grandfather write and
tell me where they are.' The same concern is to be found in a letter from JH
(3224, 1898), again written to Shaw:

> I came from Ashton union workhouse … I wish you would write to
> that home and get the address and send it … I am anxious to know
> where my mother is … some day when I am able I can have her out
> here with me and make a home for her.

DL (3224, 1899) also wanted to 'make a home' for his mother and explained to
Shaw that if he would find her for him, his employer had promised to help to
support her. He had, he said, already asked the year before. MN (3214, 1905) wrote
to Mrs Shaw sending her a dollar as a Christmas present, thanking her for sending
out her brother and then, in another letter soon afterwards, asking for her help
in arranging for her mother and two sisters to come as well: 'my mother could
get lots of work [and] in time I could pay you back'. She ended by promising to
send 50 cents 'for the missionaries'. Similar sentiments were expressed by MG
(3216, 1913). After thanking Shaw for sending her to Canada, she added, 'if I had
my Mother with me I would be a lot happier I do not know where she is. If you
get to know … please … send me a short note'.

Occasionally, information was also sent to the Home by employers to say that
the child placed with them had received a letter from their family. Mrs G (3215,
1898) wrote to the Marchmont Home from Toronto concerning a letter that had
arrived from HW's sister in Britain (which she enclosed). This asked:

> Do you think if me and Martha Ann saved enouth money for you
> to come home do you think your mistress would let you she might
> Mother does cry about you I do not know what they wanted to send
> you there for you could get on quite as well here in service Me and
> Martha Ann would have all our money for you you might ask I sure
> there is plenty of girls there I think it is a shame and I know you
> would like to come home again … mother would be pleased if you
> could come.

Evidently the 'mistress' was sympathetic and had agreed to write to the Wallaces (who were running the Marchmont Home that the Manchester Society was using) on the girl's behalf. This she did:

> … I think it was a pity to send the poor child away to Canada when her mother and father knew nothing of her coming until after she was here … you made a mistake of a year in her age, as her mother says she was fifteen. H does not wish to return to England for a year yet – but I told her if the people of the Home would send me another in her place I would be willing to let her go…. We will send you what was her year's wages all in a few days. She is well and happy here only Homesick at times.

Mrs Wallace then wrote to Shaw asking for information about the girl's mother and why H was received into the Home. Furthermore, she wanted to know whether, in fact, the sisters were likely to be able to raise the £6 necessary for a passage home and, in any case, what, she asked, was there to go back to? Shaw's reply has not survived.

As well as queries about the whereabouts and well-being of their families many children wished to have information about themselves, rarely about their backgrounds but more often about their dates of birth and their ages. MJ (3222, 1886), for example, wanted 'to know very much' when her birthday was. A related theme that is often to be found in the letters of both the boys and the girls conveys a deep sense of isolation, loneliness and homesickness, as well as disappointment at not having received hoped-for letters. These feelings were evident among those who claimed to have a good placement just as much as they were among those who were dissatisfied with where they were. This is how CJ (3214, 1921) wrote to Ackroyd, the Society's secretary, seven years after her arrival in Canada:

> … I am hoping I will get one of your Christmas letters I did not get one last year and I misted it very much I live 9 miles from a town and three miles from a village I get very lonsom at times and often wish I could hear from some of the girls or see some off them that came out hear to Canada … if you will please send me Miss Smethhurst and Miss Pickfords [staff at the Manchester Home] address I will lose no time in writing them as I wrote three letters and no answer I was feeling very Discurraged.

These feelings of loneliness and homesickness that the children recounted in their letters were not only described in terms of their separation from their families but also as a wistfulness for the Homes in which they had lived in Manchester, for the companionship of the other children and for the presence of the staff. Indeed, in the girls' letters it gradually emerged that when they referred to 'mother' they sometimes meant the matron or house mother at the Rosen Hallas Home.

AD (3222, 1887) wrote to Shaw that she had 'got such a good home' but that she still thought about 'the dear Refuge'. AT (3216, 1913) told Ackroyd that she also often thought 'about the old home in Manchester and all my friends'.

Several young people sent small (albeit large to them) sums of money to the Society without being asked to do so. JB (3225, 1901) for example, wrote to Shaw to say that he was trying to get other 'old boys' in and around Toronto to send donations. Many other young people were keen to have the Shaws, the Wallaces or the Home's staff write to them, and many asked for their photographs. Such links were obviously important to many of the children. This not only reflected their reliance on letters for news but also the need to be reassured that they were not forgotten. They needed to feel that they still had links to their past, especially when their family seemed to have disappeared. However, since one of the purposes of the Society in sending children to Canada was to separate them from what were considered to be degraded families, information about their whereabouts may have been deliberately withheld. Whatever the reasons for the loss of contact with their families, it would appear that many of the letter-writers sought to build a sense of identity and belonging through their association with the organisation. Indeed, it was not uncommon for those over the age of 18 still to write to ask for information, but more often to recount their misfortunes or to tell of their successes. Mrs AW (3220, 1916) wrote to the Marchmont Home to say how happy she was now that she was 'with a man who will take my baby has his own. She calls him Daddy he is a good steady worker and sober ... he used to be in Mrs Birt's Home....' Another woman, KW (3215, 1905), informs Wallace that she is now married and living in New York, but also that she has written to 'Mother' many times but is very sad that she has never had a reply. Her sister JW says the same.

EH (3217, 1892), now grown-up, shares her troubles in a letter to 'Mr and Mrs Shaw':

> ... I have had such a sad misfortune ... I have had a very miserable time of it. My health is not as it used to be, and I have myself and little boy [4] to support, my husband is a drunkard and I cannot live with him, he would not provide for us ... sometimes I feel that I dont care what becomes of me. I get so despondent... [she enclosed a photograph of her son].

It is disappointing that few replies from the Society have survived. We do not know therefore how, or if, the children's letters were answered. Some certainly were, because 'acknowledged' is quite often written on them, but what was said is rarely to be discovered. Nevertheless, there is a great sense of the deep need to know about family and friends and to have a significant 'connection' with someone. It belies the widespread belief at the time that once in Canada children would find a 'new life' in a 'new family' and put the past behind them.

Although it is clear that many children moved or were moved from place to place their letters give little hint of why. Nor do they ask to be moved, either in their letters or in what they said to the visitors. It may be, therefore, that the children who wrote to the Manchester Society, or to other societies, were either those who were reasonably content or, on the other hand, fearful of retribution were they to voice their complaints. However, some of the letters, especially from the girls, reveal other reasons why they did not seek to move. There were those who felt obliged to stay because they were 'needed'. CB (3220, 1911) was 25 when she wrote to Ackroyd, the secretary, describing her life:

> They have been very good to me of course they never gave me any wages but they are not able and I did not feel like leaving on that account as I know they needed me ... mother has been sick for nearly two years and has been helpless as a child.

She went on to say that her 'mother' was now 76 years old and that she had to sit up with her at night, which was 'very trying', but, she added, 'she took care of us when we were young'. A note on her letter queries: 'should this girl stay when the woman dies?'. CJ (3214, 1921) wrote to Ackroyd in a similar vein. She explained that she had:

> ... been here 7 years as Mrs L is an invalid and cannot walk at all I have to take her around in a wheel chair I am pretty well tied down as her daughters all live away from home and her one son stays hear and works the farm. I am alone with her most of the time I often think of the people in England.

She ended by saying that what she would really like was to become a nurse in a hospital.

Another aspect of children's 'entrapment' was the failure of some employers to allow them to go to school, or to go as often as they should. Hillyard, a government inspector, reported on MT (3215, 1911) who was only allowed a few weeks' school. Her mistress's explanation was that because she was ill the girl 'could not be spared'. SB (3215, 1912) tells Ackroyd that she tries 'to do better every day and keep God's will', but Hillyard writes to the Chorlton guardians that as she was 13 'she ought to be at school'.

Others who wished that they were back in England nevertheless accepted their lot as God's plan for them – testimony perhaps to the success of the Society's religious instruction. SF (3215, 1907) writes to Shaw to say that she is very happy but 'of course I some times feel as though I would like to be back with sister and brothers and father but I know that God does what is best for me'. EH (3217, 1892) sighs in a letter to Mrs Shaw:

> ... o dear i think it would be nice to see dear old england once again
> it makes me feel I would like to come back, and then something tells
> me that if it was not God's will i would not have been here, and i
> know whatever we have to do or whatever we have to bear all comes
> from above....

Such sentiments of resignation, indeed fatalism, may well have led to rather more stable placements than would otherwise have been the case, but not necessarily to contentment.

However, alongside the unhappy, distressing or wistful letters there were others that reflected a rather different picture. CL (3222, 1887) declared that she had a good home and was the only girl with six 'brothers'. She refers to 'my ma' and later calls her her 'guardian'. Likewise, EN (3215, 1898) writes to Mrs Wallace that she is 'very well and very happy. It is like a happy heaven. I get plenty to eat and the Mistress likes me very well ... and the Master likes me very well ... I have a nice little bedroom to myself.' Later in the letter she slips into calling the Master 'father'. AT (3216, 1913) says in a letter to Ackroyd that her employers are 'like a mother and father to me'. Likewise, AD (322, 1887) tells Shaw that she has 'such a good home'.

In saying how well settled they felt both boys and girls were also keen to tell of what they could now do around the farm: milking, cheese-making, driving a horse and cart, ploughing or riding. Such letters also give an insight into the kinds of farms in which they found themselves and into the daily routines that surrounded their lives. AP (3216, nd) writes to Shaw that she liked it where she was and that 'we' have '15 sheep, 16 pigs, 6 horses, 2 colts, 16 cows, 14 calves, 9 head of young cattle and about 120 hens'. Likewise, AW (3224, 1892) tells Shaw that he is:

> ... very thankful that I came out to Canada to make room for some
> more poor Boys.... I get up every morning and clean three stables
> attend to four horses and five cows and milk three of them get in the
> wood and then get ready for school but Willie [another MSBG boy
> from Shaw's organisation placed elsewhere] has to clean four stables
> attend to eleven horses and twenty eight cows milk five of them and
> get in wood and water and then get ready for school.

He explains that after he has done his work he walks one-and-a-half miles to school.

Some of the letters, from the girls in particular, reflect a desperate hope that they will be able to stay where they are and that those with whom they have been placed will like them. AD (3215, 1898) sent two letters, one to the Wallaces and the other to Shaw. In the first she says that she likes her home in Toronto and has a good master and mistress. She sends 6s for the Home. In the other letter she asks to be forgiven for giving her mistress trouble – 'being dirty' – and promises to do better: 'then they will like me better'. Similarly, MD (3215, 1898) wrote to the Wallaces in response to a critical letter that her employers had sent to them. She apologised for the trouble she caused and hoped she could stay. Similarly, the sisters K and NM (3215, 1899) tell the Wallaces that they 'are trying to be good girls and to do everything that is right'.

Before drawing conclusions from this brief exploration of the children's letters in the Manchester archive it must be reiterated that they tell us nothing – except by extension – about children who did not write or whose letters have not survived. Among other things the letter-writers may have been the most literate, although in a few cases it was evident that someone had written the letters for them. Nonetheless, it should be noted that the standard of literacy was surprisingly good, given the children's turbulent backgrounds, and is probably testimony to the basic schooling provided by the Society, by the Poor Law schools and, when they attended, by the Canadian schools.

Even though these are only extracts from a selection of letters they demonstrate recurring concerns: the desire to maintain links with family and friends, a sense of loneliness, the fear of having been abandoned, the quest for identity, wistful affection for the Manchester Homes and their staff and sadness at seeming to have been forgotten by them. Much of this is exemplified in the full text of a letter written to Leonard Shaw in 1890 by Jessie J, who was in service with a minister. This is what she wrote:

> I write these few lines to you hoping that you are all quite well as I have not been well since I left Mother first one thing and then another it makes [me] feel as if I dont care what I do and then look I am 100.60 miles [sic] away from Sarah S the only girl that I trust as a friend to me I am being to think that you have foresaken me altogether as I have roat to Mother [a member of the Home's staff] three times allready and she has never roat to [me] once yet nor Miss Fogg nor Miss Slater nor Miss Poter and I have roat to Miss Hudson and she has not roat to me so I think that you have forgotten me but I have not forgotten you and how good you was to me it is 12 months since you gave me that Bibel I ues it Sunday and it is just like new yet and I mean to keep it so as soon as I get settled I will send you some money for your goodness to me when I was not abel to work for myself and now Dear Mr Shaw I am going to ask you for ... your and Mrs Shaw pictures I would so much like to see you now as I am far away from you and Mrs Shaw and I would like one of Mothers give my best love to Mother and all the girls and allso to Mrs Shaw and Miss Poter and everybody else I do not like being hear if I could come back at all I would but I cant ... [I am] lonely by myself but I will [have] to bare it I hope you have got some good girls now you have got rid of all the bad ones at Rosen Hallas I wish I was there now Wow wouldnt I work and do all I could for to please Mother for I know that I was the

worse girl she had in the house but I know that both you and Mother has forgiven me now havent you … I am not a girl of 14 now I am 20 now so please write back as soon as you can … from your loving freind Miss Jessie J God be with you till we meet again.

At the head of this letter was written 'Ack??'

II The Unwanted and the Runaways

There is conclusive evidence throughout the archives that have been consulted that it was commonplace for children to move from place to place. The main reason lay in their employers' dissatisfaction. They were 'too slow', 'too small', 'dirty' (that is, soiling or wetting), 'disobedient', 'obstinate', 'untruthful', 'cruel to the livestock', 'forward with boys', 'unable to learn' – and so the list continued. When dissatisfaction reached a certain point a child was returned to the distribution Home or, in some cases, taken to the nearest railway station or town and left to make their own way. However, in many instances the complaints that led to the return were accompanied by a request for a 'better' replacement.

It is tempting to see the reason for a child's return as essentially self-interest on the part of their employers. In many ways it was, but their feelings and attitudes could span anger, indifference, despair or regret. For instance, Rose Standish was brought to Canada from Liverpool by the Society for Promoting Christian Knowledge (SPCK).[3] In 1891 she was placed with Mrs Biddeson of Roaring River (250 miles north west of Winnipeg). Her 'mistress' wrote to the Rev. Penbreath (who seems to have been a local agent) as follows:

> … she is far too young. I would have liked to have had one about 13 years as I am an aged woman and feel as though I cannot undertake to bring up another child so young and she is so sickly poor thing … and she is such a bad tempered child I sometimes do not know what to do with her. There is no school nearer than two miles from our place & that is too far for a little girl to go alone so of course she has not been to school.… I would like to see the child in some good home near to school, but of course I wanted a child to help me with the housework & she is no use for that in fact she makes me another one to work for. I think if you could get her a good home I should feel it a great burden lifted off my shoulders. Poor little child I feel sorry for her she is a motherless child or I really could not have put up with her at all. If I have to keep the child … I will not send her out in the world homeless. I will do my best for her as long as God spares me to do so. I should like to hear from you if you would write soon.[4]

Dyke, the Liverpool-based Dominion immigration agent, was eventually asked by his department to bring the case to the attention of the Rev. Baron of the

SPCK in the city, since he was assumed to have been responsible for arranging for Rose to go to Canada. In reply Baron explained that she

> … was in good health when she left England. She was a little young but there were several applicants for her.… I am sorry she was removed to an old lady who wanted someone who could be more help to her.… I will see to her removal on my arrival at Winnipeg or if necessary bring her home.[5]

Letters from employers often explained why they were dissatisfied with the child placed with them. In this one (from the Manchester archives) it was claimed that a boy was:

> … no earthly use on a farm. He is so terrible slow I cannot do anything with him. I have tried every plan … but it is no use, and I cannot put any dependence in him. Then he is terribly dirty, and has the habit of dirtying the bed and his clothes. I took the whip to him the other day when, a day or two after my warning him, I had to strip him to the skin and make him wash himself. You will see I cannot pay him $4 a month. I will not keep him if I have to pay him that. I do not want to get rid of the boy … please let me know at once what you will do with him and write to the boy and see if it will sharpen him a little.… I broke him off tobacco.[6]

Whether the boy stayed or not is unclear. Other employers wrote in a similar vein. One girl was returned because, her mistress complained, she was 'so headstrong that if I am not always scolding she will not heed me nor scarcely move. I do mind speaking to you this way but my nerves will not bear constant strife.… I can scarcely rest at nights.'[7]

This dissatisfaction with the children's usefulness, often combined with accounts of their difficult behaviour, did not always lead to their being returned to a distribution Home. Clay, the immigration agent at Halifax, had been told by 'respectable people' that James Francis had not only been ill-used but that he had also disappeared. After contacting Ottawa, Clay was instructed to investigate and report. He saw the employer who explained that:

> … the lad had destroyed a very large amount of property, and he was afraid to keep him any longer and so had given him a little money [22 cents], fitted him up, gave him half a ticket, and went with him as far as Spring Hill Junction, and then gave him in charge to the conductor, to transfer to the conductor from St John at Amhurst with instructions to leave him at, or near Moncton, he being then about ten years and five months old.[8]

At first the boy was found on the streets of Moncton, 'friendless, homeless and hungry'. However, when Clay located him he was on a farm 13 miles away, although the story did not end there, as we shall see later.

Another set of reasons for the requests that children should be 'returned' concerned their illnesses or disabilities. Here is one boy writing to the Wallaces at the Marchmont Home. He had, he said, been 'very sick and I have seventeen dollars in the bank but it took ten for my sickness. My master said I was not able to work on a farm … he thinks I had better go back….' [9] Some of the reasons for returning a child involved fears that they were 'going mad'. Here is Wallace writing to Shaw in Manchester about a girl who 'was becoming mentally unbalanced, singing and knocking at night', although, he added, she was 'rational some of the time'. She had been examined by doctors and recommended for admission to the Rockwood Hospital for the Insane;[10] but, asked Wallace, 'who will pay for her? She is under 18 and has been out for 3 years.'[11] In another letter Wallace tells Shaw that:

> When Miss Hertz [of the Chorlton guardians] was here in the summer she visited E … and found she was 'feeble minded'… she cannot tell the time … seems to have no memory … is very small for her age and very delicate and is quite unfit for Canadian life. The Chorlton authorities should certainly not have sent her…. I cannot place her … it is more than likely she will become a public charge.[12]

Indeed, a child's mental state, described in various ways, is not infrequently found among the reasons for sending them back to the receiving Home or, in the case of a boy from the Croydon union, for it being impossible to make a placement. Joseph, explained the immigration agent at Winnipeg, was 'about 12 or 13 years of age, a complete idiot, whom nobody will employ'. He had been 'brought out' by the Rev. Winter of the SPCK, but when approached to take the boy back he protested that he did not have sufficient funds to do so.[13] Indeed, neither employers nor the organisations were anxious to meet such costs or those arising from medical treatment, especially for those whose condition was likely to be long-standing. They were no longer an asset to the labour force and thus a liability that Canadian charitable agencies were loth to accept. Nor were children's medical expenses covered by any of the mutual aid societies that were beginning to emerge, particularly in association with the growing trade union movement. When they had workmates these might rally round to give immediate help. For example, John Newstubb, brought out by Lord Archibald Douglas under Catholic auspices when he was 17, lost a foot while working for a railway contractor. In 1887 there was no employer liability legislation, but his fellow workers subscribed enough for him to be fitted with an artificial foot.[14]

Few boys, however, worked in such occupations; most stayed on the farms, at least for their first years in Canada. Nevertheless, they were also exposed to accidents, typically with farm tools and machinery and with horses. Others, both boys and girls, suffered from frostbite because of inadequate clothing, or were crippled by ill-fitting footwear. Almost always they were then returned, being considered no longer able to do the work demanded of them. Furthermore, it was not unusual for older children, particularly the boys, to leave of their own accord: to escape ill-treatment, to get better wages, to search for brothers or sisters elsewhere in Canada or to experience the assumed excitement of the larger towns and cities. Such children were frequently described as having 'run away'. Their recovery was sometimes sought by their employers through advertisements in a local paper and rewards for their 'recapture' were occasionally offered. More often they were recorded by the societies and by the Canadian government inspectors as having 'disappeared'. The whereabouts of some were later discovered, but vigorous tracing was beyond the resources of most of the agencies. It follows that the visiting that was done could be abortive, the inspector arriving at the placement only to find the child no longer there, the employer not having informed the agency nor having any information about where they were to be found. Indeed, many appear to have disappeared without trace despite, in some cases, the efforts of immigration agents, the police or advertisements in the papers. For example, Esther Keep was brought to Canada in March 1891 from the Peckham Union by Rye, but by the end of the year her mother had heard nothing about or from her and sought information from the Local Government Board (LGB). Queries were dispatched and eventually Donaldson, the Toronto agent, was asked to make inquiries and report back.[15] He failed to find her.

When children ran away employers often sought a replacement and in doing so communicated the fact that the child had left. This, for example, is what the postmaster at Rat Portage (south of Winnipeg), the employer of George Walkley, wrote to the Department of Agriculture:

> … he went today without my consent. Can you send me a good boy that has been well brought up. I want one to cut wood, carry it in, take out parcels & make himself generally useful and if suitable and trustworthy I would learn him the business and make a clerk out of him. I want a boy stronger and quicker than Geo. Walkley and better brought up.[16]

This illustrates two important points. First, that employers could misunderstand who it was who had provided them with a British immigrant child. Certainly, the Department of Agriculture did not do so. Second, the letter exemplifies the fact that even when employers were dissatisfied with a child they were not necessarily deterred from asking for another.

Sometimes children went to neighbours, or were taken in by them when they were thought to have been ill-treated. Whatever the reason it was liable to lead to disputes, the more so when religious differences intervened. Here, for example, is Rye writing to Lowe at the Department of Agriculture:

> In May of 85 I placed a little girl of 9 years old named Catherine Camp
> with Mr Edward Robinson of Lascelles [in the province of Québec] ...
> in April of this year '89 – he reports that some very low RC neighbours
> have taken this child – & defy him to take her again.
>
> I wrote him giving him authority to take her but they laugh at him
> – can you send your district immigration agent after the child, to see
> what had better be done – if he can remove her – she had better not
> go to the Robinsons again – but be sent back here?[17]

Unfortunately, there is no evidence as to whether or not the child was recovered
for Rye or, indeed, whether the Department acceded to her wishes.

We have seen already how the Catholic Church in Britain was anxious to
extricate Catholic children from Protestant influences.[18] That quest also extended
to Canada, as in the case of William Anson. Eight-year-old William, a Catholic, was
placed by Gardner (the immigration agent at St John, New Brunswick, acting for
the Bristol Emigration Society [BES]) with a non-Catholic family. Questioned
about his decision he wrote to the Department of Agriculture to explain what
had happened. The boy had arrived 'labelled Wm. Anson 7 years old going to
Mr Gardner, St John NB'.

> ... Mr Whitwill wrote me the lads wretched mother had employed
> a Lawyer who wrote him he must get the child back or he would be
> proceeded against in Law. Mr W then wrote me to visit the child and
> report his present position – which I did ... [then] I was called upon
> by a Priest Secretary to Bishop Sweeny who brought a letter from an
> Atty ... in London asking the child ... be sent back to his mother, the
> letter stating the mother had reformed & become a good *Catholic* &
> married to a highly respectable man. I replied I did not see how this
> could be done, that I had no power to do so & if I had it would be a
> *cruel* thing to do ... (original emphases).

In any case, he said, he had informed the priest 'that something stronger than the
letter would be required, not least money to pay for the child's return ... since the
child was not put to work, but brought up ... as their own, clothed well & kept at
school'. Later, Gardner saw the Bishop, who told him that 'religion was far above
anything else'. 'Well', the immigration agent countered, 'I did not know anything
about religion when I placed the child.' He hoped that the Bishop would leave
the child undisturbed although the attempt to have him removed was:

> ... in full accordance with the present policy of the Romish Church;
> however we must do what we can to frustrate the effort and to prevent
> a wicked mother from again getting hold of the child for whose care
> she is utterly unsuited.[19]

As in so many of the cases that emerge from the records the outcome remains undocumented. But with new legislation being introduced in Britain between 1889 and 1891 curtailing the rights of parents in these matters it seems unlikely that the child's mother could have obtained an effective legal means of recovering her son.

So, the considerable movement of the children from place to place could arise for many reasons: one other was because they were removed by the agencies, either because they had been ill-treated or, in the case of girls, when they became pregnant or were thought to be in moral danger.

III Removing the Ill-treated

There is no way of knowing now how many of the child migrants of the late nineteenth and early twentieth century were ill-treated. We should also remember that what is considered to be unacceptable physical punishment today would often have passed as appropriate discipline at that time – from the use of canes or sticks to 'whipping'. Furthermore, there were more things for which such punishments were considered appropriate. Likewise, the physical labour expected of young children then would be regarded as excessive today and would be classed as ill-usage; the concept of 'emotional abuse' hardly existed. All these provisos have to be taken into account in assessing the nature and extent of the ill-treatment to which British children were exposed in Canada. The most searching assessment was made by Parr in her sample of Barnardo children. She concluded that there was case file evidence that nine per cent of the boys and 15 per cent of the girls had been subjected to excessive punishment.[20]

When there were grounds for believing that a child was being ill-treated the precipitating event was usually a letter from a concerned third party – a neighbour, one of the Canadian government inspectors in the case of Poor Law children or sometimes from local notables to whom others had conveyed their concerns. It was extremely rare for the children themselves to sound the alarm: they mostly suffered in silence or ran away. Even when the alarm had been raised those commissioned to investigate could dismiss the complaint, report that punishments were justified or fail to elicit the child's side of the story. And when legal proceedings against perpetrators were instituted, cases were usually dismissed by local magistrates despite compelling evidence of an offence having been committed.

The case of Mary Mills from Barnardos illustrates several of these aspects of ill-treatment and the responses to it. Captain Annesley, superintendent of the reception Home at Peterborough, brought a charge against Mrs McNish for assaulting Mary. A full report of the proceedings appeared in *The Cornwall Standard*.[21] Both parties were represented. Mary had been sent to Canada in 1889 at the age of 12 and later that year placed with the Rev. McNish and his wife in the town of Cornwall. Annesley did not visit her for nearly six weeks, but when he did he found her with the Hollister family nearby. In his testimony he said that the child:

... had a cut wound across the bridge of the nose which had blackened both her eyes. There was a bruise on each of her temples; a cut on the wrist, which must have been from a heavy blow as it cut nearly to the bone. It appeared as if the bone was broken to a non-professional man. There were two bruises on one arm and on the other a black place as big as the palm of my hand. It was pretty livid.... I noticed that the child had difficulty walking; saw her limbs; they were a mass of bruises right down to the heels – black and discoloured.

Under cross-examination Annesley agreed that Mary had been 'commended' to the McNishes by the Home, but denied that he knew that she 'had come from the midst of crime, nor that her father and mother had been in prison the greater part of her life, nor that she had been in a poor house'. The prosecution lawyer contended that these questions about the child's antecedents were irrelevant, but the magistrate allowed similar questions to continue to be put. Annesley explained that he had called a doctor to the child, but the doctor had told him that the Hollisters had a bad reputation and so he declined to attend. When it became clear that there was going to be a trial, two other doctors 'refused to touch the case'. Another eventually examined Mary on behalf of Barnardos but was not called by the prosecution because he was considered to be prejudiced in favour of the defence. However, the family doctor whom Mrs Hollister had called to attend Mary in the first place did give evidence that substantially confirmed Annesley's account, but adding that some of the bruises were not recent. Then followed the evidence of two neighbours who had seen the injuries that had been inflicted on Mary. They too corroborated the evidence of the previous witnesses.

Mrs Hollister was then called, but not her husband. She explained that she had seen Mary on the street with blood on her nose, had taken her home where she had examined her and found that, as well as the injury to her nose, there were 'bruises on the side of her face and on her arms and legs; they were black and blue'. Apart from calling her doctor she did not, she said, know what to do as Dr McNish was a minister. Mary herself was the next to give evidence. First she explained what had been required of her:

After I got up I lit the fires, set the tables, swept and then whatever my mistress told me. I washed dishes, and did the boots. I sometimes used to wash the clothes, sometimes to sew.... I did not attend the public school since I came here.

Then she recounted what had happened:

I received a whipping. Mrs McNish gave it to me. I was wheeling baby up and down the hall in the carriage. It is about four years old. She was standing up and I told her to sit down and she would not do it. The cat was in the carriage and jumped out and she leaned over to catch it and fell out. She was not very much hurt. I took her up to Mrs McNish. She took the stick out of the drawer and beat me. It was about as thick as a piece of the chair [pointing] … about 2 feet long and about ½ an inch thick. She struck me across the face on both sides and on the top of the head. Also on the arms, three or four times on each arm. Also on the legs, I don't know how often. After the whipping she told me to lie down, she was going to whip me again. I ran out of the house and met Mrs Hollister, and went home with her, where I have been ever since.

The defence then asked Mary about her earlier life in London. She had had a stepfather who was frequently in court for beating her mother. Mary often went for the police. In the end her mother 'ran away', leaving the children behind. Two brothers and a sister were admitted to the 'poor house', she to hospital from where 'a lady' took her to Barnardos. She had been in hospital for three months.

Mid-way through the proceedings the magistrate intervened to say that he thought that 'the whole case had been hatched up', whereon the prosecution lawyer said that it was plainly useless to continue after such a statement and withdrew. However, he was persuaded to continue and Mrs McNish was called. On the day in question she was, she said, ill in bed. She had heard a thud and knew that her youngest child had fallen. Mary brought the child to her who was not crying at the time but who did do so 'very hard' shortly afterwards. When asked how she fell the infant replied that Mary had 'pushed her off the carriage'. Then, went on the mother,

> I feared she had killed my child. I did not 'flog her'. I took a piece of shingle and gave it to her over the hands. I positively say I did not touch her face. I did not chastise her as severely as I would my own child under the same circumstances. I had not the strength.…

Her husband, Mrs McNish said, had made all the arrangements for taking the girl in the first place. She had objected to doing so 'knowing from my experience what Home girls were. I took her against my will.' She had had another Barnardo girl from the Orkney Islands but had sent her away. Mrs McNish continued by saying that she did not know that the children were 'imported' from England, only later learning that they were 'the very refuse of London'.

The defence lawyer was invited to address the court. 'The charge', he maintained, 'hung on the slender thread of the child's [Mary's] evidence uncorroborated.' He went on to denigrate the work of Barnardos and the type of child brought to Canada. The most useful contribution of the evidence offered was, he claimed, to show people the 'risk they were running in taking such girls'. Furthermore, the Hollisters 'did not stand well in the community' and the case provided 'a fine chance to degrade a minister of another congregation'. Even if Mrs McNish had inflicted all the injuries as described, the chastisement would have been warranted, and no more than a parent would administer. The whole case, the defence contended, could have serious consequences, especially for a minister.

The prosecution pointed out that there was no evidence to tarnish Annesley's character and that he had behaved entirely correctly. Mrs Hollister had also acted in a responsible way. Mrs McNish admitted that there were no bruises on Mary when she had arrived and that she *had* beaten her, but not, she claimed, as severely as was being contended. As the law stood a parent could only chastise a child in a 'reasonable and moderate' manner, and this was neither. Yet the magistrate dismissed the case.

Mary was removed to the Peterborough Home and later placed elsewhere. The conclusions to be drawn from this case are pretty clear, but they should be considered in the light of other examples of the circumstances surrounding the removal of children (or the failure to do so) from placements in which they had been ill-treated or abused in other ways. For example, Clay, the immigration agent in Halifax, had received a number of anonymous letters calling his attention to the ill-treatment of certain children placed by Birt. However, he reported that after visiting he found the accusations, 'with trifling exceptions', to be unfounded. This, he admitted, had induced him 'to treat with indifference' subsequent letters of a similar kind. Thus, when he had received another about the ill-treatment of 10-year-old James Francis he had, he said, regarded it in the same light. Nevertheless, he later felt constrained to visit because of rumours that the boy had 'disappeared', which indeed he had. However, Clay found that another family had taken the boy in and they refused to relinquish him. As a result the immigration agent left the matter in the hands of the stipendiary magistrate and city marshal at Moncton. This led to the case being referred to the Attorney-General of Nova Scotia who instructed a barrister to make enquiries and bring charges if there were evidence that James had been ill-treated. This he did, the case being heard 'before a very large crowd of people … many came from miles to be present'. The case was dismissed, however, albeit with 'a suitable rebuke' to the employer for having sent James away. The boy, it was reported, was then cleared of the defendant's claim that he had destroyed farm equipment, although James had not been charged with that offence.[22] The accused was himself a justice, which perhaps explains the widespread public interest in the proceedings. Indeed, the networks of acquaintances and friendships, as well as antagonisms between neighbours and sectarian rivalries, should not be underestimated as factors influencing the responses made to claims of ill-treatment.

Another example serves to illustrate the lack of urgency attached to removing a child who had been ill-treated and the strong tendency to 'blame the victim'. Gardner, the agent at St John, received a telegram informing him that 'the boy at Geo. Craig's is scandolous [sic] abused something should be done at once'. Four days later he forwarded the telegram to Ottawa saying that he had visited the boy, William Summerly, four months earlier when the boy had thanked him for placing him there. But Gardner also explained that 'Mr Craig to whom I sent him is in prison for smuggling horses from the US. So there are only women to control him and he has a bad temper.' Gardner then went on to say that there was nobody nearby with whom he could place William. Therefore, should he, he asked the Department, bring him back to St John and try to obtain another place for him, and what about the expenses involved? It was unwise, he pointed out, 'to have the neighbourhood to cry ill-treatment and [to provide] no relief'.[23] Yet again, the record ceases at this point.

Very occasionally older boys initiated action against a cruel employer. James Bradburn's case was reported in the *Grenfell Sun* (North West Territories [NWT]).[24] James brought a charge of assault against Samuel Heritt, claiming that he had tried to strangle him and had beaten him. Heritt was found guilty and paid the $10 fine and $5.25 costs.

These various cases suggest certain conclusions that it is reasonable to assume applied more generally. First, there is the matter of the nature of the information about ill-treatment. Given the infrequency of inspections and the children's reluctance to make accusations in front of the perpetrators, ill-usage was unlikely to be detected unless, as in the case of Mary Mills, there was palpable evidence that it had occurred. Bruises gradually disappear and not all ill-treatment would have been persistent. In any case, as has been said, the use of physical punishment for childhood misdemeanours was commonplace in those days and, up to a point, considered to be justifiable. Second, the explanations of injuries given by adults were often preferred to those of the children. Furthermore, there was a strong tendency to lay the blame on the victims, either because of their unacceptable behaviour or because of the disreputable backgrounds from which it was assumed they had come. All this leads to a third conclusion; namely, that neither the staff of the Homes nor the governments' local agents were likely to detect ill-treatment on their occasional visits. They were more likely to be alerted by letters from neighbours expressing their concern. Some of the letters were anonymous and some may have been malicious. Not all were taken seriously.

Lastly, there was the question of whose responsibility it was to investigate possible ill-treatment and then take any action that was required. Some of the emigrationists did shoulder these responsibilities, but others endeavoured to shift them to the central government's immigration agents and later to the special inspectors appointed after 1900. However, although these officers visited the Poor Law children they were only able to advise the agency or the British authorities concerned of any disquiet that they felt. Some of their reports demonstrated profound misgivings about what was happening. For example, Inspector Hillyard reporting to the Marchmont Home about AW's mistress in 1910 wrote that she was

> ... a person of violent temper who had no idea of government except by force. Last year I remonstrated with her for administering corporal punishment.... As might be expected this course of treatment has resulted in making the girl revengeful, stubborn and hateful.

The girl had told him, the inspector continued, that the day before the master had kicked her. 'I would', he stressed, 'strongly urge her removal.'[25] Similarly, Inspector Henry had reported to the same Home two years earlier that EB had

> ... a pretty hard home. Her mistress has not been any too kind, wants to return her and get a smaller girl. E also desires another place and I certainly think she should have an immediate change where the work wd be lighter and pay given.[26]

Further evidence that government inspectors like these did not have the authority to remove a child when they discovered ill-treatment is provided by the case of James Griffiths in 1906, then 16 years old. Inspector Hillyard reported that James had told him:

> ... that he had been frequently beaten and kicked and that one of the instruments of torture used was a heavy strap with a buckle at the end. On one occasion he [the employer] had struck him with a bridle to which was attached the iron bits, and again he cut him across the face with a rawhide.[27]

These were, Hillyard explained to the chief inspector of British immigrant children, 'only a few of the brutalities to which the boy has had to submit'. Furthermore, the boy was only paid $4 a month and board but was 'easily worth $8 or $10 and board'. Although it is not clear from the report which organisation had brought James to Canada, Hillyard hoped that its staff could be informed and then find the boy another placement; it would not be difficult because he was 'a smart active fellow'. What happened as a result of this account of the boy's testimony is unrecorded, but Hillyard's letter emphasises the fact that when an inspector had concerns about one of the Poor Law children he was visiting he first had to communicate with the chief inspector who then informed the relevant organisation; it was then left to the organisation to take whatever action was considered necessary. The society concerned should then have informed the Poor Law union from which a boy or girl had been sent and Ottawa should have sent the report to the Local Government Board (LGB) in London. Even when all this had been done as it should have been the inherent delays could leave children in dangerous circumstances for too long.

As well as the removal of a child who was ill-treated, there was the further matter of bringing charges against the perpetrators. Whether or not this was done seemed to depend on several considerations. First, the emigrationists were sometimes reluctant to take legal action for fear that the publicity would cast their work in an unfavourable light. Alongside this was their uncertainty about obtaining a conviction, even when the evidence was strong. Then there was the question of who should pay to bring a case to court: the agencies themselves, the

Dominion government, a provincial government or one of the various authorities involved in Britain?

For all these reasons the removal of a child because of physical abuse or the number of cases brought to court are inadequate indices of its actual scale. Likewise, the removal of girls because they became pregnant does not give a full picture of the sexual abuses to which they could have been exposed. All that can be said is that these removals give some indication of the nature of the risks and of the way in which the employers and the agencies responded when they became evident.

IV Seduction, Sexual Assault and Rape

Parr has discussed the particular vulnerability of girl immigrants who were placed in households where, although they often lived more intimately with the family than they would have done in Britain, they remained 'outside the incest taboo'. Furthermore, their vulnerability was increased because they were 'outsiders whose characters were suspect, and [whose] "moral falls" tended to confirm local beliefs rather than provoke local outrage...'. They were also 'placed beyond the reach of their mother's and sister's counsel'.[28] In her large sample of Barnardo child emigrants Parr found that 11 per cent of the girls had become pregnant (and presumably given birth) while they were still the responsibility of the Society. These were only the instances that led to pregnancy. The records of the various agencies, and of the Canadian officials, provide regular glimpses of the sexual defencelessness of immigrant girls (the similar potential vulnerability of boys is never mentioned). However, few of these cases are sufficiently well documented to determine what actually happened. This is partly because sexual matters were often described or discussed in a rather indirect fashion. However, there were three things that tended to happen when there was evidence of the 'seduction' (the word most commonly used) of a British immigrant girl. First, there was usually pressure for her to be removed, even where the offence had not occurred in the family in which she was placed. Second, the Canadian authorities usually adopted an attitude of non-intervention. Third, there was an almost total failure to gain restitution or to punish the guilty at law – even when, in exceptional cases, proceedings were initiated. For example, in 1878 the Rev. Hodnett of Perrytown wrote to the immigration authorities to inform them that a girl of 15 who had been placed with him by Rye had been seduced by a wealthy neighbour. He requested that an enquiry be instituted. MacPherson, the Kingston immigration agent, was asked to investigate. He wrote to Lowe, the Deputy Minister at the Department of Agriculture, that:

> After having seen the girl also the Doctor who examined her and having obtained an affidavit as evidence confirming the case, with other necessary information & evidence I returned to Port Hope ... and ... found the Rev Mr Hodnett who expressed himself very desirous of

being relieved of the girl at as early a date as possible. The following day I proceeded to Toronto and there reported my investigations, recommending that passes be forwarded to Miss Rye that she might … have the girl returned to … [the] Home at Niagara.[29]

And that was what happened. The case of another girl provides further illustration. She had been placed from Birt's Knowlton Home. Her subsequent seduction was reported in 1890 in the *Montreal Witness*. The case was raised by the Society for the Protection of Women and Children. They wrote to the Minister of Justice in Ottawa asking that his department institute legal proceedings but, as Lowe reported to his Montreal agent, the minister 'advised that it would not be well for the Dept to intervene…'.[30]

The societies and organisations seemed to follow various courses when seduction was discovered or suspected. In some cases they referred the matter to the official responsible for immigration and left them to take any further action. Thus, in 1887 Rye wrote to Lowe asking him: 'what became of the cases [sic] [of] seduction – [of] the very young girl who had a child at Wingham. Did the Ontario Government take any further action … it is a cruel shame if nothing more has been done.'[31] Rye's enquiry highlights one of the reasons why firm official action was not always taken; namely, the division of responsibility between the federal and provincial governments. In this case the matter had been referred to the government of Ontario 'in order to enable such steps to be taken as are necessary [for] … bringing to justice the person accused of the crime'.[32] In fact the Ontario Department of Justice did initiate proceedings but '… the prosecution failed for want of proof of the child's age'.[33] Indeed, the children rarely, if ever, had their birth certificates, nor did the Homes, added to which the children themselves were sometimes uncertain how old they were. Even when girls who were sexually abused were obviously very young the lack of firm evidence about their age usually meant that prosecutions failed, as in the case about which Rye had already enquired. She wrote to Lowe soon after the outcome, pressing him to secure an amendment to the legislation that would overcome this particular problem. In doing so she strengthened her case by announcing that she had a 'more serious case to report':

> … in Aug[st] 1885 [a man] took a child of 10 – from here – and he has been using her from December 1885 till this July – when she ran away and came here & told her story. I took her next day to Mr Hill police magistrate at the Falls, who after proper very severe examination – sent the case to trial at Welland. I attended on 17th insta the child (an absolute orphan) – the grand jury found a true bill but the petty jury dismissed the case – for want of proof of child's age.[34]

In a postscript she added: 'It will ruin this work in England if these facts are known there.' This was another reason why societies or individuals were not always keen to initiate proceedings, even when a girl's age could be established. It was not until the Ontario legislation of 1897 for the protection of British immigrant children that, as Parr points out, the problem of establishing a child's age before a court was overcome. Information on the disembarkation papers was thereafter treated as sufficient evidence of age (but could, of course, still be wrong). Three years later federal legislation made this applicable throughout Canada.[35]

It was probably the exception rather than the rule to bring cases of the seduction and sexual assault of immigrant girls to court. (This may also have been the pattern for those born in Canada too.) In 1913 DS was returned to the Marchmont Homes because she was pregnant. She accused the 'master', whereon Knight (the Wallaces' successor as superintendent) placed the matter in the hands of a solicitor.[36] The girl swore on oath that she was telling the truth, but the accused denied responsibility. The solicitor concluded that her story, which was 'revolting in the extreme', had to be believed, but no further action seems to have been taken. Two years later the same girl was in the maternity hospital in Montreal. The father of her child was reported to be a solicitor (presumably a different one). Knight wrote that he 'would like to see this reprobate brought to trial but', he pointed out, 'there are difficulties in the way, the law is very peculiar in these cases'.[37] Whether or not the matter was in fact brought to trial is unclear.

Not only were girls 'returned' if they became pregnant but also when they were 'thought' to be or when their behaviour was considered to be 'too forward'. For example, Mrs Wallace of the Marchmont Home wrote to Shaw in Manchester about EW who was brought back:

> … she *looks suspicious* but declares there is nothing wrong and her master says the same. However we have made him pay $200.00, part to be returned if all is right – so to avoid the scandal here and also the impossibility of getting her another home (original emphasis).[38]

EW was then returned to the Home in Manchester but, Wallace pointed out, 'she knows nothing of our having made the man pay or who is sending her home. Thought it best not to tell her.' The girl was found a position in service but lost it and was then in and out of the workhouse. It is unclear whether or not she actually was pregnant.

Even more concern was expressed when it was believed that a girl had taken 'to a life of immorality'. However, such girls were often elusive, and finding them in order to return them could be difficult, as in the case of Mary L. She had been sent to Canada at the age of 16 in 1887 from the Sale Industrial School where she had been since she was 10. Her emigration was arranged by the Society for Promoting Christian Knowledge (SPCK) in conjunction with the Montreal-based Women's Protection Immigration Society (WPIS). The files contain considerable correspondence on the case, partly as a result of endeavours to establish just when and where the girl was 'ruined'. Was it in England? Was it on board the ship in the company of some of the ship's officers? Or, was it after her arrival at Québec? The superintendent of the Sale Industrial School wrote that:

> the girl was pure, her moral character chaste. No dishonour had come to her in this sense.... She knew undesirable people in Manchester and we felt sooner or later after leaving School she would in all probability go to them, and we did not think well of her mother, and so to cut her off from all these influences and give her an entirely new start in life I was induced to send her out, believing I was doing the kindest and best thing for her. She was a clever girl, a good worker, and a good needlewoman and might have done exceedingly well. She was intelligent and in no way ignorant of the suffering consequent on any sinful conduct.[39]

In drawing the case to the attention of the Immigration Department in Ottawa, the Rev. Fyles (the SPCK chaplain at Québec) expressed the strong view that it was not to be tolerated

> ... that this *young girl*, entrusted to our Canadian authorities, should be left unrestrained to pursue evil courses. I would suggest ... that she should be arrested.... The Rev Bridger and an SPCK matron are expected.... On the return of these the girl might be placed in their charge, and returned to the School ... it is to be hoped she would give such information as might lead to the punishment of those who have brought about her ruin (original emphasis).[40]

This, and the previous letter reported above, encapsulate the complicated mixture of motives that influenced reactions in matters of this kind: outrage, blaming the girl, an attempt to allocate blame for what had happened to her and the wish to see Canada rid of the problem, partly in order not to prejudice the future work of child and female emigration.

One of the largely unrecorded issues is the fate of the babies born to the girls. A few would have been boarded out if their mothers continued to be employed and could pay the fees. However, even for older girls in service their wages were usually insufficient to meet the cost. Although a Children's Aid Society had been established in Toronto in 1891 (and later elsewhere) it did not admit babies, leaving that to 'infant shelters'. They, in their turn, would not usually keep children beyond the age of four. Certainly, the emigrationists were very reluctant to admit the babies of any of the girls whom they had brought to Canada to their reception Homes. First, because it was unlikely that such babies could be readily placed and, second, because keeping them for any length of time was costly and would gradually reduce their ability to absorb newcomers from Britain or to receive those who were returned to them. What usually happened was that once returned to the reception Homes the girls were sent back to Britain, where they had their babies, who were then taken into the care of the agencies responsible for their mother's emigration in the first place. It is not unreasonable, therefore, to regard this 'repatriation' as one example of the deportation of social casualties from Canada.

V Repatriation and Deportation

The repatriation of children to Britain was usually initiated by the emigration agencies. It was done as a token of their good faith; that is, as evidence that they could be relied on not to burden Canada with the unfit, the unworthy, the idle or the immoral. Most considered that this was necessary in order not to prejudice the future of their work. However, it is virtually impossible to discover just how many children were sent back to the 'Old Country' – certainly more than were recorded in the agencies' public documents. Nonetheless, additional 'deportations' do come to light in the Canadian archives because the emigrationists were keen to obtain concessionary fares for the return trip, and this required an application to the central department.

There were some instances where a combination of factors led to a child being sent back to Britain. Martha Radcliffe's father had written to various authorities in Canada asking for help in securing his daughter's return. The case was complicated because Rye had arranged for the girl to be admitted to the Mercer reformatory in Toronto, because 'she would not work – and would run away from her places'.[41] However, the girl had committed no offence. Rye said that she had no objection to the government sending the girl back to her father as long as it met the expenses involved. Lowe, at the Department of Agriculture, conveyed this information to the Department of Justice together with his view that it would be better to have the girl returned to her father.[42] He also issued a mild rebuke to Rye, saying that he doubted 'the special good that will come to any girl from residence in the Mercer institute'.[43] A few days later he wrote to her again, saying that he saw no reason for not returning Martha to her father and that she should act accordingly – and meet the cost.[44] Eventually an order was issued for Martha's release[45] and Rye duly paid for her to go back to Britain.[46]

The repatriation of 'unsatisfactory' children forms part of the larger picture of deportation in Canadian politics during this period and, indeed, later. A number of studies have suggested that it served two main purposes: the expulsion of political radicals and the shedding of surplus labour. However, Drystek advances a somewhat different view that corresponds more closely with the reasons for child deportation. His view is that the 60,000 deportations before the Second World War owed more 'to the inadequacy and parsimony of social services ... than to political repression or to labour policy'.[47] In short, deportation was a convenient way of avoiding having to support immigrants who became dependent. More generally, however, deportation was a means by which the federal government could parry demands for firmer control over both the amount and the 'quality' of immigration. This is an exact parallel to what was happening in the case of child immigration. *Some* deportations were the price to be paid for sustaining its scale. It was a politically symbolic concession to those who complained of the unfair burden that destitute or dependent immigrants placed on local resources. Deportation was a logical extension of the prohibition on the entry of 'every lunatic, idiot, deaf, dumb, blind or infirm person'.[48]

Thus, although keen to increase the scale of immigration for economic reasons, Canada wanted only the young, the able-bodied and the hardy – people who would swell the kind of labour force that would enable its agricultural and natural resources to be exploited. The land needed to be peopled, but not by the dependent. British children were regarded by government as a welcome addition unless or until they came to be viewed as a social or political liability.

VI Citizenship

Whether carried out informally by the societies or formally by the Canadian authorities the deportation of children raises the question of their civil status. In a number of the archival documents relating to this period it is stated or implied that it was not possible for an official deportation (or even an unofficial deportation) to be ordered once a young person had been resident in Canada for more than three years. Aliens who had not yet been 'naturalised' could be deported, but it was by no means clear how this applied to British immigrants and, more particularly, to lone British children since, until the 1947 Canadian Citizenship Act, Canadian nationals were considered to be British subjects. Nevertheless, the term 'Canadian national' had appeared in various pieces of legislation such as the 1914 Naturalisation Act and the 1921 Canadian National Act.[49] Furthermore, before 1947 'minors' (including women) did not have authority over their nationality: they could only become naturalised as a member of a family.

How could a British immigrant be legally deported when their British citizenship was tantamount to Canadian citizenship? Only aliens could be deported. However, the question of whether or not immigrant children were Canadian nationals, and hence entitled to the rights that that conferred, went beyond the issue of deportation. It raised the question of whether they had the same rights as Canadian-born young people – to protection, to education, to inheritance and to assistance of various kinds. Furthermore, there was the equally important matter of what their rights were generally *thought* to be and how far, in any case, these were tied to the identification of a parent or guardian. Once the children were in Canada who, if anyone, occupied this role, and who did so legally? Such ambiguities pursued some of the children into adulthood. Later examples are to be found in the evidence that the 'Home Children Canada' organisation laid before the British Committee on the Welfare of Former British Child Migrants in 1998. There was, for example, a wife's difficulty in inheriting her husband's estate because, as a 'Home boy' he did not have 'classification citizenship' and had been unaware of the fact. There was the problem faced by another wife of inheriting her husband's insurance because his date of birth (given him by the emigrating agency) was found to be incorrect. Indeed, the lack of a birth certificate seems to have complicated a number of the encounters that grown-up child immigrants had with official and commercial bodies.[50] The key question, therefore, is whether (and if so, when) the British child immigrants to Canada acquired full citizenship in the new country and how far this affected their understanding of their status as they reached adulthood. It seems likely that many would have been unsure about it, a fact that would only have added to other uncertainties about their identities.

THIRTEEN

Parents' Rights, Consent and Legislation

I A Changing Pattern

We have seen that the children who were emigrated enjoyed few rights; but in the nineteenth century this was the case for children generally. The rights that did exist were the result of the gradual curtailment of a father's historic right to do whatever he liked with his children. These limitations arose with the increasing involvement of the state in securing the education, health and protection of children. However, it was the last quarter of the nineteenth century and the early years of the next that witnessed the emergence of more far-reaching interventions whereby, under certain circumstances, a child could be removed from parental custody on a court order and placed with somebody else or with a corporate body. The grounds for such an order were couched in terms of the parents' unfitness to retain custody. In some cases the removal was clearly necessary in order to protect a child from abuse, but the precise threshold beyond which such action should be taken was largely unspecified, as were the residual rights that parents continued to have – such as giving or withholding their consent to emigration.

However, assumptions about parental 'fitness' also affected the way in which the parents of children who had been admitted to Poor Law or other institutions on a voluntary basis were treated. They could be kept at arm's length by information being withheld, by visiting being severely restricted and by the receipt and sending of letters being obstructed. Furthermore, children could be retained against the wishes of their parents without any legal basis for doing so. This informal restriction of parental rights was reflected in the manner in which many agencies dealt with the question of obtaining parental agreements to the emigration of children in their care. Some, like Barnardos, required a parent to sign an undertaking that, as a condition of their child's admission, they would allow emigration if that were considered to be appropriate. Other societies, such as Middlemores, only offered emigration so that it was apparent at the outset that this was the intention. Nonetheless, parents who sought their child's admission to such organisations could be constrained by the lack of an alternative – except the Poor Law from which many recoiled.

However, not all children who were admitted to one of the voluntary societies or to the Poor Law were referred by parents. There were innumerable intermediaries: diocesan workers, bible women, priests and local gentry, as well as relatives with whom a child lived. Those go-betweens with the means to do so would sometimes sponsor a child's admission to a voluntary Home, paying a lump sum or a regular contribution. Some would specifically sponsor their emigration by meeting the costs of an outfit and the sea passage.[1] But these intermediaries did not always explain to hard-pressed parents exactly what was involved in relinquishing their child. Sometimes parents were unable to read the documents put before them to sign, and sometimes extravagant promises were made about the better future that separation held in store for their child. There was also the matter of class and power. Reluctant parents could be swayed by the status and standing of those who proposed admission to a Home as the solution to a poverty-stricken widowhood, to an illegitimate birth or to the severe difficulties of bringing up a large family. In situations like these parents could decide to part with a child in ignorance of the possible implications. Some thought, for example, that the parting was a temporary measure until they 'got back on their feet'. All these factors conspired to affect a parent's understanding of what rights they retained and the ease with which these could be overridden.

What is apparent is that many children whose parents retained their parental rights but not custody were emigrated without their consent and not infrequently without their knowledge until after the event. It has to be acknowledged, of course, that it could be difficult to trace parents: poor people moved a great deal, while some were anxious not to reveal their whereabouts, escaping from debt, violence or the law. Nevertheless, few efforts seem to have been made to locate parents in order to obtain their consent. Resources did not stretch to doing so and, in any case, those who had 'disappeared' were usually considered to have lost interest in their children and their futures, although the truth of the matter was rarely tested. Furthermore, there was sometimes little wish to locate a parent who was considered to be 'unfit' for fear that they would press for the return of their child or refuse to consent to their being emigrated.

II The Campaign to Limit Parental Rights

During the second half of the 1880s there was an orchestrated campaign to secure legislation to curtail the rights of parents who were regarded as irresponsible or who were considered to constitute a threat to their children's well-being. Those involved in bringing this pressure on the government were initially concerned to see the promised Bill, based on the recommendations of the Aberdare Commission on Reformatories and Industrial Schools,[2] passed through Parliament but with clauses added that would extend the power of managers to retain control over their charges until the age of 18. The reason given for this was the desire to keep certain young people away from the pernicious influences of their parents.

The campaign to achieve this was mounted mainly through the organisation of delegations to call on the Home Secretary. The first was received in January 1889. Its spokesman was Brooke Lambert, the chairman of the Metropolitan Association for Befriending Young Servants. Other members included representatives of the Industrial Schools Committee of the London School Board, the National Association of Certified Reformatory and Industrial Schools, the Central Poor

Law Conference, the Girls' Friendly Society, the Association for the Promotion of Boarding Out, Rudolf of the Waifs and Strays Society; Stephenson of the NCH (National Children's Homes) and Barnardo. Their principal request was that children should be able to be returned to or be retained in industrial schools up to the age of 18 where it could be shown before magistrates that the restoration of parental control would blight a child's future.[3] As the law stood they had to be released by the age of 16.

Before the Home Secretary (Henry Matthews) met the delegation the proposal had been referred to Lushington, the under-secretary, for an opinion. He was strongly opposed to any such change, arguing that:

> ... putting it into the hands of Magistrates to send [children] back to school till 18, merely on account of the risk of their careers being prejudiced by the interference of their parents, would lead to considerable abuses – to the children the hardship of further detention, and to the Treasury a heavy charge....[4]

Nevertheless, the deputation obtained its hearing. They were sure, Lambert said, that the assertion of parental rights in the cases that they had in mind was 'a most monstrous injustice to the children'.[5] However, the Home Secretary was not convinced and the deputation failed to gain his support for its proposal. Even so, the campaign was continued in other quarters. First there was the National Vigilance Association,[6] which wanted the powers of the High Court in respect of infants to be extended to the county courts and, in some cases, to magistrates and for boards of guardians and managers of industrial schools or reformatories to be able to exercise the rights of guardianship over certain children in their care. The main aim of both proposals was to provide greater protection for children from the 'vicious practices of parents'.[7]

The National Vigilance Association met the Home Secretary in February 1889.[8] He was reminded by his civil servants that similar proposals to the second of those advanced by the Association had been received from the guardians of 120 Poor Law unions over the last few years.[9] However, it was not only the Association that followed hard on the heels of the first deputation; others came in quick succession. *The Times* reported two more towards the end of February 1889.[10] There was the National Association of Certified Reformatory and Industrial Schools (again) and the Reformatory and Refuge Union in which Whitwill of Bristol assumed a principal role. Indeed, after the Refuge Union's meeting he sent a letter to the Home Secretary summarising the points that had been made by his deputation. These included stressing the value of there being clauses in the new Bill that would allow managers to act as parents in disposing of children by apprenticeship or emigration.[11] Not to be outdone the Liverpool School Board also entered the fray, submitting a *Memorandum as to the Emigration of Children* to the Home Office in which it was proposed that where children were committed to an industrial school because of 'the criminality, desertion, or immoral character of their parents, magistrates be empowered … to order, as an alternative … the emigration of the children to a British colony…'.[12] However, this suggestion was also rejected by the Home Secretary.

There was therefore a concerted lobby in 1889 aimed at securing various legislative changes in order to increase the powers of corporate bodies over the children for whom they already had some responsibility and, by definition, to reduce those of their parents. Yet what has been described was only part of an even wider movement to secure the protection of children from 'unworthy' parents. Most notably, as we shall see, there was the campaign, spearheaded by Benjamin Waugh of the National Society for the Prevention of Cruelty to Children (NSPCC),[13] for the introduction of legislation that would enable courts to order the removal of children who had suffered cruelty at the hands of their parents.

Over and above these elements in the campaign various boards of guardians had been urging that they be given greater control over the children in their care. For instance, in December 1887 a delegation from the Manchester Poor Law Conference had met the President of the Local Government Board (LGB) to impress on him the need for them to be able to retain the custody of pauper children in cases where the resumption of parental custody would put them in physical or moral danger.

It is not clear why the movement for child protection and the curtailment of parental rights came to a head in the late 1880s. Certainly there was opposition to such changes as well as considerable unease, especially at the Home Office. Nevertheless, the many personal connections between those involved in the 'campaign', together with their persistence and determination, are certainly possible explanations for its eventual success, a success exemplified in four pieces of legislation that reached the Statute Book between 1889 and 1891 and which, among other things, opened the door more widely to those who wished to encourage child emigration unhindered by parental reluctance or opposition.

III The Legislation

The first of the four new pieces of legislation was the 1889 Prevention of Cruelty to Children Act. This marked an important stage in the development of family and child law. Until then it had only been possible to proceed in limited ways against parents who abused or ill-treated their children: the home, and what went on within it had, in this as in other family matters, remained an essentially private domain. Now, not only could cruel parents be charged and, if found guilty, punished, but magistrates could order the removal of the children and place them in the custody of a fit person until, in the case of girls they reached the age of 16 or, if they were boys, 14. However, the Act failed to clarify the notion of a fit person. In particular, it did not indicate whether corporate bodies, such as Barnardos or the NSPCC, could be regarded as a fit 'person'. At first it was their directors or principals who were specified by name in the orders. Nevertheless, once a child had been committed in this way they were, typically, absorbed into the Homes of an organisation and then treated on a par with other children in its care and considered for emigration. Indeed, the right of the fit person (in fact the society) to make that decision was greatly strengthened. Initially, no approval had to be sought from the Secretary of State and neither the parents nor the child had to be consulted. The Home Office was aware that these were shortcomings but refrained from issuing rules about the operation of the Act until there were sufficient cases to show what needed to be done. However, even by the end of 1889 Stuart-Wortley, one of two under-secretaries, noted that: 'one of the first rules we shall have to make will be that without the Secretary of State's sanction no child placed under adoption [that is, in the care of a fit person] ... shall be sent out of the United Kingdom'.[14] There was particular concern that an organisation (as a fit person) would not be able to exercise its quasi-parental responsibilities towards a child whom it had sent abroad. Furthermore, there was a query as to whether maintenance payments from parents that were granted for about half of all the fit person order cases dealt with by the courts could continue to be received by the organisation.

It should be remembered that it was almost exactly at this time that the wave of concern about the emigration of children by Barnardos without either their parents' consent or knowledge was greatest. Indeed, Home Office files on the operation of the 1889 Prevention of Cruelty to Children Act contain several cross-references to cases such as that of 14-year-old Arthur Crook whose sister had complained to the Home Secretary in March of that year that her brother was about to be sent to Canada against his wish and without her consent.[15] Similar cases were reported in *The Times* throughout 1889 and 1890, among them the now well-known Gossage and Tye affairs.[16]

For the first few years of the operation of the 1889 Prevention of Cruelty to Children Act there were therefore no legal restrictions on a 'fit person' arranging the emigration of a child in his or her charge – to Canada or anywhere else. Some children were certainly dealt with in this way, although it is impossible to discover how many until 1893, when the Home Office took the opportunity to add a clause to a Private Member's Bill in order to provide additional security for children 'against unjustifiable emigration'.[17] This became part of the 1894 Prevention of Cruelty to Children Act and obliged any 'fit person' contemplating the emigration of a committed child to obtain the Home Secretary's authorisation. This was clear enough, but it gave no hint of the hesitation and caution that prevailed within the Home Office in going even this far in allowing emigration. In the initial scrutiny of the draft Bill, Troup, a chief clerk (later to become Sir Edward Troup and an under-secretary), gave his opinion that the 'power to emigrate is useful but should be jealously safeguarded. The safeguard here is the strongest possible, viz., the sanction of the Secretary of State....' [18] However, when the draft was passed to Russell, one of the two under-secretaries, he wrote briefly but pointedly: 'I object to this power of expatriation'. Troup later added to the notes the fact that in the Solicitor-General's view the section should be included because a similar power existed in the 1891 Reformatory and Industrial Schools Act (discussed later), and that seems to have tipped the balance.

Although the terms on which a child committed to a fit person could be emigrated appeared to have been settled by the 1894 Act, it remained unclear whether the child's consent to such a step was expected (or indeed required) as it would have been had they been in the care of a public body. Nor was it evident whether the parents had to be consulted and reasons shown why any objections raised should be overridden. A few letters from magistrates' clerks to the Home Office mentioned that a mother had objected, but there is no evidence that parents were routinely consulted, let alone asked to give their permission. Indeed, even the consolidating 1908 Children Act failed to include firm direction about the matter. Although it reiterated the need to obtain the consent of the Secretary of State to a committed child's emigration it offered no guidance about the consultation (or rights) of children and parents. This is clear from correspondence between a magistrate in Cockermouth and the Home Office in 1910.[19] He wished to know why a girl who had been committed to the custody of Barnardos in 1908 on a fit person order had been emigrated without any reference to her father, whom he employed. 'I shall be obliged', he wrote, 'if you will inform me whether such action can be legally taken without the consent of the parent.' The minute giving guidance for a reply explained that 'it is not usual to consult the parents in these cases...'. However, the under-secretary to whom the draft was submitted wrote that 'the parent ought to be consulted before we decide. The justices whom we consult ought really to make the enquiry, but we cannot rely on their doing so. In this case the child has gone....' [20] Nevertheless, it was decided that new arrangements would have to be made and a letter was sent to the five societies who were regular applicants for permission to emigrate children committed to their care on fit person orders[21] explaining that, in future, before the Secretary of State sanctioned the emigration of a committed child 'its parents or guardian must be consulted and given an opportunity of consenting or objecting'.[22] The NSPCC responded first to the letter, their director, Robert Parr, saying that they were 'happy to carry out the excellent suggestions'. However, Barnardos, replying next through their director William Baker (Barnardo's successor), protested that the new procedure would impede their work and greatly increase the difficulties of lifting children out of their former environments and giving them 'a fresh life, quite removed from the possibility of coming again within the contaminating influences from which they have been rescued'.[23] Rather surprisingly Baker's letter was sent, in confidence, to the NSPCC for their comments. Parr replied that he still felt that the Home Office scheme was 'fair and proper', adding that he had 'complete confidence that the Secretary of State will act in the children's interests'.[24]

Jackson, secretary of the Middlemore Emigration Homes in Birmingham, elaborated further on the reasons for his organisation's dislike of the new procedure. 'I am of the opinion', he wrote,

... that Societies like ours will have their hands very much tied if compelled to carry out the regulations contained in your communication, and the agents of such Societies, who attend Children's Courts, will certainly hesitate to accept cases when asked to do so by the Justices, as we shall feel that our object may so easily be defeated at the will of the parents and that we may, if the parent refuses consent to the emigration of the child, be compelled to keep such child in our Homes until it attains its sixteenth year.[25]

Reassured perhaps by the NSPCC's positive reaction, the Home Office's reply to these objections explained that it was not intended

... that the protests of a parent against the emigration of a child entrusted to the care of your Society should ordinarily prevail: but it is only right that the parent should have an opportunity of putting forward any argument in support of the contention that the child should be allowed to return to him in due course.[26]

It is interesting to observe that although this letter, setting out the new procedures, was sent to only five organisations, it was referred to in the Home Office files as a 'regulation'. Whether or not it had the force of law it was treated henceforth as if it did, although the issue of the child's consent was not settled until the 1933 Children and Young Persons Act that made clear that a committed child's emigration would not be allowed unless the Secretary of State was satisfied that their consent had been obtained before justices as well as their parents having been consulted, or it being shown that it was impracticable to do so.

One effect of the Prevention of Cruelty legislation was to ensure a steady supply of children from the courts to a relatively small number of organisations after 1889: to Barnardos and to the NSPCC in particular. Children remained in their custody until they were 16 (in 1894 boys were put on a par with girls) and while they had charge of them they exercised certain parental rights, including the right to arrange emigration, albeit with the Secretary of State's consent in each case after 1894.

In the event how many committed children were emigrated? From 1894 we know the number of applications for their emigration that were submitted to the Home Secretary. Between 1894 and 1907 there were 905, of which 889 (98 per cent) were approved.[27] It was not until 1895, however, that the number of fit person orders made was published. Hence, only then can the number of approvals for emigration be calculated as a proportion of all such orders.[28] During the period 1899-1909 this emerged as a staggering 90 per cent.[29] Sixty-four per cent of the children who were subject to a fit person order and emigrated in these years were sent abroad by Barnardos, 16 per cent by Middlemores and 13 per cent by the NSPCC. The Waifs and Strays Society accounted for four per cent. The remaining three per cent included all the other organisations and individuals.[30]

The committed boys and girls went overseas in roughly equal numbers, although there were slightly more boys than girls. Unfortunately the approval letters rarely give the children's ages. However, from time to time the Home Office itself, or the committing justices whom they consulted, raised questions about the tender years of some of the children who were proposed for emigration. In 1899, for instance, Barnardo was asked about two girls, one of whom was 10 and the other 11. The letter said that the Secretary of State wished to know 'what object is gained by sending them out before they are old enough to be put to work'.[31] Barnardo must have provided a satisfactory reply because approval was forthcoming within the week. In another instance, two years later, a similar exchange occurred about a boy of eight. The Secretary of State presumed 'that when the emigration of children is procured at this early age, they are boarded out in such places and circumstances as admit of their education receiving proper attention'.[32] This time Barnardo had to wait a month for approval, but young Isiah Birch duly went to Canada. Occasionally, the justices also raised doubts about the desirability of emigrating the youngest of the committed children. The chief magistrate at Bow Street Police Court in London was one, but he was reassured by the Home Office that 'the practice of sending children to Canada from the Barnardo Home at an early age is not new, and ... the Department has always confidently left the future care of such children to Dr Barnardo...'.[33] In another case 'with regard to D. Powell', the committing justices wrote to Barnardo to express their view 'that the boy is too young for emigration, but the Secretary of State thinks that no doubt you can furnish a re-assuring account of the working of your system of emigrating very young children'.[34]

Although few in number, such examples serve to demonstrate the unwillingness of the Home Office to withhold permission despite its earlier misgivings. There was the case of Robert Greenwood, a committed boy. Letters about him passed between the Home Office and Barnardos during the spring of 1900. Barnardo was asked for his observations on Robert's emigration since he had a brother in an industrial school and the two 'were very much attached to one another, and ... it would be a pity to dispose of one in such a way as to permanently separate the two ...'.[35] Later, there was another letter about Robert, this time raising a new issue. He had had a rheumatic infection that had affected his heart and had been sent to a convalescent home to recuperate. Was the boy, asked the Home Office, physically fit for emigration?[36] Barnardos replied that Robert had already been sent to Canada unintentionally, although the Secretary of State's permission had not been obtained. Should he be brought back to Britain? An assistant under-secretary replied that the Secretary of State 'trusts great care will be taken to prevent the recurrence of such a mistake in future, but in this case he gives his sanction'.[37] As with other categories of child emigration, once the committed child was in Canada the matter was regarded as a *fait accompli* about which nothing further could be done. Another example was of a mother who protested to the Home Office and sought their help in securing the return of her daughter, Ellen Ring, who had been committed to Barnardos and sent to

Canada. Upon investigation it was discovered that this had been done without the permission of the Home Secretary. Because of this Mrs Ring was informed that he was unable to assist her,[38] but she was given no advice about other legal steps that she might take. And there the matter seems to have rested.[39]

A steady flow of letters from parents and relatives reached the Home Secretary in the years spanning the turn of the century, usually to ask that he withhold his approval to the emigration of their committed child, niece or nephew. In no instance were any of their representations successful, although further enquiries were sometimes set in train as a result. Occasionally relatives engaged the services of a solicitor to represent their objections, but with no more success. In response to these and other protests parents were usually told that the Secretary of State saw no grounds for withholding his approval, but sometimes it was also made clear that if the parent or relative felt that there were grounds for the revocation of the order they should have applied to a court before emigration became a matter for their concern.[40] But just how could a parent or relative seek the revocation or variation of an order once the child was in Canada? By and large, severance was the order of the day, not rehabilitation.

A second development of a similar kind to the 'cruelty' Act was the 1889 Poor Law (Amendment) Act. Its key feature was that:

> Where a child is maintained by the guardians … and was deserted by its parent, the guardians may … resolve that such child shall be under the control of the guardians until it reaches the age, if a boy, of sixteen, and if a girl of eighteen years, and thereupon until the child reaches that age all powers and rights of such parent in respect of that child shall … rest in the guardians.

This section – often referred to as the Poor Law adoption procedure – is the origin of the law which, until the 1989 Children Act, allowed local authorities to assume parental rights and duties in respect of children in their care.[41] They did not have to apply to a court when they wished to take this step; they simply proceeded by resolution. Parents had to be notified and if they objected the issue was adjudicated in court. In 1889, however, they could only make a complaint after the event. If this were upheld then the resolution was revoked. Furthermore, in 1889 'desertion' was held to include cases where a parent was imprisoned under a sentence of penal servitude or was imprisoned in respect of an offence committed against the child. When rights and duties were assumed by a board of guardians the parents were not relieved of the responsibility of contributing towards their child's maintenance, although on assessment many were found to be too poor to pay.

This was a remarkable piece of legislation because it effectively allowed guardians to extinguish parents' rights by administrative fiat, prompting a senior civil servant at the Home Office in 1944 to comment that 'it is always a subject of wonder how it ever passed the scrutiny of Parliament'.[42] In fact there was virtually no debate when the Commons considered the Bill during the summer of 1889, and there was only a desultory discussion in the Lords.

The changes of 1889 were surprising given, as the Webbs pointed out, that the LGB 'clung to the principle of parental authority'.[43] As late as 1887, Ritchie, President of the Board, had said:

> No doubt there are some instances in which the interests of children are prejudiced by their parents claiming them from the guardians, but I should not be prepared to propose legislation which would enable a board of guardians to withhold a child from its parent when claimed by him.[44]

That, however, was exactly what he did in bringing the Poor Law (Amendment) Bill to the Commons two years later, perhaps encouraged to do so by the report of the House of Lords Select Committee on Poor Relief, published in 1888, which suggested that 'power might be given to the Guardians to retain in their custody children who, having been deserted by their Parents at an early age, are claimed by them after the lapse of a long period'.[45] For whatever reason the legislation took the form that it did, it gave local guardians the power (among other things) to arrange for the emigration of a child whom they had 'adopted' without any hindrance from parents or any reference to the courts or to the LGB. Unfortunately, it is impossible to differentiate those 'adopted' children who were emigrated by Poor Law authorities from others whom they dealt with in this way.

The 1891 Custody of Children Act[46] was the third statute to affect parental rights. It was short, just four clauses, the provisions of which arose, in large part, from the Barnardo court cases of the late 1880s in which several parents had applied for writs of *habeas corpus*, a procedure that it was thought others might follow. Its purpose was to limit the ability of parents to apply to a court for a writ or order for the production of their child by an organisation in whose care they had been placed. First, if the court considered that the parent had abandoned or deserted their child, or was unfit to be granted custody, then it could refuse to make an order for the child to be 'delivered up'. Second, if it did make such an order it could make a further order that the parent pay the body that had been bringing up the child the full or part cost that had been incurred. This was a major deterrent to a parent making an application in the first place. Obviously, it made it unlikely that poor parents would now contemplate making an application for a writ. Even if they did, they might still be unsuccessful in recovering their child if they were then unable to repay the cost of the child's care. It is also noteworthy that, unlike the Prevention of Cruelty legislation, the parent did not have to have been cruel or physically neglectful to be adjudged 'unfit'. Indeed, the balance was shifted towards a parent having to prove his or her fitness against claims to the contrary.

Like the other pieces of legislation of the period that have been discussed, this also helped organisations to retain children against their parents' wishes and therefore more easily arrange for their emigration. However, yet again, it is not possible to determine how many children were sent to Canada or elsewhere with the aid of these provisions. As with the 1889 Poor Law Act they might actually have served to reduce the overall number being emigrated, given that it may now have seemed unnecessary to resort to such a measure in order to forestall the reunification of a child with its parents. However, there were doubtless still concerns about a young person returning to parents on their discharge from the care of an organisation.[47] In the light of this possibility permanent severance through emigration may have remained an attractive option.

The last of the four pieces of legislation that followed in such quick succession was the 1891 Reformatory and Industrial Schools Act. It emerged from a Private Member's Bill that was introduced in the Lords by Lord Monkswell (chairman of the Committee of Management of the Feltham Reformatory). It dealt with only one issue; namely, the abolition of 'the right of parents of children in Industrial and Reformatory Schools ... to have these children home again after their period of detention'.[48] In large part this is what the campaigners who had petitioned the Home Secretary earlier had been seeking. However, the question of emigration was more closely implicated in this later move. For example, Monkswell explained that at the end of their detention there were just three things that could be done with young people: return them home, arrange for their employment away from home or secure their emigration. He believed that the last option was 'the best plan' but even here, he went on,

> ... the law does all it can to thwart and baffle us in our endeavours to give these boys [those at Feltham] the opportunity of making a better future for themselves, for the consent of the parents has to be obtained, and we find that in only one case out of four will the parents consent to ... emigration....[49]

Earl Stanhope, speaking on behalf of the industrial schools and as a manager of one in Kent, maintained that the Bill was 'most valuable' in enabling managers 'to apprentice boys without their parents having power to exercise a veto ... and also for enabling managers to emigrate boys to Canada or elsewhere'.[50] Once more, however, it is impossible to say how many boys and girls were emigrated with the aid of this legislation, but easier emigration was something that its architects clearly had in mind.

IV Parents' Complaints and Where They Stood

We have seen that it was not unusual for children to be emigrated without their parents' consent. The high profile Tye and Gossage cases that brought Barnardo to court to explain and defend his actions have been well described elsewhere and in the press at the time.[51] However, there were others, unrecorded except in the public archives. Two examples provide a glimpse of the lengths to which some parents went in order to recover their emigrated children, albeit ultimately without success.

In the summer of 1886 Childers, the Home Secretary, received a letter from Charles Elton, MP, which dealt with complaints by Robert and Mary Dodd of Fiddington in Somerset, as well as from Mr Waterman, Mary's father. The details of the case were written out by the local rector (the Rev. Parkinson) and read over to Mary who testified that they were correct. Her statement ran as follows:

> J. Collard and Mary Waterman of Spaxton had 8 children – J. Collard was killed in 1870 leaving Mary Collard with 8 children –
>
> The Parish allowed Mary Collard 9s per week, the eldest boy earned 5s per week in farm labour.… On the request of Miss Jeffries of Taunton, who promised to allow her 3/6d per week if she would send four of her children to Dr Barnardo's Home, signed a paper, not knowing what it contained – giving consent to the four children to go to Dr Barnardo. Miss Jeffries was to pay Dr Barnardo 4/6d for each child per week. Robert Dodd with three children married widow Collard in 1871.…
>
> Frank Collard [a son] …was sent by Dr Barnardo to Canada against the express orders of his parents in 1884 and has not been heard of since. Mary Dodd heard from Miss Jeffries and not from Dr Barnardo in May 1886 that Blanche and Clara Collard [daughters] were to be sent out in July – she went to Miss Jeffries about June 5 and forbid her children being sent to Canada. On June 9 Robert Dodd wrote to Dr Barnardo forbidding the children being sent to Canada and ordered them to be sent home and he would provide for them.… His brother-in-law – a policeman of Chelsea – went to Stepney [Barnardos' headquarters] on July 2 to forbid the children being sent to Canada as emigrants and demanded them to be given up to him to be conveyed to Fiddington.…
>
> Dr Barnardo declined to give them because he was not a relation and their parents were doubtful characters.…
>
> Mrs Dodd went to London on July 13/14 and sought to see Barnardo directly. She was sent to Ilford to see the matron. She was assured that they would not be emigrated and sent home.… The children went to Canada on July 22. After that Mrs Dodd went to solicitors.[52]

Elton asked the Home Secretary to investigate the case, adding in his letter that 'the assumption that Dr Barnardo makes as to it being undesirable to return the children to their parents on the grounds of their being agricultural labourers appears to be quite unwarrantable…'. He also pointed out that 'a like complaint comes from …Waterman of Spaxton respecting his daughter Elizabeth aged 15 who was sent out on the same day against his express orders'.

The Dodds' solicitor wrote to Barnardo asking for an account of the matter. He received a defensive reply saying that the Collard children had been surrendered voluntarily and that he had acted on the rights conveyed to him by the 'instrument' that Mrs Dodd had signed. This included provision for him to send the children to Canada. He pointed out that two brothers had already been sent (Mrs Collard's statement only mentioned one) and that, in any case, he did not know of the mother's objection. The girl had wished to be included in the emigration party. Finally, he did not see, he said, how the mother could manage any more children with a labouring husband and a large family.[53] Barnardo's letter was included in the papers sent to the Public Prosecutor who, in due course, conveyed his views to the Home Office. He felt that it was impossible to express a firm opinion on the basis of the available evidence. However, the tone of his letter conveyed little sympathy for Mrs Dodd's complaint. It was undeniable, he wrote, that she had voluntarily placed four of her children in Barnardo's care and that she had signed 'an agreement of some kind'. Her claim that she did not know its purport was, he thought, 'remarkable having regard to the attitude she now takes up'. It seemed to him that the mother had acted wisely and in the children's best interests in parting with them. However, he concluded, 'now that their education is completed and possibly they might be of use to her and earn their own living she wishes to have them back…'.[54]

Troup, the senior clerk at the Home Office, composed a minute in the light of this reply. In it he concluded that:

> There seems to be no ground for a criminal charge; and it is very undesirable that the Secretary of State should intervene in the disagreement between Dr Barnardo and the parents of the children in his home…. Dr Barnardo's letter does not give a very favourable impression of his straightforwardness, but no doubt he does good in the majority of cases. Probably the matter will have to be dropped; but for the present.[55]

Despite further letters to the Secretary of State from Elton and from the Rev. Parkinson, as well as a continuing exchange between the Dodds' solicitors and Barnardo, the parents of these particular child emigrants were unable to obtain a satisfactory resolution of their complaint. As in other similar cases, the fact that the children were already in Canada amounted to a powerful *fait accompli*.

Five things should be noted, aside from the unknown destinies of the children. First, this was one of several cases with which the Home Office was asked to deal; but since the Barnardo Homes did not come under the jurisdiction of any department of central government the only official action that could be taken was via the Public Prosecutor through the courts. The legal status of Barnardo's document that Mary Dodd had signed was at no time questioned. She maintained that when she signed it in the presence of Miss Jeffries it was not read over to her and no mention was made of emigration. Jeffries had merely said that the children would be sent to London, fed, clothed and educated. The girls would be put to service and the boys taught a trade. On later enquiries Jeffries had refused to provide the detailed substance of the form in question.

Second, the steps that an illiterate mother and stepfather, an agricultural labourer in a remote part of rural Somerset, took to prevent the emigration of their children were remarkable, even if they seem to have been assisted and advised by their local rector. They approached their MP and enlisted his support, they arranged for a relative to visit Barnardos, the mother travelled to London and thence out to Ilford and the couple took their case to a local solicitor.

The third noteworthy feature of the case is the intermediary role played by the shadowy figure of Miss Jeffries (described by Barnardos as a 'correspondent'). As we have seen, the intervention of such go-betweens was not that unusual.

A fourth conclusion can reasonably be drawn from the correspondence; namely, that Barnardo did not deal 'straightforwardly' with the enquiries made of him. Certainly the officials at the Home Office took that view. For example, it subsequently emerged from a letter written by one of the daughters to her mother that the other sister did not accompany her to Canada and was hence still in London at the time of the request for the girls' return. Barnardo said that they had both gone to Canada. It may well have been the conviction that he was acting in the children's best interests that led to such prevarication, but this made it doubly difficult for people like Mrs Dodd to press her case or, indeed, even to know how matters stood. The fact that Barnardo and others were involved in 'good works' as well as being committed evangelicals seems to have led some to feel themselves above the law and above the standards against which they were accustomed to judge the children and adults with whom they dealt.

Finally, the case reflects the general impact of poverty, accentuated by widowhood and large families, on the decisions of parents to part with their children. In addition, however, the importance of the earnings of older children to the survival of such families is yet again apparent. No wonder the parents wanted to have their children back when they reached an age to earn and when they no longer constituted a burden on fragile family resources.

Within the Home Office a number of other 'special cases' continued to draw attention to the issue of parents' rights with respect to their children's emigration, even after the radical changes introduced in the legislation of 1889-91. Barnardos continued to be in the limelight. In September 1897, for example, Mrs Hole of Kilburn in London, a widow with several children, called at the Home Office to ask that her 11-year-old son Frederick be restored to her since he was shortly to go to Canada. She was seen by one of the clerks who, in his minute, recorded that she had placed her child with Barnardos two years earlier when she was destitute. She did not know the terms of the 'agreement' she was asked to sign as she could not read. 'She is now', the minute recorded, 'in a better position & thoroughly respectable, and does not want her boy sent away; she can maintain him.' Mrs Hole had been told that the Secretary of State had no authority in the matter but that if the agreement were invalid she should seek 'relief' through the courts.[56] Nonetheless, it was decided that Barnardo should be invited to give his observations on the case, a procedure that had been employed on previous occasions. He did consent to delay the emigration but contended that Mrs Hole had understood the nature of the agreement that she had signed. However, as he explained, it was his policy that children would not be admitted to his Homes unless parents gave consent to emigration.[57] Even if parents like Mrs Hole understood these terms, they must have felt themselves confronted with Hobson's choice and signed hoping or expecting that there would be no reason to send their sons or daughters to Canada. Yet, after 1891, simply by being unable to reimburse the society for the cost of their children's maintenance they could be prevented from resuming their care. It is doubtful whether most parents appreciated how difficult it could be to reclaim their children.

The Home Office was by no means satisfied that Barnardo exercised his 'rights' wisely. In the Hole case a senior clerk wrote in a minute on Barnardo's response that:

> It is doubtless right & necessary that Dr B should secure to himself ample legal control of the children committed to his homes, but it is questionable whether he ought to exercise his powers to the full, without regard to the circumstances under which such control was obtained & the (apparently) altered circumstances of the parents.... The insistence of a *Charity* on its *legal right* to place the Atlantic between a child & its mother does not look well (original emphasis).[58]

His senior, Henry Cunynghame, one of two assistant secretaries, added that 'it will not do for mothers when in difficulty to make agreements which they afterwards wish to rescind when the child is in a position to earn money'.[59] It seemed to have been overlooked that Frederick was still only 11 years old.

Nearly two weeks after her first call at the Home Office Mrs Hole returned to enquire what progress there had been in the matter. In the meantime, however, the Home Office had written to the Commissioner of Police asking him to provide an assessment of her character. He replied that she was found to be very respectable, the two children living with her being clean and healthy and her home well kept. Furnished with this additional information the clerk questioned Mrs Hole again, in particular about the agreement that she had signed.

> She persisted that it was not read over to her; she told the Home officials that she could not read, & they replied 'Never mind. Sign your name here' or words to that effect. She would not have left the boy at the Homes had she been aware that by doing so she would surrender all rights of control over him.[60]

He went on in his minute as follows:

> The agreement under which the child is detained has probably been drawn up under competent legal advice, but might not its validity be successfully challenged.... Only strong reasons could justify the forcible and possibly life-long separation of a respectable widow & her only [sic] son ... should not some steps be taken to compel or induce the Doctor to abandon his intention of sending the boy out of the country?[61]

However, the clerk's senior did not think that the Secretary of State could do more than communicate the substance of the police report to Barnardo; but the clerk was not content to let matters rest. Just over a week later he prepared another minute. In it he drew attention to the fact that in law a parent could only contract away his power over his child if it were for the good of the child. However, he went on,

> If this case became the subject of legal proceedings, the question would mainly turn on what is for the child's best interest, & what is fair to all parties.... No doubt the mother wishes for the boy's assistance in wage-earning. I am by no means sure that to a limited extent, a widow is not entitled to look to her eldest son. Upon the whole I think no more can be done in this case, but it is a pity that Dr B so often strains his rights to their fullest extent.[62]

And there, everyone concerned at the Home Office agreed, matters had to stop. Mrs Hole did not call again and Barnardo seems not to have replied to the letter informing him of her good character.

Few parents would have been as persistent as Mrs Dodd and Mrs Hole, but this does not indicate indifference to the fate of their children. Even with considerable help, success in recovering their children, or preventing their emigration, was elusive. Some certainly did agree to, or acquiesce in, their children's trans-shipment, but with what despair or fatalism we do not know.

Part VII
A Chapter Closes

FOURTEEN

Into the Twentieth Century

I The Quest for Improvements

By 1887 it seemed as if the differences between the British authorities and the Dominion government concerning the proper supervision of Poor Law children in Canada had been resolved. Yet a nagging dissatisfaction remained among the LGB's officers that led to renewed efforts to persuade the Dominion to provide more frequent inspection and to continue it up to the age of 16. One of those who was most outspoken in his criticism of the prevailing arrangements was W.E. Knollys, the chief inspector. In 1895 he appeared before the Poor Law Schools Committee to give evidence on a range of matters connected with the education and care of Poor Law children.[1] Part of that evidence concerned their emigration. What he said revealed the nature of his unease and probably that of his department. For example, in answer to a question put by Mundella,[2] the chairman, he replied that:

> ... all boards of guardians should look upon themselves *in loco parentis*
> to every child under their care till it comes to reasonable years.... And
> I cannot, myself, look without some compunction upon the fact that
> in these cases [emigration] they lose all control of the children....[3]

In answer to another question he explained that only about 75 per cent of the children who should have been reported on were seen and that no second reports had so far been forthcoming.[4] When reports did reach the LGB they were scrutinised and then copies sent to the union or parish from which a child had been emigrated, with attention drawn to anything untoward.[5] Thus, the responsibility for dealing with any inadequacies or abuses was laid at the door of the local guardians. One wonders what kind of action the numerous boards of guardians involved could take, except through the emigrating societies with which they had made the arrangements; and that meant that any action to right the wrongs noted in the reports depended on the ability and willingness of these societies to do so. As we have seen the Canadian inspectors carried no such responsibility.

There were, however, other deficiencies in the system of furnishing reports that Knollys did not mention. One was the Canadian practice of only carrying out a first inspection in the calendar year following that of the child's arrival. As the commissioner of immigration in Winnipeg pointed out in 1910, the arrangement amounted to 'a license to brutal men to thrash and treat them [boys] like dogs ... a boy could be killed as easily the first year he is in the country as in the second'.[6]

The practice of waiting until the year after a child's arrival before an inspection was made was linked with another. This was the collection of reports into yearly batches for transmission to the LGB. The combination of these two procedures led to considerable delay in information reaching Britain and, eventually, the Poor Law guardians involved. The 'uselessness' of the reports in this respect was stressed by the clerk of the Fareham union in writing to the LGB in 1904. The report on one boy, he pointed out, was 16 months old and although it said that he was of good character, in fact he had been returned to England by then for the rape of a little girl of five.[7] This, and similar complaints were forwarded to the Governor-General, the long-drawn-out outcome of which was that instead of bundles of handwritten reports being sent once a year they were in future sent every six months and typed.[8]

These various expressions of concern about the well-being of children sent to Canada reflected similar misgivings about the circumstances of Poor Law children boarded out in Britain. Mary Mason, the LGB's inspector of boarding out, listed the problems in her annual reports. It was not true, she wrote in 1895, that boarded-out children:

> ... had the eye of the neighbours upon them, and that any ill-treatment or neglect will become known. In the first place, many cottages are isolated.... In the second, a great deal may go on inside the walls which even a next door neighbour does not know, and in the third, neighbours, as a rule, do not like to draw quarrels ... upon themselves....[9]

The following year she elaborated on her concern:

> However undesirable it may be in other respects to mass children together, it has this advantage, that they have friends and fellows in misfortune if badly treated, while an ill-treated child boarded-out is alone with its oppressors.[10]

These anxieties applied with equal force, if not more so, to the situation of children sent to Canada and were likely to have coloured the chief inspector's evidence before the Mundella committee of inquiry. Despite this, when its report was published in 1896[11] the virtues of emigration were extolled, drawing heavily on what was said by witnesses like Samuel Smith and Barnardo. Nevertheless, it did recommend that special attention be paid to the education and inspection of child emigrants, for example, that the child's schoolteacher should send certificates of attendance periodically to the authorities in London.[12] In the matter of inspection the committee came down in favour of the responsibility being laid firmly on the emigration societies. It recommended that they be required to appoint their own inspectors, some of whom should be women.[13]

Soon after the report was published the LGB asked the Colonial Office to submit a proposal to the Governor-General that each Poor Law child be visited annually by officers of the Dominion until they were 16 years old. The Canadian government declined to extend its responsibilities in this way, the main objection being 'the enormous' increase in expense that this would entail. It pointed out that in Canada there was

> ... a growing, although probably ill-founded, prejudice against this class of immigration; that various public bodies in the country have suggested its entire prohibition; and that any very material increase of its cost to Canada would almost certainly lead to that result.[14]

At the Colonial Office the reasons given by the Canadian government against an extended period of supervision were considered to be conclusive.[15] It was therefore suggested to the LGB that either a grant be given to cover the extra costs or that the Board should employ one of its own inspectors to carry out inspections in Canada. However, neither of these suggestions commended themselves. The Board's views (or at least those of its senior staff) may be gleaned from their response to the first request for approval to the emigration of Poor Law children to be received in 1897.[16] Knollys prepared a forceful minute for Owen, the permanent secretary, in the following terms:

> As the Board have made up their minds that the supervision and inspection in Canada are inadequate and unsatisfactory, I do not see how we can properly go on authorising expenditure for the purposes of emigration ... until we are satisfied that the matter will be put on a better footing....[17]

Somewhat surprisingly Owen wrote back that he did not think that the emigration of Poor Law children should be stopped, although he agreed that more frequent inspection was desirable.[18] Nevertheless, Knollys stuck to his guns and broached the issue with Henry Chaplin, President of the Board, writing that it was not right that 'the Board should take upon themselves further responsibility as regards the emigration of children, except in those cases where they are satisfied that the inspection will be ... effective'.[19] Chaplin, however, did not think that the Board's sanction should be withheld while they waited for a satisfactory settlement with Canada to be reached.[20] Knollys responded with a four-page minute, part of the contents of which deserve to be quoted at length. He maintained that there was

> ... no proper means of knowing what the treatment of the children is
> – take the case of Patrick Brady aged 12 ... placed with a labourer (!!)
> reported as being unwanted and poorly clad – working in a factory
> – we have no date as to when the child was placed ... who set him

to work in a factory – nor as to the date when he was visited – all we know is that we sanctioned his emigration in 1893, & we hear this in 1897. Take again the case of J. W. Hill ... placed with a farmer – he complained of ill treatment & exposure, he was brought back to Ottawa by the farmer himself and had to be sent to the childs Hospital suffering from sore feet from exposure, & was afterwards returned to Mr Wallace's Home. We have no dates as to when he was placed in this Home, how soon after he was visited – we sanctioned the emigration in March '94, we have this report in March 1897.[21]

He added a list of other such cases and argued that until there was better supervision and better information no more Poor Law children should be sent to Canada. This led to a partial improvement in that it was agreed that the Dominion should receive *per capita* payments in order to cover the cost of each annual inspection after the first and until the children reached 16.[22] However, the cost of these grants had to be met in advance by the local guardians. Despite this the number of Poor Law children going to Canada began to grow, from 143 in 1899 to 568 in 1913, giving a total between these years of 5,756.[23] Several factors seem to have contributed to this somewhat unexpected result. One was the more depressed state of the juvenile labour market in Britain during these years. Another may have been the tightening of the safeguards for the children (at least in principle) that reassured the LGB as well as some previously hesitant guardians. The elaboration and codification of these additional requirements (a combination of Canadian conditions and LGB policies) were set out in a circular to guardians in 1903.[24] A third reason for the rise in the number of Poor Law children sent to Canada in the early years of the twentieth century may be found in the more open encouragement that the Canadian government now seemed to be giving. For instance, in its annual report for 1903-04 the LGB explained that it had been informed by the Dominion government that 'at no previous time in Canada have there been so many opportunities as at present for absorbing in a satisfactory manner young emigrants of the class sent by Boards of Guardians'.[25] This probably reflected a growing shortage of agricultural labour in the Dominion as migration, particularly youthful migration, to the towns and cities accelerated. In addition, opposition to juvenile immigration was waning partly, as Whyte has argued, because it was now dwarfed by the enormous increase in immigration in general.[26] Indeed, between 1900 and 1913 the overall number of immigrants entering Canada grew almost tenfold, from 41,680 to 400,870.[27]

A further boost to the emigration of Poor Law children was probably imparted in 1908 by the report of a committee under the chairmanship of T. J. Macnamara, which had been asked to look into all aspects of the provisions made for Poor Law children.[28] These included the district schools, the cottage Homes, boarding out and emigration. The achievements of the last of these arrangements were warmly applauded.[29] Macnamara's enthusiasm for Canada and its opportunities may well have owed something to the fact that he was born in Québec, where his soldier father had been posted, and where he lived for the first eight years of his life.[30] Even so, his report, as it concerned emigration, was remarkably sanguine.

As the years advanced towards and into the First World War it was clear that although the Canadian government wished to attract more juvenile immigrants from Britain it remained unwilling to do much more to improve its inspection system. For example, in 1910 its immigration branch in London suggested that were a number of women inspectors to be appointed it would dispel some of the reluctance of boards of guardians to propose children for emigration and that, it was maintained, might mean that as many as 65,000 could become 'available'(a wildly unrealistic figure). However, the proposal was not accepted in Ottawa and, even by 1913, there were still only four Canadian government inspectors visiting Poor Law children, none of whom was a woman. That notwithstanding, some attempts were made to improve the image of inspection, among which was the chief inspector's 1914 memorandum to this small team. In it he reminded them that the primary purpose of inspections was 'to certify [that] everything is alright with the child'. To this end the inspectors were to see where the child slept, to speak to them on their own, visit their school, take notes and listen patiently 'to all that is said both for and against the child'. Nevertheless, the authority of the 'foster parent and employer' was to be upheld, 'and the child must obey them'.[31]

Despite these various attempts to improve the visiting of Poor Law children the system still remained inadequate and it seems likely that similar deficiencies existed with respect to the inspection of other children who were not the responsibility of boards of guardians in Britain. At least the Poor Law children had the chance of being seen by two visitors, that is, if both the voluntary organisations involved in taking them and the Canadian inspectors fulfilled their responsibilities.

II Many or Few?

By the turn of the century and until the outbreak of war in 1914 economic and social conditions in Britain were favourable to imperial emigration: demographic change had swollen the potential labour force without a comparable growth in demand. Technical and scientific developments had diminished the need for 'hands' and appropriate training for more skilled work was still in its infancy. The 'unemployment problem' loomed large on the political agenda and many voices were heard advocating emigration, especially to the Empire, as a laudable solution. William Booth had done so early on in his book *In Darkest England and the Way Out*.[32] Later, others, such as Rider Haggard, were to add their particular schemes to the clamour. The government was pressed to embrace state-aided emigration, but only the 1905 Unemployed Workmen Act offered a limited opportunity for local unemployment committees to sponsor selected applicants and their families for settlement overseas. Even so, overall emigration from the UK grew rapidly between 1900 and 1913, with the number going to Canada increasing tenfold. Doubtless this reflected a quest for employment and better prospects, but it was encouraged by the popular imperialist sentiment of the time and epitomised in the person of Joseph Chamberlain who had been appointed Colonial Secretary in the newly elected Conservative administration of 1895. He argued that the development of the Empire was vital for the preservation of national power and survival. For this the 'unity of Empire' was crucial, and this was to be strengthened by a greater British presence in both colonies and dominions.

Given such a propitious climate for emigration, and Empire emigration in particular, it seems reasonable to ask why more British children were not dispatched to Canada. Nowadays it is usually the opposite question that is asked, namely, why were so many sent? This partly reflects today's negative opinion about such a movement; but if we set this aside and consider the circumstances in the early years of the new century it is the first of these questions that demands to be answered. Let us do so by looking at the case of the Poor Law children and then at what was happening in the voluntary sector.

One reason why a larger number of Poor Law children were not sent to Canada (or indeed elsewhere) was that only a minority of them were 'available' for emigration. For instance, the figure of 65,000 possible candidates that had been suggested by the Canadian Immigration Office in London overlooked the actual composition of the population of children in the care of the guardians. Many of them were only short-term residents. There were, for example, the so-called 'ins and outs', admitted one week, discharged a few weeks later and then readmitted. Although not strictly 'ins and outs', many other children were only in public care for relatively brief periods. The number likely to spend their childhoods in Poor Law provision was, therefore, far less than the total at any one time. Indeed, boards of guardians had a financial incentive *not* to retain children but to return them to their parents or relatives unless it were judged that this would expose them to physical or moral danger. Certainly, emigration also terminated the guardians' financial responsibility but not, it should be borne in mind, their responsibility for a child's welfare, a responsibility that both the LGB and many Poor Law unions took seriously.

A second explanation for the modest increase in the number of Poor Law children being emigrated during a time in the early twentieth century when, overall, British emigration to Canada was burgeoning, is to be found in the 'rules' laid down by the LGB about the ages at which such children could be sent abroad. These sprang in particular from a concern about the safety (usually interpreted as moral safety) of girls once they had left the country. This, of course, had been reflected in the 1883 circular that had set an upper age for their emigration at 12, although certain exceptions were made when, for example, an older girl was considered to be in moral danger if returned home or when it was thought right to allow an older sister to accompany younger brothers and sisters to Canada. Furthermore, a concession was made in the case of the Canadian Catholic Emigration Society. Its secretary had assured the LGB in 1897 that girls over 12 who were sent to Canada would receive prior training, would be regularly inspected by their agents and that they would be placed in urban settings in and around Montreal.[33] This, it was argued, ensured better supervision and protection than the common practice of choosing rural areas. Having heard what was intended the proposal was allowed, with the proviso that the girls should 'be under the special care of the ladies of the confraternity' [sic].[34]

Although many of the LGB's archives for the period 1900-17 have not survived, it is possible to piece together from the registers of correspondence how the 'rules' about exceptions to the age restriction for girls began to be tightened.[35] From about 1904 the LGB required an undertaking that whenever the rule was relaxed the girl would be visited by a lady resident (Bristol correspondence). By 1905 (Hunslet) they were adding that she should also live in the neighbourhood of the home where the girl was placed. Further conditions were imposed in 1907 (miscellaneous correspondence) to the effect that such girls should be visited at least twice a year and that the 'lady' involved should 'definitely engage to befriend her'. By 1910 the Board was also requiring that such a woman should not be responsible for more than one girl and that she should remain in contact with her until she reached 18 (Bradford). These additional conditions probably made it less likely that exceptions to the 12-year-old limitation on the emigration of girls would be sought by local guardians or approved by the LGB.

Policy was also evolving at the other end of the age range. As we have seen already, some magistrates had been exercised from the beginning about whether children of five or six could be considered to be able to give a meaningful agreement to their emigration when, as Poor Law children, they were obliged to do so before justices. Likewise, the Home Office generally viewed this as impossible in the case of the youngest industrial school children. By the 1890s a firmer policy was taking shape at the LGB. To start with those under four years of age were considered to be unsuitable for emigration and the LGB was regularly refusing to permit the emigration of such young children. For example, Ellen Wallace (of the Marchmont Home in Canada) was in London in 1891 and offered to take back several infants from the Paddington Union, but its clerk was told that this was not considered to be desirable and permission was duly refused.[36] Certainly, by the turn of the century, the LGB's policy regarding the emigration of the youngest children had set the minimum age at seven, a ruling that applied to both boys and girls.

As well as this, however, there was a growing resistance in some boards of guardians to the emigration of young children in their care. For example, in 1909 the Greenwich board of guardians in London considered a proposal to send certain children between the ages of seven and nine to Canada. This was strongly opposed by one member, W.H. Reynolds, who declared that their education would be neglected and that, if they were placed on farms, 'it would be taken for granted that the farmer could hope to make a profit out of their work, and they be dealt with as slaves'. He was not alone in his view, the proposal being defeated by a large majority.[37] However, such local opposition to the emigration of the younger Poor Law children reflected a growing dissatisfaction among certain boards of guardians with the whole practice of emigration. Among other things this was related to the increasing presence of socialist members on these boards. For example, Catherine Garrett, together with others from the Chorlton board of guardians, launched an attack on the system through the columns of the *Manchester Guardian*. 'We Socialists', she wrote,

> ... do not condemn ... Canada nor emigration there; what we do condemn is the robbing of young children, because they are poor, of their childhood, the depriving them of the educational advantages of their native country, the placing of them in situations to work for their living at ages which would not be tolerated in England – namely, from seven years. No one can deny that the policy is one of economy, bought at a fearful price of a child's toil.... We condemn the inadequacy of the wages paid them (when they are paid at all), the isolation of them, in the case of brothers and sisters separated hundreds of miles, and the generally unsatisfactory nature of the inspection and supervision over their employers.[38]

Yet there were often contrary opinions, in this case from Olga Hertz (chairman of the Chorlton Cottage Homes Committee) who had been sent to Canada to report on the union's children already there. Despite criticising their erratic education and the scantiness of inspection she concluded that 'by sending them to Canada we are giving them happier and healthier surroundings than we can provide for them at home'.[39] However, the socialists' view prevailed and children of school age were henceforth debarred from being emigrated from the Chorlton union.

Thus, the age range of Poor Law children who were emigrated became more and more compressed, especially with respect to girls. Nevertheless, there were still influential voices commending such emigration. For example, although acknowledging the inadequacy of inspection in Canada the majority report of the 1909 Royal Commission on the Poor Laws[40] concluded that there were benefits to be derived from children being sent there. This was all the more surprising in the light of the evidence of Mary Mason, the Poor Law inspector of boarded-out children. She was at pains to impress on the commissioners the great dangers involved. In her opinion the Canadian inspectors could not visit as often as was necessary over such wide areas and, as they were all men, she was convinced that they could not report properly on the condition and treatment of the girls.[41] Despite this, the commissioners persisted in the view that boards of guardians should take advantage of what emigration had to offer. This echoed the 1903 circular, but it also served to emphasise the contemporary zeal for Empire emigration, a backcloth against which more cautionary views were liable to become lost. Time and again, for example, although the dangers to which child emigrants were prey are acknowledged in LGB papers, there remained an underlying sense that 'in principle' juvenile emigration should be encouraged. One finds therefore a strong tendency for official pronouncements to be at least ambiguous and sometimes at odds with the evidence available.

Let us turn now to consider the pattern of child emigration that was evolving in the voluntary sector as the new century unfolded. One notable change was the death of most of those who had led or contributed to the child emigration movement. Shaw died in 1902, Rye, Whitwill and Quarrier in 1903, Macpherson in 1904, and Barnardo in 1905. Birt died in 1911 and Stephenson in the following year. However, Middlemore and Fegan survived until 1924 and 1925 respectively, while Rudolf outlived them all until 1933. What effect, if any, did these rapidly occurring disappearances have on juvenile emigration and on the associated organisations more generally? One approach to the question is to return to the distinction that has been drawn between the enterprises that were 'organised' and those that were not, even though there were some which did not fall so clearly into one or other of these categories. Nevertheless, this characterisation does help to explain what happened after the deaths, in quick succession, of such dominant figures.

There were, as we have seen, some emigrationists who were essentially private entrepreneurs, often shunning the constraints of a conventional organisation and therefore lacking a corporate identity. Their *modus operandi* was summed up by Annie Macpherson. Writing to the Canadian High Commissioner (Lord Strathcona) in 1898 to defend herself against accusations that she was ignoring the new Canadian regulations concerning child immigration, she reminded him that from the outset she had undertaken the work 'as a freelance'.[42] Yet without a corporate identity that work was in danger of being cut short when the freelance retired or died. We have already seen that this happened in the case of the Bristol Emigration Society and with Stirling. Even so, not all the freelance ventures faded from the scene when their instigators withdrew or died. Some were absorbed by larger enterprises that had become more formalised. This is what happened when, after a serious illness, Rye retired in 1895 and passed her Homes to the Waifs and Strays Society. Such amalgamations were common in British child welfare during the latter part of the nineteenth and early twentieth centuries. For instance, during this time the annual reports of the Waifs and Strays Society regularly reported the transfer to its administration of small independent Homes whose founders no longer had the energy, enthusiasm or means to go on. Eventually, many of the managers or patrons of small under-endowed Homes were eager to relinquish 'the worry' to 'a business-like organisation'.[43] Another way in which some of the unorganised enterprises overcame the deaths of their charismatic founders (at least for a while) was by family succession, especially where relatives had already been drawn into the work. For example, when Macpherson died in 1904, her three nephews, James, Edward and William Merry (sons of her sister Rachel) took up the reins.[44] Even so, in 1920 the undertaking was merged with the Liverpool Sheltering Homes, which, in turn, were acquired by Barnardos soon afterwards.

In fact, the formalisation of their administrations is one of the key explanations for the survival of those children's societies that were closely identified with a founding individual. Barnardos, for example, had become incorporated under the

Companies Acts in 1899 despite the stubborn opposition of its leader who was adamant that he should run things 'on the same individual lines as he had always done'.[45] However, it was the organisation's growing indebtedness that convinced his committee that they had to protect themselves against financial liability and thereby move to depersonalise the work.[46] There had to be a corporate rather than solely a figurehead identity. The importance of this in ensuring continuity after Barnardo's death was summed up by William Baker, his successor. At first, he admitted, he had wondered whether the work would fall with the founder. In the event, he wrote, matters proceeded 'almost without a hitch'. Why? Because, he explained, the organisation had 'been incorporated, so as to have an entity of its own' and, with a council of leading business men and philanthropists, he was sure that there was no fear for its future.[47]

Similar developments had contributed to safeguarding the work of the Manchester and Salford Boys' and Girls' Society after Shaw's death in 1902. From the outset he, perhaps to a greater extent than his more independently minded contemporaries, recognised the need for a management structure into which he would fit as one of its parts rather than arrogating to himself a comprehensive authority. This, however, also reflected his appreciation of the need to secure the backing of influential local figures from the worlds of business, local government, the church and the police. There was a management committee from the start, albeit that Shaw was one of its members. Furthermore, he assumed the title of honorary secretary throughout, rather than director. In these senses the Manchester Society was somewhat less personalised than most of the others. Indeed, it is noteworthy that Shaw's name did not appear in the Society's title.

In the case of the Catholic enterprises the emigration work continued because it was embedded in a Church hierarchy and was further strengthened by the amalgamations that occurred in the early years of the twentieth century. In short, there was a superior authority to which people such as Father Nugent, Father Seddon and Father Berry were answerable, first at a diocesan level and eventually to the archbishop. A certain limit, therefore, was imposed on the extent to which their activities could become either freewheeling or unduly personalised. Similarly, although Stephenson's name was associated with the creation of the Methodist NCH (National Children's Homes) and with its emigration work, the organisation was regarded as a constituent part of the Wesleyan Church, whose policies could be considered in the national conference.

Although, as has been noted, Fegan, Middlemore and Rudolf lived beyond the years of the First World War, and hence beyond the years of this study, it is interesting to see how similar factors determined the fortunes of their organisations after their deaths. Fegans (now Fegans Child and Family Care) had become fairly formalised early on, with trustees and a council, but, like Barnardos, the enterprise was facing considerable debt by the 1890s and, like Barnardos' council, Fegans' had insisted on protecting themselves from personal liability through incorporation, secured in 1899,[48] well before the founder's death in 1925. The course of the Middlemore Homes was different. Its founder had exercised a far-reaching influence over the work for many years, being chairman, treasurer and director, but by the time of his death in 1924 others had already succeeded him in the administration and it was they who decided in the mid-1920s to delegate the emigration work to the Fairbridge Society and to concentrate their efforts on Birmingham-based schemes.[49] Rudolf, by comparison with other 'founders', had always assumed a rather low profile as secretary of the Waifs and Strays which, in common with the Catholic agencies and the NCH, was, of course, part of an embracing church with all that that meant for a continuing corporate rather than a figurehead identity.

Let us now retrace our steps to those transitions of leadership that happened in the years before the outbreak of war in 1914 and consider what effect, if any, these had on the scale of child emigration. Overall, the number of children emigrated to Canada from the turn of the century rose sharply to a peak of 3,264 in the financial year 1905–06, when, it should be noted, the highest number of children in the care of the Poor Law in England and Wales (50,000) was also reached.[50] In the next two years the emigration figure declined by about 1,000, remaining at around 2,500 a year until the outbreak of war. Even so, the outflow continued to be dominated by Barnardos, which, between 1900 and 1916, accounted for almost 45 per cent of the total of 33,180.[51]

However, with the exception of Barnardos and Quarriers there were no noticeable changes in the number of children emigrated by the societies when their founders died or retired. In Barnardos' case there had been a steady yearly increase up to and including 1905, the year of his death. Indeed, that year had seen the ceiling of 1,314 reached. The following year saw a fall of 11 per cent, followed by a drop of eight per cent and then 13 per cent in the next two. Although numbers varied slightly thereafter, that is from 1908 until 1913, each year saw 11 per cent of all the children being looked after by Barnardos being emigrated: in 1905 it had stood at 17 per cent. This does suggest that Barnardo's death was associated with a slackening of the drive for emigration. On the other hand, Quarrier, it will be recalled, had been so opposed to the Ontario regulations of 1897 concerning child immigration that he had refused to continue the work. No children went from his Home to Canada from 1898 until 1904, but in 1904 Quarriers' committee decided to resume emigration. It is reasonable to conclude therefore that it was Quarrier's death in 1903 that enabled this to be done. The only other agency to show some slowing down in its emigration after the founder's death was the Liverpool Sheltering Homes where the greatest annual exodus coincided with the year of Birt's death (1911). Thereafter the number began to fall away. However, since the differences are quite small it would be unwise to read too much into them. Furthermore, as in the case of Birt, for instance, some of the founders had become ill and therefore probably less involved several years before their deaths.

Thus, although in some cases the death of the societies' figureheads did seem to weaken the enthusiasm for child emigration, in others it did not. Not only organisational but also other factors doubtless exercised an influence on the emerging pattern. However, it is difficult to attribute any of this to wider social and economic considerations such as the state of the juvenile labour market, developments in education policy, or poverty and destitution. It is not that these factors had no effect; they probably did, but because the number of children emigrated was small compared with the child population as a whole, or even with the number in some form of substitute care, it is hard to determine which influences were significant. Take, for example, the market for children's labour. Certainly, in Canada the demand for British young people continued unabated. In the first decades of the twentieth century requests for the children grew rapidly, from 4,400 in 1900–01 to 19,400 in 1905–06. Thereafter the requests fell somewhat until 1910–11, but after that they ran at about 30,000 a year, reaching a maximum of 31,725 in 1915–16.[52] Such applications far exceeded the number of children available, but that meant that, had they wished or been able to, the emigrationists could have found a placement for any child they wanted to send to Canada (with the exception of those under about 10 years of age, for whom there was little or no demand).

The position with respect to the juvenile labour market in Britain was less clear-cut. For instance, the raising of the school leaving age to 12 in 1899 (and to 14 in those areas in which local school boards chose to exercise powers granted them in the following year) may have had a dampening effect on the readiness to arrange emigration. Although the new attendance requirement could be partially circumvented through the 'half-time school half-time work' dispensation (which survived until 1918), it was still a requirement that children should attend school. Furthermore, the 'half-time' concession was mainly invoked in certain agricultural areas and in the textile towns of Lancashire and Yorkshire, where there was still a demand for child labour. For instance, the 1911 Census[53] recorded 31,800 children between the ages of 10 and 12 'occupied' in some work and another 114,600 of those aged between 13 and 14. However, the textile industries accounted for 54 per cent of child labour among the under 12s. The 1911 Census also revealed that domestic service still occupied a prime position in the labour market for girls in Britain. In 1911 nearly 250,000 of those under the age of 18 were engaged in 'domestic indoor service', nearly a fifth of all female domestic servants. Hence, unless they were 'incorrigible' or disabled in some way there was little problem in finding work for girls in Britain; whether they kept it or not was another matter. Indeed, as we have seen, the usual reason offered for sending the girls to Canada was not to find them work but to separate them from 'undesirable' parents or from circumstances in which they were considered to be morally vulnerable.

The situation with regard to boys as the new century dawned was more complicated. The main societies and the Poor Law authorities continued to express great concern that too many school-leavers were going into dead-end jobs (for example, as messengers, delivery boys, boot-blacks, pages or street traders). This is borne out by details provided in the 1911 Census that put the number of boys under 18 who were occupied in these jobs at 152,700, of whom 24,870, that is,

16 per cent, were under 14, and the largest number (52,680) comprised 14-year-olds, mostly the immediate school-leavers.

One way in which such casual and largely unsupervised work could be avoided was by steering boys towards the armed forces or the merchant navy. The various training ships contributed to securing such employment: first, because they kept boys until they were 16 (when, normally, they could enlist), thereby deferring their entry into the labour market and, second, because they equipped them with rudimentary skills for service at sea. However, the nature of the military service market for boys had begun to change by the twentieth century. For instance, the demand for boy sailors declined as sail gave way to steam, as the loss of life at sea became less and as the ships became technically more sophisticated. This changed situation was explored in 1907 by a committee that looked into the supply of boys for the merchant navy. Its report pointed out that whereas, for example, in 1870 there had been over 18,000 indentured apprenticeships in the merchant service, this figure had fallen to 5,000 by 1905. 'Shipowners', the committee explained, 'at the present time decline to carry boys on the grounds that it does not pay them to do so',[54] and this was despite the introduction of a government subsidy (the boy sailor scheme) introduced under the 1898 Merchant Marine Fund Act. Its purpose was not simply to encourage the employment of boys at sea but to reduce the number of foreigners serving in the merchant navy. Although an alternative source of cheap adult labour, they could not be used as reservists for the Royal Navy in time of war and, as Anglo-German competition for naval supremacy grew after the turn of the century, this became a matter of concern to the Admiralty.[55]

There was also the question of the 'fitness' of boys for military service. At the turn of the century the Boer War had exposed the poor state of health of potential recruits, with many of those wishing to enlist being rejected on medical grounds. So great was the concern that an inter-departmental committee was appointed to examine 'physical deterioration', essentially among the working classes.[56] It seems reasonable to assume that among the 'Home' boys somewhat similar levels of unfitness would have prevailed, but while this would have prevented their enlistment it should also have been likely to have barred them from emigration.

So, although by the twentieth century the British juvenile labour market was changing, many of its nineteenth-century features remained. Girls were still sought in certain sectors, especially domestic service, but the prospects for boys were uncertain, especially between the ages of 14 and 18. Emigration still offered itself as a reasonable option for those whose opportunity for secure work in Britain looked unpromising. Nonetheless, it remains an open question whether or not such labour market factors in Britain, somewhat changed though they were by the new century, had any influence on the scale of child and youth emigration. Certainly, some of the societies maintained that their emigration work was intended, among other things, to address the recurrent problem of youth unemployment.

The political quest for Empire settlement, together with difficulties in finding employment for boys in Britain, merged to create a context in which the still buoyant demand for child labour in Canada might have been expected to have been more fully satisfied than it was, but there were countervailing influences. As we have seen, there was the raising of the school-leaving age, the death of some of the most enthusiastic advocates of emigration from the leadership of certain voluntary organisations and, as with the Poor Law children, the fact that, for one reason or another, fewer young people were 'available' for Canada or elsewhere in the Empire. In addition, some of the societies began to adopt policies that imposed restrictions on the age at which children in their charge could be sent abroad. For example, the Waifs and Strays Society declared in their annual report for 1909 that, henceforth, they would no longer emigrate girls until they were 14.[57] This was quite the opposite to the policy of the LGB which, by then, was not allowing girls to be sent overseas beyond that age. Clearly, the assessments of the relationship between their age and the 'risk' that they ran had produced different conclusions.

Thus, as there had always been, there were pulls and pushes influencing the scale of child emigration. It was the inter-relationship between these that affected the scale of child emigration from Britain. The constraining factors have not been given as much prominence as those that were perceived as advancing the cause of the movement: hence the reason for asking why *more* children were not sent to Canada, especially in the early twentieth century. Had there been no war in 1914 the balance between the 'pulls' and the 'pushes' might have changed, not least because, just before the outbreak of hostilities, newcomers were appearing on the scene anxious to promote child emigration.

III The Newcomers

Founded in 1878, the Salvation Army (SA)[58] was the most notable organisation to embark on child emigration in the early years of the twentieth century. William Booth, the architect of the Salvation Army, was a strong advocate of emigration as an important part of the solution to 'the social question', although the organisation did not become much involved in this activity until after his seminal book on the 'way out of darkest England',[59] that is, until the 1890s. Even then progress was slow, partly because the principal scheme being proposed was to establish farm colonies overseas.[60] Indeed, several were founded in the United States[61] and in 1904 the British government was persuaded to appoint Rider Haggard (novelist and Salvationist) to report on these in order to assess whether similar colonies might be set up in the Empire, in particular in the Canadian north west, possibly with support from public funds. His favourable report was submitted in 1905[62] but was then referred to a departmental committee whose conclusion, published the following year,[63] was that the scheme was impractical. Instead, it was recommended that individual emigration should be encouraged. Furthermore, it advised that juvenile emigration should be expanded. In the light of these conclusions 'the Salvation Army abandoned the concept of the back to the land colony in favour of a vigorous promotion of emigration, particularly to Canada'[64] and began to consider the emigration of unaccompanied children. The framework for such a shift in policy was already in place. In 1903 a separate Migration and Settlement Department had been set up under the direction of David Lamb who, in the same year, travelled to Canada to assess the prospects for emigration. However, at this stage the work was still focused on adults: 1,500 went to the Dominion under the Army's auspices in 1905 and in the next year 13,000.[65] By 1911 it was claimed that 50,000 people had been assisted to emigrate, most going to Canada.[66]

However, it was not until 1907 that the SA actually became involved in the emigration of children, again principally to Canada.[67] Four years later a department was created in the London headquarters to encourage and organise it. By 1915 the Army claimed that it was placing a greater number of children in Canada than 'certain other Societies who have been established many years'.[68] It was also claimed that the emigration of young children was a special feature of this work, in particular Poor Law children. 'Boards of Guardians throughout the country have been seen and the subject exhaustively discussed, resulting – in many cases – in children being brought forward for Emigration by Guardians who in the past have been opposed to Emigration.'[69]

At the outset the Canadian Department of the Interior extended a warm welcome to the SA's initiative. There were two particular reasons for this. The first was because, by then, the organisation had considerable experience in the emigration of families and young adults, and second, because it also possessed an established network of offices and staff throughout most of the populated parts of the Dominion. There was an officer in charge of child immigration in Toronto as well as a receiving and distribution Home, the Newcomers' Inn, which, in 1913, was praised by Bogue Smart, the Canadian chief inspector.[70] In short, there was a substantial and pre-existing organisation onto which the work of child emigration could be grafted. Indeed, in 1913 the Dominion superintendent of immigration (William Scott) felt able to write that there was 'no organisation better equipped to place out and supervise the children than the Salvation Army',[71] and the Minister of the Interior had also lent his strong endorsement, telling the Canadian House of Commons that the Salvation Army was a reliable institution that took care of those whom it brought out.[72] However, two years later (1915) certain concerns had begun to surface. Bogue Smart complained that although he had discussed the matter with its officers 'time after time', the Salvation Army had still failed to provide him with adequate placement addresses and had failed to inform him when changes were made. 'The trouble with the organisation in question', he concluded, 'appears to … be the lack of system.'[73] The following year (1916) a particular case led to the superintendent of immigration writing a warning letter to the Army. Herbert Sills from Edmonton (London) had had an appendectomy but was quickly discharged from hospital and placed in employment in a Toronto garage. However, he was not fully recovered and but for the proprietor's wife getting him readmitted to hospital his condition would have worsened. 'I am constrained to point out', wrote the superintendent, 'that in this case there certainly appears to have been ... reprehensible carelessness or neglect'. Furthermore, it was pointed out that a city garage 'was not considered to be a desirable place for a boy like Sills when there [is] an abundance of healthier and more desirable openings with the farmers of the Province'.[74] However, any further action on the part of either the Department of the Interior or the Salvation Army was overtaken by the exigencies of war.

When it interrupted its work of juvenile emigration in 1916 because of hostilities, the Salvation Army had taken 500 children, mostly boys, to Canada[75] and had placed them widely throughout the country, from New Brunswick to British Columbia. However, three-fifths of the young emigrants had arrived after 1912 and it was clear that but for the war the Salvation Army would have done more. Indeed, in 1911 one of the contributors to its meeting of the Salvation Army's International Social Council asked rhetorically: 'Can there be a greater opportunity for Christ's work than this child emigration project offers?'[76] The project was resumed after the war, but it was then to Australia that most of the young people went – typically boys from 14 to 19 who had had some preliminary training at the Army's farm school.

As well as the Salvation Army the Church Army (CA) (formed in 1882 through the determination of Wilson Carlile) was almost a replica of the Salvation Army with its uniform, its captains and sisters and firm discipline. The major difference was that whereas by 1885 the CA had become 'an integral part of the Church of England, entering the parishes only on the invitation of the incumbent, the Salvation Army [was] ... a religious group without any affiliation to a denomination'.[77] The aim of the CA was to bring the Church of England closer to the poor, particularly through its schemes of social relief. It was also concerned with the unemployment or blind-alley jobs that plagued young boys and in 1909 a Boys' Aid Department was opened in order to find work for those on its register. Some went to its training farm where they could be prepared for emigration,[78] but exactly how many were sent out to Canada and Australia is unclear.

The question remains, however, why neither the Salvation Army nor the Church Army became engaged in child emigration until towards the end of the first decade of the twentieth century. One explanation applies to both, namely, that neither was established specifically as a child-saving organisation. Each was involved more generally with the social casualties of the time – children were included only inasmuch as their families were the object of concern. By contrast, the child emigrationists who went before them devoted themselves almost wholly to the plight of children. In the case of the Church Army there was also the fact that within the Church of England the Waifs and Strays Society already existed. Indeed, it is somewhat surprising that it was felt necessary to add another child emigration arm to the work of the established Church. The explanation may lie in the mounting concern in the early years of the new century with the unemployment of older young people.

Although there were other 'newcomers', their contribution to the child emigration movement was limited. They were individualistic and small-scale and some, like Ellinor Close's farm scheme in New Brunswick, collapsed after only a few years. Brief details of many of these are provided by Marjorie Kohli in *The Golden Bridge*.[79] Furthermore, apart from the Salvation Army, the new ventures that sprang up in the early twentieth century hardly had an opportunity to add to the volume of child emigration before the war brought their activities to a halt, albeit temporarily in some cases.

Part VIII
A Review

FIFTEEN

Explanation and Assessment

I Why?

How best is this episode in the history of British children to be explained? Previous chapters have demonstrated the interwoven nature of the factors that shaped it, but there is no single or simple explanation. Nevertheless, it behoves the commentator to offer a view of the major elements in this complicated and involved emigration saga.

The existence of profound poverty in Britain during the years 1867-1917 must be recognised as an important predisposing condition. It was exacerbated by insecure employment (or none at all), by low wages and by single parenthood, in particular that caused by widowhood and desertion. The effects of extensive poverty were especially evident among children. Not only were these publicly visible but also regarded as a potential threat to social order. Superimposed on this was a child-saving movement, driven forward by the evangelical revival from the 1850s onwards and thereby closely linked with the desire to 'save' children in the religious sense. This was buttressed by a belief that children *could* be saved through exposure to religious teaching and God-fearing example, whereas considerably more doubt existed with respect to adults, especially if they were addicted to alcohol and 'sunk in depravation'. It is difficult for us today to appreciate the pervasiveness of the evangelical fervour that gripped many of the middle classes and sections of the artisan population. That movement, however, was not homogeneous. It sprang from several roots, was divided and each variation vigorously defended. This led to sectarian rivalry, to competition for financial support as well as for membership. Both the Catholic Church and the established Church felt threatened by such non-conformist zeal and responded with countermeasures. Each religious faction was keen to outdo its rivals, and this included outdoing them in the realm of child saving.

What, then, can one say about the motives of those who established and sustained these child-saving schemes? We shall never know for certain and perhaps, for historical purposes, it is unnecessary to know. However, the driving force of evangelism did offer opportunities for the realisation of personal ambitions as well as religious fulfilment. Most, if not all, appear to have convinced themselves that what they did was disinterested and a manifestation of God's design for them. Most maintained that they had been 'called' to the work. This applied to both the men and the women who became involved, but in the case of the women there was another dimension. As middle-class ladies they were denied a place in most spheres of public life and indeed in useful employment, but a career could be constructed in the field of welfare work, especially in that concerned with women and children, and this was more easily done (in the sense of its social acceptability) when its rationale was religious endeavour.

Why, however, should such individuals have included the *emigration* of poor children in their schemes for saving children from the ravages of destitution, from neglectful or abusive parents and from a religious void? There was certainly the influence of the 'climate of the times', a climate that reflected a concern about the dangerous potentialities of the so-called 'surplus population', together with a wish to see the inter-generational continuities of pauperism, crime and brutalism broken. In these respects there was a clamour in favour of emigration *in general*: it appeared to offer a cheap and effective remedy to a mixture of social problems. There was also the conviction that emigration would strengthen the Empire. It is not hard, therefore, to see how child emigration fitted so well into these prevailing preoccupations.

One other factor accelerated the development of all forms of emigration; namely, the greater speed, safety and cheapness of sea transport. By the start of the main child emigration movement in and around 1870 sail had largely given way to steam, especially on the trans-Atlantic routes, and fierce competition for this trade tended to bring down fares. It was not for this reason alone, however, that the 'child emigrationists' chose Canada as the favoured destination. The other major reasons are to be found in assumptions about the nature of Canadian society, the stage of its economic development and, by comparison, the difficulties associated with other possible destinations. Even by the latter half of the nineteenth century Canada was relatively un-urbanised or industrialised. It remained a thinly populated land, the economy of which still depended on agriculture and the garnering of raw materials. Seen from a British perspective it could appear (or be presented as) a country retaining the assumed virtues of a rural existence, uncorrupted by the immorality and other depravations associated with urban industrial life. There was, it should be borne in mind, a strong attachment in Britain to the image of a golden age of rural tranquillity, with its healthy environment and upstanding morality. Agricultural life was a 'good' life and many philanthropists strove to recreate it through the establishment of farm colonies, rural resettlement schemes and farm training schools. One only has to look at the frontispiece of Booth's *In Darkest England and the Way Out* to appreciate the strength of this imagery and its powerful appeal to those who sought both a moral and a social solution to the ills that abounded. Furthermore, of course, the countryside was seen as a place where honest work went hand-in-hand with religious probity.

Canada seemed to offer all these virtues, especially if its towns and cities could be avoided. Surely, it was argued, so many reformative influences came together in that country that it provided an ideal destination for endangered poor children, a destination which, in addition to its other attractions, gave the chance of making a 'new start' with prospects of advancement. Indeed, this was the formula that had already attracted many to Canada's shores. Not least, there was ample land which, made available through land grant systems, could enable poor immigrants to establish themselves on family farms. In due course, it was maintained, some of the immigrant children (in particular the boys) could take advantage of this and thereby better themselves.

During this period of child emigration Canada needed people, and people of an age who, through their labour, could contribute to its economic development. They certainly did not want the old, the 'halt' or the 'lame', or those who were likely to pursue an idle or criminal life. In short, no actual or potential social casualties were required. Over and above this was the question (both for Britain and for Canada) of ensuring a significant majority of British 'stock' who would regard themselves as citizens of the Empire, with abiding loyalties to the 'old country'. Yet, by the turn of the century a large number of immigrants were arriving from many other European countries. Canada certainly needed them, but was ambivalent about their origins. Racial and linguistic issues intruded, not least with respect to Québec's aspirations for a larger francophone population.

As long as they carried none of the hallmarks of pauperism, of disease or of potential criminality, British children commended themselves as additional labour, appropriate to the support of family farming, as well as having the additional advantage of being British. Yet not all the child candidates for emigration were free from the social blemishes that Canada was so concerned about and that were thought to increase the danger of national degeneration. They had to 'pass muster' – through medical examinations and by being portrayed by the emigrationists as carefully selected; indeed, in Barnardo's words, as being 'the flower of the flock'. For its part, the Canadian government faced the problem of convincing an often sceptical population that the children who came (and for some of whom they paid *per capita* grants) were indeed the flower of the flock. The trade unions saw them as cheap labour that threatened to undercut wages or to reduce employment, while certain doctors, civic dignitaries and, later, social workers, regarded them as a potentially contaminating influence and prime candidates for hospitals, asylums or prisons. Hence, the Canadian government was obliged to tread a fine line between the encouragement of young immigrant farm labour and a readily aroused political opposition to any such policy. In this situation the value to the Canadian authorities of the 'private' activities of the British emigrationists lay in the ease with which successive governments could partially absolve themselves from a responsibility for the influx of unaccompanied children.

Finally, together with all its other attractions for child emigration, Canada remained the destination that posed the least practical and political problems. Early on the US had closed its doors to any such trans-shipment; South Africa had ample cheap or free black labour; Australia and New Zealand involved long and expensive sea passages; and India, like South Africa, had a superfluity of cheap labour. Thus, questions of Empire, labour markets, communications and rural imagery merged to make Canada the preferred destination for child emigrants, at least until after the 1914-18 war when the balance of these factors began to change, leading to a shift towards Australia.

It is, of course, not only the child emigration movement that needs to be explained, albeit in all its complexity, but also its scale. One's first reaction upon learning that some 80,000 children were sent to Canada over the 50 years from 1867 is to wonder at such a large exodus. In fact, as has been suggested, one might equally well wonder why the number was not considerably larger. Certainly, many of the emigrationists sought to expand their activities and many others believed that more children could be recruited. Furthermore, as we have seen, both the basic conditions in Britain and in Canada were favourable to an expansion. So, what, then, kept down the number? The answer, in a nutshell, is twofold. First, there were never as many children available for emigration as was usually believed. We have seen that a considerable proportion of the children in the care of the Poor Law were there for comparatively short periods. Likewise, those looked after by the voluntary societies were relatively small in number. In addition, not all the children were fit enough or old enough to be considered for emigration. Second, various constraints surrounded the schemes for child emigration. In the first place there were the administrative checks. At different times considerable misgivings about what was being done were entertained by the Local Government Board (LGB) and by the Home Office in Britain, and although their ability to prevent the expatriation of particular children was somewhat limited both departments did exercise a restraining influence that could persuade Poor Law guardians or industrial schools to think twice about volunteering their children for Canada. Indeed, directives and circulars set upper and lower age limits and during the 1880s, the LGB imposed a moratorium on the emigration of all Poor Law children.

Other pockets of opposition existed in certain Poor Law unions, sometimes on matters of principle, sometimes on the basis of the needs of local labour markets and sometimes because of a lack of confidence in the emigrationists who approached them. Even among some of the children's societies (such as the Waifs and Strays) the emigration 'solution' was not embraced as enthusiastically as it was by others: the age of the children was more carefully circumscribed and, in particular, the vulnerable position of girls once they were in Canada tended to cause concern and therefore hesitancy.

Not all the children sent to Canada had left their families well before emigration. Certain parents were persuaded to allow their offspring to be sent to Canada in order to give them 'a better chance' than they had at home. Typically, these were hard-pressed parents of large families, especially lone mothers. Nonetheless, the scope for recruiting children in this way was limited. Whatever the blandishments, parents were usually reluctant to part with their children in so complete a manner, although some did agree to their being 'taken into care' without realising that they might then be emigrated. So, parental and family opposition to such a course did exist and was sometimes able to thwart the aspirations of the emigrationists. Indeed, where a serious attempt was made to obtain parental consents these were often unforthcoming. The requirement that children in public care should appear before magistrates to give their consent to being emigrated also influenced the number emigrated. Some did say 'no' and where they did this seems to have been respected.

Thus, in Britain a number of factors served to limit the scale of child emigration. Furthermore, as we have seen, in Canada the political sensitivities were such that governments were careful not to be seen to be encouraging too many child immigrants and the emigrationists, being aware of this, seem to have avoided bringing large parties of children to the Dominion at any one time. Indeed, Barnardo, the most active of them, became the target of Canadian criticism because, among other things, he was perceived to be 'flooding' the country with his young charges.

II Outcomes and Evaluation

Considerable efforts are currently being made to establish the 'outcomes' for children who are, or have been, the responsibility of the state or other corporate bodies. In particular, there is a desire to know which consequences follow which interventions, or the lack of them, in order to discover 'what works' in the best interests of the child. Despite such a surge of interest the research necessary to establish aggregate (rather than individual) outcomes faces a number of difficulties.[1] For example, just when can it be decided that an 'outcome' has been reached? Furthermore, what data are required for that purpose? It is therefore not always a straightforward matter to determine an outcome and then to evaluate it, not least because there is rarely a basis for comparison; that is, in this case, to know what happened to children in similar circumstances who were not emigrated. Then there is the distinction between how one person evaluates their experience and how a researcher evaluates the collective experience of greater numbers. There will always be exceptions to the generalisations.

Inevitably, therefore, both establishing the general outcome of child emigration between 1867 and 1917 and then its evaluation pose problems. For a start information is both selective and sparse and those who were caught up in the trans-shipments are no longer alive to bear witness. Furthermore, when it comes to an evaluation there is the danger that the past will be judged through present-day eyes. Social and economic conditions have changed radically and our understanding of child development and of the impact of privation, deprivation and upheaval has been much refined. Even within the 50 years of this study there were considerable changes, most notably in the introduction of compulsory education, improvements in public health measures and the gradual establishment of specific services for children. Bearing all this in mind, there are three ways of approaching the determination and assessment of the outcomes of child emigration to Canada over 100 years ago. First, there are a few studies that have addressed the issue. Second, there are some contemporary testimonies of those who were sent and, third, there are the more recent accounts of those who were expatriated (mainly to Australia) and whose experiences throw light on its emotional impact.

The first reasonably well-designed study was commissioned by the Canadian Council on Child Welfare and undertaken by Breckenridge McGregor. The results were published in 1928 under the title *Several Years After*.[2] Although Rooke and Schnell[3] have argued that its purpose was to demonstrate the corrupting influence of British immigrant children on the health, morality and genetic stock of the country, it was the first attempt to discover what had happened to the children. It set out to trace the histories of 200 of them who had arrived in 1910 and another 200 in 1920. They were to be selected in proportion to the scale of involvement of eight of the emigration agencies and with a representative number of Poor Law and non-Poor Law children, as well as a two-to-one split in favour of boys. In the event the plan could not be realised: information was able to be collected on only 311 of the 400, and even then most of it fell short of what it had been hoped to obtain. The biggest stumbling block was the refusal of four of the societies to co-operate (Barnardos, the Salvation Army, the National Children's Homes and Fegans). This was probably because they were suspicious about the purpose and thus the objectivity of the study.

Despite the dearth of information about the children's backgrounds and subsequent fortunes certain conclusions were drawn from what could be discovered. For instance, the homes of prospective employers were not usually visited prior to placement; that too much reliance was placed on references from, and subsequent oversight by, local clergy; that the emphasis was on finding a child for a home rather than a home for a child; that erratic school attendance was common, and that it was 'a mistake to suppose that the employers in applying for the child are actuated by altruistic motives. There is no more reason why this should be expected of them than of the business man who applies for an office boy.'[4]

Such a situation goes a long way to account for the principal reason found in the study for a child being 'returned' to the distribution Home; namely, that they were 'unsatisfactory'. Yet none of these conclusions gave a longer-term description of 'outcomes'. Indeed, McGregor concluded that despite her search for information she could not put a figure on the 'success' or otherwise of child immigration, but she was quick to point out that neither could the societies, notwithstanding their glowing claims.[5]

As the number of children sent to Canada declined in the inter-war years, interest in the question of how they, and those who had gone before them, fared also declined. It was not until the 1970s that further light began to be shed on the destinies of Britain's emigrant children in Canada. The major contribution to this was Joy Parr's PhD thesis, subsequently published as *Labouring Children* in 1980.[6] It was based on an examination of a five per cent sample of the files of children taken to Canada by Barnardos between 1882 and 1908, giving 997 in all. These records offered an insight into what life was like for immigrant children, lives that were shaped by their ambiguous status in the families for whom they worked as well as by the discrepancy between the employers' expectations and the children's ability or willingness to meet them. Parr also collected a reasonable amount of aggregate information about the children's health, about the extent of corporal punishment, about school attendance and about pregnancies among the girls. There was also some material about their circumstances in adulthood.

Nearly 18 per cent of the children had problems with their health while in Canada, a reduction of the rate of 26 per cent that was recorded prior to their emigration. In particular, while in Canada there was a marked decline in 'the cases of contagious diseases endemic to children's institutions of the time', but it was noticeable, Parr emphasised, that there was also a reduction in 'consumption, scrofula and frailty'. The exception to this trend was 'that mental disturbance and mental weakness' were reported more frequently in Canada – rising from a rate of five per cent before leaving Britain to nine per cent thereafter.[7] However, three cautionary notes need to be sounded about these figures. First, there is the reliability of the records. Second, there was a 'missing data' rate of 19 per cent throughout. Third, the children's health was likely to have been better monitored in Britain than it was in Canada because most had lived in institutions where there would have been a premium on reporting contagious diseases and infections. What is notable, however, is the increase in 'mental problems', even though the actual number of cases counted from the records was quite small. But not all conditions that would be included today were included then. Furthermore, because of this, and because visits to the children were so infrequent, the incidence of 'mental disturbance' was likely to have been underestimated, only being noted when it became severe.

Since health data were recorded on the files prior to a child's emigration it was possible for Parr to establish whether or not a pre-existing condition persisted in Canada. For 28 per cent of the children with eye, ear, nose or throat problems before they left, these continued after emigration. Likewise, almost 31 per cent of the children who had been classed as 'delicate' or in poor general health remained so in Canada. Given figures like these then, on health grounds alone, the emigration of a substantial minority of the children was hard to justify. Indeed, given the facts about the children's health *before* their emigration one has to question the adequacy of the medical scrutiny to which they were subject. Of course, diagnostic aids were not what they are today and the doctors may well have hurried through their inspections, taking note of only the more obvious illnesses or disabilities. Nevertheless, if, as Barnardo claimed, those proposed for emigration were specially chosen then their selection suggests that those who were left behind, but who were otherwise potential candidates, were in poorer health.

In the case of corporal punishment the Barnardo records indicated that for nine per cent of the boys and 15 per cent of the girls this had been what Parr classed as 'excessive'; that is, where there were 'substantiated charges of ill-treatment resulting in reprimand of the master or removal of the child'.[8] The difference between the rate for boys and that for girls was, as she suggests, likely to have been a reflection of the higher threshold of the dividing line between 'reasonable' and 'excessive' punishment set for the boys. Furthermore, the records only included 'reported and substantial cases' so that the quoted figures have to be treated as minimum proportions. In addition, there was no information concerning this aspect of the children's treatment in a little over a quarter of the sample.

It has been evident in previous chapters that irregular schooling was a major shortcoming in the lives of the emigrant children, and that although concern about it was often expressed the problem persisted. Indeed, 70 per cent of those in Parr's sample who were 13 to 15 years old when they arrived, and for whom information was available, had never been to school in Canada. Among the 10- to 12-year-olds the rate was 30 per cent. However, those who were under 10 when they landed fared better: only three per cent never having attended school thereafter. Nevertheless, for all the age groups having some schooling, occasional or interrupted education was common. For instance, the rates that Parr established for this were 29 per cent for those under 10 on arrival, 44 per cent for the 10- to 12-year-olds and 25 per cent for those between 13 and 15.[9] If those who were 16 or older at emigration are excluded then, for the rest, the rate of non-attendance was 40 per cent and that for irregular attendance 34 per cent, making almost three-quarters who experienced less than complete schooling.[10] However, it should be noted that when 'regular attendance' was recorded it rarely meant full-time attendance. Both the 'indentures' that were drawn up for the children and Canadian practice in rural areas defined this as an 'acceptable' proportion of the year. Bearing this in mind Parr questions whether the British emigrant children were much worse off in the farming districts than their Canadian classmates.[11] This may have been so, but it seems likely that they were worse off in terms of their schooling than their Barnardo contemporaries who remained in Britain.

When she turned to the extent to which the girls became pregnant while minors, Parr found a recorded rate of 11 per cent, with a further two per cent where it was intimated that this was the case. Girls arriving in Canada between the ages of 13 and 15 appear to have been the most vulnerable.[12] Although the incidence of pregnancy in the sample was 'markedly higher than that among other Canadian women of similar ages in 1926' (the first year for which comparable figures were available), it was the extent of illegitimate births that stood out. This was, Parr explained, 'eight times higher than among Canadian adolescents as a whole and even more atypically high by comparison with other rural residents of similar ages'.[13] What is unclear, however, is what the equivalent rate of pregnancy was among Barnardo girls of a similar age who were not emigrated or, indeed how, at the time, such a figure would have compared with that for girls of this age sent out to domestic service in Britain. Canadian farms may have offered healthier surroundings but the girls' isolation and status made them especially vulnerable to sexual exploitation.

Thus, Parr was only able to gather a limited amount of aggregate information that gave an indication of what happened to the emigrant children while they remained children. The data that she could gather led her to conclude that 'if the childhood years alone [are] … considered, the juvenile immigration policy was a dubious business'. But, she continued, 'the sponsors of the movement were not primarily interested in the child's early years'.[14] They would have argued that the measure of their success was to be found in the years beyond childhood. Only then, it was usually claimed, would it be evident whether or not the better opportunities that Canada was considered to offer had materialised. Typically, those opportunities were believed to lie on the land, the crowning point of which for the boys was farm ownership and for the girls a farm marriage. Hence, how the children fared as adults could be considered to be the touchstone of the success or otherwise of child emigration.

However, once the young people reached their adult years contact with Barnardos began to decline and records became sporadic or ceased altogether. Even so, Parr gathered what information she could about their subsequent lives, but primarily in terms of their occupations. These were noted at the point of the last contact with the organisation. Obviously, as she acknowledged, this raised two problems. First, it was unlikely that those who remained in contact were a representative group and, second, the age at which final contact was made varied considerably. Nonetheless, what Parr was able to learn provided a rough indication of occupational outcomes. Indeed, there was some information on a third of the women and a fifth of the men 20 years after the end of their so-called apprenticeship.[15] If one takes the group of 94 men who were between the ages of 27 and 36 at final contact, 70 per cent had labouring or other unskilled jobs (but only a few were unemployed). Only six had become agricultural proprietors and a further five were tenant farmers or sharecroppers. By contrast, of the 146 who were over 36 when last in contact, 23 (or 16 per cent) had succeeded in becoming owners of farms or smallholdings. However, most young men whom Barnardos had sent as children quickly left farm life. Parr found that only 11 per cent of those who were last known of between 27 and 36 years of age had remained in this work.[16] Sixty-seven per cent were employed in towns and cities. Among this group about one in eight had established themselves as artisans, clerks, foremen and such like.[17]

The young women were much more likely to have gravitated to the urban centres than the men. Alongside the drift to the towns and cities there was a pronounced movement away from employment in domestic service: factories and shops were preferred. However, there was less upward occupational mobility than among the men. None of the women were known to have become teachers. Only two per cent had completed training as nurses and only seven per cent had become stenographers. Overall, 15 per cent had secured some clerical or professional training.[18] However, the occupational analysis of the fortunes of the women could not be taken very far: most were married in their mid-twenties, although few became farm wives.

We are handicapped, as ever, in drawing conclusions about the success or otherwise of Barnardos' emigration scheme from these occupational data as there is an absence of comparable information about those who were not emigrated. And how did their working lives compare with those who were Canadian-born and of a similar age and background? We cannot tell. Even so, Parr cautiously concluded that, especially for the men, there were occupational 'gains'. Nevertheless, her question as to whether these (or, indeed, other 'gains') could compensate for earlier hardships and anguish remains pertinent.

III Hearing From the Survivors

Of course, none of the 'outcome' data that we have been discussing say much about the emotional impact of unaccompanied emigration on the children and, later, on their adult lives. However, a rather different study was published in 1979 that gathered 'the personal stories' of people who had been sent to Canada between the years 1871 and 1930. This was Phyllis Harrison's *The Home Children*.[19] She placed a notice in 40 newspapers inviting survivors, or their descendants, to write to her about their experience. One hundred and five did so. The accounts are both moving and vivid. Above all they provide an insight (as did the children's letters included in chapter 13) into what it *felt* like to be an emigrant child and indeed, for many, how the emotions experienced at that time lived on into old age. However, before we hear from Harrison's respondents, a few statistics will provide the framework.

Seventy-three per cent of the letters were from or about men and 27 per cent from or about women. Sixty-nine per cent of them had been brought to Canada in the period 1870-1915, the rest from 1920 to 1930. Overall, 48 per cent had been 12 years of age or younger when they landed, the girls typically being younger than the boys. However, no details about ages were given in nearly 30 per cent of the letters. The most frequently mentioned items of information concerned the organisation that had arranged the emigration. Barnardos dominated the picture, being responsible for almost half of the emigrations. Sixteen per cent of the letter-writers did not say, or could not remember, who brought them to Canada. Overall, three-quarters of the respondents said that they (or those they wrote about) had worked on farms, certainly until they were 18 (83 per cent of the boys and 57 per cent of the girls). Only six per cent had definitely not been placed on farms. The remainder either did not include this information or had had a mixture of farm and non-farm work.

There was considerable mobility. Hardly any of the people had stayed in one place until they were 18. Unhappiness, the end of a short-term engagement, being considered 'unsatisfactory', running away or being removed because of ill-treatment, all contributed to this history of unsettlement. Indeed, a pattern of 'moving around' and restlessness, particularly among the boys, was liable to continue into adult life. In the 1930s the Depression increased this trend as work was sought throughout the country and in the United States. Almost half of the letters (47 per cent) described long sequences of moves, from one family to another and from one place to another. Another 37 per cent described periods of instability interspersed with times of stability and *vice versa*. Only 16 per cent of the respondents, mainly women, reported stable and long placements, some less from contentment than from a fear of leaving or from not knowing how that might be done.

Eighteen per cent of the letters described harsh physical treatment (boys and girls in equal proportion) and a fifth of the women who replied said, or strongly implied, that they had been sexually abused by some man in the families to which they were sent. Even with these kinds of facts, and those provided by Parr, it soon becomes evident from the letters that an evaluation of child emigration to Canada is not a straightforward matter. For example, it was not unusual for a harsh and unsympathetic placement to be followed by another where the child found kindness, was sent to school and not overworked; but the next might be similar to the first. Even in the same household the husband could be brutal but the wife protective, and there were instances of the reverse as well. Can, or should, good and bad experiences be homogenised into one general assessment, with some of the positives offsetting some of the negatives as well as the opposite? Indeed, the question is made even more difficult when one follows the letter-writers into old age. A loving marriage, children and grandchildren could be, and for some were, considered to compensate for earlier harrowing, unhappy or traumatic experiences. As one correspondent wrote: 'I'm happily married and have no regrets now',[20] and as another explained, 'I married at 25 the woman who made up to me for the love I did not receive as a child'.[21]

Some letters captured the ambiguities and ambivalences involved in making an assessment of a lifetime's experiences. Here is what one man wrote:

> I wouldn't go back to England now if you gave me a free ticket and a life pension. But looking back over my life, I believe no organisation should have been allowed to ship out children under 18 years of age. After that they have some chance to defend themselves against labour-hungry and dollar-hungry farmers.[22]

Furthermore, in reading the testimonies in Harrison's book one finds some accounts that look back and highlight positive aspects of their authors' lives. For example, one man wrote that his 'life as an orphan boy was very good',[23] and there was the woman who wrote of her foster parents that 'they were wonderful people and I shall never forget them and what they did for me'.[24] However, only five said that they had been 'adopted' as she had been. Others, although recounting an unloving and lonely childhood, considered that their lives had turned out well as a result of their own efforts and resolve, especially, as one man put it, through 'hard work and self-education',[25] or, as another explained, 'I made up my mind to make the best of it and be a Canadian'.[26]

Together with a minority of upbeat accounts such as these, there were those that were deeply sad and where that sadness and distress had persisted through to retirement and beyond. Those who wrote about such distress tended to do so in some detail. Typically, they emphasised their feelings of loneliness, of being unloved, of being stigmatised as a 'Home child' and of feeling a deep sense of psychological damage. Here are some illustrative extracts:

The feeling of utter loneliness would be hard to describe.[27]

I was sure I would die of loneliness.[28]

I grew up without companionship and, worse still, without parental love.[29]

I was given to understand that an orphan was the lowest type of person on earth … and the insults I had to take … have always stayed with me. It's only the bruises on the outside I don't feel anymore….[30]

Am I glad I came? One has to experience loneliness to evaluate it.[31]

My background of life has given me a restless nature. As I grew up there was always the question in my mind. Why, for what reason did our family have to be broken up?[32]

Thus, if one endeavours to assess what the letters suggested about 'outcomes' well after retirement, there was a mixture of good and bad experiences. Certainly, many correspondents described childhoods of excessive hard work and long hours (43 per cent did so specifically), of little or no schooling (nearly 30 per cent) and of wages not being paid, or being paid at a lower rate than had been agreed. In any case, wages were usually sent to the societies to be kept in trust until the young emigrants reached the age of 18. Some said that even then they did not get what was due to them. Nevertheless, as already explained, events in later life were often described in more favourable ways even though, in Parr's terms, only 12 of the 105 cases could be classed as 'occupationally' successful. But few had remained in farming, except for those who had managed to acquire their own holding, often in the face of much hardship.

Of course, in trying to make an assessment of child emigration one has to bear in mind that many of the things that befell those who went to Canada also befell others who stayed in the Homes in Britain or, indeed, children in the wider community in both countries. Corporal punishment was common and widely accepted as an appropriate form of discipline. Indeed, several of those who wrote to Harrison described harsh physical punishments in the British Homes before they left, although others remembered kindness and care. And sexual abuse was not the unique experience of some of the British children in Canada.[33] Likewise, hard work and long hours could also be the lot of Canadian-born children who were brought up on family farms, as could erratic schooling. What stands out so vividly in these letters, however, is the sense and reality of isolation, loneliness and friendlessness, not only in relation to adults but also with regard to other children. This was likely to have been superimposed on feelings of devaluation and stigmatisation as an outsider. In Goffman's terms they felt 'discredited' because of their background and because of the assumptions that were often made about their immutable imperfections.[34] Furthermore, because they possessed few details about their past lives they had fragile identities, the only one readily available being that of a discredited Home child.

There is a strong impression from the letters that Harrison received that it was not the heavy work and long hours that these former young immigrants considered to have been so damaging, but the emotional wounds that they suffered. It was these that caused so much pain then and later in their adult lives. However, this aspect was less prominent in a small study published in 1981 by Gail Corbett in which she recorded interviews with 22 people who had been sent to Canada by Barnardos between 1903 and 1937.[35] Both these studies were, of course, based on a small and selective collection of voices. The lives of the children that they described often seemed to depend on the luck or the misfortune of their placements and then on what happened as they grew up; but their lives were also shaped by the emotional damage that they had suffered and by whether or not they had been able to come to terms with it.

IV Later Voices

In 1989 a documentary film called *Lost Children of the Empire* was screened on television with an accompanying book written by Bean and Melville bearing the same title.[36] Interest in the subject had been aroused through the work of Margaret Humphreys, a Nottingham social worker who, in 1987, had set up, almost single-handedly, the Child Migrants Trust, the aims of which were to help those 'lost children' discover more about their personal histories and, if possible, reunite them with at least some of their relatives. An account of the work of the Trust was published by Humphreys in 1994 as *Empty Cradles*.[37] Both this and Bean and Melville's book include extracts from the many interviews with those who contacted the organisation. These provide a heartrending insight into the emotional impact that emigration had on these people who, as children, had been trans-shipped to Australia, to Canada, to New Zealand and to what was formerly Rhodesia. However, most of the accounts are from those who went to Australia. This is important to remember because, unlike in Canada, these children went to residential institutions run, for example, by the Christian Brothers, by orders of nuns and by the Fairbridge organisation. Normally they were kept there until they were 16, when they were placed out, often on farms.

The dominant message that is gained from what those who contacted the Trust said was of the pain of a lost identity. Here is a selection from the interviews that illustrate the point:

> I'm 45 years old, with two children of my own, and still I have no identity.[38]
>
> You [they] could have told me who I am – that's important to me, to know who I am.[39]
>
> Just help me to die knowing who I am. Let me have a birth certificate [Canada].[40]

The anguish of not having an identity was closely related to the belief or wish that, somewhere, there *were* relatives:

> There must be someone, I must be related to someone, even if it's an aunt or an uncle, I feel I'm a nobody, a nothing, without any roots at all.[41]
>
> I've always felt that I'm less than other people who can talk about at least an auntie or uncle. I can never say that.[42]
>
> It would be nice to know that I belong to someone....[43]

However, because the purpose of the Trust was to help those who had either lost contact with their families, or simply knew nothing about them, it is not surprising that the question of identity should loom large in what they said. Nevertheless, identities had also been undermined because, as children and even later as adults, those who approached the Trust said that they had often been denied key information and told that they were orphans when, eventually, it transpired that many were not. As well as this it was not unusual for those who contacted the Trust to be without birth certificates as well as being without the citizenship of the country to which they had been sent and without a formal recognition of a British nationality either. These impediments to the formation of an identity are tellingly described in Perry Snow's Canadian account of his father's fruitless quest for his 'stolen identity'.[44]

Not all the children who were emigrated more recently (or as Snow and others prefer to call it, 'deported') were quite as bereft of information about their past, but the issue of identity nonetheless figured in their accounts of the effect of their trans-shipment. Certainly, the idea of having a 'spoiled identity' was linked with queries of 'Why me?', 'What did I do wrong?' and therefore to 'Why was I not wanted either by family or by my country of birth?' Here are a few examples of the ways in which these questions were put by those who contacted the Child Migrants Trust:

> I got terribly withdrawn as it seemed nobody wanted me, only for the work I did.[45]
>
> Why did they send me? What did I do wrong?[46]
>
> I've often wondered why and who sent me...? What was wrong with me that no-one wanted me?[47]
>
> Your 'circumstances' are always a dark mystery and there is tremendous guilt that you have done something dreadful to have been rejected by your parents.[48]
>
> ... mostly I wondered what I'd done wrong.[49]

These are feelings that might well be entertained by children who were separated from their families but not emigrated; but emigration, and especially then placement in institutions or remote farms, compounded the sense of abandonment.

Indeed, loneliness is a recurrent theme, although some acknowledged that being in an institution provided the opportunity for friendships and thereby a measure of mutual support.

The feeling of loneliness was described in various ways by those who sought the help of the Child Migrants Trust. Sometimes it was simply put as: 'I was very homesick and lonely'.[50] And the homesickness was not necessarily for a family home. For instance, as one woman said: 'I never knew home life at home, but I never had such homesickness in my life'.[51] Such loneliness was, for some, related to the sense of being trapped, of being unable to escape from what had befallen them. These are the words of one woman who arrived in Canada at the age of 14:

> With no money, you can't do anything. And you haven't any friends and no way of making them because they would never let you out. They were always there with you, you were never with anyone alone to be able to tell them.[52]

Like Harrison's respondents those who contacted Humphreys often described their feelings in terms of what would immediately be recognised as a sense of stigma. They were 'outsiders', strangers who spoke differently and who, in any case, often carried the burden of a 'spoiled identity'. This is how one woman, arriving in Canada in 1913 explained it: 'You weren't considered as good as the rest of the kids, because you had no home of your own and no parents ... You don't know what this does to you. I have never got over it'.[53]

Taking all these emotional repercussions together it is not surprising that those who approached the Child Migrants Trust often spoke (or wrote) about an enduring feeling of unworthiness. These are some of the ways in which this was expressed: 'At the back of my mind is the fact that I'm a nobody. I've got no roots.'[54] And, similarly, 'I feel I'm a nobody, a nothing, without any roots at all.'[55]

Of course, these are doubly selected extracts. They are the words of those who contacted the Trust and then my choice from among them. We must be careful, therefore, in concluding that all the children sent overseas suffered the same emotional anguish. Nevertheless, even for the resilient among them and for those who found themselves with kind and generous people, damage was likely to have been done, and for one very good reason. Expatriation to an unknown and strange country was often superimposed on the emotional upheavals that many had already experienced prior to their emigration. Indeed, various research, particularly since the 1970s, and summarised by Rutter, has demonstrated both the cumulative effect of multiple stresses and the fact that 'one stress (biological or social) actually increases the likelihood of [the] occurrence of others'.[56] These personal testimonies bear witness to these effects, but they also suggest, again, that material hardship alone left fewer scars than the emotional consequences of alienation, of abuse (both physical and sexual), of the sense of rejection and of the lack of love. As one woman put it: 'the hurt is inside'.[57]

V Confirmation

Many of those who had contacted the Child Migrants Trust, and some of those whose accounts have been quoted, also gave evidence to the Health Committee of the House of Commons that was appointed in 1997 to examine the issue of the welfare of former British child migrants. Its report was published in the same year.[58] It received submissions from nearly 250 of these now-elderly people. The committee also visited Australia and New Zealand and heard directly from 200 of those who had been sent there as children. The great majority who submitted evidence went to Australia (84 per cent) where almost all (98 per cent) were placed first in an institution. Those who had been dispatched to New Zealand (11 per cent) were boarded out or placed directly into farm work. The rest had gone to Canada and Rhodesia. A few had been sent away before the Second World War, but most after 1947.[59]

What they said echoed the evidence that has already been discussed. However, accounts of severe physical abuse and persistent sexual abuse were more common. Twenty per cent of the men who wrote described extremely harsh physical treatment (not just smacking), as did 25 per cent of the women. Sexual abuse, often of the most depraved kind, was recounted by 24 per cent of the men and 16 per cent of the women. Very few said that they had *not* been abused in one or other of these ways, and there may have been others who were but who found it too painful to describe what had happened to them. It seems likely that it was the fact of being gathered together in institutions in Australia, particularly those run for boys by the Christian Brothers in Western Australia, that provided a context in which abusers were free to engage in 'exceptional depravity', as the Health Committee's report described it.[60] The institutionalisation of the children, usually until they were 16, was significantly different from the practice in Canada where almost all were quickly scattered to different places. Because of this their experiences would have been more mixed, as Harrison's study suggests. Another difference between the two countries appears to have been the younger ages at which the children were sent to Australia in the more recent period. Of those who explained to the Health Committee how old they were on arrival, 40 per cent said that they were 10 or under. Only two per cent had been 15 or older. It might be argued that the ensuing trauma for such young children would have been greater than it was for the somewhat older group who were earlier sent to Canada.

For reasons like these, therefore, one should be cautious in drawing conclusions about the emotional consequences of emigration by those who had been shipped to Canada from what was reported by those who were dispatched to Australia much later. Nevertheless, the way in which the Health Committee's uncompromisingly critical report summarised the psychological damage inflicted on the post-war child migrants did not seem to be greatly out of step with much of the Canadian evidence. This is how the report put it:

The consequences of child migration for many include difficulties in forming or maintaining relationships; fear of closeness and sharing emotions; a need to be understood; psychiatric disorders including many attempts at suicide and alcoholism; and feeling socially handicapped. We have also heard accounts of inability to accept authority or hold down a job, a propensity to itinerant lifestyles.[61]

The sense of a loss of identity, the denial of information and the deception about their origins that was practised were also profoundly important issues that its witnesses pressed on the committee. In short, this inquiry was left 'in no doubt that hardship and emotional deprivation were the common lot of child migrants, and that cases of criminal abuse were not infrequent'.[62] Yet the consequences of these experiences were more far-reaching than this indictment suggests. First, there was the scale. Forty-six per cent of the men who wrote to the committee said that they had suffered significant emotional problems, as did 42 per cent of the women. Second, many said that these problems had remained with them throughout their lives. Third, there was, what one respondent termed, the 'ripple effect'; that is, the anguish that was caused to many parents (in particular the mothers) by the severance from their children, but also the repercussions borne by the spouses and children of those who had been child emigrants. A few extracts from the poignant letters submitted as evidence to the Health Committee make all these points:

> I've been grieving a lifetime for a lost country, lost family, lost childhood, lost identity....
>
> Deep down I have always felt an outcast.
>
> The pain of the past doesn't get easier, and in fact the older I get the enormity of it hits me more.
>
> Don't believe the crap about children handling things well. They don't have the communication skills to express their terrors and pain so they internalise and become walking time-bombs.
>
> There are no words to express anyone's feelings of dread not to belong to anybody in this world.... *Nothing. Nothing*, not a B person to care about you ... it *never never* gets any better.
>
> I suffered loss of childhood and a lifetime of emotional scarring.
>
> ... every day in my young life I craved to belong to someone and someone to belong to me.
>
> I grew up with little self confidence, never feeling love, always never good enough, imperfect.
>
> As I grow older I find it is getting harder and harder ... it pervades our lives and the lives of those we touch.
>
> The loneliness and isolation was devastating.

These quotations[63] are illustrative of the kinds of feelings that many others who wrote expressed, as well as of those whom Gill interviewed in Australia in the late 1980s.[64] Certainly, in all these various accounts a few people were positive about their experience or positive now in the latter part of their lives. Some had come to terms with the past with the help of their spouses but had not put it out of their minds. Others had become successful through remarkable efforts, but they too could not dismiss the past or completely ignore its effects.

It is now an inescapable conclusion that the re-establishment of these emigration schemes in 1947, largely by the voluntary children's societies,[65] was a grave wrong, especially in the light of what was, by then, understood about child development. That has now been acknowledged by all concerned: apologies have been offered and the magnitude of the hurt that was perpetrated recognised. Indeed, the Health Committee opened its report by quoting the Chief Executive of Barnardos, who, in his evidence, had said: 'It was barbaric; it was dreadful. We look back on it in our organisation with shock and horror.'[66]

VI A Reckoning

The conclusions to be drawn from all these sources is that the most profound iniquity of the emigration movement lay in the psychological damage that it inflicted on the children. Furthermore, their trans-shipment to another country without adequate support or protection did nothing to mitigate the emotional upheavals that many had already suffered in Britain. Emotional hurt was likely to have been heaped on already existing emotional hurt. Indeed, the children sent abroad were likely to have been among the least able to deal with the inevitable stresses and strains that that entailed.

In making an assessment of the emigration schemes to Canada over the years from 1867 to 1917, therefore, it is these effects that demand to be regarded as the key criterion, notwithstanding the physical hardships, exploitation and the denial of adequate schooling that many endured at the time. Interpreted through a twenty-first-century understanding of the impact of traumatic experiences and of the likely results of multiple deprivations, the verdict on the practice of sending already vulnerable children to another country would be uncompromisingly severe. However, such an indictment would run the risk of having the benefit of hindsight. With that in mind we must ask whether the emotional effects on a child of being separated from familiar people, places and culture and consigned to an unknown family that was essentially seeking to benefit from his or her labour, would have been the same 100 years or more ago as they would be likely to be today? Although the context has changed would the trauma of being uprooted, of feeling alone and unvalued not have had similar consequences? If this is a valid way of looking at things then it is legitimate to evaluate what happened from the vantage point of our present understanding.

Nevertheless, alongside this issue there is a second and somewhat different question that has to be addressed; namely, are the actions of the emigrationists a century ago equally susceptible to being evaluated in the light of what we know about child development today? The issue turns on the extent of the awareness of the emotional implications for the children of what was claimed to be their 'rescue'. What appreciation of the damaging consequences for the children of being emigrated could one expect there to have been in the second half of the nineteenth century? There are at least two ways of approaching the question. First, what was the state of the prevailing understanding on the matter? And, second, if there were some such understanding on the part of the emigrationists were other factors considered to be so insistent that the child's psychological well-being was regarded as of secondary importance?

During this time the medical profession generally subscribed to the view that the causes of stress and insanity were essentially physical in origin. Such a belief was certainly reflected in Clouston's 700-page compendium on 'mental disease' that was first published in 1883. However, there was only a limited discussion of conditions that might fall short of manifest madness, and nor were there more than passing references to children. However, one chapter was devoted to 'The Insanities of Puberty and Adolescence'. These, it was claimed, often sprang from 'the decadence of the period'. Nevertheless, there were, Clouston explained, 'developmental neuroses' which occurred 'during the growth period of the brain'.[67] However, he considered that:

> The nutritive energy of the brain is so great in youth, its recuperative power so vigorous, and its capacity for rest in sleep so powerful, that its mental functions are not often upset ... and when upset, they soon are set to rights again.[68]

In short, the message from this influential text was that children rarely suffered from 'insanity' but that there could be 'developmental neuroses' brought on by irregularities in the growing brain, in the process of which unfortunate hereditary blemishes could appear. In all of this there was a confusion between what today would be classed as psychological conditions and those of a physical nature. However, given the 'natural tendency' for the youthful brain to recover, Clouston's view was that children and adolescents were likely to survive any developmental setbacks.

If, as it seems reasonable to assume, this represented the state of most professional thinking at the time, then it would follow that any 'mental consequences' associated with a child's uprooting would be assumed to be short-lived as long as they did not carry severe hereditary imperfections. The emigrationists could hardly be expected to take a different view. Hendrick has summed up the prevailing way of thinking as a preoccupation with 'bodies'.[69] First and foremost, children were seen as 'homeless and ragged; ... starved, neglected and sometimes murdered by paid carers...'. They were sick, disabled, cruelly treated or delinquent and, one might add, quite untouched by religious teaching. It is understandable that such perceptions could take precedence over what might have been thought of as the less pressing question of what children felt, even had there been a theoretical framework that might have encouraged the emigrationists to take account of this aspect of their interventions. In brief, as Hendrick put it, 'the mind-body relationship was not pursued'.[70] Nevertheless, in Dora Black's history of child and adolescent psychiatry she advances the view that a professional concern with the psychological origins of stress did start to emerge at around the turn of the century. Only then, she writes, did a 'serious medical interest [begin] to be shown in the emotional and intellectual problems of young people and [in] the importance of a developmental perspective in understanding disorder'.[71] Even so, there appears to have been a continuing professional preoccupation with insanity, certainly until the shell-shock victims of the 1914–18 war forced a recognition of the ravages of traumatic stress. Progress was slower in the case of children, psychological interest in whom tended to centre on testing their intelligence and the related issue of diagnosing mental deficiency. After all, it was not until 1927 that the first child guidance clinic was established in Britain.[72] It might have been expected that the inauguration of the school health service in 1907 would have accelerated progress in the recognition of the emotional ills of some children, but its major concern, perhaps understandably, was with, for example, ear, nose and throat conditions, speech defects, dental problems, orthopaedic deformities, epilepsy and nutritional deficiencies.[73]

So, with respect to the state of a psychological understanding of the emotional stresses to which a child could be subject, it is probably unfair to accuse the instigators of child emigration 100 years or more ago of culpable indifference. Nevertheless, looked at from other points of view, enough flaws in the schemes soon became evident to have given a clear signal that all was not well: the lack of supervision, the children's frequent moves, the examples of harsh treatment, the denial of education and the failure of many employers to observe the terms of the 'indentures' that they had signed. All these should have been enough to have raised serious doubts, quite apart from questions of the emotional damage that might be done to uprooted vulnerable children. Misgivings *were* expressed in some quarters, but other confident voices were usually sufficient to carry the day, sustained as they were by the glowing reports provided by those who had a keen interest in portraying the movement as a successful means of resolving a cluster of social and economic problems.

Perhaps the risks involved in emigrating a child were foreseen but discounted because the risks of not doing so were deemed to be greater. As we have seen, these were considered to be both numerous and severe. There were three main groups of risks: first, the material, moral and spiritual jeopardy in which many poor children were believed to live; second, the dangers to social order that these deficiencies represented; and, third, the related risks associated with a 'surplus' population. It would have been difficult for middle-class Victorians not to have been influenced by such prevailing concerns. Alongside this, of course, went the attractions that Canada appeared to offer, attractions that were coloured by several beliefs: by the conviction of the 'child savers' that permanent separation from pernicious surroundings was the means to the ends that they sought, by what might be termed ideas of the 'rural idyll', by financial savings and by the pervasive influence of imperial sentiments. Together with all of this, emigration promised an *immediate* remedy to so many of the ills that were believed to beset certain children. It also offered a solution to some of the administrative problems that faced the organisations that became involved in emigration. Taken together, therefore, these factors represented a coalition of forces that, in many instances, overrode the doubts expressed in some quarters about the wisdom of sending vulnerable children to an unfamiliar country thousands of miles away. Typically, however, the emigrationists were swept along by a self-justifying conviction that what they were doing was right, a conviction that was fortified by religious certainties.

So how should we judge this child emigration movement, whose origins and course we have described? With hindsight, a damning verdict is inescapable. Nevertheless, those who orchestrated and supported the system were creatures of their time, moved by a variety of motives, some of which were more dubious than others. It is perhaps understandable that little attention was paid to the psychological damage that could be inflicted on children, many already separated from their families, by sending them to a far-off country. But much *was* known about the other kinds of risks that were associated with such expatriation without its promoters being deterred by that knowledge. As a result, many of the uprooted children would have suffered greatly.

One cannot help wondering how the convictions that are entertained today about the needs of vulnerable children and how these are or should be met might, in their turn, be judged 100 years from now.

Notes

one   **The Background**

1. For these early years see Wagner, G. (1982) *Children of the Empire*, London: Weidenfeld & Nicholson, ch 1.
2. See Shaw, A.G. (1966) *Convicts and the Colonies*, London: Faber & Faber.
3. See Blackburn, G. (1993) *The Children's Friend Society*, Northbridge, Australia: Access Press.
4. See Montague, C.J. (1904) *Sixty Years in Waifdom or, the Ragged School Movement in English History*, London: Murray.
5. Neff, C. (2000) 'Youth in Canada West: a case history of Red Hill Farm school emigrants, 1854-1868', *Journal of Family History*, vol 25, no 4.
6. See 1834 Poor Law (Amendment) Act, section lxii.
7. See Hitchins, F.H. (1931) *The Colonial Land and Emigration Commission*, Philadelphia, PA: Philadelphia University Press.
8. *Ibid*, p 203.
9. See Carrier, N.H. and Jeffrey, J.R. (1953) *External Migration: A Study of the Available Statistics, 1815-1950*, London: HMSO, table D/F/G(1), p 95.
10. See Summers, A. (1975) *Damned Whores and God's Police: The Colonisation of Women in Australia*, Harmondsworth: Penguin.
11. See Robbins, J. (1980) *The Lost Children: A Study of Charity Children in Ireland, 1700-1900*, Dublin: Institute of Public Administration, especially chs 8-11.
12. *Ibid*, p 179.
13. *Ibid*, pp 200-21.
14. 1849 Poor Law (Amendment) Act, section xx.
15. Webb, S. and Webb, B. (1963) *English Poor Law Policy*, London: Cass edn, p 142.
16. Carrothers, W.A. (1965) *Emigration from the British Isles*, London: Cass, p 305.
17. PRO, MH 19/22/5197. Sinclair to Hawes, 29.10.49 and 27.12.49.
18. PRO, MH 19/22/48314. CLEC to PLC, 5.12.52; also 7637, 2.3.53.
19. PRO, MH 19/22/24273. Hall to Courtney, 22.6.52.
20. PRO, MH 19/22/34929. Lumley memorandum, nd.
21. PRO, MH 19/22/15705. CLEC to PLB, 3.5.56, reply 15.5.56.
22. *Second Report of the British and Colonial Emigration Fund*, 1870, at NAC, RG 17/2397/assisted emigration.
23. See Malchow, H.L. (1979) *Population Pressures: Emigration and Government in Late Nineteenth-Century Britain*, Palo Alto, CA: Society for the Promotion of Science and Scholarship, ch 2.
24. OR (Lords), 16.4.69, 'Pauperism and Emigration', cols 943-71.

25. OR (Commons), 1.3.70, 'Emigration', cols 1002-77.
26. As note 24, cols 944-5.
27. *Ibid*, col 946.
28. *Ibid*, col 953.
29. *Emigration: Circular to Various Governors*, BPP, xlix, 1870, 179, p 595.
30. From annual reports of the PLC, PLB and LGB.
31. NAC, RG 17/2393/Emig Corr. 1865-66. Clerk of the Limerick Union to Buchanan, 19.4.65.
32. *Ibid*. Buchanan to the clerk of the Limerick Union, 12.5.65 and Buchanan to Bourke, 12.5.65. See aso Clark, A. (2005) 'Wild workhouse girls and the liberal imperial state in mid-nineteenth century Ireland', *Journal of Social History*, vol 39, no 2.
33. As note 31. Wills' report, nd, c. May, 1865.
34. *Ibid*. Macpherson's report.
35. *Ibid*. Clerk of the Limerick Union to Buchanan, 10.6.65.
36. NAC, RG 17/1499/11. Taché to Dixon, 22.5.68.
37. Hammerton, A. (1979) *Emigrant Gentlewomen*, London: Croom Helm, p 126.
38. Rye, M.S. (1862) 'Female middle class emigration', *The English Woman's Journal*, vol 10, July. For the Female Emigration Society see Clarke, P. (1985) *The Governesses: Letters from the Colonies, 1862-82*, London: Hutchinson, ch 1.
39. Diamond, M. (1999) *Emigration and Empire: The Life of Maria S. Rye*, London and New York, NY: Garland, p 29.
40. *Ibid*, p 166.
41. PRO, MH 12/11687/12773. Clerk of the Wolverhampton guardians to PLB, 13.4.68.
42. As reported in *The Wolverhampton Express*, 18.4.68 and *The Wolverhampton Chronicle*, 13.5.68.
43. PRO, MH 12/11687/18575. Clerk of the Wolverhampton guardians to PLB, 8.5.68.
44. Dixon was appointed immigration agent for the UK in 1866 and stationed at Liverpool and then Wolverhampton from 1867-68. In 1869 he was posted to London. He died in 1873.
45. PRO, MH 12/11687/21159. Dixon to PLB, 19.5.68.
46. PRO, MH 12/11687/21892. Clerk of the Wolverhampton guardians to PLB, 22.5.68.
47. NAC, RG 17/22/1920. Rye to Macdonald 22.6.68.
48. NAC, RG 17/1499/39. Chapais memorandum, 25.6.68.
49. NAC, RG 17/22/1970. Rye to Taché, 9.7.68.
50. NAC, RG 17/23/2049. Rye to Taché, 19.8.68.
51. NAC, RG 17/24/2169. Dixon to Stafford, 1.10.68.
52. PRO, MH 12/11687/47605. Clerk of the Wolverhampton guardians to PLB, 5.10.68.
53. PRO, MH 12/11687/48535. Dixon to PLB, 13.10.68.

54. PRO, MH 12/11687/54080. CO to PLB, 12.11.68.
55. NAC, RG 17/24/2185. Dixon to Taché, 14.10.68.
56. NAC, RG 17/25/2252. Dixon to Stafford, 12.11.68.
57. *The Times*, 29.9.68. Diamond, *op cit*, points out that the manager (Morris) was a friend of Rye's.
58. NAC, RG 17/29/2585. Dixon to Taché, 12.5.69.
59. As note 29.
60. See Gelber, N. (nd) *Canada in London: An Unofficial Glimpse of Canada's Sixteen High Commissioners, 1880-1980*, London: Canada House. Also Skilling, H.G. (1945) *Canadian Representation Abroad*, Toronto: Ryerson Press.
61. See Long, M.H. (1931) 'Sir John Rose and the informal origins of the Canadian High Commission in London', *Canadian Historical Review*, March.

two   **Early Initiatives**

1. Wagner (1982), *op cit*, p 39.
2. Lowe, C.M. (nd) *God's Answers: A Record of Miss Annie Macpherson's Work*, London: npb (reprint 'LR') and Birt, L.M. (1913) *The Children's Home Finder*, London: Nisbet.
3. Macpherson, A. (1866) *The Little Matchbox Makers*, London: private.
4. Logan, E. and Macpherson, A. (1869) *Emigration the Only Remedy for Chronic Pauperism in the East of London*, London: private.
5. Loring Brace, C. (1872) *The Dangerous Classes of New York, and Twenty Years' Work Among Them*, New York, NY: Wynkoop/Hallenbeck [republished 1973, Washington: NASW, p 225].
6. NAC, RG 17/30/2710. Noted in Patterson to Rye, 2.7.69.
7. *Ibid*, Rye to Secretary of State, 5.7.69.
8. NAC, RG 17/30/2733. Rye to Rose, 29.6.69.
9. NAC, RG 17/1499/243. Taché to Rye, 14.7.69.
10. *Ibid*, Dixon to Taché, 21.10.69.
11. NAC, RG 17/30/2939. Dixon to Stafford, 21.10.69.
12. *Ibid*, Rye to Stafford, 20.10.69.
13. NAC, RG 17/27/2447. Dixon to Stafford, 25.3.69.
14. NAC, RG 17/36/3296. Dixon to Taché, 26.3.70.
15. See Birt, *op cit*, ch iv.
16. Lowe, *op cit*, p 109.
17. Prochaska, F.K. (1980) *Women and Philanthropy in Nineteenth Century England*, Oxford: Oxford University Press, p 222.
18. See Stephenson, T.B. (1883) *The Story of the Children's Home and Princess Alice Orphanage*, London: NCH; Bradfield, W. (1913) *The Life of the Reverend Thomas Bowman Stephenson*, London: Kelly; Horner, F. (1919) *Shadow and Sun*, London: Epworth/NCH.
19. See Barritt, G.E. (1972) *The Edgeworth Story*, Harpenden: NCH.
20. *Annual Report, 1872*, p 8.

21. *Annual Report, 1876-77,* p 18.
22. Bradfield, *op cit,* p 138.
23. As note 20, p 9.
24. As note 21, p 17.
25. Stedman Jones, G. (1984) *Outcast London: A Study in the Relationship between the Classes in Victorian Society,* Harmondsworth: Peregrine.
26. Bennett, J. (1949) *Father Nugent of Liverpool,* Liverpool: Liverpool Catholic Children's Protection Society, p 29.
27. *Ibid.*
28. St John, E. (1929) *Manning's Work for Children: A Second Chapter in Catholic Emancipation,* London: Steed/Ward, p 13.
29. *The Tablet,* 29.6.66 and 3.7.66.
30. See Bennett, J. (1950) 'The care of the poor', in Beck, G.A. (ed), *The English Catholics, 1850-1950,* London: Burns/Oates, and Inglis, K.S. (1963) *The Churches and the Working Classes in Victorian England,* London: Routledge and Kegan Paul, pp 122–30.
31. St John, *op cit,* p 95.
32. PRO, MH 12/5983/440038. Schenck to Granville, 4.10.71.
33. *Ibid,* Winterbotham to LGB, 9.10.71.
34. PRO, MH 12/5983/46459. Lumley minute, 27.10.71.
35. *Annual Report of the Halifax Branch of the Colonial and Continental Church Society,* 1876, pp xiii and 69.
36. ANQ, Travaux Publics, Correspondance Reçue, EOO25/60/226. Birt to de Boucherville, 31.12.77.
37. PANS, RG 7/4/146b/72. Hill to Laurie, 8.8.76; JPHANS, 1877, appendix 1, p 17 and *Halifax Morning Herald,* 26.8.76.
38. NAC, RG 17/1511/303. Lowe to Laurie, 3.9.75 and 141/14766. Laurie to Lowe, 13.9.75.
39. NAC, RG 17/350/37331. Laurie to Lowe, 19.9.82.
40. Birt, *op cit,* p 133.
41. PANS, RG 7/4/147a/54. Hill to Lowe, 5.9.77.
42. See Urquart, J. (1900) *The Life-Story of William Quarrier: A Boy's Resolve and What Became of It,* London: Partridge; Gammie, A. (1936) *The Romance of Faith: The Story of the Orphan Homes of Scotland and the Founder William Quarrier,* London: Pickering/Inglis; Ross, A. (1971) *The Power I Pledge,* Glasgow: Quarriers; Magnusson, A. (1984) *The Village: A History of Quarrier's,* Glasgow: Quarriers; also Abrams, L. (1998) *The Orphan Country,* Edinburgh: Donald, ch 4.
43. *Glasgow Herald* and *North British Daily Mail,* 1.9.71.
44. Ross, *op cit,* pp 58–9.
45. *Annual Report, 1872,* p 11.
46. *Annual Report, 1875,* p 8.
47. *Annual Report, 1878,* p 12.
48. *Annual Report, 1879,* p 20.

49. *Report of the Select Committee on the Poor Laws (Scotland)*, BPP, xi, paper 301, 1869, cols 1780-1.

50. MacDonald, H.J. (1996) 'Boarding-out and the Scottish Poor Law', *The Scottish Historical Review*, vol lxxv, 2, no 200.

51. QA, Quarrier, W. (1884) *Occasional Paper*, Glasgow: Orphan Homes of Scotland.

52. Nonetheless, in Quarriers' *Annual Report* for 1908 (p 37) in an article from *The Christian* it is noted that 'Quarrier had been possessed by a determination to bring about a time when "every orphan child in Scotland should be removed from the poorhouse"'.

53. See Anon (1972) *One Hundred Years of Child Care: The Story of the Middlemore Homes, 1872-1972*, Birmingham: Middlemore.

54. *Ibid*, p 6.

55. NAC, MG 29/E. 8/1. Middlemore to Dixon, 7.4.73.

56. *Annual Report, 1873*, p 6.

57. NAC, RG 17/657/74802. Middlemore to Lowe, 24.8.90 and 1675/Gi/85–90. Gibbens to Lowe, nd.

58. NAC, RG 17/1680/Me-Mi, 1891-5. Middlemore to Lowe, 8.5.94.

59. *Halifax Herald*, 21.5.96.

60. As note 53, p 11.

61. As note 57.

62. As note 53, p 4.

63. *Annual Report, 1875*, p 3.

64. *Annual Report, 1878*, p 8.

65. *Annual Report, 1882*, p 6.

66. See for example, NAC, MG 29/E18/ 5/558. Lowe to Burgess, 22.6.94.

67. See Lacey, C.A. (1986) *Barbara Leigh Smith Bodichon and the Langham Place Group*, London: Routledge Kegan Paul.

68. We know more about Rye's family background thanks to Diamond's biography (*op cit*).

three   **Checks and Balances**

1. 1850 Poor Law Act.

2. PRO, MH 12/2869/26746. Clerk of the Wareham-Purbeck guardians to PLB, 7.6.70 and 14.6.70.

3. For example, PRO, MH 12/3874/24808, 8.4.73 (Hannah Pearce's consent).

4. PRO, MH 12/7817/1874. Fry minute, 26.5.74.

5. PRO, MH 12/12776/14319 and 17901. Clerk of the Brighton guardians to PLB, 1.4.71 and 26.4.71. Also 19017. PLB to the clerk, 2.5.71.

6. PRO, MH 12/7373/13670. Clerk of the St Mary's Islington guardians to LGB, 7.3.72 and subsequently.

7. PRO, MH 12/7373/11735, 13934 and 13670. Encls Seddon to LGB, 24.2.72.

8. PRO, MH 12/3876/62668. Fry minute re letter from clerk of the Bristol guardians, 6.10.75.

9. PRO, MH 12/3872/30860. Clerk of the Bristol guardians to LGB, 30.6.70.

10. *Ibid*. PLB to the clerk of the Bristol guardians, 6.7.70.

11. PRO, MH 12/3928/6923. The form is included in clerk of the Cheltenham guardians to LGB, 3.2.71.

12. PRO, MH 12/1157/30276. Clerk of the Stockport guardians to LGB, 26.4.77. See Cruikshank, M. (1981) *Children and Industry: Child Health and Welfare in the North-West Textile Towns During the Nineteenth Century*, Manchester: Manchester University Press.

13. PRO, MH 12/3928/14835. Clerk of the Cheltenham guardians to PLB, 31.3.70 (dated 31.5.70).

14. PRO, MH 12/345/26104. Clerk of the Windsor guardians to LGB, 29.8.71.

15. PRO, MH 12/7373/13670. Clerk of the Islington guardians to the LGB, 7.3.72; and MH 12/6997/13887, clerk of the Chelsea guardians to LGB, 8.3.72.

16. PRO, MH 12/7447/22685. Clerk of the Kensington guardians to LGB, 2.1.72.

17. PRO, MH 12/345/26104. Rye to LGB, 15.6.72 and note.

18. PRO, MH 12/9460/18828. LGB to the clerk of the Nottingham guardians, 8.4.72.

19. As note 17. LGB to British and Colonial Fund, 19.4.72 and Fund to Board thereafter.

20. PRO, MH 12/12909/35125. Clerk of the East Preston guardians to LGB, 28.5.73.

21. Wagner (1982), *op cit*, pp 50-1; and Parr, J. (1980) *Labouring Children*, London/Kingston: Croom Helm/McGill Queens, p 31.

22. Deduced from Rye's letter to LGB in *The Emigration of Pauper Children to Canada*, BPP, lxxi, 1877, c 2620.

23. LMA, issue BG.10, 1874, minutes for 12.3.74, p 5.

24. MacDougall was a Canadian lawyer, newspaper owner and politician.

25. As note 23, 26.3.74, pp 39-41.

26. *Ibid*, 2.4.74, pp 51-2.

27. *Local Government Chronicle*, 20.9.73.

28. As note 23. Minutes for 9.4.74, p 62.

29. PRO, MH 25/25/22281. Grainger to LGB, 28.3.73.

30. Mentioned in PRO, MH 19/86 (no piece no). 'Memorandum on the Emigration of Poor Law Children under Miss Rye', 14.5.74, np.

31. Lambert, R. (1963) *Sir John Simon and English Social Administration, 1816-1904*, London: MacGibbon/Kee, pp 524-5.

32. Webb, S. and Webb, B. (1963) *English Poor Law History, Part II*, vol I, London: Cass edn, pp f200-1.

33. Preston-Thomas, H. (1909) *The Work and Play of a Government Inspector*, Edinburgh/London: Blackwood, pp 55-6.

34. As note 30.

35. *Ibid.*
36. *Ibid.*
37. *Ibid.*
38. See Boase, F. (1892) *Modern English Biography*, Truro: Netherton/Worth, col 284.
39. Quoted in Turner, W. (1976) 'Miss Rye's children and the Ontario Press, 1875', *Ontario History*, vol 68, no 3.
40. Mackay, T. (1904) *History of the English Poor Law, vol III, 1834-1898*, London: Murray, p 382.
41. See *Annual Report of the Local Government Board*, BPP, xxv, 1874, c 1071, appendix, report 15, pp 171-9, 'Swansea Union – Boarding-out of pauper children'.
42. *Ibid*, Doyle to Llewlyn, 9.4.75.
43. *Report on the Special Enquiry into Schools at Mettray and Dusseltal*, 28.3.73. This is mentioned in several places but no copy found.
44. *Report to the President of the Local Government Board by Andrew Doyle … as to the Emigration of Pauper Children to Canada*, BPP, lxiii, HC 9, 1875.
45. *Ibid*, p 20.
46. *Ibid*, p 21.
47. *Ibid*, p 18.
48. *Ibid*, p 34.
49. PRO, MH 25/26/70295. Barclay to LGB, 23.10.75. Enclosures Campbell to Barclay (nd) and Rye to Barclay, 11.10.75.
50. As note 44, p 28.
51. PRO, MH 12/12546/32002. Clerk of the St Olave's board of guardians to LGB, 2.5.77 and 3.7.77; and replies 5.5.77 and 4.6.77. LGB minute 19.5.77 and President's note 20.5.77.
52. PRO, MH 12/9026/44612, 69410 and 73931. Clerk of the Glendale board of guardians to LGB, 10.5.81 and 18.7.81 and replies 19.10.81 and 22.10.81.
53. *The Times*, 2.7.77.

four   The Issue of Inspection

1. *Report of the Proceedings of the Committee of the House of Commons on Immigration and Colonisation* (10.3.75), *JHCC*, appendix 4, p 9.
2. NAC, RG 17/1958, *Reports to the Privy Council*, no 94, 9.6.75.
3. Parr, (G.)J. (1977) *The Home Children: British Juvenile Immigrants to Canada, 1868-1924*, Yale, CT: Yale University PhD, p 61.
4. *Ibid*, p 63. *The Times*, 2.7.77.
5. PRO, MH 19/6/7425. Salt to Lambert, 5.2.78.
6. *Ibid*. Doyle to Salt, 11.2.78.
7. PRO, MH 19/6/51572. CO to LGB, 15.7.78.

8. *Ibid.*
9. PRO, MH 19/6/52572. Bauke minute, 13.8.78.
10. See PRO, MH 19/7/17419. Lowe to Colmer, 25.1.83.
11. PRO, MH 19/7/30243. Clerk of the St Georges guardians to Dilke, 21.3.83.
12. PRO, MH 19/7/32771. Clerk of the St Pancras guardians to LGB, 5.4.83.
13. PRO, MH 19/7/34413. Tassie to LGB, 4.4.83.
14. As note 11. Dilke minute.
15. Dilke's caution may have reflected critical articles in the press. For example, the London *Globe* warned that it was necessary that the expatriation of the children should not be used as a 'mere machine for ridding ratepayers of a burdensome responsibility. The children have as much right to be considered as the ratepayers ... the Local Government Board appears wholesomely cautious.' The *Wolverhampton Chronicle* sounded an equally disapproving note. (Both reports 10.4.83).
16. LGB, *Memorandum of Conditions upon which the Local Government Board are Prepared to assent tentatively to the Emigration of a Limited Number of Orphan and Deserted Pauper Children to Canada*, 1883.
17. See *Annual Report of the Local Government Board*, BPP, xxxvii, 1884, c 4166, p xlix.
18. PRO, MH 19/7/42693. Bauke to Sendall, 15.5.84.
19. PRO, MH 19/7/10990. Sendall to Owen, 30.1.85.
20. *Ibid.* Owen to Dilke, 31.1.85.
21. PRO, MH 19//7/111283. Gee to Colonial Secretary, 19.11.83.
22. *Ibid.* Dangerfield to Gee (copy), 9.1.82; received 30.11.83.
23. PRO, MH 19/7/117769. Gee to Colonial Secretary, 10.12.83.
24. *Ibid.* Letter from Matlock with Gee's letter, nd.
25. *Ibid.* LGB to CO, 22.12.83.
26. PRO, MH 19/8/12501. Owen to Dilke, 12.2.86.
27. PRO, MH 19/8/42670. CO to LGB, 30.4.86 (enclosing report of the Privy Council).
28. Parr (1977), *op cit*, p 66.
29. As note 26. Owen to Dilke, 5.5.86.
30. *Ibid.* LGB to CO, 8.5.86.
31. *Liverpool Mercury*, 11.8.86.
32. As note 26, 79859. High Commissioner to CO, 20.8.86.
33. *The Times*, 23.11.86. The Howard Association was important because it counted many magistrates among its membership. Concerned principally with penal reform it regarded juvenile emigration as a useful way of forestalling delinquency. Later, by amalgamation, it became the Howard League for Penal Reform.
34. As note 26, 106737. Tallack to Ritchie, 7.11.86.
35. See Smith, S. (1902) *My Life Work*, London: Hodder/Stoughton, ch xviii.
36. *The Times*, 14.12.86.
37. As note 26, 21373. CO to LGB, 28.2.87.

38.   *Ibid.* Wodehouse memorandum, 3.3.87.

39.   *Ibid.* Owen memorandum to Dilke, 4.3.87.

40.   LGB, *Memorandum of Conditions upon which the Local Government Board assent to the Emigration of Orphan and Deserted Pauper Children to Canada*, 1888.

41.   Figures from the *Report of the Departmental Committee on the Education and Maintenance of Pauper Children in the Metropolis* (henceforth *Poor Law Schools Committee*), vol II, 'Minutes', BPP, xliii, 1895, c 8032, p 662 (Knollys' evidence).

five   The Second Wave of Organised Protestant Child Emigration

1.   See Wagner, G. (1979) *Barnardo*, London: Weidenfeld & Nicholson; Rose, J. (1987) *For the Sake of the Children*, London: Hodder/Stoughton; and Barnardo, S. and Marchant, J. (1907) *The Memoirs of the Late Dr Barnardo*, London: Hodder/Stoughton.

2.   Derived from Barnardos' Annual Reports at LUA, D239, A3.

3.   See Wagner (1979), *op cit*, ch 9 for Barnardo's court cases between 1889 and 1891.

4.   Wymer, N. (1954) *Father of Nobody's Children: A Portrait of Dr Barnardo*, London: Hutchinson, p 241.

5.   For an account of the 'Arbitration Case' that necessitated Barnardo's acceptance of greater formalisation of his activities see Wagner (1979), *op cit*, ch 8.

6.   Wagner (1979), *op cit*, p 183.

7.   *Ibid.*

8.   See Parker, R.A. (1975) 'Social administration and scarcity', in E. Butterworth, and R. Holman, (eds) *Social Welfare in Modern Britain*, Glasgow: Fontana/Collins, pp 204-12.

9.   Barnardo, T.J. (1889) *Something Attempted Something Done*, London: Barnardos/Shaw, p 181.

10.   *Annual Report, 1884-85*, pp 11-12.

11.   See Barnardo, T.J. (nd) *The Rescue of Waifs*, London: Barnardos, pp 11-12.

12.   Barnardo (1889), *op cit*, p 183.

13.   *Annual Report, 1881-82*, p 6.

14.   Barnardo (1889), *op cit*, p 186.

15.   NAC, RG 17/348/37126. Fielder to Lowe, 24.8.82.

16.   NAC, RG 17/349/37236. Lowe to Fielder, 30.8.82.

17.   The report is reproduced in 'Our first emigrants', *Night and Day*, nm, 1882. Referred to in Rose (1987), *op cit*, p 87.

18.   NAC, RG 17/411/44833. Barnardo to Tupper, 26.6.84. See Saunders, E.M. (ed) (1916) *The Life and Letters of the Rt Hon Sir Charles Tupper*, London: Cassell.

19. *Ibid.* Tupper to Pope, 11.7.84.
20. NAC, RG 17/1642/946. Lowe to Barnardo, 14.8.84.
21. See *Canadian Gazette*, 28.5.85 (p 178) for an example of Tupper's encouragement.
22. NAC, RG 17/487/53503. Tupper to Carling, 3.6.86. See also Barnardo (1889), *op cit*, p 195.
23. LUA, D239/C2 (vi) 12d, 'Extracts from the minutes of the General Committee regarding Canada', p 252, 16.11.87. See also Barnardo and Marchant, *op cit*, p 170.
24. Derived from LUA, D239, C2/6/56.
25. See *Annual Reports of the Department of the Interior, 1897* and *1911*, SP (Canada) 1898 and 1912, reports 13 and 25 respectively and pp 157 and 112.
26. Parr (1977), *op cit*, pp 192 and 195.
27. *Ibid*, p 178.
28. Calculated from LUA, D2/1a/192, 'Boys' registers', and D2/1a/246, 'Girls' registers'.
29. See Parr (1980), *op cit*, p 85.
30. A copy of the form setting this out is at NAC, RG 76/51/22091. Smart to Pedley, 12.5.02.
31. *Annual Report of the Department of the Interior, 1896*, SP (Canada) 1897, report 10, p 98.
32. *Annual Report of the Department of the Interior, 1898*, SP (Canada) 1899, report 13, p 157.
33. As note 28.
34. *Ibid.*
35. Parr (1977), *op cit*, p 125.
36. LUA, D239/C1/1, pp 65–6. Fowler to Barnardo, 25.7.05.
37. See Rose (1987), *op cit*, '… the children were sent back to the homes when they left school to learn a trade and this often proved a wrench' (p 117). 'They had to leave their cottage and their foster parents and their homes, the only home they'd ever known. They were so distraught' (staff comment, 1930s, p 124).
38. Corbett, G.H. (1981) *Barnardo Children in Canada*, Peterborough: Woodland, p 92.
39. See LUA, D239, C2/6/56 for these figures and possible errors.
40. Rose (1987), *op cit*, p 101.
41. *Ibid.*
42. *Ibid*, pp 100–4.
43. LUA, D239, C2/6/16. McCall to Black, 8.12.16 and Mayers to Black, 5.12.16.
44. Rose (1987), *op cit*, p 103.
45. As note 43. Hobday's report, c June 1919.

46. It seems possible that 25,000 is an over–estimate. From 1901 to 1905 the registers give a total of 5,278 whereas the figures in the annual reports add to 5,718 – eight per cent more.

47. This cannot be an exact calculation because the number 'in care' given in the annual reports is for the end of each year whereas the number emigrated is the total *throughout* the year.

48. See Pike, W.T. (ed) (1899) *Contemporary Biographies: Manchester and Salford at the Close of the Nineteenth Century*, Manchester: Pike, p 259; Edmondson, W. (1921) *Making Rough Places Smooth: Fifty Years Work of the Manchester and Salford Boys' and Girls' Refuges and Homes, 1870-1920*, Manchester: Sherratt/Hughes.

49. See Fernie, D.A. (1993) 'John Rylands of Manchester', *Bulletin of the John Rylands University Library of Manchester*, vol 75, no 2.

50. TTA, *Annual Reports* of the Society, 362/7/M1.

51. *Annual Report, 1887* (1886), p 33.

52. *Annual Report, 1871*, p 17.

53. *Annual Report, 1873* (1872), pp 16-17.

54. *Annual Report, 1884* (1883), pp 17-18.

55. *Ibid*.

56. *Ibid*, p 18.

57. *Annual Report, 1891* (1890), p 15.

58. Figures from *Annual Reports*.

59. *Annual Reports, 1905-07*.

60. As note 54, p 19.

61. Parr (1980), *op cit*, pp 146-7.

62. Hertz was one of the first women to be elected a guardian. See Hollis, P. (1987) *Ladies Elect: Women in English Local Government, 1865-1914*, Oxford: Clarendon Press, pp 225-7.

63. *Annual Reports* for these years.

64. As note 51, p 19.

65. Birt, *op cit*, pp 65-6.

66. *Report of the Departmental Committee on the Education and Maintenance of Pauper Children in the Metropolis*, BPP, xliii, 1896, c 8027, vol II, pp 596-601.

67. *Ibid*.

68. *Annual Report, 1895* (1894), p 15.

69. Figure from *Annual Report of the Department of the Interior, 1907*, SP (Canada) 1908, report 25, pp 110-11.

70. *Annual Report of the Department of the Interior, 1900*, SP (Canada) 1901, report 5, p 101.

71. As note 66, p 596.

72. *Ibid*.

73. See lists of donations in *Annual Reports*.

74. See Jones, A. and Rutman, L. (1981) *In the Children's Aid: J.J. Kelso and Child Welfare in Ontario*, Toronto: Toronto University Press; also Splane, R.B. (1965) *Social Welfare in Ontario, 1791-1893: A Study in Public Welfare Administration*, Toronto: Toronto University Press, pp 266-77.

75. The reduction in child emigration that at first followed the Ontario Acts was noted in LGB circular *Emigration of Children by Boards of Guardians* (1903) p 8.

76. *Annual Report, 1898* (1897), p 24.

77. *Annual Reports, 1914* (covering 1912-13), pp 44 and 18 respectively.

78. *Annual Report, 1915* (1914), p 12.

79. See Rose (1987), *op cit*, p 311.

80. See Fullerton, W.Y. (1908) *J.W.C. Fegan*, London: Marshall/Morgan/Scott; also obituaries in *The Christian*, 17.12.25 and *The Life of Faith*, 16.12.25.

81. FA, Fegan, J.W. (1901) 'The Late Lord Blantyre', *The Rescue*, p 7. This house journal was sub-titled *A Monthly Record of Christian Efforts in Connection with Mr Fegan's Homes, amongst our Juvenile Home-Heathen*.

82. Fullerton, *op cit*, p 106.

83. FA, Fegan, J.W. (1887) 'Emigration chat', *The Rescue*, January, pp 11-12. Gooderham also left $10,000 to Fegans in his will (*Loving and Serving*, May 1906, p 11).

84. FA, Fegan, J.W. (nd) *A Visit to Our Sons Across the Sea*, in *Booklets*.

85. First there was *The Rescue*, then *Loving and Serving* and finally *The Red Lamp*.

86. *Loving and Serving*, November 1905, p 9.

87. *Loving and Serving*, July 1906, p 9.

88. FA, Fegan, J.W. (nd) *A Murderer's Boy*.

89. Fullerton, *op cit*, ch xi.

90. NAC, RG 76/58/2571. Greenaway memorandum, nd, c 1900.

91. FA, 'Young emigrants and farewell meetings', *The Rescue*, June 1885, pp 2-3.

92. FA, 'Minute books', 1895-1922.

93. *Ibid*. Greenaway to Smart, 21.3.17.

94. FA, from 'List of boys emigrated to Canada'.

95. FA, from 'Admission registers', 1900 and 1910.

96. As note 94.

97. *The Rescue*, December 1895, p 12.

98. *Loving and Serving*, June 1914, p 3.

99. *The Rescue*, January 1887, p 14.

100. *Loving and Serving*, July 1906, p 9.

101. FA, Fegan, J.W. (nd, c 1920) *After-Math*.

102. As note 86.

103. *Loving and Serving*, various, 1907-09.

104. See Anon (1922) *The First Forty Years: A Chronicle of the Church of England Waifs and Strays Society, 1881-1920*, London: SPCK; also Stroud, J. (1971) *Thirteen Penny Stamps: The Story of the Church of England Children's Society from its Beginnings as 'Waifs and Strays'*, London: Hodder/Stoughton. For the Society's attitude towards parents and children see Ward, H. (1990) *The Charitable Relationship: Parents, Children and the Waifs and Strays Society*, Bristol: Bristol University PhD.

105. Stroud, *op cit*, pp 29-30.

106. *Ibid*, p 30.

107. See Chadwick, O. (1970) *The Victorian Church*, vol 2, London: Black, especially ch 3.

108. *Ibid*, vol 1, p 5.

109. Stroud, *op cit*, pp 85-6.

110. See Ward, *op cit*. For example (p 9), 'Children were referred largely by single, middle class women, as part of their traditional duty towards the poor'.

111. Stroud, *op cit*, p 64.

112. *Ibid*, p 54.

113. Reproduced in Anon (1922), *op cit*, pp 8-9.

114. See *Daily News*, 22.7.84.

115. For some background see Home Office, *Report of the Enquiry into the Conduct of Standon Farm Approved School*, BPP, xiv, 1947, cmd 7150.

116. Figures from *Annual Reports* held at LUA, D541, D1.

117. Anon (1922), *op cit*, p 107. Although no authorship is given it is generally accepted that it was written by Rudolf.

118. Ward, *op cit*, p 328.

119. *Ibid*, p 333.

120. *Ibid*, p 336.

121. LUA, D521, L1, 'Emigration agenda minute book' (1910-21).

122. *Annual Report, 1888*, p 10.

123. *Annual Report, 1910*, pp 14-15.

124. See Jones and Rutman, *op cit*. As the Superintendent of Neglected and Dependent Children in Ontario, Kelso interpreted his responsibilities as covering British immigrant children as well (p 93).

125. *Annual Report, 1893*, p 13.

126. *Annual Report, 1898*, p 17.

127. In his report on the Niagara Home in 1904 Smart observed that there were 33 girls in residence, 'the majority of tender age'. *Report of the Department of the Interior, 1904*, SP (Canada) 1905, p 92.

128. NAC, RG 76/6648/205185. Rudolf to Smart, 7.12.07.

129. *Ibid*. Falk to Smart, 6.12.10.

130. *Ibid*. Scott to Falk, 14.12.10.

131. *Ibid*. Rudolf to Smart, 27.1.11.

132. *Ibid*. Smith to Rudolf, 8.2.11.

133. HC, Session 1997-98, Third Report, Health Select Committee, *The Welfare of Former British Child Migrants*, vol 2, 'Minutes of evidence', HC 755-II, SO 1997, p 173. Also NAC, RG 76/78/6648, pt 5.

134. Anon (1922), *op cit*.

135. *Report of the Department of the Interior, 1901*, SP (Canada) 1902, p 118.

136. NAC, RG 76/6648/205185. Smart to Rudolf, 5.9.05.

137. *Ibid*, Smart to Rudolf, 12.3.06.

138. *Ibid*, Rudolf to Smart, 24.3.06.

139. *Report of the Department of the Interior, 1912*, SP (Canada) 1913, p 109.

140. As note 135, p 174.

141. As note 138. Falk to Smart, 6.12.10.

142. *Ibid*, Smart to Rudolf, 5.9.05.

143. CSA, 'Our emigration work', *Waifs and Strays*, no 40, August 1887.

144. A more public dispute erupted between Rudolf and Barnardo in 1895 when Barnardo charged Rudolf with denigrating his organisation (Ward, *op cit*, p 84); another went on throughout 1903 (Stroud, *op cit*, p 131).

six The Catholic Response

1. See Inglis, *op cit*, ch 3.

2. See St John, *op cit*; also Strachey, L. (1918) *Eminent Victorians*, London: Chatto/Windus.

3. First the Westminster Diocesan Fund for the Poor, later the Diocesan Education Fund.

4. St John, *op cit*, p 108.

5. From 1869 no child under 12 cared for by the Poor Law was allowed to change their religion.

6. St John, *op cit*, p 136.

7. *Annual Report, 1882*, p 3 (held in NCSA).

8. *Annual Report, 1892*, p 5.

9. NCSA, item 7.

10. Information from the Society's *Annual Reports* and from *Annual Reports of the Department of the Interior*. There were gaps but estimates were made in reaching 2,400.

11. Bennett (1949), *op cit*, p 9.

12. PRO, MH 12/5996/78923. Sendall minute, 14.8.84.

13. *Annual Report, 1888*, p 5. Also *1893*, p 3.

14. *Annual Report of the Department of the Interior, 1901*, SP (Canada) 1902, report 25, p 105.

15. NAC, RG 76/65/46944. Pereira to Brennan, 21.2.98.

16. NAC, RG 76/65/32906. Note, 15.6.98.

17. NAC, RG 76/65/73781. Pereira to Brennan, 2.2.99 and *Ottawa Journal*, 26.1.99.

18. NAC, RG 76/65/74027. Brennan to Pereira, nd (1899), enclosing inspector's report.

19. NAC, RG 76/65/74027. Pearl to Brennan, 27.1.02.

20. NAC, RG 17/290/29957. Stafford to Lowe, 8.9.80.

21. See Waugh, N. (1911) *These, My Little Ones: The Origin, Progress and Development of the Incorporated Society of the Crusade of Rescue and Homes for Destitute Catholic Children*, London: Sands.

22. NAC, RG 17/391/42130. Seddon to Lowe, 10.12.83.

23. NAC, RG 17/526/58288. Colmer to Carling enclosing Seddon's letter, 15.2.87.

24. *Ibid*. For example, Seddon to the clerk of the Kensington board of guardians, 10.2.87.

25. LMA, HO BG Emigration, 534/1. Seddon to the clerk of the board of guardians of St Giles and Bloomsbury, 17.5.88.

26. *Ibid*.

27. *Montreal Witness*, 21.10.91.

28. *Ibid*, 22.10.91.

29. As note 25.

30. Figures from *Annual Reports of the Department of the Interior*.

31. See CCSWA, *Annual Reports of the … Society of the Crusade of Rescue*.

32. As note 30.

33. Douglas (1850-1938) was uncle to Lord Alfred Douglas who became known for his homosexual relationship with Oscar Wilde.

34. PRO, MH 25/139/xc 026770. St John to LGB, 28.5.97.

35. *Ibid*.

36. NAC, RG 17/1685/78361. 'Second report on the visitation of the children emigrated to Canada', 31.10.90, pp 1-3.

37. One of these priests (Labelle) was also, in 1890, Deputy Minister of Agriculture for the Province of Québec. 'We have', he wrote to Rossall, 'room for millions and millions of immigrants.' *Ibid*, p 7.

38. As note 36. 'First report on the visitation of the children emigrated to Canada', 24.10.89, p 2.

39. *Ibid*. Figures from further reports. Details of the third party did not include ages.

40. Figures from *Reports of the Department of the Interior, 1894, 1895* and *1896*, SP (Canada) 1895-97, reports 13 and pp 7, 8 and 81.

41. See CCRS (1986) *The Catholic Children's Rescue Society Centenary, 1886-1986*, Manchester: CCRS, p 26.

42. I am indebted to Jim Richards for pointing out this possibility.

43. NAC, RG 17/285/252093, pt I, reports, nd except the year 1902.

44. CCSWA, Bans, E. and Thomas, A.C. (1902) *Catholic Child Emigration to Canada*, London: npb.
45. See Waugh, *op cit*, p 141.
46. As note 43. Thomas to Smart, 30.3.03.
47. CCSWA, Bans, E. and Thomas, A.C. (1904) *Further Notes on Catholic Child Emigration*, London: npb.
48. For example, at the 1904 Conference of Catholic Guardians (Report at CCSWA) Hudson maintained that 'through emigration children were rescued from the gutters of our cities; from drunkenness and immorality and foul words, and want and cruelty and filthiness of soul and body, and all the horrors of a world that cares for neither God nor man' (np, npb).
49. Bans and Thomas (1904), *op cit*, p 5.
50. NCSA, Arden, C. (1904) *Report to the Committee of the Catholic Emigrating Society* (sic), p 5. In committee minutes, ACCSL.
51. NCSA, CEA, *Annual Report of the Canadian Agent, 1904*, p 4.
52. As note 50, p 7.
53. Bans and Thomas (1904), *op cit*, p 3.
54. As note 51, p 7.
55. NAC, RG 76/241/450298. Arden to Smart, 19.11.05. Also *Ottawa Journal*, 15.11.05.
56. Bans and Thomas (1904), *op cit*, p 3.
57. NCSA, Thomas, A.C. (1905) *Wise Imperialism: Or, the Advantages of Child Emigration within the Bounds of the Empire*, London: npb, p 3.
58. NAC, RG 76/241, pt I/450298. Smart to Scott, 9.9.05.
59. See *Report of the Department of the Interior, 1917*, SP (Canada) 1918, report 25, p 85.
60. Waugh, *op cit*, p 147.
61. Malchow, *op cit*, p 86.
62. Boyd, J.H. (1883) *State-directed Emigration*, Manchester: npb.
63. Malchow, *op cit*, p 111.
64. PRO, HO 45/A 13312/26 for circular.
65. PRO, MH 12/3173/89889. Clerk of the Lanchester Union to LGB, 13.9.84.
66. *Ibid*, 93868. Clerk to LGB, 25.9.84; consent 95217.
67. PRO, MH 12/2947/94942. Sendall minute, 29.9.84.
68. *Ibid*, 100838. Clerk of the Auckland Union to LGB, 18.10.84.
69. *Ibid*, 104619. Clerk to LGB, 31.10.84, reply 29.11.84.
70. PRO, MH 12/6309/94374. Clerk of the Toxteth Union to LGB, 27.9.84.
71. *Ibid*. Sendall notes, 30.9.84.
72. *Ibid*. Sendall memorandum, 4.10.84.
73. *Ibid*. Dilke note, 4.10.84.
74. PRO, MH 12/6309/no piece no. Seddon to Sendall, 6.10.84.
75. *Ibid*, 94374. LGB to clerk of the Toxteth Union, 7.10.84 and circular.
76. *Ibid*, 97576. Carr to LGB, 9.10.84.

77. *Ibid.* Boyd's letters of 10.10.84 (98140); 11.10 (98953); 14.10 (99401); 15.10 (99482); and 21.10 (101699).

78. *Ibid.* Sendall minute, 6.1.85.

seven   The 'Unorganised' Emigrationists

1. See Stirling, E.M. (nd) *Our Children in Old Scotland and Nova Scotia*, London: Haddon (in NAS). See also NAS, GD/409/1-5, minutes and details of Edinburgh and Leith Children's Aid and Refuge.

2. *The Glasgow Herald*, 28.2.83.

3. *Ibid*, 8.3.83.

4. See NAS, GD/409/1/1, minutes, 6.11.85.

5. Stirling, E.M. (1887) *Our Children*, at NAS, GD/409/5/2, p 26.

6. *Ibid*, p 12.

7. Papers at NAS, CS/2/240/M1/5.

8. See NAS, GD/409/5/4, *Report of the Edinburgh and Leith Children's Aid and Refuge for the Prevention of Cruelty to Children*, 1889, p 5.

9. NAS, GD/409/1/1, minutes, 6.9.88.

10. NAS, CS/240/D4/1.

11. *Ibid.* Gray to Stirling, 27.11.88.

12. *Ibid.* Stirling to Gray, 28.11.88.

13. Before Justice Richie, Supreme Court of Nova Scotia, February 1891.

14. *Ibid.*

15. The Lord Chief Justice of Nova Scotia presided and was one of the judges to find in favour of Stirling.

16. *Report by Mr H. Mellish, Detective Officer … of his Search for the Children of the Petitioner*, 1891, at NAS, CS/240/D4/1.

17. NAC, RG 76/64/2932, pt 1. Pady to Department of the Interior, 4.4.94.

18. *Ibid.* 'Private and confidential report on the work of the Canadian Emigration Bureau', 15.11.93, unattributed.

19. *Winnipeg Daily Tribune*, 16.8.94.

20. As note 17. Colmer to Carling, 9.4.90.

21. *Ibid.* Carling to Tupper, 6.5.90.

22. *Ibid.* LGB to Tupper, 5.5.90.

23. *Ibid.* Smith to Lowe, 22.5.90.

24. *Ibid.* Pady to Department of the Interior, 20.6.90.

25. *Ibid.* Pereira to Pady, 3.7.90.

26. *Report of the Department of the Interior, 1894*, SP (Canada) 1895, report 13, p 92.

27. As note 17. Bennett to Smith, 9.5.93.

28. *Ibid.* Unattributed to Boardman, 3.7.93.

29. As note 17. Pereira to Pady and Pereira to Doyle, 8.7.93.

30. *Ibid.* Doyle to Pereira, 17.8.93.

31. *Ibid.* Pady to Pereira, 8.7.93.
32. *Ibid.* Pady to Department of the Interior, 28.8.93. Pereira to Pady, 24.10.93.
33. *Ibid.* Gretton to Colmer, 7.11.93.
34. *Report of the Poor Law Schools Committee*, vol II, *op cit*, pp 690-1.
35. See Mowat, C.L. (1961) *The Charity Organisation Society: Its Ideas and Work, 1869-1913*, London: Methuen, pp 45 and 90. One of the aims of the COS was to monitor the *bona fides* of charitable organisations.
36. As note 17. Paterson to Colmer, 17.11.93.
37. *Ibid.* Alkman to Smith, 8.12.93.
38. *Ibid.* Alkman to Smith, 18.1.94.
39. *Winnipeg Tribune*, 16.8.94 and 17.8.94.
40. As note 17. Pereira to Colmer, 6.4.94.
41. *Ibid.* LGB to Pady, 1.6.94.
42. *Ibid.* Doyle to the Department of the Interior, 1.5.94.
43. *Ibid.* Pady to the Department of the Interior, 22.6.94.
44. *Ibid.* Pereira to Smith, 28.6.94 and Smith to Pereira, 10.7.94.
45. *Ibid.* Pereira to Colmer, 17.7.94.
46. For a brief history see Woodroofe, K. (1966) *From Charity to Social Work*, London: Routledge and Kegan Paul, ch 2.
47. See Williams, M. (1920) *Mary Clifford*, London/Bristol: Arrowsmith, especially ch v.
48. Whitwill was a Bristol City councillor from 1870 to 1891, first as a Conservative and then as a Liberal. He became a JP in 1875. He was a trustee of the Bristol Grammar School and the Red Maids School, agent for the Belgium and Greek consulates and president (and major initiator) of the Bristol Hospital for Sick Children and Women. He had established a steamer service from Bristol to New York (the Great Western Steamship Company) and later to Boston, Philadelphia, Baltimore and Montreal. However, the company was wound up in 1895 in the face of competition from larger ships sailing from Liverpool. See Neale, W.G. (1968) *At the Port of Bristol*, vol 1, Bristol: Port of Bristol Authority. Also Pike, W.T. (1898) *Contemporary Biographies: Bristol in 1898*, vol I, Bristol: Pike, p 77.
49. *Bristol Mercury*, 10.2.83 and 14.2.83.
50. The Barton Regis Union was in Bristol (formerly the Clifton Union). It was dissolved in 1902 to be merged with the Bristol Union.
51. Hollis, *op cit*, p 233.
52. *Ibid*, p 258.
53. *Report of the Department of the Interior, 1902*, SP (Canada) 1903, report 25, p 104. Typically, the children were aged from 9 to 14 with somewhat more boys than girls.

54. Margaret Forster remained the committee's agent. Several of its members served on the Barton Regis board of guardians where Mary Clifford remained a prominent member. See Malos, E. (1983) 'Bristol women in action: 1839-1919', in Anon, *Bristol's Other History: 1840-1940*, Bristol: Bristol Broadsides.

55. As note 53.

56. NAC, RG 76/99/13204, pt I. Pereira to Gardner, 10.7.94.

57. *Ibid*. Gardner to Pereira, 13.7.94.

58. *Ibid*. Mitchell to Colmer, 11.5.95 and Whitwill to Dyke, 9.5.95.

59. *Ibid*. Pereira to Gardner, 19.2.98.

60. *Ibid*. Gardner to Pereira, 1.3.98.

61. *Ibid*. Smart to Pedley, 7.1.01.

62. *Ibid*. Lantalum to Pedley, 11.1.01.

63. *Ibid*. Pereira to Gardner, 20.11.96.

64. *Ibid*. Clay to Department of the Interior, 19.11.94.

65. *Ibid*. Scott to Preston, 2.10.03.

66. *Ibid*. Forster to Preston, 18.11.03.

67. *Ibid*. Smart to Scott, 7.12.03.

68. NAC, RG 76/288/258859, pt II. Blair to Smart, nd, c 1904.

69. NAC, RG 76/100/13204, pt II. Note and telegram, 29.5.96.

70. *Ibid*. Whitwill to Gardner, 26.7.96.

71. *Report of the Department of the Interior, 1911*, SP (Canada) 1912, report 25, pp 112-13.

eight   The Canadian Demand for Child Labour

1. See Fowke, C. (1946, reprint 1978) *Canadian Agricultural Policy: The Historical Pattern*, Toronto: Toronto University Press.

2. The table is derived from census reports for the period, but see in particular *Census of Canada, 1921*, vol 2, pp 3-4, table 2. The sharp increase in the number of small farms of under 10 acres in 1891 is probably explained by the worsening economic depression and the increasing resort to part-time farming or the return to semi-subsistence farming by those made unemployed.

3. Derived from census reports.

4. *Census of Canada, 1901*, vol 2. Compiled from tables i and viii, p 64 *passim*.

5. *Special Report on the Immigration of British Children* (Kelso), SP (OLA) 1898, pp 15-16.

6. Figures from Urquart, M.C. and Buckley, K.A. (1965) *Historical Statistics of Canada*, Toronto: CUP/Macmillan, Series S 24-38, p 528.

7. See Berton, P. (1970) *The National Dream: The Great Railway, 1871-81*, Toronto: McClelland/Stewart.

8. *Report of the Minister of Agriculture ... for the Year 1882*, SP (Canada), 1883, appendix 10, report 14, sub-report 7, p 131.

9. As note 6; summarised from series A 211-20, p 21.

10. Compiled from the respective census reports, and from Fowke, *op cit*, pp 188-9 and appendix C.

11. Nicholson, G. W. (1962) *The Canadian Expeditionary Force, 1914-1919*, Ottawa: Queen's Printer, table C.

12. *Census of Canada, 1911*, vol vi, table iv, pp 30-1.

13. *Ibid* for the basis of these calculations.

14. *Report of the Department of the Interior for 1897*, SP (Canada), A 1898, report 13, p 157.

15. *Report of the Department of the Interior for 1914*, SP (Canada), A 1915, report 25, p 93.

16. *Report of the Work Under the Children's Protection Act for 1893*, SP (OLA) 1894, report 47, p 34.

17. *Report of the Work Under the Children's Protection Act for 1894*, SP (OLA) 1895, report 29, p 10.

18. *Ibid*, p 34.

19. *Report of the Work Under the Children's Protection Act for 1896*, SP (OLA) 1897, report 16, p xii.

20. *Census of Canada, 1901*, vol iv, table xviii.

21. As note 19, pp xii-xiii.

22. *Report of the Work Under the Children's Protection Act for 1899*, SP (OLA) 1900, report 39, p 44.

23. Calculated from 'Occupations' in the respective census reports.

24. *Report of the Minister of Agriculture ... for the Year 1870*, SP (Canada), 1871, appendix 6, report 64, sub-report 2, p 36.

25. *Report of the Work Under the Children's Protection Act for 1905*, SP (OLA) 1906, report 43, p 29.

26. Barber, M. (1980) 'The women Ontario welcomed: immigrant domestics for Ontario homes, 1870-1930', *Ontario History*, vol lxxii, no 3.

27. See Dryhouse, C. (1981) *Girls Growing Up in Late Victorian and Edwardian England*, London: Routledge and Kegan Paul, especially ch 3.

28. *Report of the Work Under the Children's Protection Act for 1900*, SP (OLA) 1901, report 14, p 81.

29. Parr (1977), *op cit*, p 178.

30. *Report of the Work Under the Children's Protection Act for 1903*, SP (OLA) 1904, report 43, p 79.

31. NAC, MG 29/E8/10/6. *Toronto Mail* clipping and note, 21.3.87.

32. NAC, RG 17/589/66513. Merry to Lowe, nd, report for 1888.

33. As note 17, p 32.

34. Parr (1977), *op cit*, p 179.

35. *Ibid.*

36. *Report of the Work Under the Children's Protection Act for 1907,* SP (OLA) 1908, report 35, p 97.

37. As note 15, p 183.

38. *Annual Report of the Department of the Interior for 1894,* SP (Canada) 1895, report 13, Herbert's sub-report, p 106.

39. *Annual Report of the Department of the Interior for 1907,* SP (Canada) 1908, report 24, p 114.

40. *Ibid,* p 117.

41. Parr (1977), *op cit,* p 202.

42. *Annual Report of the Department of the Interior for 1908,* SP (Canada) 1909, report 25, p 108.

43. *Annual Report of the Department of the Interior for 1911,* SP (Canada) 1912, report 25, p 100.

44. *Report of the Work Under the Children's Protection Act for 1904,* SP (OLA) 1905, report 43, p 73.

45. As note 39, p 88.

46. See Phillips, C.E. (1957) *The Development of Education in Canada,* Toronto: Gage, especially pp 187-8.

47. *Statistical Yearbook of Canada, 1889* (1890), Ottawa: Queen's Printer, p 390.

48. Stamp, R.M. (1982) *The Schools of Ontario, 1876-1976,* Toronto: Toronto University Press, p 21.

49. *Truancy and Juvenile Crime in Cities,* DHE, vol xv, no 2, 1860. Quoted in Prentice, A. (1977) *The School Promoters: Education and Social Class in Mid-Nineteenth Century Upper Canada,* Toronto: McClelland/Stewart, p 37.

50. See Prentice, A. and Houston, S. (eds) (1975) *Family, School and Society in Nineteenth Century Canada,* Toronto: Oxford University Press, especially pp 178-82.

51. Stamp, *op cit,* p 37.

52. Haythorne, G.V. and Marsh, L.C. (1941) *Land and Labour: A Social Survey of Agriculture and the Farm Labour Market in Central Canada,* Toronto: McGill/ Oxford University Press, p 82.

53. Condensed from Urquart and Buckley, *op cit,* tables V1-20 and A28-43, pp 587-9 and 16 respectively.

54. *Ibid.*

55. *Census of Canada, 1901,* vol IV, 'Vital statistics', table xiii.

56. See Gaffield, C. (1982) 'Schooling, the economy, and rural society in nineteenth century Ontario', in J. Parr (ed) *Childhood and Family in Canadian History,* Toronto: McClelland/Stewart, p 79.

57. *Annual Report of the Department of the Interior for 1898,* SP (Canada) 1899, report 13, p 89.

58. *Report by Andrew Doyle as to the Emigration of Pauper Children to Canada, op cit,* pp 24-5.

59. Parr (1977), *op cit*, found that 30 per cent of those who were under 10 when they were emigrated were reported as receiving only irregular schooling, while the same proportion of those between 10 and 12 had none at all (p 223).

60. *Report of the Work Under the Children's Protection Act for 1908*, SP (OLA) 1909, report 35, p 27.

61. *Report of the Work Under the Children's Protection Act for 1911*, SP (OLA) 1912, report 26, pp 112–13.

62. *Act to Regulate the Immigration into Ontario of Certain Classes of Children*, 1897.

63. See Parr (1977), *op cit*, p 224.

64. See *The Ontario* [Law] *Reports*, vol xxviii; 'Hall v Public School Trustees of Stisted', p 134.

65. *Ontario Appeal Reports*, vol xxiv, p 47.

66. *Annual Report of the Department of the Interior for 1911*, SP (Canada) 1912, report 25, p 104.

67. *Report of the Work Under the Children's Protection Act for 1913*, SP (OLA) 1914, report 27, p 92.

nine Canadian Opposition to Child Immigration

1. See Palmer, D.B. (1985) 'Labour in nineteenth century Canada', in Cherwinski, W.J. and Kealey, G.S. (eds) *Lectures in Canadian Labour and Working-class History*, Toronto: Committee on Labour History/Hogtown Press, pp 51–7.

2. See French, D. (1962) *Faith, Sweat and Politics: The Early Trade Union Years in Canada*, Toronto: McClelland/Stewart.

3. See Kennedy, D. (1956) *The Knights of Labour in Canada*, London, Canada: University of Western Ontario Press.

4. For example, NAC, RG 17/1673/Dem–Don, Donaldson to Lowe, 10.12.87.

5. See O'Donoghue's letter to the *Manchester Guardian*, 4.5.85.

6. In NAC, RG 17/454/49539.

7. See *Toronto Mail*, 6.10.88.

8. *Ibid*.

9. For example, *Reynold's News*, 9.1.89.

10. Parr (1977), *op cit*, p 103.

11. NAC, RG 17/629/71381. Dower to Minister of Agriculture, 2.12.89.

12. Copy in NAC, MG 29/E18/10/6.

13. *Report of the Royal Commission on the Relation Between Capital and Labour*, 1889.

14. *Report of the Commissioners Appointed to Enquire into the Prison and Reformatory System of Ontario*, SP (OLA), 1891.

15. *Ibid*, p 215.

16. *Ibid*, p 744.

17. NAC, RG 76/121/23624. O'Donoghue to Minister of the Interior, 5.8.95.

18. NAC, RG 76/121/23624. Davis to Department of the Interior, 23.8.95.
19. *Report of the Select Standing Committee on Agriculture and Colonisation, JHCC*, 1895, appendix 3, p 221 – letter from Owen to Burgess, 24.4.95.
20. See NAC, RG 76/121/25399; also Parr's summary of the case in the *Canadian Dictionary of Biography* (Green), vol xii, 1990, Toronto: Toronto University Press.
21. See NAC, RG 76/121/23624. O'Donoghue to the Minister of the Interior, 3.3.96.
22. *Ibid*.
23. *Ibid*. O'Donoghue to Sifton, 21.3.97. Sifton's comments had appeared in *The Canadian Gazette*, 31.12.96.
24. Parr (1977), *op cit*, p 106, quoted from Sifton note, 26.3.97; as note 21.
25. *Ibid*, p 105.
26. *Ibid*, pp 105–6.
27. Jones and Rutman, *op cit*, p 94.
28. *Report on the Immigration of British Children … by the Superintendent of Neglected and Dependent Children of Ontario*, SP (OLA), 1898.
29. *Ibid*, p 11.
30. Urquart and Buckley, *op cit*, table A254, p 23. Immigration had risen from a trough of 16,800 in 1895 to a peak of 400,900 by 1913.
31. *Ibid*, pp 60 and 105.
32. *Ibid*, p 111.
33. Langdon, S. (1975) *The Emergence of the Canadian Working Class Movement*, Toronto: New Hogtown Press, p 7.
34. See French, *op cit*, p 43.
35. For instance NAC, RG 17/537/59773. Howland (Mayor of Toronto) to Carling, 25.5.87.
36. For example NAC, RG 17/1564/211. Lowe to Mayor of Toronto, 18.5.88 in reply to his of 10.5.88.
37. As note 28, p 10.
38. See Wallace, E. (1957) *Goldwin Smith*, Toronto: Toronto University Press.
39. NAC, RG 17/404/43689. Pell to Lowe, 19.5.84.
40. NAC, RG 17/1544/226. Lowe to Pell, 21.5.84.
41. NAC, RG 17/398/42967. Hollis to Pope, 29.2.84.
42. NAC, RG 17/398/42987. Cruikshank to Pope, 25.3.84.
43. NAC, RG 17/395/42586. Donaldson to Lowe, 9.2.84.
44. NAC, MG 29/E18/27/307. Lowe to Donaldson, 28.5.84.
45. NAC, RG 17/395/42588. Spence to Lowe, 13.2.84.
46. NAC, RG 17/462/50480. Cox to Carling, 30.11.85.
47. See Parr (1980), *op cit*, p 153.
48. Parr (1977), *op cit*, pp 99–100.
49. *Report of the Select Standing Committee on Agriculture and Colonisation, JHCC*, 1888, appendix 5, p 10.
50. *Ibid*, p 12.

51. *Ibid.*
52. *Ibid.*
53. *Ibid*, p 13.
54. *Ibid*, p 14.
55. *Ibid.*
56. *Ibid*, p 15.
57. *Ibid.*
58. *Ibid.*
59. McLaren, A. (1990) *Our Own Master Race: Eugenics in Canada, 1885-1945*, Don Mills: OUP, pp 50-2.
60. NAC, RG 17/1681/Run-Rz. Rye to Lowe, 12.9.88. 'I really cannot resist writing to tell you that Dr Ferguson is going to take *one of my despised & horribly diseased*!!! girls for his servant!' (original emphasis). Rye had also reported to Lowe that Goldwin Smith's wife too had asked for a girl, but that she had had 'great pleasure' in refusing her. See NAC, RG 17/1681/Run-Rz. Rye to Lowe, 5.6.88 and 10.6.88.
61. *Report of the Select Standing Committee on Agriculture and Colonisation, JHCC*, 1889, appendix 4, p 35.
62. *Ibid*, pp 40-3.
63. *Report of the Select Standing Committee on Agriculture and Colonisation, JHCC*, 1894, appendix 4.
64. *Ibid*, p 207.
65. *Ibid*, p 208.
66. See Dickin McGinnis, J. (1988) 'From salvasan to penicillin: medical science and VD control in Canada', in Mitchinson, W. and Dickin McGinnis, J. (eds) *Essays in the History of Canadian Medicine*, Toronto: McClelland/Stewart, pp 126-47.
67. See Davidson, R. and Hall, L. (eds) (2001) *Sex, Sin and Suffering: Venereal Disease and European Society since 1870*, London: Routledge.
68. *Ibid*, p 6.
69. *Report of the Royal Commission on Venereal Disease*, BPP, xvi, 1916, cd 8189 ('Evidence', 8190).
70. *Ibid*, p 17.
71. *Ibid*, p 14 and table 3, appendix ix, p 122.
72. *Ibid*, p 65.
73. Hall, L. (2001) 'Venereal diseases and society in Britain, from the Contagious Diseases Acts to the National Health Service', in Davidson and Hall, *op cit*, p 120.
74. Turner, *op cit*.
75. *Ibid*, p 181.
76. *Ibid*, quoted on p 189, from *Toronto Globe*, 2.10.75.
77. Wagner (1982), *op cit*, p 134.
78. *Ibid*, p 135, from *Toronto News*, 6.5.84.
79. *Ibid*, from *The Toronto Globe*, 9.10.84.

80. Clipping in NAC, MG 29/E18/10/6. Not dated, but 1891.
81. Parr (1977), *op cit*, p 99.
82. Ontario Department of Agriculture, *Bulletin*, 53, 1895, pp 5-8.
83. For example, *Hamilton Spectator* and *Montreal Gazette*, 25.7.95.
84. NAC, RG 76/119/22877. James to Burgess, 26.6.95.
85. *Ibid*. Burgess to James, 30.6.95.
86. NAC, RG 76/119/23017. Burgess circular to all the correspondents, 20.7.95.
87. NAC, RG 76/119/23502. McPhee to Burgess, 27.7.95.
88. NAC, RG 76/119/23531. Amos to Burgess, 31.7.95.
89. NAC, RG 76/119/23606. White to Burgess, 5.8.95.
90. NAC, RG 76/119/22877. Pereira to Doyle, 10.3.98.
91. NAC, RG 76/119/54693. Doyle's reports, nd.
92. Shortt, S.E. (1972) 'Social change and political crisis in rural Ontario: the Patrons of Industry, 1889-1896', in Swainson, D. (ed) *Oliver Mowat's Ontario*, Toronto: Macmillan.
93. *The Farmers' Sun*, 13.2.95 and 26.6.95, quoted in Shortt, *op cit*, p 217.
94. Parr (1980), *op cit*, p 58.

ten **The Management of the Opposition in Canada**

1. *Toronto Mail*, 11.5.88.
2. NAC, RG 17/1681/Run-Rz. Rye to Lowe, 16.5.88.
3. NAC, RG 17/1655/120. Lowe to Rye, 22.5.88.
4. *Debates of the Senate of Canada*, 16.5.88, pp 742-96.
5. *Ibid*, p 742.
6. NAC, RG 17/1682/Sa. Sanford to Lowe, 16.5.88.
7. NAC, RG 17/1682/Sa. Lowe memorandum with Sanford to Lowe, 17.5.88.
8. As note 4, p 744.
9. *Ibid*, pp 752-3.
10. *Ibid*, p 756.
11. *Ibid*, p 761.
12. *Ibid*, p 764.
13. *Ibid*, p 765.
14. *Ibid*, p 766.
15. *Ibid*, p 782.
16. *Ibid*, p 786.
17. *Toronto Mail*, 15.5.88 and *Star* (London), 24.5.88.
18. *Toronto Mail*, 24.5.88.
19. *Toronto Mail*, 30.5.88.
20. NAC, RG 17/578/65212. Stafford to Lowe, 28.5.88.

21. NAC, RG 17/1564/227. Lowe to Stafford, 30.5.88.
22. NAC, RG 17/579/65336. Stafford to Lowe, 4.6.88.
23. NAC, RG 17/1678/McN-McZ. Macpherson to Lowe, 9.6.88.
24. NAC, RG 17/1655/454. Lowe to Macpherson, 13.7.88.
25. NAC, RG 17/1655/166. Lowe to Rye, 28.5.88.
26. *Report of the Select Standing Committee on Agriculture and Colonisation, JHCC,* 1889, appendix 4.
27. NAC, RG 17/584/65983. Macpherson to Lowe, 19.7.88.
28. *Toronto Mail,* 9.6.88.
29. NAC, RG 17/1681/Run-Rz. Rye to Lowe, 5.6.88.
30. NAC, RG 17/1655/255. Lowe to Rye, 8.6.88.
31. As note 29. Rye to Lowe, 10.6.88.
32. *Ibid.* Rye to Lowe, 12.9.88.
33. *Ibid.* Rye to Lowe, 1.11.88.
34. NAC, RG 17/1656/56. Lowe to Rye, 3.11.88.
35. As note 29. Rye to Lowe, 7.11.88.
36. NAC, RG 17/1566/64. Carling to Tupper, 9.7.88.
37. Kealey, G. (ed) (1973) *Canada Investigates Industrialism,* Toronto: Toronto University Press, p ix.
38. NAC, RG 17/608/68823. Rye to Lowe, 15.2.89.
39. NAC, RG 17/607/68686. Birt to Laurie, 27.2.89 – copy with Laurie to Lowe, 18.3.89.
40. *Ibid.*
41. NAC, RG 17/1657/29. Lowe to Laurie, 22.4.89.
42. NAC, RG 17/1657/193. Lowe to Birt, 15.5.89.
43. NAC, RG 17/695/79666. Dyke to Carling, 22.7.91.
44. *Liverpool Daily Post,* 17.7.91.
45. *Report of the Department of the Interior 1893,* SP (Canada) 1894, p 7.
46. NAC, RG 76/119/22857 for the questionnaire.
47. NAC, RG 76/119/86032. Jury's report, 12.6.99.
48. NAC, RG 76/119/86032. Murray's report, 1.3.99.
49. See Lloyd, V. (1974) *The Camera and Dr Barnardo,* London: Barnardos. Some 55,000 children were photographed starting in 1874.
50. See, for example, the 26 selections from such letters in Barnardo (1889), *op cit.*
51. See Wagner (1979), *op cit,* p 245.
52. NAC, RG 76/94/10216. Pereira to Smith, 30.11.93.
53. *Ibid.* Pereira to Owen, 30.11.93.
54. *Ibid.* Pereira to Hiam, 30.11.93.
55. *Ibid.* Hiam to Pereira, 13.12.93.
56. *Ibid.* Struthers to Smith, 15.12.93.
57. *Ibid.* For example, Burgess to Fortier, 29.12.93.
58. *Ibid.* Burgess to Daly, 9.1.94.
59. *Ibid.* Pereira to Barnardo, 22.1.94.

60. *Ibid.* Pereira to Hiam, 22.1.94.
61. *Ibid.* Pereira to Smith, 22.1.94.
62. *Ibid.* Pereira to MacPherson, 1.2.94.
63. *Ibid.* Pereira to Rye, 1.2.94.
64. *Ibid.* Meiklejohn to Pereira, 7.2.94.
65. *Ibid.* Owen to Pereira, 6.2.94.
66. *Ibid.* Rye to Pereira, 5.2.94 and Pereira to Rye, 13.2.94.
67. *Ibid.* Rye to Pereira, 14.2.94.
68. *Ibid.* Pereira to MacPherson, 17.2.94 and MacPherson to Pereira, 5.3.94.
69. *Ibid.* Pereira to various NWMP, 9.2.94.
70. *Ibid.* Smart to Struthers, 8.1.94.
71. *Ibid.* Barnardo to Pereira, 23.5.94.
72. *Ibid.* Cox to Pereira, – 2. 94 (no day).
73. *The Colonist*, December 1893. A monthly journal 'devoted to the interest of Manitoba and its Territories'.

eleven   The Reformatories and Industrial schools

1. For the history see Carlebach, J. (1970) *Caring for Children in Trouble*, London: Routledge and Kegan Paul, ch 1; and Rose, G. (1967) *Schools for Young Offenders*, London: Tavistock, ch 1.
2. This requirement continued to apply until 1894 when it was made optional. It was removed in 1899.
3. 1880 Industrial Schools Amendment Act.
4. See Parker, R.A. (1990) *Away from Home: A Short History of Child Care*, Ilford: Barnardos, ch 3.
5. Carpenter, M. (1851) *Reformatory Schools for the Children of the Perishing and Dangerous Classes and for Juvenile Offenders*, London: Gilpin.
6. Figures from various *Annual Reports of the Inspector of Reformatory and Industrial Schools of Great Britain*.
7. *Report of the Royal Commission on Reformatories and Industrial Schools*, BPP, xxxviii, 1884, c 3876. Vol I 'Report' and vol II 'Minutes of evidence' (c 3876-1).
8. As note 6.
9. *The Times*, 18.9.80.
10. Quoted in Gardiner, A.G. (1923) *The Life of Sir William Harcourt (1827-1886)*, vol I, London: Constable, p 389.
11. Bodleian Library Oxford, Harcourt MS, dep 95, folio 216.
12. RC, vol II, para 22.
13. *Ibid.*

14. *Ibid*, para 26.
15. *Report on the State of the Law Relating to the Treatment and Punishment of Juvenile Offenders*, 1881. At PRO, HO 45/9607/A 2720.
16. RC, vol I, para 41.
17. RC, vol II, para 4138.
18. *Ibid*, para 3769.
19. *Ibid*, para 4414.
20. *Ibid*, para 4064.
21. *Ibid*, paras 6950-1.
22. RC, vol I, para 47.
23. RC, vol II, para 4413.
24. *Ibid*, paras 4401-2.
25. *Ibid*, para 11457.
26. *Ibid*, para 10568.
27. *Ibid*, para 12854.
28. RC, vol I, para 43.
29. 1886 Reformatory and Industrial Schools Act, sections 18 and 27.
30. RC, vol II, para 2879.
31. *Ibid*, paras 4139-43.
32. *Ibid*, para 4417.
33. *Ibid*, para 6946.
34. RC, vol I, para 41.
35. *Ibid*, para 42.
36. *Ibid*, para 44.
37. PRO, HO 45/9617/A 13312/25.
38. PRO, HO 144/133/A 34834/1.
39. PRO, HO 45/9617/A 13312/33.
40. PRO, HO 45/9617/A 13312/18.
41. PRO, HO 158/8/A 22484/X 1122, 22.11.84.
42. *Ibid*, 20.12.82.
43. PRO, HO 45/96291/A 22484/8-13. Harcourt to Aberdare, 27.12.84.
44. *Ibid*, January 1885.
45. *An Explanatory and Supplementary Circular as per Circular of 22nd November, 1884*. As at note 41.
46. PRO, HO 45/9672/A 46505B/1. Beaumont to Secretary of State, 5.12.85.
47. *Ibid*, A 46505B/1B. Tupper to Granville, 4.4.86.
48. *Ibid*, A 46505B/1D. Tupper to Granville, 22.6.86.
49. *Ibid*, A 46505B/2. Lansdowne to Holland, 14.7.86.
50. *Ibid*, A 46505B/3. Tupper to CO, 17.8.87.
51. *Ibid*, HO to Tupper via the CO, partially undated approved draft, September 1887.
52. *Ibid*, A 46505B/6. Lansdowne to Holland, 28.11.87.
53. *Ibid*, A 46505B/11.
54. *Ibid*, A 46505B/1.

55. *Ibid*, A 46505B/12.
56. The Glasgow Juvenile Delinquency Board was established in 1878 for 'Preventing and Suppressing Juvenile Delinquency in the City...'.
57. NAC, RG 76/123/24641/41617. Pereira to Colmer, 24.8.97.
58. PRO, HO 45/10361/154821/192.
59. See Harper, M. (1988) *Emigration from North-East Scotland*, vol 2, Aberdeen: Aberdeen University Press, p 206.
60. NAC, RG 76/104/16900/AG 96172. Smith to Scott, 7.9.09.
61. *Ibid*. Scott to Smith, 17.9.09.
62. *Report of the Inspector of Reformatories and Industrial Schools*, part II, BPP, xlvi, 1909, cd 4929, pp 32-3.
63. As note 60. Scott to Trevarthen, 13.5.10.
64. *Ibid*, memorandum. Robertson to Fortier, 13.5.10.
65. NAC, RG 76/111/34066. Craster to Hoolan, 3.2.97 and Gardner to Pereira, 22306, 15.6.95.
66. For a general view of the 'culture' within the Home Office at this time see Pellew, J. (1982) *The Home Office: 1848-1914 – From Clerks to Bureaucrats*, London: Heinemann. Appendix B has information about Home Office officials.
67. For a detailed explanation of the financial issues see *Report of the Inter-department Committee on the Provision of Funds for Reformatory and Industrial Schools*, vol I 'Report' and vol II 'Evidence', BPP, liv, 1906, cd 3143 and 3144.
68. As note 62.

twelve   What Befell the Children

1. These archives (TTA) are in the Manchester Central Library (MCL). The references to the letters in the text are the piece numbers under M 189. A condition of the use of these archives was that children's names should not be revealed.
2. PRO, MH 19/2947 (no piece no.) contains 2,000 such reports.
3. The fact that the SPCK provided 'escorts' for some parties of children during their voyage was linked to the Society's provision of chaplains on emigrant ships.
4. NAC, RG 17/678/77465. Biddeson to Penbreath (copy), 9.2.91.
5. NAC, RG 17/681/77805. Noted in Dyke to Small, 19.3.91.
6. TTA, M 189/3224, 1893.
7. *Ibid*, 3216, nd.
8. NAC, RG 17/387/41760. Clay to Department of Agriculture, 23.11.83.
9. TTA, M 189/3223, 1892.
10. The Rockwood hospital was in Kingston, Ontario.
11. TTA, M 189/3216, 1916.
12. TTA, M 189/3216, 1909.
13. NAC, RG 17/549/61521. Grahame to Lowe, received 29.8.87.

14. NAC, RG 17/526/58285. Douglas to Tupper, 11.2.87 and Colmer to Douglas, 15.2.87.
15. NAC, RG 17/1594/205. Small to Donaldson, 12.1.92.
16. NAC, RG 17/692/79209. Bennett to Small, 11.8.91 (letter enclosed).
17. NAC, RG 17/1681/Run-Rz, 1887-94. Rye to Lowe, 10.5.89.
18. In Britain the Gossage case provided a spur to such disputes. In 1888 Barnardo had allowed Harry Gossage, an infant, to be 'adopted' by a Canadian 'gentleman' who was not a Catholic. The mother's permission had not been obtained. Encouraged by the Catholic Church, the mother applied for a writ of *habeas corpus* and the court found in her favour. Despite that, the boy was not produced, Barnardo arguing that he could no longer be found.
19. *Ibid.* Whitwill to Gardner, 18.12.89 (enclosure).
20. Parr (1977), *op cit*, p 21.
21. *The Cornwall Standard*, 29.11.89. Cornwall is a town south of Ottawa.
22. NAC, RG 17/387/41760. Clay to Minister of Agriculture, 23.11.83. Although Moncton is in New Brunswick, the Attorney-General of Nova Scotia was involved because the boy had been placed out from that province.
23. NAC, RG 17/642/72928. Gardner to Small, 2.5.90.
24. *Grenfell Sun*, 7.2.96.
25. TTA, M 189/3215, 1910.
26. TTA, M 189/3215, 1908.
27. NAC, RG 17/724 pt 3/48432.
28. Parr (1980), *op cit*, p 116.
29. NAC, RG 17/212/21843. Macpherson to Lowe, 16.1.78.
30. NAC, RG 17/1576/113. Lowe to Daly, 2.8.90. Earlier correspondence 1690/336. Lowe to Watt, 20.7.90.
31. NAC, RG 17/552/61830. Rye to Lowe, 7.10.87.
32. NAC, RG 17/1560/197. Lowe to Powell, 23.7.87.
33. NAC, RG 17/555/62351. Deputy Minister of Justice to Lowe, 29.12.87.
34. NAC, RG 17/555/62351. Rye to Lowe, 5.11.87.
35. Parr (1980), *op cit*, p 115.
36. TTA, M 189/3220, 1913.
37. *Ibid*, M 189/3217, 1893.
38. *Ibid*, M 189/3220, 1915.
39. NAC, RG 17/572/64465. Lyons to Fyles, 22.3.88.
40. *Ibid*. Fyles to Lowe, 3.4.88.
41. NAC, RG 17/525/58142. Rye to Lowe, 22.2.87.
42. NAC, RG 17/1558/192. Lowe to Burbidge, 16.2.87.
43. NAC, RG 17/1651/435. Lowe to Rye, 16.2.87. For a brief history of the Mercer reformatory see Splane, *op cit*, pp 169-71.
44. NAC, RG 17/1651/494. Lowe to Rye, 23.2.87.
45. NAC, RG 17/529/58644. Powell to Lowe, 30.3.87.
46. NAC, RG 17/527/58307. Rye to Lowe, 4.3.87.

47. Drystek, H.F. (1982) 'The simplest and cheapest mode of dealing with them: deportation from Canada before World War II', *Social History*, vol xv, no 30, p 427. Drystek records that between April and September 1930 a total of 81 British boys were officially deported and another 20 returned by the organisations that brought them.
48. Classes proscribed in the 1869 Immigration Act.
49. Citizenship and Immigration Canada (2000) *Forging our Legacy: Canadian Citizenship and Immigration, 1900-1977*, Ottawa: Citizenship and Immigration Canada, pp 64-5.
50. *The Welfare of Former British Child Migrants*, vol II, *op cit*, p 75.

thirteen **Parents' Rights, Consent and Legislation**

1. For a commentary on the role of 'intermediaries' see Ward, *op cit*.
2. *Report of the Royal Commission on Reformatories and Industrial Schools*, *op cit*.
3. PRO, HO 45/B 5314/20. Brooke Lambert to Ruggles-Brise, 2.1.89.
4. *Ibid*, Lushington minute, 16.1.89.
5. PRO, HO 45/B 5134/29. Record of the meeting, 29.1.89.
6. The National Vigilance Association was founded in 1885 'for the repression of criminal vice and public immorality and for the care and protection of minors'.
7. PRO, HO 45/B 5314/24. Coote to Matthews, 19.1.89.
8. See *The Times*, 13.2.89.
9. As note 7. Troup to Lushington, 4.2.89.
10. *The Times*, 1.3.89.
11. PRO, HO 45/B 5314/39. Whitwill to Matthews, 2.3.89.
12. PRO, HO 45/B 5314/37. Liverpool School Board to Home Secretary, 28.2.89.
13. For a history see Behlmer, G. (1982) *Child Abuse and Moral Reform in England, 1807-1908*, Stanford, CA: Stanford University Press.
14. PRO, HO 45/9814/B 7399/5. Stuart-Wortley minute.
15. PRO, HO 45/9814/B 7399/1 and HO 144/B 6159/1.
16. See Wagner (1979), *op cit* and *The Times*' law reports of 24.1, 28.1, 5.11. 11.11, 13.11 and 14.12.90.
17. PRO, HO 45/9764/B 825E/1.
18. *Ibid*.
19. PRO, HO 45/10598 and 188663/10.
20. *Ibid*.
21. The five were: the NSPCC, Barnardos, Middlemores, the Waifs and Strays, and the Catholic Emigration Association.
22. As note 19.
23. *Ibid*.
24. *Ibid*.
25. *Ibid*.

26. *Ibid*.
27. I extracted the material from PRO, HO 152/Miscellaneous Domestic Correspondence/1-14 and PRO, HO 167/Child Entry Books.
28. For the number of fit person orders made see *Judicial Statistics* (1895-1909), part I – *Criminal Statistics*, 'Courts of summary jurisdiction: proceedings in quasi-criminal matters'.
29. This was the period for which I collected data.
30. As note 27.
31. PRO, HO 152/2/188. Cunynghame to Barnardo, 21.8.99. Approval in 203, 24.8.99.
32. PRO, HO 152/9/28. Cunynghame to Barnardo, 26.10.02. Approval in 246, 29.10.02.
33. PRO, HO 152/7/908. Cunynghame to the chief magistrate, Bow Street court, 19.4.02.
34. PRO, HO 152/3/5. Murdoch to Barnardo, 14.3.00.
35. *Ibid*.
36. PRO, HO 152/3/267. Murdoch to Barnardo, 28.4.00.
37. PRO, HO 152/3/267 and 194. Murdoch to Barnardo, 16 and 28.4.00.
38. PRO, HO 167/3/764. Byrne to Barnardo, 18.6.09.
39. PRO, HO 152/14/765. Byrne to Ring, 18.6.09.
40. For example PRO, HO 152/3/496. Murdoch to Wardle, 2.6.00.
41. Continued as section 2 of the 1948 Children Act and section 3 of the 1980 Children Act.
42. PRO, MH 102/1378. Harris minute on *The Break-up of the Poor Law and the Care of Children and Old People* (13.6.44).
43. Webb and Webb (1963), *op cit*, p 203.
44. OR (Commons), 28.5.87, col 857.
45. *Report of the Select Committee on Poor Law Relief*, HC (HL) 363, BPP, xv, 1888, p 23.
46. The Act remained in force until 1989 although little used in later years.
47. The Act did not specify the age at which the prohibition should expire but it can be assumed that it was 16 or 18.
48. OR (Lords), 5.6.91, col 1696.
49. *Ibid*, col 1698.
50. *Ibid*, col 1700.
51. See Wagner (1979), *op cit*.
52. PRO, HO 144/A 34834/6. Elton to Home Secretary, 31.8.86.
53. *Ibid*. Barnardo to Trevor, 22.7.86.
54. PRO, HO 144/A 34834/7. Cuffe to Leigh-Pemberton, 13.9.86.
55. *Ibid*. Troup minute, 16.9.86.
56. PRO, HO 144/B 25118/1. Minute of Hole's visit, 21.9.97.
57. PRO, HO 144/B 25118/3. Barnardo's letter and Byrne minute, 23.9.97.
58. *Ibid*. Byrne minute.
59. *Ibid*. Cunynghame minute, 22.9.97.

60. PRO, HO 144/B 25118/5. Minute of Hole's visit, 6.10.97 and reply from the Commissioner of Police.
61. *Ibid*.
62. *Ibid*. Minute, 18.10.97.

fourteen **Into the Twentieth Century**

1. *Poor Law Schools Committee*, vol II, *op cit*.
2. See Armitage, W.H. (1951) *A.J. Mundella: The Liberal Background to the Labour Movement*, London: Benn.
3. As note 1, paras 16,166-7.
4. *Ibid*, para 16,170.
5. *Ibid*, para 16,174.
6. NAC, RG 76/65/3115/ 5. Walker to Smart, 4.1.10.
7. NAC, RG 76/324/318481/2. Clerk of the Fareham board of guardians to LGB, 7.7.04.
8. As note 6. Scott to Smart, 1.4.05.
9. *Report of the Local Government Board, 1894–5*, BPP, l, 1895, c 7867, appendix B/32, pp 90-1.
10. *Report of the Local Government Board, 1854-6*, BPP, xxxvi, 1896, c 8212, appendix B/70, pp 232-3.
11. As note 1, but vol 1, 'Report', c 8027.
12. *Ibid*, para 515.
13. *Ibid*, p 138.
14. PRO, CO 42/840/18386. Burgess to Scott, 30.7.96.
15. *Ibid*. Branston minute, 2.9.96, and CO to LGB, 15.9.96.
16. PRO, MH 12/2959/24618. Clerk of the Auckland guardians to LGB, 18.2.97.
17. *Ibid*. Knollys minute, 2.3.97.
18. *Ibid*. Owen minute, 3.3.97.
19. *Ibid*. Knollys minute, 4.3.97.
20. *Ibid*. Russell and Chaplin minutes, 8 and 15.3.97.
21. *Ibid*. Knollys minute, 18.3.97.
22. LGB (1898) *Costs of Inspection of Children Sent Out to Canada*.
23. From Parr (1977), *op cit*, p 67.
24. LGB (1903) *Emigration of Children by Boards of Guardians*.
25. *Report of the Local Government Board, 1903-4*, BPP, xxv, 1904, cd 2214, appendix A/7.
26. Whyte, D. (1978) *The Evolution of Federal Juvenile Immigration Policy, 1894-1920*, Toronto: Toronto University dissertation, p 21.
27. Knowles, V. (1992) *Strangers at our Gates: Canadian Immigration and Immigration Policy, 1540-1990*, Toronto: Dundrum, table A1, pp 188-9.
28. *Children Under the Poor Law*, BPP, xlii, 1908, cd 3899.
29. *Ibid*, para 466.

30. See Betts, R. (1999) *Dr Macnamara, 1861-1931*, Liverpool: Liverpool University Press.

31. NAC, RG 76/65/3115/5. 'The Inspection of British Immigrant Children', 29.1.14.

32. Booth, W. (1890) *In Darkest England and the Way Out*, London: Salvation Army.

33. PRO, MH 25/139/13480. Knollys minute, 2.1.97.

34. *Ibid*. Knollys to Proctor, 11.3.97. See *Boys and Girls*, vol 1, no 4, 1897 for an account of the scheme.

35. Certain registers did survive however (MH 15 and miscellaneous) and from their indices it is possible to identify the subject, the guardians with whom the issue arose and the year, but not the precise date.

36. PRO, MH 12/12352/12925. LGB to the clerk of the Paddington board of guardians, 20.2.91.

37. NAC, RG 76/65/3115/ 5. Clipping, British paper (unspecified), 30.9.09.

38. *Manchester Guardian*, 19.4.10. Garrett to editor; also 4.4.10.

39. As note 37. *Report to the Chorlton Board of Guardians on a Visit to Emigrated Children in Canada*, nd.

40. *Report of the Royal Commission on the Poor Laws and the Relief of Distress*, BPP, xxxvii, 1909, cd 4499 (majority report).

41. *Ibid*, pt 4, para 426.

42. NAC, RG 76/64/3081/1. Macpherson to Strathcona, 24.10.98.

43. Stroud, *op cit*, pp 93-4.

44. Birt (1913), *op cit*, p 234.

45. Wagner (1979), *op cit*, p 271.

46. *Ibid*, ch 15.

47. Barnardo and Marchant, *op cit*, appendix A, pp 338-9.

48. FA, Council Minute Books, vol 1, 1895-1904.

49. See Anon (1972), *op cit*.

50. From *Annual Reports of the Local Government Board*, 1900-14.

51. *Report of the Department of the Interior, 1917*, SP (Canada) 1918, 'Report of the Chief Inspector of British Immigrant Children', p 85.

52. *Annual Reports of the Department of the Interior, 1900-1, 1905-6, 1915-16*, SP (Canada) 1902-17, 'Reports of the Chief Inspector of British Immigrant Children', reports 25, pp 95, 110 and 86 respectively.

53. *Census of England and Wales, 1911*, 1913, cd 7018, vol x (part 1), 'Occupations'.

54. *Report of the Committee Appointed by the Board of Trade to Inquire into the Supply and Training of Boy Seamen for the Merchant Navy – I*, 'Report', BPP, lxxv, 1907, cd 3722, para 4.

55. *Ibid*, para 17.

56. *Report of the Inter-departmental Committee on Physical Deterioration*, vol 1, BPP, xxxii, 1904, cd 2175.

57. CSA, *Annual Report*, 1909, p 15.

58. See Sandall, R. (1955) *The History of the Salvation Army, vol III 1883-1953: Social Reform and Welfare Work*, London: Nelson; Moyles, R.G. (1977) *The Blood and the Fire in Canada: A History of the Salvation Army in the Dominion, 1882-1976*, Toronto: Martin. Also Walker, P.J. (2001) *Pulling Down the Devil's Kingdom: The Salvation Army in Victorian Britain*, Berkeley, CA: University of California Press.

59. Booth, *op cit*, chs 2 and 4.

60. See Harper, *op cit*, vol 2, for an account of the schemes.

61. See Spence, C. (1955) *The Salvation Army Farm Colonies*, Tucson: University of Arizona Press.

62. *Report on the Salvation Army Colonies in the United States and at Hadleigh, England, with Scheme of National Land Settlement*, BPP, liii, 1905, cd 2562. For background see Haggard, H.R. (1910) *Regeneration*, London: Longmans/Green, pp 80-6.

63. *Report of the Departmental Committee ... to Consider Mr Rider Haggard's Report on Agricultural Settlements in British Colonies*, BPP, lxxvi, 1906, cd 2978.

64. Spence, *op cit*, p 113.

65. Harper, *op cit*, p 213.

66. Lamb, D. (1917) 'Child emigration', in Anon, *Aspects of Social Work in the Salvation Army*, London: Salvation Army, p 83.

67. NAC, RG 76/494/768363, pt I. Note, 5.2.08, also Howell to Scott, 7.4.09.

68. *Ibid.*

69. *Ibid.*

70. *Ibid.* Memorandum, nd.

71. *Ibid.* Scott to the clerk of the St Mary Islington board of guardians, 9.1.13.

72. Referred to by Mapp, Colonel (1917) 'Filling up Canada', in Lamb, *op cit*, p 167.

73. As note 67. Bogue Smart to Scott, 10.9.15.

74. *Ibid.* Scott to Vallance, 12.8.16.

75. From figures in annual reports of the Department of the Interior.

76. Lamb, *op cit*, p 93.

77. See Heasman, K. (1962) *Evangelicals in Action: An Appraisal of their Social Work*, London: Bles.

78. Heasman, K. (1968) *Army of the Church*, London: Lutterworth, p 65.

79. Kohli, M. (2003) *The Golden Bridge: Young Immigrants to Canada, 1833-1939*, Toronto: Natural Heritage Books.

fifteen   **Explanation and Assessment**

1. See Parker, R.A. (ed) (1991) *Assessing Outcomes in Child Care*, London: HMSO. Also Parker, R.A. (1998) 'Reflections on the assessment of outcomes', *Children and Society*, vol 12, nnb, pp 192-201.

2. Breckenridge McGregor, J. (1928) *Several Years After: An Analysis of the Histories of a Selected Group of Juvenile Immigrants Brought to Canada in 1910 and in 1920, by British Emigration Societies*, Ottawa: Canadian Council on Child Welfare.

3. Rooke, P.T. and Schnell, R.L. (1981) 'The King's children in English Canada: a psychosocial study of abandonment, rejection and colonial response (1869–1930)', *Journal of Psychohistory*, vol 8, no 4.

4. As note 2, p 27.

5. *Ibid*, pp 30 and 34.

6. Parr (1977 and 1980), *op cit* (2nd edn 1994).

7. Parr (1977), *op cit*, p 230, table viii-3.

8. *Ibid*, p 218.

9. *Ibid*, p 223.

10. *Ibid*, p 223, table viii-2.

11. *Ibid*.

12. *Ibid*, p 236.

13. *Ibid*, p 239.

14. Parr (1980), *op cit*, p 123.

15. *Ibid*, p 126, table 7.1.

16. *Ibid*, p 130.

17. Parr (1977), *op cit*, pp 248–50.

18. *Ibid*, pp 129–30.

19. Harrison, P. (ed) (1979) *The Home Children*, Winnipeg: Watson/Dwyer.

20. *Ibid*, p 93.

21. *Ibid*, p 156.

22. *Ibid*, p 144.

23. *Ibid*, p 232.

24. *Ibid*, p 239.

25. *Ibid*, p 229.

26. *Ibid*, p 133.

27. *Ibid*, p 101.

28. *Ibid*, p 135.

29. *Ibid*, p 155.

30. *Ibid*, p 162.

31. *Ibid*, p 261.

32. *Ibid*, p 112.

33. See Jackson, L. (2000) *Sexual Abuse in Victorian England*, London: Routledge.

34. See Goffman, E. (1963) *Stigma: Notes on the Management of a Spoiled Identity*, Englewood Cliffs, NJ: Prentice/Hall.

35. Corbett, *op cit*.

36. Bean, P. and Melville, J. (1989) *Lost Children of the Empire: The Untold Story of Britain's Child Migrants*, London: Unwin/Hyman.

37. Humphreys, M. (1994) *Empty Cradles*, London: Doubleday.

38. *Ibid*, p 89.

39. *Ibid*, p 131.
40. *Ibid*, p 133.
41. *Ibid*, p 99.
42. *Ibid*, p 140.
43. *Ibid*, p 191.
44. Snow, P. (2000) *Neither Waif Nor Stray: The Search for a Stolen Identity*, upublish.com, p 7.
45. Bean and Melville, *op cit*, p 11.
46. Humphreys, *op cit*, p xiv.
47. *Ibid*, p 113.
48. *Ibid*, p 294.
49. *Ibid*, p 207.
50. Bean and Melville, *op cit*, p 147.
51. *Ibid*, p 142.
52. *Ibid*, p 145.
53. *Ibid*, p 11.
54. Humphreys, *op cit*, p 96.
55. *Ibid*, p 99.
56. Rutter, M. (1981) *Maternal Deprivation Reassessed* (2nd edn), Harmondsworth: Penguin, p 210.
57. Bean and Melville, *op cit*, p 120.
58. *The Welfare of Former British Child Migrants*, *op cit*.
59. These and other percentages were calculated from unpublished evidence to the committee lodged in the House of Lords Record Office. They are based on 233 letters.
60. As note 58, vol I, para 51.
61. *Ibid*, para 66.
62. *Ibid*, para 73.
63. Specific references to the letters are not given in order to preserve their authors' anonymity.
64. Gill, A. (1998) *Orphans of the Empire*, Sydney: Vintage.
65. Figures in the *The Welfare of Former British Child Migrants* (vol I, para 13) show between 7,000 and 10,000 children being sent to Australia from 1947-67. Only 423 were in the care of local authorities (1952-67): Home Office, *Children in the Care of Local Authorities in England and Wales*, annual statistics.
66. As note 58, vol I, para 1.
67. Clouston, T. (1892) *Clinical Lectures on Mental Disease* (3rd edn), London: Oliver/Boyd, p 570.
68. *Ibid*, p 571.
69. Hendrick, H. (1994) *Child Welfare: England, 1872-1989*, London: Routledge, p 3.
70. *Ibid*.

71. Black, D. (1993) 'A brief history of child and adolescent psychiatry', in Black, D. and Cottrell, D. (eds) *Seminars in Child and Adolescent Psychiatry*, London: Gaskell. Quoted in Williams, R. and Kerfoot, M. (2005) 'Setting the scene: perspectives on the history and policy for child and adolescent mental health services in the UK', in their *Child and Adolescent Mental Health Services*, Oxford: Clarendon, p 13.

72. See Neve, M. and Turner, T. (2002) 'History of child and adolescent psychiatry', in Rutter, M. and Taylor, E. (eds) *Child and Adolescent Psychiatry*, Oxford: Blackwell.

73. See for example, Cohen, H.M. (1947) 'The work of the school health services', in Moncrieff, A. and Thomson, W.A. (eds) *Child Health*, London: Eyre/Spottiswood.

References

1 Books and Articles

Abrams, L. (1998) *The Orphan Country*, Edinburgh: Donald.

Anon. (1990) *Canadian Dictionary of Biography*, Toronto: Toronto University Press.

Anon. (1922) *The First Forty Years: A Chronicle of the Church of England Waifs and Strays Society, 1881-1920*, London: SPCK.

Anon. (1972) *One Hundred Years of Child Care: The Story of the Middlemore Homes, 1872-1972*, Birmingham: Middlemore.

Armitage, W.H. (1951) *A.J. Mundella: The Liberal Background to the Labour Movement*, London: Benn.

Bans, E. and Thomas, A.C. (1902) *Catholic Child Emigration to Canada*, London: npb.

Bans, E. and Thomas, A.C. (1904) *Further Notes on Catholic Child Emigration*, London: npb.

Barber, M. (1980) 'The women Ontario welcomed: immigrant domestics for Ontario homes, 1870-1930', *Ontario History*, vol lxxii, no 3.

Barnardo, S. and Marchant, J. (1907) *Memoirs of the Late Dr Barnardo*, London: Hodder/Stoughton.

Barnardo, T.J. (1889) *Something Attempted Something Done*, London: Barnardos/Shaw.

Barnardo, T.J. (nd) *The Rescue of Waifs*, London: Barnardos.

Barritt, G.E. (1972) *The Edgeworth Story*, Harpenden, NCH.

Bean, P. and Melville, J. (1989) *Lost Children of the Empire: The Untold Story of Britain's Child Migrants*, London: Unwin/Hyman.

Behlmer, G. (1982) *Child Abuse and Moral Reform in England, 1807-1908*, Stanford, CA: Stanford University Press.

Bennett, J. (1949) *Father Nugent of Liverpool*, Liverpool: Liverpool Catholic Children's Protection Society.

Bennett, J. (1950) 'The care of the poor', in G.A. Beck (ed) *The English Catholics, 1850-1950*, London: Burns/Oates.

Berton, P. (1970) *The National Dream: The Great Railway, 1871-81*, Toronto: McClelland/Stewart.

Betts, R. (1999) *Dr Macnamara, 1861-1931*, Liverpool: Liverpool University Press.

Birt, L.M. (1913) *The Children's Home-Finder*, London: Nisbet.

Black, D. (1993) 'A brief history of child and adolescent psychiatry', in Black, D. and Cottrell, D. (eds) *Seminars in Child and Adolescent Psychiatry*, London: Gaskell.

Blackburn, G. (1993) *The Children's Friend Society*, Northbridge, Australia: Access Press.

Boase, F. (1892) *Modern British Biography*, Truro: Netherton/Worth.

Booth, W. (1890) *In Darkest England and the Way Out*, London: Salvation Army.

Boyd, J.H. (1883) *State-Directed Emigration*, Manchester: npb.

Bradfield, W. (1913) *The Life of the Reverend Thomas Bowman Stephenson*, London: Kelly.

Breckenridge McGregor, J. (1928) *Several Years After: An Analysis of the Histories of a Selected Group of Juvenile Immigrants Brought to Canada in 1910 and 1920, by British Emigration Societies*, Ottawa: Canadian Council on Child Welfare.

Carlebach, J. (1970) *Caring for Children in Trouble*, London: Routledge and Kegan Paul.

Carpenter, M. (1851) *Reformatory Schools for the Children of the Perishing and Dangerous Classes and for Juvenile Offenders*, London: Gilpin.

Carrier, N.H. and Jeffrey, J.R. (1953) *External Migration: A Study of the Available Statistics, 1815-1950*, London: HMSO.

Carrothers, W.A. (1965) *Emigration from the British Isles*, London: Cass.

CCRS (1986) *The Catholic Children's Rescue Society Centenary, 1886–1986*, Manchester: CCRS.

Chadwick, O. (1970) *The Victorian Church*, vol 2, London: Black.

CIC (Citizenship and Immigration Canada) (2000) *Forging Our Legacy: Canadian Citizenship and Immigration, 1900-1977*, Ottawa: CIC.

Clark, A. (2005) 'Wild workhouse girls and the liberal imperial state in mid-nineteenth century Ireland', *Journal of Social History*, vol 39, no 2.

Clarke, P. (1985) *The Governessess: Letters from the Colonies, 1862-82*, London: Hutchinson.

Clouston, T. (1892) *Clinical Lectures on Mental Disease* (3rd edn), London: Oliver/Boyd.

Cohen, H.M. (1947) 'The work of the school health services', in Moncrieff, A. and Thomson, W.A. (eds) *Child Health*, London: Eyre/Spottiswood.

Corbett, G.H. (1981) *Barnardo Children in Canada*, Peterborough, Canada: Woodland.

Cruikshank, M. (1981) *Children and Industry: Child Health and Welfare in the North-West Textile Towns During the Nineteenth Century*, Manchester: Manchester University Press.

Davey, C. (1968) *A Man for All Children: The Story of Thomas Bowman Stephenson*, London: Epworth.

Davidson, R. and Hall, L. (eds) (2001) *Sex, Sin and Suffering: Venereal Disease in European Society since 1870*, London: Routledge.

Diamond, M. (1999) *Emigration and Empire: The Life of Maria S. Rye*, London and New York: Garland.

Dickin McGinnis, J. (1988) 'From salvasan to penicillin: medical science and VD control in Canada', in Mitchinson, W. and Dickin McGinnis, J. (eds) *Essays in the History of Canadian Medicine*, Toronto: McClelland/Stewart.

Dryhouse, C. (1981) *Girls Growing Up in Late Victorian and Edwardian England*, London: Routledge and Kegan Paul.

Drystek, H.F. (1982) 'The simplest and cheapest mode of dealing with them: deportation from Canada before World War II', *Social History*, vol xv, no 30.

Edmondson, W. (1921) *Making Rough Places Smooth: Fifty Years Work of the Manchester and Salford Boys' and Girls' Refuges and Homes, 1870-1920,* Manchester: Sherratt/ Hughes.

Fernie, D.A. (1993) 'John Rylands of Manchester', *Bulletin of the John Rylands University Library of Manchester,* vol 75, no 2.

Fowke, C. (1946, reprinted 1978) *Canadian Agricultural Policy: The Historical Pattern,* Toronto: Toronto University Press.

French, D. (1962) *Faith, Sweat and Politics: The Early Trade Union Years in Canada,* Toronto: McClelland/Stewart.

Fullerton, W.Y. (1908) *J. W.C. Fegan,* London: Marshall/Morgan/Scott.

Gaffield, C. (1982) 'Schooling, the economy and rural society in nineteenth century Ontario', in Parr, J. (ed) *Childhood and Family in Canadian History,* Toronto: McClelland/Stewart.

Gammie, A. (1936) *The Romance of Faith: The Story of the Orphan Homes of Scotland and the Founder William Quarrier,* London: Pickering/Inglis.

Gardiner, A.G. (1923) *The Life of Sir William Harcourt (1827-1886),* vol I, London: Constable.

Gelber, N. (nd) *Canada in London: An Unofficial Glimpse of Canada's Sixteen High Commissioners, 1880-1980,* London: Canada House.

Gentilcore, R.L. (ed) (1993) *Historical Atlas of Canada,* Toronto: Toronto University Press.

Gill, A. (1998) *Orphans of the Empire,* Sydney: Vintage.

Goffman, E. (1963) *Stigma: Notes on the Management of a Spoiled Identity,* Englewood Cliffs, NJ: Prentice/Hall.

Haggard, H.R. (1910) *Regeneration,* London: Longmans/Green.

Hall, L. (2001) 'Venereal diseases and society in Britain from the Contagious Diseases Acts to the National Health Service', in Davidson, R. and Hall, L. (eds) *Sex, Sin and Suffering: Venereal Disease in European Society since 1870,* London: Routledge.

Hammerton, A. (1979) *Emigrant Gentlewomen,* London: Croom Helm.

Harper, M. (1998) *Emigration from North-East Scotland,* vol 2, Aberdeen: Aberdeen University Press.

Harrison, P. (ed) (1979) *The Home Children,* Winnipeg: Watson/Dwyer.

Haythorne, G.V. and Marsh, L.C. (1941) *Land and Labour: A Social Survey of Agriculture and the Farm Labour Market in Central Canada,* Toronto: McGill/ Oxford University Press.

Heasman, K. (1962) *Evangelicals in Action: An Appraisal of their Social Work,* London: Bles.

Heasman, K. (1968) *Army of the Church,* London: Lutterworth.

Hendrick, H. (1994) *Child Welfare: England, 1872-1989,* London: Routledge.

Hitchins, F.H. (1931) *The Colonial Land and Emigration Commission,* Philadelphia, PA: Philadelphia University Press.

Hollis, P. (1987) *Ladies Elect: Women in English Local Government, 1865-1914,* Oxford: Clarendon Press.

Horner, F. (1919) *Shadow and Sun*, London: Epworth/NCH.

Humphreys, M. (1994) *Empty Cradles*, London: Doubleday.

Inglis, K.S. (1963) *The Churches and the Working Classes in Victorian England*, London: Routledge and Kegan Paul.

Jackson, L. (2000) *Sexual Abuse in Victorian England*, London: Routledge.

Johnson, S.C. (1966) *Emigration from the United Kingdom to North America, 1763-1912*, London: Cass (new imprint).

Jones, A. and Rutman, L. (1981) *In the Children's Aid: J.J. Kelso and Child Welfare in Ontario*, Toronto: Toronto University Press.

Kealey, G. (ed) (1973) *Canada Investigates Industrialism*, Toronto: Toronto University Press.

Kennedy, D. (1956) *The Knights of Labour in Canada*, London, Canada: University of Western Ontario Press.

Knowles, V. (1992) *Strangers at our Gates: Canadian Immigration and Immigration Policy, 1540-1990*, Toronto: Dundrum.

Kohli, M. (2003) *The Golden Bridge: Young Immigrants to Canada, 1833-1939*, Toronto: Natural Heritage Books.

Lacey, C.A. (1986) *Barbara Leigh Smith Bodichon and the Langham Place Group*, London: Routledge Kegan Paul.

Lamb, D. (1917) 'Child emigration', in *Some Aspects of Salvation Army Social Work*, London: Salvation Army.

Lambert, R. (1963) *Sir John Simon and English Social Administration, 1816-1904*, London: MacGibbon/Kee.

Langdon, S. (1975) *The Emergence of the Canadian Working Class Movement*, Toronto: New Hogtown Press.

Lloyd, V. (1974) *The Camera and Dr Barnardo*, London: Barnardos.

Logan, E. and Macpherson, A. (1869) *Emigration the Only Remedy for Chronic Pauperism in the East of London*, London: private.

Long, M.H. (1931) 'Sir John Rose and the informal origins of the Canadian High Commission in London', *Canadian Historical Review*, March.

Loring Brace, C. (1872) *The Dangerous Classes of New York, and Twenty Years, Work Among Them*, New York, NY: Wynkoop/Hallenbeck [republished in 1973, Washington: NASW].

Lowe, C.M. (nd) *God's Answers: A Record of Miss Annie Macpherson's Work*, London: npb ('reprint LR').

MacDonald, H.J. (1996) 'Boarding-out and the Scottish Poor Law', *The Scottish Historical Review*, vol lxxv, 2, no 200.

Mackay, T. (1904 edn) *History of the English Poor Law, vol III, 1834-1898*, London: Murray.

Mackay T. (ed) (1908) *The Reminiscences of Albert Pell*, London: Murray.

Macpherson, A. (1866) *The Little Matchbox Makers*, London: private.

Magnusson, A. (1984) *The Village: A History of Quarrier's*, Glasgow: Quarriers.

Malchow, H.L. (1979) *Population Pressures: Emigration and Government in Late Nineteenth-Century Britain*, Palo Alto, CA: Society for the Promotion of Science and Scholarship.

Malos, E. (1983) 'Bristol women in action: 1839-1919', in Anon, *Bristol's Other History: 1840-1940*, Bristol: Bristol Broadsides.

Mapp, Colonel (1917) 'Filling up Canada', in *Some Aspects of Salvation Army Social Work*, London: Salvation Army.

McLaren, A. (1990) *Our Own Master Race: Eugenics in Canada, 1885-1945*, Don Mills: Oxford University Press.

Mitchell, B. and Deane, P. (1971) *Abstract of British Historical Statistics*, Cambridge: Cambridge University Press.

Montague, C.J. (1904) *Sixty Years in Waifdom or, the Ragged School Movement in English History*, London: Murray.

Mowat, C.L. (1961) *The Charity Organisation Society: Its Ideas and Work, 1869-1913*, London: Methuen.

Moyles, R.G. (1977) *The Blood and the Fire in Canada: A History of the Salvation Army in the Dominion, 1882-1976*, Toronto: Martin.

Neale, W.G. (1968) *At the Port of Bristol*, vol 1, Bristol: Port of Bristol Authority.

Neff, C. (1997) *The Children's Friend Society in Upper Canada, 1833-42*, Sudbury: Laurentian University.

Neff, C. (2000) 'Youth in Canada West: a case history of Red Hill Farm school emigrants, 1854-1868', *Journal of Family History*, vol 25, no 4.

Neve, M. and Turner, T. (2002) 'History of child and adolescent psychiatry', in Rutter, M. and Taylor, E. (eds) *Child and Adolescent Psychiatry*, Oxford: Blackwell.

Nicholson, G.W. (1962) *The Canadian Expeditionary Force, 1914-1919*, Ottawa: Queen's Printer.

Palmer, D.B. (1985) 'Labour in nineteenth century Canada', in Cherwinski, W.J. and Kealey, G.S. (eds) *Lectures in Canadian Labour and Working Class History*, Toronto: Hogtown Press.

Parker, R.A. (1975) 'Social administration and scarcity', in Butterworth, E. and Holman, R. (eds), *Social Welfare in Modern Britain*, Glasgow: Fontana/Collins.

Parker, R.A. (1990) *Away from Home: A History of Child Care*, Ilford: Barnardos.

Parker, R.A. (ed) (1991) *Assessing Outcomes in Child Care*, London: HMSO.

Parker, R A. (1998) 'Reflections on the assessments of outcomes', *Children and Society*, vol 12, nnb.

Parr, (G.)J. (1977) *The Home Children: British Juvenile Immigrants to Canada, 1868-1924*, Yale, CT: Yale University PhD.

Parr, J. (1980) *Labouring Children*, London/Kingston: Croom Helm/McGill Queens.

Pellew, J. (1982) *The Home Office: 1848-1914 – From Clerks to Bureaucrats*, London: Heinemann.

Phillips, C.E. (1957) *The Development of Education in Canada*, Toronto: Gage.

Pike, W.T. (ed) (1898) *Contemporary Biographies: Bristol in 1898*, vol 1, Manchester: Pike.

Pike, W.T. (ed) (1899) *Contemporary Biographies: Manchester and Salford at the Close of the Nineteenth Century*, Manchester: Pike.

Pinchbeck, I. and Hewitt, M. (1973) *Children in English Society*, vol II, London: Routledge Kegan Paul.

Prentice, A. (1977) *The School Promoters: Education and Social Class in Mid-Nineteenth Century Upper Canada*, Toronto: McClelland/Stewart.

Prentice, A. and Houston, S. (eds) (1975) *Family, School and Society in Nineteenth Century Canada*, Toronto: OUP.

Preston-Thomas, H. (1909) *The Work and Play of a Government Inspector*, Edinburgh/London: Blackwood.

Prochaska, F.K. (1980) *Women and Philanthropy in Nineteenth Century England*, Oxford: Oxford University Press.

Quarrier, W. (1884) *Occasional Paper*, Glasgow: Orphan Homes of Scotland.

Robbins, J. (1980) *The Lost Children: A Study of Charity Children in Ireland, 1700-1900*, Dublin: Institute of Public Administration.

Rooke, P.T. and Schnell, R.L. (1981) 'The King's children in English Canada: a psychosocial study of abandonment, rejection and colonial response (1869-1930)', *Journal of Psychohistory*, vol 8, no 4.

Rose, G. (1967) *Schools for Young Offenders*, London: Tavistock.

Rose, J. (1987) *For the Sake of the Children*, London: Hodder/Stoughton.

Ross, A. (1971) *The Power I Pledge*, Glasgow: Quarriers.

Rutter, M. (1981) *Maternal Deprivation Reassessed* (2nd edn), Harmondsworth: Penguin.

Rye, M.S. (1862) 'Female middle class emigration', *The Englishwoman's Journal*, vol 10, July.

Sandall, R. (1955) *The History of the Salvation Army, vol III, 1883-1953: Social Reform and Welfare Work*, London: Nelson.

Saunders, E.M. (ed) (1916) *The Life and Letters of the Rt Hon Sir Charles Tupper*, London: Cassell.

Shaw A.G. (1966) *Convicts and the Colonies*, London: Faber & Faber.

Shortt, S.E. (1972) 'Social change and political crisis in rural Ontario: the Patrons of Industry, 1889-1896', in Swainson, D. (ed) *Oliver Mowat's Ontario*, Toronto: Macmillan.

Skilling, H.G. (1945) *Canadian Representation Abroad*, Toronto: Ryerson Press.

Smith, S. (1902) *My Life Work*, London: Hodder/Stoughton.

Snow, P. (2000) *Neither Waif Nor Stray: The Search for a Stolen Identity*, upublish.com

Spence, C. (1955) *The Salvation Army Farm Colonies*, Tucson: University of Arizona Press.

Splane, R.B. (1965) *Social Welfare in Ontario, 1791-1893: A Study in Public Welfare Administration*, Toronto: Toronto University Press.

Stamp, R.M. (1982) *The Schools of Ontario, 1876-1976*, Toronto: Toronto University Press.

Stedman Jones, G. (1984) *Outcast London: A Study in the Relationship Between the Classes in Victorian Society*, Harmondsworth: Peregrine.

Stephenson, T.B. (1883) *The Story of the Children's Home and Princess Alice Orphanage*, London: NCH.

Stirling, E.M. (nd) *Our Children in Old Scotland and Nova Scotia*, London: Haddon.

St John, E. (1929) *Manning's Work for Children: A Second Chapter in Catholic Emancipation*, London: Steed/Ward.

Strachey, L. (1918) *Eminent Victorians*, London: Chatto/Windus.

Stroud, J. (1971) *Thirteen Penny Stamps: The Story of the Church of England Children's Society from its Beginnings as 'Waifs and Strays'*, London: Hodder/Stoughton.

Summers, A. (1975) *Damned Whores and God's Police: The Colonisation of Women in Australia*, Harmondsworth: Penguin.

Turner, W. (1976) 'Miss Rye's children and the Ontario Press, 1875', *Ontario History*, vol 68, no 3.

Urquart, J. (1900) *The Life-Story of William Quarrier: A Boy's Resolve and What Became of It*, London: Partridge.

Urquart, M.C. and Buckley, K.A. (1965) *Historical Statistics of Canada*, Toronto: Cambridge University Press/Macmillan.

Wagner, G. (1979) *Barnardo*, London: Weidenfeld & Nicholson.

Wagner, G. (1982) *Children of the Empire*, London: Weidenfeld & Nicholson.

Walker, P.J. (2001) *Pulling Down the Devil's Kingdom: The Salvation Army in Victorian Britain*, Berkeley, CA: University of California Press.

Wallace, E. (1957) *Goldwin Smith*, Toronto: Toronto University Press.

Ward, H. (1990) *The Charitable Relationship: Parents, Children and the Waifs and Strays Society*, Bristol: Bristol University PhD.

Waugh, N. (1911) *These, My Little Ones: The Origin, Progress and Development of the Incorporated Society of the Crusade of Rescue and Homes for Destitute Catholic Children*, London: Sands.

Webb, S. and Webb, B. (1963) *English Poor Law History, Part II*, vol I, London: Cass (reprint).

Webb, S. and Webb, B. (1963) *English Poor Law Policy*, London: Cass (reprint).

Whyte, D. (1978) *The Evolution of Federal Immigration Policy, 1894-1920*, Toronto: Toronto University dissertation.

Williams, M. (1920) *Mary Clifford*, London/Bristol: Arrowsmith.

Williams, R. and Kerfoot, M. (2005) 'Setting the scene: perspectives on the history and policy for child and adolescent mental health services in the UK', in their *Child and Adolescent Mental Health Services*, Oxford: Clarendon Press.

Woodroofe, K. (1966) *From Charity to Social Work*, London: Routledge and Kegan Paul.

Wymer, N. (1954) *Father of Nobody's Children: A Portrait of Dr Barnardo*, London: Hutchinson.

2 Principal UK Official Publications – Special Reports, etc

[Some reports will have separate volumes of evidence with a different command number. These are not listed.]

Report of the Select Committee on the Poor Laws (Scotland), BPP, xi, 301, 1869.

Emigration: Circular to Various Governors, BPP, xlix, 179, 1870.

Report on the Special Enquiry into Schools at Mettray and Dusseltal, 1873.

Report to the President of the Local Government Board by Andrew Doyle … as to the Emigration of Pauper Children to Canada, BPP, lxiii, HC 9, 1875.

The Emigration of Pauper Children to Canada, BPP, lxxi, c 2620, 1877.

Report on the State of the Law Relating to the Treatment and Punishment of Juvenile Offenders, Home Office, unpublished, 1881.

Memorandum of Conditions upon which the Local Government Board are Prepared to assent tentatively to the Emigration of a Limited Number of Orphan and Deserted Pauper Children to Canada, LGB, 1883.

Report of the Royal Commission on Reformatories and Industrial Schools, c 3876, 1884.

Memorandum of Conditions upon which the Local Government Board assent to the Emigration of Orphan and Deserted Pauper Children to Canada, LGB, 1888.

Report of the Select Committee on Poor Law Relief, HC (HL) 363, BPP, xv, 1888.

Report of the Departmental Committee on the Education and Maintenance of Pauper Children in the Metropolis, BPP, xliii, c 8027, 1896.

Costs of Inspection of Children Sent Out to Canada, LGB circular, 1898.

Emigration of Children by Boards of Guardians, LGB circular, 1903.

Report of the Inter-departmental Committee on Physical Deterioration, cd 2175, 1904.

Report on the Salvation Army Colonies in the United States and at Hadleigh, England, with Scheme of National Land Settlement, BPP, liii, cd 2562, 1905.

Report of the Departmental Committee … to Consider Mr Rider Haggard's Report on Agricultural Settlements in British Colonies, BPP, lxxvi, cd 2978, 1906.

Report of the Inter-departmental Committee on the Provision of Funds for Reformatories and Industrial Schools, BPP, liv, cd 3143, 1906.

Report of the Committee Appointed by the Board of Trade to Inquire into the Supply and Training of Boy Seamen for the Merchant Navy, cd 3722, 1907.

Children Under the Poor Law, BPP, xlii, cd 3899, 1908.

Report of the Royal Commission on the Poor Laws and the Relief of Distress, BPP, xxxvii, cd 4499, 1909.

Report of the Royal Commission on Venereal Disease, BPP, xvi, cd 8189, 1916.

Report of the Enquiry into the Conduct of Standon Farm Approved School, BPP, xiv, cmd 7150, 1947.

Report of the Health Select Committee on the Welfare of Former British Child Migrants, HC 755, 1997.

3 UK Regular Official Publications

Annual Reports of the Colonial Land and Emigration Commission
Annual Reports of the Inspector of Reformatories and Industrial Schools
Annual Reports of the Local Government Board
Annual Reports of the Poor Law Board
Census Reports
Children in the Care of Local Authorities in England and Wales (statistics)
The Judicial Statistics
The Official Record: Commons and Lords (ie *Hansard/Parliamentary Debates*)

4 Annual Reports of UK Organisations

Barnardos Homes
Catholic Emigration Association
East End Emigration and Relief Fund
East London Family Fund
Edinburgh and Leith Children's Aid and Refuge for the Prevention of Cruelty
  to Children
Fegans Homes
Manchester and Salford Boys' and Girls' Refuges and Homes
Middlemore Emigration Home
Miss Rye's Emigration Home for Destitute Little Girls
NCH (National Children's Homes)
Quarriers Homes
Society of the Crusade of Rescue and Homes for Destitute Children
Southwark Catholic Emigration Society
Waifs and Strays Society (Church of England)
Westminster Fund for Poor Children, later the Westminster Diocesan Education
  Fund

5 'House' Journals of UK Children's Organisations

Boys and Girls, Southwark Catholic Emigration Society
Night and Day, Barnardos
The Rescue, Loving and Serving and *The Red Lamp*, Fegans
Waifs and Strays, Waifs and Strays Society

6 British Newspapers and Periodicals

Bristol Mercury
The Christian
The Chronicle
Daily News

The Glasgow Herald
The Globe
Liverpool Daily Post
The Liverpool Mercury
The Local Government Chronicle
The Manchester Guardian
The North British Daily Mail
Revival
Reynold's News
The Star
The Tablet
The Times
The Wolverhampton Chronicle
The Wolverhampton Express

7 Canada: Federal and Provincial Official Reports, Records, etc

a Federal

Journals of the House of Commons (sessional papers)
Annual Reports of the Department of Agriculture
Annual Reports of the Department of the Interior
Canadian Gazette
Censuses of Canada
Debates of the Senate
Report of the Royal Commission on the Relation Between Capital and Labour, 1889
Statistical Year Book of Canada

b Ontario

Annual Reports of the Commissioner of Agriculture and Public Works
Annual Reports of the Immigration Department
Annual Reports of the Inspector of Prisons and Charities
Annual Reports of the Work Under the Children's Protection Act
Appeal (Law) Reports
Bulletins of the Department of Agriculture
Ontario Law Reports
Report of the Commissioners Appointed to Enquire into the Prison and Reformatory System, 1891
Sessional Papers, Ontario Legislative Assembly
Special Report on the Immigration of British Children, 1898

c Nova Scotia

Journals and Proceedings of the House of Assembly of the Province of Nova Scotia

d New Brunswick

Journals of the House of Assembly of the Province of New Brunswick

e Québec

Documents de la Session de l'Assemblée de Québec

8 Canadian Newspapers and Periodicals

The Colonist
The Cornwall Standard
The Farmers' Sun
The Grenfell Sun
The Hamilton Spectator
The Halifax Morning Herald
The Montreal Gazette
The Montreal Witness
The Ottawa Journal
The Toronto Globe
The Toronto Mail
The Toronto News
The Winnipeg Daily Tribune

9 Archival Sources

UK

Birmingham Record Office
Bodleian Library (Oxford)
Catholic Children's Society (London)
Children's Society (London)
Fegans Child and Family Service (Tunbridge Wells)
House of Lords Record Office
City of London, London Metropolitan Archives
Manchester Central Library
National Archives of Scotland (Edinburgh)
National Archives, Public Record Office (London)
Nugent Care Society (Liverpool)
Quarriers (Glasgow)

University of Liverpool Special Collections and Archives

Canada

Archives Nationales du Québec (Québec)
Archives of New Brunswick (Moncton)
Archives of Ontario (Toronto)
National Archives of Canada (Ottawa)
Public Archives of Nova Scotia (Halifax)

Index

(★ indicates a named child)